Barcelona

"All you've got to do is decide to go
and the hardest part is over.

So go!"

TONY WHEELER, COFOUNDER – LONELY PLANET

D1052419

THIS EDITION WRITTEN AND RESEARCHED BY

**Regis St Louis,
Sally Davies, Andy Symington**

Contents

(left) Plaça Reial (p66)

(above) Festes de la Mercè (p25)

(right) Seafood paella

Welcome to Barcelona

Barcelona is an enchanting seaside city with boundless culture, fabled architecture, and a world-class drinking and dining scene.

Architecture of the Ages

Barcelona's architectural treasures span 2000-plus years. Towering temple columns, ancient city walls and subterranean stone corridors provide a window into Roman-era Barcino. Fast forward 1000 years to the Middle Ages by taking a stroll through the shadowy lanes of the Gothic quarter. In other parts of town bloom the sculptural master-pieces of Modernisme, a mix of ingenious and whimsical creations. Barcelona has also long inspired artists, including Salvador Dalí, Pablo Picasso and Joan Miró, whose works are on bold display in the city's many museums.

A Moveable Feast

Barcelona's great artistic traditions don't end at the canvas. The masters of molecular gastronomy – Albert Adrià, Carles Abellan et al – are part of the long and celebrated tradition of Catalan cooking. Simple, flavourful ingredients are transformed into remarkable delicacies and then served up in captivating settings. You can feast on hearty, rich paella at an outdoor table overlooking the sea or step back to the 1920s at an elegant art nouveau–filled dining room. Barcelona's wide-ranging palate adds further complexity: Basque-style tapas bars, Galician seafood taverns, avant-garde Japanese restaurants and sinful chocolate shops are all essential parts of the culinary landscape.

Under the Iberian Sun

The deep blue Mediterranean beckons. Sun-drenched beaches make a fine backdrop to a jog, bike ride or long leisurely stroll along the seaside – followed by a refreshing dip, of course. You can also enjoy the view from out on the water while kayaking, stand-up paddleboarding or taking it easy on a sunset cruise. Looming behind the city, the rolling forest-covered Collserola Hills provide a scenic setting for hiking, mountain biking or just admiring the view. Closer to the city centre, hilltop Montjuïc offers endless exploring amid botanic and sculpture gardens, an old castle and first-rate museums with panoramic views at every turn.

Twenty-Four Hour Party People

The night holds limitless possibilities in Barcelona. Start with sunset drinks from a panoramic terrace or dig your heels in the sand at a rustic *chiringuito*. As darkness falls, live music transforms the city: the rapid-fire rhythms of flamenco, brassy jazz spilling out of basements, and hands-in-the-air indie-rock at vintage concert halls. Towards midnight the bars fill. Take your pick from old-school taverns adorned with 19th-century murals, plush lounges in lamp-lit medieval chambers or boisterous *cava* (wine) bars. If you're still standing at 3am, hit the clubs and explore Barcelona's unabashed wild side.

Why I Love Barcelona

By Regis St Louis, Author

I love the sea, and taking an early morning jog along the Mediterranean is my favourite way to start the day. I'm also a bit of a history nerd, and relish strolling the cobblestone lanes of the Gothic quarter, thinking about all the people in past centuries who walked these same streets. And then there's the food and drink – the first-rate tapas bars, the abundant and inexpensive wine, the superb and reasonably priced multicourse lunches. Add to all this Catalan creativity (Modernisme, Miró, Dalí), bohemian bars and stunning nearby getaways and you have, quite simply, one of the world's most captivating cities.

For more about our authors, see p304.

Above: Carrer del Bisbe, in the Barri Gòtic (p56)

Barcelona's
Top 10

Modernista Architecture *(p146)*

1 Few cities are defined by their architecture to quite the same extent as Barcelona. The weird and wonderful undulations of Antoni Gaudí's creations are echoed in countless Modernista flights of fancy across the city. You'll find shimmering mosaics, wild details (in stained glass, iron, ceramic) and sculptural elements that reference nature, mythology and medieval days. Gateway to these astonishing architectural works is L'Eixample, which was a blank canvas for some of Spain's finest buildings in the late 19th and early 20th centuries. LA PEDRERA (P131)

⊙ *La Sagrada Família & L'Eixample*

La Sagrada Família *(p124)*

2 One of Barcelona's icons, the Modernista masterpiece remains a work in progress more than 80 years after the death of its creator, Antoni Gaudí. Fanciful and profound, inspired by nature and barely restrained by the Gothic style, Barcelona's quirky temple soars skyward with a playful majesty. Stepping through its sculpted portals is like walking into a fairy tale, where a forest of columns branch towards the ceiling and light shimmers through brilliant stained-glass windows. Rich with beautifully wrought detail and packed with symbols, the basilica invites hours of contemplation.

⊙ *La Sagrada Família & L'Eixample*

JAMES EMMERSON/GETTY IMAGES ©

2
PROGNONE/GETTY IMAGES ©

La Catedral (p62)

3 A masterpiece of Catalan Gothic architecture, La Catedral is rightly one of the first stops on any visit to the Ciutat Vella (Old City). You can wander wide-eyed through the shadow-filled interior, with a dozen well-concealed chapels, an eerie crypt and a curious garden-style cloister that's home to 13 geese (which are deeply connected with the mythology of Barcelona's co-patron saint, Santa Eulàlia). Outside, there's always entertainment afoot, from *sardana* dancing on weekends to periodic processions and open-air markets, and street musicians are never far from the scene.

◉ *La Rambla & Barri Gòtic*

Mercat de la Boqueria (p81)

4 This temple of temptation is one of Europe's greatest permanent produce fairs. Restaurant chefs, homemakers, office workers and tourists all stroll amid the seemingly endless bounty of glistening fruits and vegetables, gleaming fish counters, dangling rolls of smoked meats, pyramids of pungent cheeses, barrels full of olives and marinated peppers, and chocolate truffles and other sweets. In the back, a handful of popular tapas bars serve up delectable morsels. There's always a line, but it's well worth the wait.

◉ *El Raval*

MANFRED GOTTSCHALK/GETTY IMAGES ©

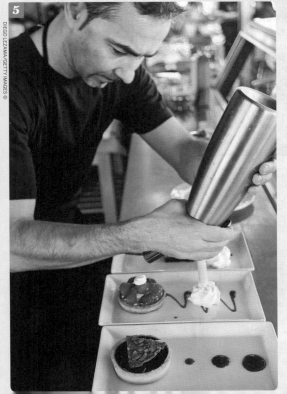

New Catalan Cuisine *(p33)*

5 Barcelona's most celebrated chefs blend traditional Catalan recipes with new cooking techniques to create deliciously inventive masterpieces. Leading the way are Albert Adrià, the molecular gastronomy whiz behind Tickets, and Carles Abellan, who elevated the humble tapas to high art in restaurants like Tapas 24. The result: Barcelona is fast becoming one of the world's great culinary destinations. No matter where you go in the city, you won't be far from a memorable meal. And the critics agree: the city has two dozen Michelin-starred restaurants.

Eating

6

7

Strolling La Rambla (p58)

6 Sure it is the most touristy spot in town. But you can't come to Barcelona and not take the 1.2km stroll down the famous pedestrian boulevard that stretches towards the sea. It's pure sensory overload – with a parade of people amid open-air cafes, fragrant flower stands, a much-overlooked mosaic by Miró and the rather surreal human sculptures. If you can take your eyes off the boulevard, you'll notice key venues lining both sides of the street, including the elegant Gran Teatre del Liceu, the sprawling Mercat de la Boqueria and several major galleries.

👁 *La Rambla & Barri Gòtic*

Museu Picasso (p94)

7 For a portrait of the artist as a young man, head to the Museu Picasso, which showcases perhaps the world's best collection of the master's early work. Picasso lived in Barcelona between the ages of 15 and 23, and elements of the city undoubtedly influenced his work, from the colourful but simply painted frescoes hanging in the Museu Nacional d'Art de Catalunya to the imaginative *trencadis*-style mosaics (pre-cubist some say) of Gaudí. The museum's setting – inside five contiguous medieval mansions – adds to the appeal.

👁 *La Ribera*

Nightlife in Sant Antoni (p193)

8 Barcelona is a city known for reinvention, but none of its neighbourhoods has seen a regeneration as dramatic as that of the unremarkable grid of streets around the splendid old Mercat Sant Antoni. It started with the tentative opening of a couple of hip cafes on Carrer del Parlament, but over the last couple of years this has bloomed into a lively strip of bars and restaurants, with an influx of hipster pleasure-seekers and entrepreneurs, and this in turn has kickstarted a slew of openings in surrounding streets. BAR CALDERS (P193)

🍷 *Montjuïc, Poble Sec & Sant Antoni*

Camp Nou *(p167)*

9 For the sports-minded, little can compete with the spectacle of a match at FC Barcelona's massive football stadium. With a loyal fan base and an incredibly gifted team led by the likes of Lionel Messi, Camp Nou always hosts a good show – even if you can't make it to a game, it's still worth visiting. The 'Camp Nou Experience' is an interactive museum and stadium tour that takes you through the locker rooms and out onto the pitch, hallowed ground for many Catalans.

◉ *Camp Nou, Pedralbes & La Zona Alta*

MARK AVELLINO/GETTY IMAGES ©

SIQUI SANCHEZ/GETTY IMAGES ©

Magical Montjuïc *(p177)*

10 When the temperature rises, head up the hill of Montjuïc for fresh air and breathtaking views over the city, best enjoyed from the dizzy heights of one of its cable cars. At any time of year it makes for a great day out, with endless parkland, themed gardens and museums to suit every taste, whether your fire is lit by sport, art or ancient remains. If you have kids in tow, meanwhile, the kitsch wonderland of the Poble Espanyol is a must. PANORAMIC VIEW OF THE HARBOUR AND MONTJUÏC

◉ *Montjuïc, Poble Sec & Sant Antoni*

What's New

Adrià's Growing Empire

Celebrated chef Albert Adrià shows no sign of stopping. Bodega 1900, one of his latest restaurant openings, is dedicated to vermouth and high-end pub fare. Plans for other Adrià eateries are in the works. (p191)

Drink of the Gods

The fashionable drink of choice these days is *vermut* (vermouth), which has enjoyed a strong resurgence in recent years. The anytime drink goes nicely with tapas, particularly at Bormuth (p102) or Mitja Vida (p171).

Bellesguard

Another of Gaudí's masterpieces has opened to the public. The neo-Gothic Bellesguard has an imposing stone facade modelled on the medieval castle that once stood here. Join a guided tour to see inside. (p169)

Museu del Disseny de Barcelona

Barcelona's newest museum was on the verge of opening at press time. Dedicated to design of all sorts, exhibitions cover decorative arts, ceramics, fashion and graphic arts. (p115)

Born Centre Cultural

Recently unveiled excavations, set inside a 19th-century marketplace, reveal what life was like for Catalans in the early 1700s in the Born Centre Cultural. Also on-site is an excellent new restaurant. (p99)

Cause for Celebration

Several new festivals have entered Barcelona's summer calendar in the last few years. Festival Piknic Electronik features DJs and outdoor revelry on Montjuïc; Festival Pedralbes stages big-name concerts in a lush garden. (p24)

Dine in Someone's Home

Locals with culinary skills are hosting dinner parties on EatWith. For about what you'd pay in a restaurant, you can get in on the action. There are hundreds of offerings in Barcelona. (www.eatwith.com)

Boutique Beauties

A crop of new boutique hotels has opened in the Barri Gòtic, bringing an ample dose of style. The beautifully designed DO (p212), Hotel Mercer (p213) and Ohla Hotel (p213) have lovely rooms, roof terraces and superb restaurants.

Modernista Makeover

At long last, several architectural treasures in L'Eixample have opened their doors to visitors: Casa Amatller (p129) and Casa Lleó Morera (p129), essential parts of the so-called Manzana de la Discordia.

Reinventing Catalan Cuisine

Culinary maestro Carles Abellan (of Tapas 24 and Comerç 24 fame) continues to add to the city's roster of great restaurants, with Suculent, one of his latest successes. (p87)

For more recommendations and reviews, see **lonelyplanet.com/barcelona**

Need to Know

For more information, see Survival Guide (p247)

Currency
Euro (€)

Language
Spanish and Catalan

Visas
Not required for US, Canadian, Australian, New Zealand or South African visitors for stays of up to 90 days. EU nationals can stay indefinitely.

Money
ATMs are widely available (La Rambla has many). Credit cards accepted in most hotels, shops and restaurants.

Mobile Phones
Local SIM cards can be used in unlocked European and Australian phones. Other phones must be set to roaming.

Time
Central European Time (GMT/ UTC plus one hour).

Tourist Information
Oficina d'Informació de Turisme de Barcelona (Map p290; ☑93 285 38 34; www.barcelona turisme.com; underground at Plaça de Catalunya 17-S; ☺9.30am-9.30pm; Ⓜ Catalunya) provides maps; sights information; tours, concert and events tickets; and last-minute accommodation.

Daily Costs

Budget: less than €50
➡ Dorm beds: €16–€28
➡ Set lunches: from €9
➡ Bicycle hire per hour: €5

Midrange: €50–€200
➡ Standard double room: €80–€140
➡ Two-course dinner with wine for two: €50
➡ Walking and guided tours: €15–€25

Top end: over €200
➡ Boutique and luxury hotels: €200 and up
➡ Multicourse meal at top restaurants per person: €80
➡ Concert tickets to Palau de la Música Catalana: around €50

Advance Planning

Three months before Book hotel and reserve a table at a top restaurant.

One month before Check out reviews for theatre and live music and book tickets.

One week before Browse the latest nightlife listings, art exhibitions and other events to attend while in town. Reserve spa visits and organised tours.

A few days before Check the forecast on weather.com.

Useful Websites

➡ **Barcelona** (www.bcn.cat/ en) Town hall's official site with plenty of links.

➡ **Barcelona Turisme** (www. barcelonaturisme.com) City's official tourism website.

➡ **Lonely Planet** (www. lonelyplanet.com) Destination information, hotel bookings, traveller forum and more.

➡ **Porktie** (www.porktie. com) Recommendations of restaurants, bars and shops.

➡ **Spotted by Locals** (www.spottedbylocals.com) Insider tips.

WHEN TO GO

Summer (July and August) is peak tourist season, when crowds swarm the city, and its beaches. For pleasant weather, come in late spring (May).

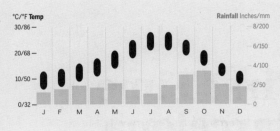

°C/°F Temp   Rainfall Inches/mm

Arriving in Barcelona

El Prat airport Frequent aerobuses make the 35-minute run into town (€5.65) from 6am to 1am. Taxis cost around €25.

Estació Sants Long-distance trains arrive at this big station near the centre of town, which is linked by metro to other parts of the city.

Estació del Nord Barcelona's long-haul bus station is located in L'Eixample, about 1.5km northeast of Plaça de Catalunya, and is a short walk from several metro stations.

Girona-Costa Brava airport The 'Barcelona Bus' operated by Sagales (one way/return €16/25, 90 minutes) is timed with Ryanair flights and goes direct to Barcelona's Estació del Nord.

Reus airport Buses operated by Hispano-Igualdino (one way/return €16/25, 90 minutes) are timed with Ryanair flights and go direct to Barcelona's Estació d'Autobuses de Sants.

For much more on **arrival** see p248

Getting Around

➡ **Metro** The most convenient way to get around. Trains run from 5am to midnight Sunday to Thursday, till 2am on Friday and 24 hours on Saturday. Targeta T-10 (10-ride passes) are the best value at €10.30; otherwise, it's €2.15 per ride.

➡ **Bus** A hop-on, hop-off Bus Turístic (p252), which leaves from Plaça de Catalunya, is handy for those wanting to see the city's highlights in one or two days.

➡ **Taxi** You can hail taxis on the street or at taxi stands. Major streets to wave them down include La Rambla, Via Laietana, Plaça de Catalunya and Passeig de Gràcia.

➡ **On foot** To explore the old city, all you need is a good pair of walking shoes.

For much more on **getting around** see p250

Sleeping

Barcelona has a wide range of sleeping options, from inexpensive hostels in the old quarter to luxury hotels overlooking the waterfront. Good-value options include the small-scale B&B-style apartment rentals scattered around the city. Typical prices for a midrange room for two are about €80 to €140 per night. Wherever you stay it's wise to book well ahead. If you plan to travel around holidays like Christmas, New Year's Eve, Easter or in summer, reserve a room three or four months ahead of time.

Useful Websites

➡ **Airbnb** (www.airbnb.com) This global network has hundreds of rooms and apartments listed in Barcelona.

➡ **Oh-Barcelona** (www.oh-barcelona.com) Good-value selection of hotels, hostels and apartment rentals.

➡ **Barcelona 30** (www.barcelona30.com) Economical options for staying on a budget.

➡ **Lonely Planet** (www.lonelyplanet.com) Huge range of hotels, hostels, guesthouses, B&Bs and apartments.

For much more on **sleeping** see p209

First Time Barcelona

For more information, see Survival Guide (p247)

Checklist

➡ To get the best deal, be sure to check all airlines before booking a flight.

➡ Find out if you can use your phone in Spain and ask about roaming charges.

➡ At the very least, book your first few nights of accommodation to ensure an easy start to your stay.

➡ Check the calendar to figure out which festivals to attend or avoid.

➡ Organise travel insurance.

What to Pack

➡ Passport and/or national ID card (EU citizens)

➡ Driving licence

➡ Phrasebook

➡ Money belt

➡ Mobile phone (and charger)

➡ Earplugs for noisy weekend nights

➡ Good walking shoes

➡ Sunglasses

➡ Reading material (try page-turners by Carlos Ruiz Zafón or Manuel Vázquez Montalbán)

➡ A rain jacket or umbrella

Top Tips for Your Trip

➡ Plan your visiting times to avoid the worst of the crowds. Go early in the morning or late in the day for the top Gaudí sites and the Museu Picasso.

➡ When possible, book tickets online. This will allow you to bypass the queues.

➡ Be mindful of siesta time (generally between 1pm and 4pm). Plan your shopping for mornings or early evenings.

➡ Travel smart; keep valuables tucked away and out of sight. Pickpocketing is a concern in busy, touristy areas.

What to Wear

In Barcelona just about anything goes, and you'll rarely feel uncomfortable because of what you're wearing. That said, Catalans are fairly fashion conscious and well dressed. Most folks dress smart casual, with something perhaps a bit dressier if going somewhere special for the evening.

If you're planning on clubbing, bring something stylish (T-shirts, sandals or sneakers are a no-go). Meanwhile, La Catedral advertises a policy of no admittance to those in sleeveless tops and shorts. The rule isn't always enforced, but it's best not to take the risk.

Be Forewarned

➡ Violent crime is rare in Barcelona, but petty crime (bag-snatching, pickpocketing) is a major problem.

➡ You're at your most vulnerable when dragging around luggage to or from your hotel; make sure you know your route before arriving.

➡ Be mindful of your belongings, particularly in crowded areas.

➡ Avoid walking around El Raval and the southern end of La Rambla late at night.

➡ Don't wander down empty city streets at night. When in doubt, take a taxi.

➡ Take nothing of value to the beach, and don't leave anything unattended.

Money

Credit cards are widely accepted in Barcelona, although there may be a minimum amount of €5 or €10. When paying with a credit card, a photo ID is often required, even for chip cards where you're required to enter your PIN (for US travellers without chip cards, just indicate that you'll give a signature). ATMs are widespread, and most allow you to use international debit or credit cards to withdraw money in euros. Remember also that there is usually a charge (around 1.5% to 2%) on ATM cash withdrawals abroad.

For more information, see p253.

Plaça Reial (p66)

Taxes & Refunds

Value-added tax (VAT) is a 21% sales tax levied on most goods and services. For restaurants and hotels it's 10%. Most restaurants usually include VAT in their prices, but it is not also included in hotel-room prices, so be sure to ask when booking. It's sometimes possible for visitors to claim a refund of VAT paid on goods; see p254 for details.

Tipping

➡ **Restaurants** Catalans typically leave 5% or less at restaurants. Leave more for exceptionally good service.

➡ **Taxis** Optional, but most locals round up to the nearest euro.

➡ **Bars** It's rare to leave a tip in bars, though a bit of small change is always appreciated.

Etiquette

Barcelona is fairly relaxed when it comes to etiquette. A few basics to remember:

➡ **Greetings** Catalans, like other Spaniards, usually greet friends and strangers alike with a kiss on both cheeks, although two males rarely do this. Foreigners may be excused.

➡ **Eating & Drinking** Waiters won't expect you to thank them every time they bring you something, but they will expect you to keep your cutlery between courses in more casual restaurants and bars.

➡ **Visiting Churches** It is considered disrespectful to visit churches as a tourist during Mass and other worship services. Taking photos at such times is a definite no-no.

➡ **Escalators** Always stand on the right to let people pass, especially when using the metro.

Language

English is widely spoken in Barcelona. Even Catalans with only a few English words are generally happy to try them out. Learning a little Spanish before you come will greatly enhance your experience, not least in your ability to converse with locals. Even better if you can learn some Catalan. English signage is available at most museums (though not all). Many restaurants have English-language menus, though simpler places may have them only in Spanish and Catalan.

See Language (p257) for more information.

Top Itineraries

Day One

La Rambla & Barri Gòtic (p56)

On day one spend the morning exploring the narrow medieval lanes of the Barri Gòtic. Have a peek inside **La Catedral** – not missing its geese-filled cloister – and stroll through the picturesque squares of **Plaça de Sant Josep Oriol** and **Plaça Reial**. Discover Barcelona's ancient roots in the fascinating **Museu d'Història de Barcelona**. Before lunch have a wander down La Rambla to take in the passing people parade.

 Lunch Cafè de l'Acadèmia (p73) serves outstanding Catalan fare.

La Ribera (p92)

In the afternoon, wander over to La Ribera, which is packed with architectural treasures. Take a look inside the majestic **Basílica de Santa Maria del Mar**. At the **Museu Picasso**, beautifully set inside conjoined medieval mansions, you can spend a few hours taking in the early works of one of the great artists of the 20th century.

 Dinner Elbow your way up to the bar for gourmet tapas at Cal Pep (p103).

La Ribera (p92)

Before having a late dinner (as is the custom in Spain), catch a show inside the **Palau de la Música Catalana**, one of the great Modernista masterpieces of Barcelona. Afterwards end the night with drinks at **El Xampanyet**.

Day Two

L'Eixample (p122)

On day two start with a morning visit to **La Sagrada Família**, Gaudí's wondrous work in progress. It's worth paying a little extra for a guided tour (or audio guide) for a deeper understanding of Barcelona's most famous sight.

 Lunch The fabulous Cinc Sentits (p136) serves up creative perfection.

L'Eixample (p122)

After lunch, explore more of the great Modernista buildings by taking a stroll down L'Eixample's **Passeig de Gràcia**. Have a look at the three most famous buildings that make up the **Manzana de la Discordia**. Then visit one of Gaudí's house museums on the street – either **Casa Batlló** or **La Pedrera** further up the avenue.

Dinner Enjoy excellent wines and tasty sharing plates at Viblioteca (p162).

Camp Nou, Pedralbes & La Zona Alta (p165)

In the evening catch a football match at **Camp Nou**, the home of the top-ranked FC Barcelona. Amid the roar of the crowds, prepare for a serious adrenalin rush, especially if Barça is playing arch-rivals Real Madrid. Afterwards head back to L'Eixample for a drink at the classy **Les Gens Que J'Aime** before moving on to the big beats at **City Hall**.

Day Three

Barceloneta & the Waterfront (p109)

 On your third day in Barcelona it's time to take in the lovely Mediterranean. Start the morning with a stroll, jog or a bike ride along the waterfront. Beach-facing restaurants and cafes provide refreshment along the way.

> **Lunch** Join seafood-loving locals at always-buzzing Can Maño (p117).

Barceloneta & the Waterfront (p109)

 Stroll through Barceloneta, stopping for a peek inside the **Mercat de la Barceloneta**. Afterwards visit the **Museu d'Història de Catalunya** and peel back the centuries on an interactive journey into Catalan history.

> **Dinner** La Vinateria del Call (p73) has a magical medieval setting.

La Rambla & Barri Gòtic (p56)

At night catch a live band inside the Gothic quarter. **Harlem Jazz Club** and **Jamboree** are good bets for jazz and world music. If you still have energy, check out a few bars in the neighbourhood, including **Ocaña**, which has a beautiful setting on Plaça Reial.

Day Four

Montjuïc (p177)

 Start the day with a scenic cable car ride up to Montjuïc, followed by a stroll past flower and sculpture gardens to the **Museu Nacional d'Art de Catalunya** (**MNAC**). Take in the magnificent Romanesque frescos, vivid Gothic paintings and works by 17th-century Spanish masters.

> **Lunch** O'Gràcia! (p161) is a charming neighbourhood spot for Catalan fare.

Gràcia (p154)

After getting a taste of Montjuïc, hop on the metro up to Gràcia and wander through its enchanting village-like streets. Cafes, bookshops and vintage shops all make for some worthwhile exploring. The bars surrounding its plazas come to life around sundown.

> **Dinner** Feast on beautifully prepared Catalan dishes at Suculent (p87).

El Raval (p79)

Take in the bohemian side of Barcelona in El Raval. Browse record shops and vintage stores, enjoy a live band at the **Jazz Sí Club**, or watch an indie feature at the **Filmoteca de Catalunya**. Finish the night over a few housemade vermouths at **La Confitería**, or at dance favourite **Moog** for something livelier.

If You Like...

Markets

Mercat de la Boqueria One of Europe's largest food markets, with a countless array of tempting delicacies, plus tapas bars at the back. (p81)

Mercat de Sant Antoni A massive but largely tourist-free food market that also hosts a flea market on Sunday. (p194)

Mercat de Santa Caterina La Ribera's bountiful food market, with its wavy colourful roof and archaeological fragments from the 1400s. (p99)

Els Encants Vells A sprawling flea market with plenty of treasures and trash on the edge of Poblenou. (p121)

Mercadillo de la Plaça de Sant Josep A colourful collection of artworks sold by local artists on weekends in the Plaça de Sant Josep Oriol. (p66)

Port Antic A tiny weekend antiques market on the waterfront, at the foot of La Rambla. (p121)

Feria de Artesanía del Palau de Mar This waterfront market is a fine nautical place to browse for handicrafts and souvenirs. (p121)

Parks & Gardens

Parc de la Ciutadella Pretty landscaped grounds with a dramatic fountain, curious artwork, the Catalan parliament building and a zoo. (p100)

Park Güell A green wonderland with fine views over the city and the surreal sculptural architecture courtesy of Gaudí. (p156)

HENDRIK WEBERS/GETTY IMAGES ©

Parc de la Ciutadella (p100)

Jardí Botànic One of Montjuïc's many lush gardens, this one full of Mediterranean flora as well as plants from similar climates. (p189)

Parc de la Creueta del Coll Near Parc Güell, this is a family favourite with pool, snack bar and trails. (p169)

Parc de Collserola A vast scrubby woodland with trails for bikers and runners and superb views over the city. (p172)

Jardins del Laberint d'Horta Picturesque gardens with artificial lake and waterfalls and challenging labyrinth a bit out of the city centre. (p171)

Museums

Museu d'Història de Catalunya Interactive exhibits cover 2000-plus years of Catalan history: Romans, Arabs, feudal times, civil war and the post-Franco era. (p112)

Museu d'Història de Barcelona Stroll over ruins of Roman-era Barcino, then see fine Catalan Gothic architecture inside a former royal palace. (p65)

CosmoCaixa A fun science museum that's a big hit with families – especially its recreated patch of Amazonian rainforest. (p170)

Museu-Monestir de Pedralbes A peaceful old convent with a 14th-century cloister and old-world religious artwork. (p168)

Poble Espanyol This kitschy leftover from the 1929 World Exhibition provides an overview of Spain's diverse cultures. (p186)

Museu Blau A spacious natural history and science museum with interactive exhibits and a huge animal collection – dinosaurs included. (p116)

Art & Design

Vinçon Beautiful furniture and home design from a famed Barcelona brand. (p141)

Fundació Joan Miró A temple to the great artist, complete with outdoor sculpture gardens. (p184)

Fundació Antoni Tàpies Fascinating collection of a great Catalan artist set in a Modernista building. (p129)

Sala Parés Reputable gallery that's been going strong for over 100 years. (p78)

Museu del Disseny de Barcelona Dedicated to decorative arts, this is the city's newest museum, set in a controversial ultramodern building. (p115)

Centre de Cultura Contemporània de Barcelona A must for art lovers, the CCCB hosts excellent cutting-edge exhibitions. (p84)

Museu d'Art Contemporani de Barcelona (MACBA) A packed collection of 20th-century artwork in a modern Richard Meier–designed building. (p82)

Museu Nacional d'Art de Catalunya (MNAC) Stunning collection of Romanesque art dating back 900 years. (p179)

CaixaForum Inside a modernist building designed by Puig i Cadafalch, this place hosts fantastic exhibitions. (p185)

Contemporary Architecture

Torre Agbar Jean Nouvel's striking cucumber-shaped tower dominates the new high-tech zone of 22@. (p115)

Teatre Nacional de Catalunya The design of this stately theatre is a perfect medley of Ancient Greece with high modernism. (p120)

For more top Barcelona spots, see the following:
- ⇒ Eating (p33)
- ⇒ Drinking & Nightlife (p39)
- ⇒ Gay & Lesbian (p43)
- ⇒ Entertainment (p45)
- ⇒ Shopping (p48)

PLAN YOUR TRIP IF YOU LIKE...

El Fòrum A blue triangular building by Herzog & de Meuron that manages to be both organic and weirdly futuristic. (p115)

Plaça de les Glòries Catalanes One of the latest projects to transform a messy urban area, with a new market and museum. (p241)

Panoramic Views

Temple del Sagrat Cor It's worth the trip to the top of Tibidabo for this mesmerising lookout. (p172)

Transbordador Aeri An old-fashioned cable car (with modern cables) affording sublime views from its dangling trajectory. (p189)

Torre d'Alta Mar Serves up classic seafood dishes amid eagle's-nest views overlooking the waterfront. (p117)

Castell de Montjuïc One of many great spots on Montjuïc to gaze upon city and sea. (p185)

Mirablau Well-known Mirablau, at the foot of Tibidabo, has magnificent views out over the city. (p175)

Staying out Late

Moog A small, fun and relatively attitude-free downtown club that's a great spot for dancing. (p89)

Ocaña Perfectly positioned on scenic Plaça Reial, with a wildly designed interior and two stylish drinking dens below. (p73)

Opium Mar A perennial club favourite for its seaside location, open-air deck and thumping dance floor. (p119)

Harlem Jazz Club Hear live eclectic sounds till late in the morning at this old-shool Gòtic gem. (p75)

La Confitería A fin-de-siècle mural-covered bar that was once a confectioner's shop. (p88)

Marula Cafè A small, eclectic, dance-loving space in the Barri Gòtic with a serious penchant for funk and soul. (p74)

El Paraigua Head to the brick-vaulted chambers underground for free late-night music on weekends. (p75)

Barcelona Pipa Club Always a lively place to stop in for a late-night libation in the Barri Gòtic. (p74)

Fashion

La Manual Alpargatera The birthplace of espadrilles, and the world's best place to get a pair of the iconic Catalan rope-soled canvas shoes. (p78)

L'Arca A treasure chest of high-end vintage clothes dating back to the 1920s. (p77)

L'Illa Diagonal One of the top shopping malls for designer fashions; there's also an amazing food court on the lower level. (p50)

Adolfo Domínguez Browse for beautifully made men's and women's ready-to-wear at this elegant Passeig de Gràcia boutique. (p144)

Regia This perfumery has been around since 1928, and even has its own perfume museum on-site. (p145)

Obach This old-fashioned shop in the Barri Gòtic sells a fine array of hats for men and women. (p78)

Bagués-Masriera Beautifully crafted jewellery in the architecturally stunning Casa Amatller. (p145)

FC Botiga If dressing up means sporting your team's colours, don't miss this temple to all things FC Barça. (p78)

Chocolate

Museu de la Xocolata This museum is a requisite stop for every chocolate lover. There's even a shop on-site selling the good stuff. (p101)

Cacao Sampaka One of the city's finest temples to chocolate, with a cafe where you can imbibe thick *xocolata calenta* (hot chocolate). (p144)

Escribà An icon in the *barcelonin* world of sweets, Escribà has two locations filled with creations that are (almost) too beautiful to eat. (p135)

Hofmann Pastisseria Lots of chocolate goodies, pastries and other temptations await you in this shop in La Ribera. (p108)

Foix de Sarrià This brilliant pastry shop has been whipping up chocolate tortes and other finery since the 1860s. (p173)

Surprising Places

Museu Frederic Marès Barcelona's biggest curiosity cabinet, with a wild collection of religious sculpture, architectural fragments and 19th- and 20th-century ephemera. (p67)

Observatori Fabra Book for dinner under the stars in this Zona Alta observatory. (p170)

El Rey de la Màgia A century-old magic shop full of mystery and intrigue. (p108)

Sinagoga Major One of Europe's oldest synagogues, this secretive place lay hidden for hundreds of years. (p68)

Bosc de les Fades Like a page torn from a fairy tale, this Barri Gòtic bar makes an enchanting setting for a drink. (p75)

Herboristeria del Rei A cinematic spice and herb shop that's been around since 1823. (p78)

Speakeasy True to its name, this well-respected L'Eixample restaurant lies hidden behind a cocktail bar. No passwords required. (p136)

La Caseta del Migdia An outdoor bar with great views tucked amid the greenery way up on Montjuïc. (p193)

Month by Month

January

Barcelonins head to the Pyrenees for action on the ski slopes, while others simply enjoy a bit of post-holiday downtime (school holidays go to 8 January).

✨ Reis/Reyes

On 5 January, the day before Epifanía (Epiphany), children delight in the Cavalcada dels Reis Mags (Parade of the Three Kings), a colourful parade of floats and music, during which countless sweets are launched from the floats into the crowds.

✨ Festes dels Tres Tombs

In addition to live music and *gegants* (papier-mâché giants worn over the shoulders of processionists), the festival dedicated to Sant Antoni features a parade of horse-drawn carts in the neighbourhood of Sant Antoni (near the Mercat de Sant Antoni) every 17 January.

February

Often the coldest (and seemingly longest) month in Barcelona, February sees few visitors. Nonetheless, some of the first big festivals kick off, with abundant Catalan merriment amid the wintry gloom.

✨ Carnestoltes/Carnaval

Celebrated in February or March, this festival (www.bcn.cat/carnaval/en) involves several days of fancy-dress balls, merrymaking and fireworks, ending on the Tuesday before Ash Wednesday. Over 30 parades happen around town on the weekend. Down in Sitges a wilder version takes place.

✨ Festes de Santa Eulàlia

Around 12 February this big winter fest (santaeulalia.bcn.cat) celebrates Barcelona's first patron saint with a week of cultural events, including parades of *gegants,* open-air art installations, theatre, *correfocs* (fire runs) and *castells* (human castles).

April

Spring arrives with a flourish, complete with wildflowers blooming in the countryside, Easter revelry and school holidays, although April showers can dampen spirits. Book well ahead if coming around Easter.

✨ Día de Sant Jordi

Catalonia honours its patron saint, Sant Jordi (St George), on 23 April. Traditionally, men and women exchange roses and books – and La Rambla and Plaça de Sant Jaume fill with book and flower stalls.

May

With sunny pleasant days and clear skies, May can be one of the best times to visit Barcelona. The city slowly gears up for summer with the opening of the *chiringuitos* (beach bars).

✯ L'Ou com Balla

On Corpus Christi (late May or June), L'Ou com Balla (the Dancing Egg) bobs on top of flower-festooned fountains around the city. There's also an early evening procession from La Catedral and traditional Catalan folk dancing.

✯ Festa de Sant Ponç

To commemorate the patron saint of bee keepers and herbalists, locals fill Carrer de l'Hospital in El Raval on 11 May with the chatter and bustle of a street market.

☆ Primavera Sound

For one week in late May or early June, the open-air Parc del Fòrum and other locations around town stage an impressive line-up of international bands and DJs (www.primaverasound.com).

✯ Ciutat Flamenco

One of the best occasions to see great flamenco in Barcelona, this concentrated festival (ciutatflamenco. com) is held over four days in May.

June

Tourist numbers are well on the rise as Barcelona plunges into summer. Live music festivals and open-air events give the month a festive air.

☆ Festival Pedralbes

New in 2013, this fest (www.festivalpedralbes. com) takes place in lovely gardens and stages big-name performers (George Benson, Carla Bruni, Kool & the Gang) from mid-June to early July.

☆ Festival Piknic Electronik

Every Sunday from June through September, you can enjoy a day of electronic music at an outdoor space on Montjuïc (piknic-electronik.es/en). It attracts a mix of young families and party people.

✯ La Revetlla de Sant Joan/Verbenas de Sant Joan

On 23 June locals hit the streets or hold parties at home to celebrate the Revetlla de Sant Joan (St John's Night), which involves drinking, dancing, bonfires and fireworks (santjoan.bcn.cat).

✯ Pride Barcelona

The Barcelona Gay Pride festival (www.pridebarcelona. org) is a week of celebrations held towards the end of June with a crammed program of culture and concerts, along with the traditional Gay Pride march on the last Sunday of the month.

☆ Sónar

Usually in mid-June, Sónar (www.sonar.es) is Barcelona's massive celebration of electronic music, with DJs, exhibitions, sound labs, record fairs and urban art. Locations change each year.

July

Prices are high and it's peak tourist season, but it's a lively time to be in the city with sun-filled beach days, open-air dining and outdoor concerts.

✯ Festival del Grec

The major cultural event of the year is a month-long fest

(grec.bcn.cat) with dozens of theatre, dance and music performances held around town including at the Teatre Grec amphitheatre on Montjuïc, from which the festival takes its name.

August

The heat index soars; *barcelonins* leave the city in droves for summer holidays, as huge numbers of tourists arrive. It's a great time to hit the beach.

✯ Festa Major de Gràcia

Locals compete for the most elaborately decorated street in this week-long Gràcia festival (www.festamajorde-gracia.cat) held around 15 August. Also featured are free outdoor concerts, street fairs and other events.

✯ Festes de Sant Roc

For four days in mid-August, Plaça Nova in the Barri Gòtic becomes the scene of parades, the *correfoc*, a market, traditional music and magic shows for kids.

September

After a month off, *barcelonins* return to work, although several major festivals provide ample amusement. Temperatures stay warm through September, making for fine beach days.

✯ Festa Major de Sants

The district of Sants hosts a five-day fest (www.festa majordesants.net) with concerts, dance parties,

Top: Festes de la Mercè
Bottom: Festa Major de Gràcia

correfocs and elaborately decorated streets.

🎖 Diada Nacional de Catalunya

Catalonia's national day curiously commemorates Barcelona's surrender on 11 September 1714 to the Bourbon monarchy of Spain, at the conclusion of the War of the Spanish Succession.

🎖 Festes de la Mercè

Barcelona's co-patron saint is celebrated with fervour in this massive five-day fest (merce.bcn.cat). The city stages sporting events, free concerts, dance performances, human towers of *castellers,* parades of *gegants* and a fiery *correfoc.*

🎖 Festa Major de la Barceloneta

Barcelona's other big September celebration honours the local patron saint, Sant Miquel, on 29 September. It lasts about a week and involves plenty of dancing and drinking.

December

As winter returns *barcelonins* gear up for Christmas, and the city is festooned with decorations. Relatively few visitors arrive, at least until Christmas, when the city fills with holidaying out-of-towners.

🛍 Fira de Santa Llúcia

Held from early December to Christmas, this market has hundreds of stalls selling Christmas decorations and gifts, including the infamous Catalan Nativity scene character, the *caganer* (the crapper).

With Kids

Barcelona is great for older kids and teens – the Mediterranean attitude means they are included in many seemingly adult activities, like eating late meals at bars or restaurants. Babies will love the welcoming Mediterranean culture, and toddlers will be showered with attention.

RICHARD CUMMINS/GETTY IMAGES ©

L'Aquàrium (p112)

Dining Out

Barcelona – and Spain in general – is super friendly when it comes to eating with children. Locals take their kids out all the time and don't worry too much about keeping them up late, so going out to eat or to sip a beer on a terrace on a summer evening needn't mean leaving children with minders – and they're bound to strike up a friendship or two! Spanish kids tend to eat the Mediterranean offerings enjoyed by their parents, but many restaurants have children's menus that serve up burgers, pizzas, tomato-sauce pasta and the like. Good local – and childproof – options commonly found on tapas menus are the *tortilla de patatas* (potato omelette) or *croquetas de jamón* (croquettes with ham).

Best Kid-Friendly Eateries

La Nena
A fantastic cafe for chocolate and all manner of sweet things (p160).

Fastvínic
Great eatery (p135) for an off-peak lunch or quick dinner, while the kids entertain themselves by drawing on the glass wall.

Granja M Viader
No kid will be left unimpressed by the thick hot chocolate here (p88).

Butifarring
This eatery (p71) serves up grilled sausages made with top-quality ingredients.

Granja La Pallaresa
Along a street famed for its chocolate cafes, this place (p77) is a favourite for crispy churros dipped in steaming chocolate.

Best Parks & Open Spaces

Parc de la Ciutadella
This park (p100) has a zoo, a pond and a playground.

Parc d'Atraccions
This fabulous funfair (p172) is excellent for adrenalin-loving kids and grown-ups.

Parc de la Creueta del Coll
Excellent park (p169) for its splashing pool, swings and snack bar.

Font Màgica
The light show (p186) is guaranteed to make the little ones shout 'Again!'

Platja de la Nova Icària
One of a string of beaches (p112) between Barceloneta and El Fòrum.

Best Kid-Friendly Museums

CosmoCaixa
A fantastic science museum (p170) whose interactive displays fascinate kids of all ages.

Museu de la Xocolata
This museum (p101) is all about chocolate – need we say more?

Zoo de Barcelona
You'll find all the animals you can think of in this relatively small zoo (p101), from yawning hippos, to spluttering elephants and frowning gorillas.

L'Aquàrium
This a fantastic aquarium (p112), one of Europe's largest, with tank after tank of glimmering, colourful fish.

Poble Espanyol
Kids and parents can enjoy going through a mini Spain (p186) together.

Best Ways to See the City

By Bike
Barcelona has tonnes of bike tours and outlets that hire bikes with little trolleys in the front, for transporting the little ones (p32).

On Segway
Parents and older kids and teens can mount these futuristic-looking vehicles and scoot around town (p31).

By Bus
Barcelona's bus tours are great for older kids – hop on, climb up to the open top floor and see the views (p252).

NEED TO KNOW

➡ Get a babysitter at **Tender Loving Canguros** (www.tlcanguros.com).

➡ Nappies, dummies, creams and formula can be bought at any of the city's many pharmacies. Nappies are cheaper in supermarkets.

➡ Make sure you have your child's **EHIC card** (www.nhs.uk/ehic) before you travel within the EU.

➡ Barcelona's metro is accessible and great for families with buggies. Be mindful of pickpockets.

➡ The narrow streets of the Ciutat Vella are less buggy-friendly than the rest of Barcelona.

By Cable Car
Travel to Montjuïc from Barceloneta beach through the air. The Transbordador Aeri is bound to be loved by all ages (p113).

Best Shopping

Imaginarium
An international chain (www.imaginarium.ie) that has shops dotted around Barcelona (and Spain), it sells toys and clothes. There's even a branch in **Barri Gòtic** (Map p276; Carrer del Pi 7; ☺10am-8.30pm Mon-Sat; MLiceu). Some locations have a cafe for babies and kids.

Papabubble
Watch candy being made the old-fashioned way at this inviting little shop (p78) in the old city.

El Ingenio
Imaginations run wild here (p78) amid the shelves packed with puppets, masks, yo-yos and novelty items.

El Rei de la Màgia
A cabinet of curiosity for all budding magicians (p108).

Taller de Marionetas Travi
A small, enchanting shop (p76) full of handmade wooden and papier-mâché marionettes.

Like a Local

Whether you're a frequent visitor or a first-timer, taking a local approach when it comes to eating, drinking and other amusements offers a rewarding way to experience the city.

FC Barcelona fans cheer on their team

When to Dine

In Barcelona, and elsewhere in Spain, meal times run late. Most restaurants don't open for dinner until 8.30pm or 9pm and close at midnight or 1am; peak dining time is around 10pm. Locals commonly have lunch between 1pm and 4pm. This is then followed by a siesta (a loll on the beach or in one of the parks is a fine choice when the weather is pleasant). Locals aren't big on breakfast – a croissant and a *cortado* (espresso with milk) is a typical way to start the day.

Water & Wine

Lunch or dinner, wine is always a fine idea, according to most *barcelonins*. Luckily, many restaurants offer *menú del día* (menu of the day, or fixed price) lunches that include a glass of red or white. If you become a regular, waiters may give you complimentary refills or even leave the bottle. Of course, you can also opt for another drink. A word on water: no one drinks it straight from the tap (taste it and you'll know why). Order *agua mineral*, either *con gas* (bubbly) or *sin gas* (still).

Tapas

When hunger pains arrive in the afternoon or early evening, locals head out for a predinner tapa. This means heading to the local favourite for a bite of anchovies, sausage, squid, mushrooms, roasted peppers or dozens of other tempting morsels. Wine, *cava* or beer all make fine accompaniments. Many tapas spots are lively stand-around-the-bar affairs (Bormuth (p102) and Vaso de Oro (p116) are great places to start).

Local Meal Spots

La Rambla is fine for a stroll, but no local would eat there. The same holds for Carrer Ferran and other tourist-packed streets in Barri Gòtic. The Gòtic does, however, have some local-favoured gems, particularly on the narrow lanes of the east side – such as Onofre (p72) and Cafè de l'Acadèmia (p73). For more authentic neighbourhood dining, browse the streets of El Born, Barceloneta, El Raval and Gràcia.

Weekends

Many *barcelonins* head out of town on the weekends. That could mean skiing in the Pyrenees in winter, or heading up the Costa Brava in summer. Those that stick around might hit up flea markets or produce markets, head to the beach or have an outing in the park. The parks are liveliest on weekends, when local musicians, picnickers, pop-up markets and playing children add to the city's relaxed air. Culture-craving locals might hit an art opening – openings at CCCB (p84) and MACBA (p82) are good fun – see a rep film (Filmoteca de Catalunya, p89, has intriguing fare) or catch a concert, like at Jazz Sí Club (p90) or Sala Apolo (p193).

The Sunday Feast

Sunday is typically the most peaceful day for Catalans, and a fine occasion for gathering with family or friends over a big meal. Lunch is the main event, and many restaurants prepare Sunday-only specials. Lots of places close on Sunday nights too, so it's worth lingering over a long multi-course meal – a rich paella at Barraca (p117) or Can Ros (p117), followed by a long leisurely stroll along the waterfront is always a hit.

Festivals & Other Events

One of the best ways to join in for local amusement is to come for one of the city's big festivals. During summer (June to August), Música als Parcs features 30 or so open-air concerts at a dozen parks in Barcelona, and free concerts are held at various venues around the city. Stop in at a tourist office for the latest schedule. Other great open-air concerts that goes through summer include Festival Piknic Electronik (p24) and Festival Pedralbes (p24).

Local Listings

If you can read some Spanish (Castilian), browse the latest art openings, film screenings, concerts and other events in the *Guia del Ocio* (www.guiadelocio.com), *Time*

NEED TO KNOW

➡ **Miniguide** (miniguide.es) Guide on culture, food, nightlife, fashion and more; published 10 times a year.

➡ **Barcelona Cultura** (barcelona cultura.bcn.cat) Upcoming cultural fare, including concerts, exhibitions and festivals.

➡ **Spotted by Locals** (www.spotted bylocals.com/barcelona) Reviews of favourite spots – restaurants, bars, cinemas, galleries and more, written by local residents/expats.

➡ **Barça Central** (http://barca central.com) The latest news about FC Barcelona.

➡ **In & Out Barcelona** (www.inand outbarcelona.net) New restaurants, bars, cafes, shops and clubs with lovely photos – but in Spanish.

Out Barcelona (www.timeout.cat) or the daily papers like *La Vanguardia* (www.lavanguardia.com) and *El Periodico* (www.elperiodico.com). Friday papers list the weekend's events (most with pull-out supplements), and are often worth a read even if your Spanish is limited.

Football

FC Barcelona plays a prominent role in the city's imagination. Heading to a match at Camp Nou (p176) is the best way to catch a bit of Barcelona fever, but watching it onscreen at a tavern can be just as much fun depending on the crowd. For the most fervent fan base, head to Barceloneta, El Raval, Gràcia or Sarrià, where you'll find lively spots to catch a game. The daily journal *Marca* (www.marca.com) gives the latest on sporting news.

Sardana

The traditional Catalan folk dance *sardana* still attracts a small local following. On weekends aficionados gather in front of La Catedral for group dancing to a live 10-piece band. The action happens at 6pm on Saturday and noon on Sunday and lasts about an hour.

For Free

With planning, Barcelona can be an affordable place to travel. Many museums offer free days, and some of the best ways to experience the city don't cost a penny – hanging out on the beach, exploring fascinating neighbourhoods and parks, and drinking in the views from hilltop heights.

Walking Tours

Numerous companies offer pay-what-you-wish walking tours. These typically take in the Barri Gòtic (p69) or the Modernista sites of L'Eixample (p132). A few recommended outfitters include Runner Bean Tours (p31), **Feel Free Tours** (www.feelfreetours.com), **Orange Donut Tours** (www.orangedonuttours.com; ⊘tours 11am & 3pm), **Discover Walks** (www.discoverwalks.com; ⊘10.30am, 3pm & 5pm Fri-Mon Apr-Oct) and **Travel Bound** (www.travelbar.com).

Festivals & Other Events

Barcelona has loads of free festivals and events, including the Festes de la Mercè and the Festes de Santa Eulàlia (see p23 for more listings). From June to August, the city hosts Música als Parcs (Music in the Parks), a series of open-air concerts held in different parks and green spaces around the city. Over 40 different concerts feature classical, blues and jazz groups. Popular venues include Parc de la Ciutadella, Parc de Joan Miró (Carrer de Tarragona, Sant Antoni) and Parc Turó (Avenida de Pau Casals 19, Sant Gervasi). Stop in at the tourist office or go online (www.bcn.cat) for a schedule.

Museums

Entry to some sights is free on occasion, most commonly on the first Sunday of the month, while quite a few attractions are free from 3pm to 8pm on Sundays. Others are always free. The following listed are most likely to attract your attention.

Always Free Museums

➡ Centre de la Imatge (p59)
➡ Centre d'Art Santa Mònica (p59)
➡ Basílica de Santa Maria del Mar (p97)
➡ Estadi Olímpic Lluís Companys (p187)
➡ Col·lecció de Carrosses Fúnebres (p189)
➡ Museu d'Història de la Immigració de Catalunya (p116)
➡ Palau del Lloctinent (p64)
➡ Temple Romà d'August (p68)
➡ Antic Hospital de la Santa Creu (p84)
➡ Font Màgica (p186)
➡ Jardins de Mossèn Cinto de Verdaguer (p190)
➡ Cementiri del Poblenou (p112)
➡ Universitat de Barcelona (p131)

Free Museums Sometimes

➡ Museu d'Història de Catalunya (p112)
➡ Museu Nacional d'Art de Catalunya (p179)
➡ Museu Picasso (p94)
➡ La Catedral (p62)
➡ Museu Frederic Marès (p67)
➡ Castell de Montjuïc (p185)
➡ Museu-Monestir de Pedralbes (p168)
➡ Jardins del Laberint d'Horta (p171)
➡ Museu de la Música (p113)
➡ Museu d'Història de Barcelona (p65)
➡ Museu Marítim (p111)
➡ Ajuntament (p64)

Guided Tours & Walks

There are many ways to get a more in-depth look at the city, whether on a specialised walking tour through the Ciutat Vella, on a bicycle excursion around the centre or on a hop-on, hop-off bus tour all across town.

Bike tour, Plaça del Rei (p69)

Walking Tours

The Oficina d'Informació de Turisme de Barcelona (p255) organises a series of guided walking tours. One explores the Barri Gòtic (adult/child €16/free); another follows in Picasso's footsteps and winds up at the Museu Picasso, to which entry is included in the price (adult/child €22/7); and a third takes in the main jewels of Modernisme (adult/child €16/free). There's also a 'gourmet' tour of traditional purveyors of fine foodstuffs across the old city (adult/child €22/7). Stop by the tourist office or go online for the latest schedule. Tours typically last two hours and start at the tourist office.

More specialised tours are also bookable through the tourist office: themes include running, shopping, literary Barcelona, tapas tours, civil-war tours, the Gothic quarter by night, Park Güell and half a dozen other options.

My Favourite Things (☏637 265405; www.myft.net; tours from €26) offers tours for no more than 10 participants based on numerous themes: anything from design to food. Other activities include flamenco and salsa classes and bicycle rides in and out of Barcelona.

Runner Bean Tours (Map p276; ☏636 108776; www.runnerbeantours.com; ⊘tours 11am year-round & 4.30pm Apr-Sep) has several daily thematic tours. It's a pay-what-you-wish tour, with a collection taken at the end for the guide. The Old City tour explores the Roman and medieval history of Barcelona, visiting highlights in the Ciutat Vella. The Gaudí tour takes in the great works of Modernista Barcelona. It involves two trips on the metro. Runner Beans also has ghostly evening tours and a Kids and Family Walking Tour; check the website for departure times.

Scooter & Go-Cart Tours

Cooltra (p251) offers three different scooter tours around the city (€40 to €50): city highlights, Modernista architecture and a beach tour.

Barcelona Segway Fun (Map p276; ☏670 484000; www.barcelonasegwayfun.com; meeting point: Sots Tinent Navarro 26; tours €30-57; Ⓜ Jaume I) offers urban and even country tours on two-wheel people-movers! A one-hour tour costs €30 and leaves from Barri Gòtic at 11am daily. The 90-minute and two-hour tours also depart from here.

GoCar (Map p284; 🗷93 269 17 92; www.gocartours.es; Carrer de Freixures 23; tours 2½/8hr €70/160; ☉9am-9pm) has GPS-guided 'cars' (actually two-seat, three-wheel mopeds) that allow you to tour around town, park where motorbikes are allowed and listen to commentaries on major sites as you go. The GPS system makes it virtually impossible to get lost.

Boat Tours

Several companies take passengers on short jaunts out on the water. These depart several times daily (with many departures in the summer) from Moll de les Drassanes near the southern end of La Rambla. **Las Golondrinas** (Map p286; 🗷93 442 31 06; www.lasgolondrinas.com; Moll de les Drassanes; 35min tour adult/child €6.80/2.60; ⓜDrassanes), BC Naval Tours (p121) and other companies offer scenic catamaran trips around the harbour and beyond. Avoid going on a windy day, when the seas can be rough.

Trixi Tours

These three-wheeled cycle **taxis** (Map p276; 🗷699 984726; www.trixi.info; Plaça dels Traginers 4; 1/2hr tour €25/45) operate around the Ciutat Vella, the waterfront and much of the city centre (noon to 8pm daily March to November). They can take two passengers on guided tours ranging from 30 minutes to three hours. You can find them in front of La Catedral.

Bus Tours

Bus Turístic (p252) is a hop-on, hop-off service that stops at virtually all of the city's main sights. Audio guides (in 10 languages) provide running commentary on the 44 stops on the three different circuits. The service operates from Plaça de Catalunya and Plaça del Porta de la Pau.

Tickets are available online and on the buses, and cost €27 (€16 for children from four to 12 years) for one day of unlimited

rides, or €35 (€20 for children) for two consecutive days. Buses run from 9am to 8pm (7pm in winter) and the frequency varies from every five to 25 minutes.

The two key routes take about two hours each; the blue route runs past La Pedrera on Passeig de Gràcia and takes in La Sagrada Família, Park Güell and much of the Zona Alta (including Pedralbes and Camp Nou). The red route also runs up Passeig de Gràcia and takes in Port Vell, Port Olímpic and Montjuïc.

Barcelona Guide Bureau (🗷93 315 22 61; www.barcelonaguidebureau.com; Via Laietana 54) places professional guides at the disposal of groups for tailormade tours of the city. Several languages are catered for. It also offers a series of daily tours, from a five-hour highlights of Barcelona tour (adult/child €59/30, departing at 10am) to a trip to Montserrat, leaving Barcelona at 3pm and lasting about four hours (adult/child €47/23).

Bicycle Tours

Barcelona is awash with companies offering bicycle tours. Tours typically take two to four hours and generally stick to La Sagrada Família, the Ciutat Vella and the beaches. Operators include the following:

Barcelona By Bicycle (Map p284; 🗷93 268 21 05; www.bicicletabarcelona.com; Carrer de l'Esparteria 3; tour €22)

Barcelona By Bike (Map p288; 🗷671 307325; www.barcelonabybike.com; Carrer de la Marina 13; tours €22; ⓜCuitadella/Vila Olimpica)

BarcelonaBiking.com (Map p276; 🗷656 356300; www.barcelonabiking.com; Baixada de Sant Miquel 6; bike hire per hr/24hr €5/15, tour €21; ☉10am-8pm, tour 11am daily; ⓜJaume I or Liceu)

CicloTour (Map p280; 🗷93 317 19 70; www.barcelonaciclotour.com/eng; Carrer dels Tallers 45; tours €22; ☉11am daily, 4.30pm mid-Apr–Oct, 7.30pm Thu-Sun Jun-Sep)

Fat Tire Bike Tours (Map p276; 🗷93 342 92 75; http://fattirebiketours.com; Carrer Sant Honorat 7; bike hire per hr/half-day €3/8, tour €24; ☉10am-8pm; ⓜJaume I or Liceu)

Terra Diversions (Map p296; 🗷93 416 08 05; www.terradiversions.com; Carrer de Santa Tecla 1bis) Mostly mountain-bike tours outside the city.

Quimet i Quimet (p191)

Eating

Barcelona has a celebrated food scene fuelled by a combination of world-class chefs, imaginative recipes and magnificent ingredients fresh from farms and the sea. Catalan culinary masterminds such as Albert Adrià and Carles Abellan have become international icons, reinventing the world of haute cuisine, while classic old-world Catalan recipes continue to earn accolades in dining rooms and tapas bars across the city.

New Catalan Cuisine

Avant-garde chefs have made Catalonia famous throughout the world for their food laboratories, their commitment to food as art and their crazy riffs on the themes of traditional local cooking.

Here the notion of gourmet cuisine is deconstructed as chefs transform liquids and solid foods into foams, create 'ice cream' of classic ingredients by means of liquid nitrogen, freeze-dry foods to make concentrated powder versions and employ spherification to create unusual and artful creations. This alchemical cookery is known as molecular gastronomy, and invention is the keystone of this technique.

Diners may encounter olive oil 'caviar', 'snow' made of gazpacho with anchovies, gellified parmesan turned into spaghetti, or countless other concoctions.

The dining rooms themselves also offer a reconfiguration of the five-star dining experience. Restaurateurs generally aim to create warm and buzzing spaces, with artful design flourishes, without the stuffiness and formality typically associated with high-end dining.

Celebrity Chefs

Albert Adrià, brother of Ferran of El Bulli fame, has brought culinary fame to Barcelona with his growing empire of restaurants. Tickets (p192) is a delectable showcase of whimsy and imagination, with deconstructed tapas dishes like liquid olives, 'air baguettes' (made with Iberian ham) and cotton-candy-covered trees with edible dark chocolate 'soil'.

Other great chefs continue to redefine contemporary cuisine. The Michelin-starred chef Carles Abellan, creator of Comerç 24 (p105),

NEED TO KNOW

Price Ranges

In our listings, we've used the following price codes to represent the cost of a main course:

€	less than €10
€€	€10 to €20
€€€	over €20

Opening Hours

Most restaurants open from 1pm to 4pm and from 8.30pm to midnight.

Reservations

At midrange restaurants and simpler taverns you can usually turn up without booking ahead. At high-end restaurants, and for dinner especially, it is safer to make a booking. Thursday to Saturday nights are especially busy.

Tipping

A service charge is often, but not always, included in the bill. Catalans and other Spaniards are not overwhelming tippers. If you are particularly happy, 5% on top is generally fine.

Menú del Día

The *menú del día*, a full set meal with water and wine (and usually with several meal options), is a great way to cap prices at lunchtime. They start from around €8 to €10 and can move as high as €25 for more elaborate offerings.

Menú de Degustación

At high-end restaurants you can occasionally opt for a *menú de degustación*, a tasting menu involving samples of different dishes. This can be a great way to get a broader view of what the restaurant does and has the advantage of coming at a fixed price.

Tapas 24 (p137) and other restaurants, playfully reinterprets traditional tapas with dishes like the *melón con jamón,* a millefeuille of layered caramelised Iberian ham and thinly sliced melon.

Another star of the Catalan cooking scene is Jordi Vilà, who continues to wow diners at Alkímia (p138) and Vivanda (p173) with reinvented Catalan classics. Other major players on the Catalan dining scene are Jordi Artal at Cinc Sentits (p136) and Xavier Pellicer at ABaC (p173) and Barraca (p117).

Tapas Bars

Tapas, those bite-sized morsels of joy, are an essential pillar in Barcelona's culinary scene. Like all elements of Catalan cuisine, the breadth of choice when it comes to tapas is extraordinary. Tapas bars are found all across the city. Most open earlier than restaurants – typically around 7pm – making them a good predinner (or instead-of-dinner option). Some open from lunch and stay open without a break through late-evening closing time.

As per the 'bar' designation, these places are less formal than restaurants, and drinking is an essential component in the experience.

ORDERING TAPAS

Ordering tapas generally works like this: you take your seat at the bar or one of the cafe-style tables usually on hand, order drinks – try the slightly fizzy white wine *(txacolí),* a glass of *cava* (sparkling wine), a housemade *vermut* (vermouth) or a refreshing *caña* (draught beer) – and ask for a plate.

Many of the tapas are *montaditos* (a sort of canapé), which can range from a creamy Roquefort cheese and walnut combination to a chunk of spicy sausage. They all come with toothpicks. These facilitate their consumption, but serve another important purpose too: when you're ready to leave, the toothpicks are counted up and the bill presented.

While a *tapa* is a tiny serving, if you particularly like something you can have a *ración* (rations; large tapas servings) or *media ración* (half-rations; smaller tapas servings). Remember, that two or three *raciones* can easily constitute a full meal; the *media ración* is a good choice if you want to experience a broader range of tastes.

In addition to plates displayed on the bar, some tapas venues will also offer hot dishes fresh from the kitchen. The bar staff will typically go around the bar and see if anyone is interested. If you see something you like, take it!

Other places only bring out hot plates when ordered. Have a look at the menu, which might be a posted chalkboard listing the day's specials. If you can't choose, ask for *la especialidad de la casa* (the house speciality), and it's hard to go wrong.

Classic Catalan Cuisine

Traditional Catalan recipes showcase the great produce of the Mediterranean: fish, prawns, cuttlefish, clams, pork, rabbit, game, first-rate olive oil, peppers and loads of garlic. Classic dishes also feature unusual pairings (seafood with meat, fruit with fowl): cuttlefish with chickpeas, cured pork with caviar, rabbit with prawns, goose with pears.

Great Catalan restaurants can be found in nearly every neighbourhood around town. The settings can be a huge part of the appeal – with candle-lit medieval chambers in the Ciutat Vella and Modernista design in L'Eixample setting the stage for a memorable feast. Although there are plenty of high-end places in this city, foodie-minded *barcelonins* aren't averse to eating at humbler, less elegant places – which sometimes cook up the best meals.

Seafood Restaurants

There are a wealth of restaurants specialising in seafood. Not surprisingly, Barceloneta, which lies near the sea, is packed with eateries of all shapes and sizes doling out decadent paellas, cauldrons of bubbling molluscs, grilled catch of the day and other delights. Nearest the sea, you'll find pricier open-air places with Mediterranean views, but plunge into the narrow lanes to find the real gems, including bustling family-run places that serve first-rate plates at great prices.

Catalan Specialities

STARTERS

➡ **Calçots amb romesco** Sweet and juicy spring onions cooked up on a barbecue

➡ **Escalivada** Red peppers and aubergines, grilled, cooled, peeled, sliced and served with an olive oil, salt and garlic dressing

➡ **Esqueixada** Salad of *bacallà/bacalao* (shredded salted cod) with tomatoes, red peppers, onions, white beans, olives, olive oil and vinegar

MAIN COURSES

➡ **Arròs a la cassola/arroz a la catalana** Catalan paella, cooked without saffron

➡ **Arròs negre** Rice cooked in black cuttlefish ink

TOP TAPAS PLATES

If you opt for *tapes*/tapas, it is handy to identify some of the common items:

➡ **boquerons/boquerones** white anchovies in vinegar – delicious and tangy

➡ **bombes/bombas** meat and potato croquettes

➡ **carxofes/alcachofas** artichokes

➡ **gambes/gambas** prawns, either done *al all/al ajillo*, with garlic, or *a la plantxa/plancha*, grilled

➡ **navalles/navajas** razor clams

➡ **patates braves/patatas bravas** potato chunks bathed in a slightly spicy tomato sauce, sometimes mixed with mayonnaise

➡ **pop á feira/pulpo a la gallega** tender boiled octopus with paprika

➡ **truita de patates/tortilla de patatas** potato-filled omelette; one with vegetables is a *tortilla de verduras*

➡ **xampinyons/champiñones** mushrooms

➡ **Bacallà a la llauna** Salted cod baked in tomato, garlic, parsley, paprika and wine

➡ **Botifarra amb mongetes** Pork sausage with fried white beans

➡ **Cargols/caracoles** Snails, often stewed with *conill/conejo* (rabbit) and chilli

➡ **Fideuà** Similar to paella but with vermicelli noodles as the base. Often accompanied by *allioli* (pounded garlic with olive oil) that you can mix in as you wish

➡ **Fricandó** Pork and vegetable stew

➡ **Sarsuela/zarzuela** Mixed seafood cooked in *sofregit* (fried onion, tomato and garlic sauce) with seasonings

➡ **Suquet de peix** Fish and potato hotpot

DESSERTS

➡ **Crema catalana** A cream custard with a crisp burnt-sugar coating

➡ **Mel i mató** Honey and fresh cream cheese

Market Dining

Barcelona has some fantastic food markets. Foodies will enjoy the sounds, smells and most importantly tastes of the Mercat de

Eating by Neighbourhood

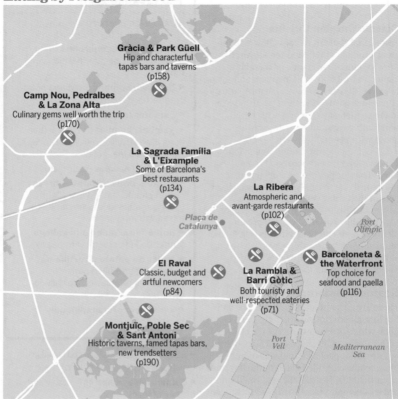

Gràcia & Park Güell
Hip and characterful
tapas bars and taverns
(p158)

**Camp Nou, Pedralbes
& La Zona Alta**
Culinary gems well worth the trip
(p170)

**La Sagrada Família
& L'Eixample**
Some of Barcelona's
best restaurants
(p134)

La Ribera
Atmospheric and
avant-garde restaurants
(p102)

*Plaça de
Catalunya*

*Port
Olímpic*

El Raval
Classic, budget and
artful newcomers
(p84)

**La Rambla &
Barri Gòtic**
Both touristy and
well-respected eateries
(p71)

**Barceloneta &
the Waterfront**
Top choice for
seafood and paella
(p116)

**Montjuïc, Poble Sec
& Sant Antoni**
Historic taverns, famed tapas bars,
new trendsetters
(p190)

*Port
Vell*

*Mediterranean
Sea*

la Boqueria (p81). This is probably Spain's biggest and best market, and it's conveniently located right off La Rambla. Here you can find temptations of all sorts: plump fruits and veggies, fresh-squeezed juices, artisanal cheeses, smoked meats, seafood and pastries. The best feature: an array of tapas bars and food stalls where you can sample amazingly fresh ingredients cooked to perfection. Some other great market options:

➡ Mercat de Sant Antoni (p194)

➡ Mercat de Santa Caterina (p99)

➡ Mercat de la Llibertat (p158)

How to Eat Like a Local

Barcelonins aren't big breakfast eaters. Most folks tend to stop in at a bar on the way to work for a pastry and a *cafe amb llet* (coffee with milk). Lunchtimes are a more decadent affair. At the restaurant, which typically serves lunch from 1pm to 4pm, locals might opt for the good-value *menú del día,* a multicourse meal that often includes wine, dessert and coffee. Dinner can be a sit-down affair (restaurants serve from 9pm to 11.30pm on average) or something more casual – tapas and drinks at a neighbourhood bar.

Eating can be an art in Barcelona, and here are a few local tips: always ask for the local speciality; never be shy about looking around to see what others have ordered before choosing; and always ask the waiters for their recommendations.

One of the best ways to eat like a local is to dine in a *barcelonin's* home. New sites like EatWith (www.eatwith.com) list hundreds of prospective hosts who throw dinner parties. A full meal with wine costs €20 to €40 per person.

Lonely Planet's Top Choices

Cinc Sentits (p136) Tasting menus that showcase the best of Catalan cooking.

Tickets (p192) The celebrated restaurant by Albert Adrià, showcasing Barcelona's best *nueva cocina española*.

Tapas 24 (p137) Carles Abellan creates some of Barcelona's best tapas.

Pla (p73) Delectable fare in a candle-lit medieval dining room.

La Vinateria dell Call (p73) Charming spot hidden down a narrow Gothic lane.

Best by Budget

€

Les Tres a la Cuina (p158) Gràcia gem serving unique, Slow Food–minded dishes.

La Cova Fumada (p116) Barceloneta hole-in-the-wall with excellent small plates.

€€

Suculent (p87) Carles Abellan's bistro serving excellent Catalan cooking.

Casa Delfin (p103) Delicious Mediterranean fare in an atmospheric setting.

€€€

Alkímia (p138) Magnificent Catalan cuisine by Michelin-starred Jordi Vilà.

Koy Shunka (p73) Avant-garde Japanese fare, probably Barcelona's best.

Best for Tapas

Bormuth (p102) Serves both the classic and the new wave, plus tasty vermouths.

Quimet i Quimet (p191) Mouth-watering morsels served to a standing crowd.

Ajoblanco (p173) Creative tapas dishes and great cocktails.

Bar Pinotxo (p87) Pull up a bar stool at this legendary Boqueria joint.

Tapas 24 (p137) Everyone's favourite gourmet tapas bar.

Best for Catalan

Vivanda (p173) Magnficent Catalan cooking with year-round garden dining.

El Glop (p160) A buzzing neighbourhood spot in Gràcia.

Roig Robí (p162) A pillar of traditional Catalan cooking.

Cafè de l'Acadèmia (p73) High-quality dishes that never disappoint.

Best for Basque

Euskal Etxea (p104) Authentic San Sebastián–style tapas joint.

Ipar-Txoko (p161) Sumptuous cooking served in a warmly lit dining room.

Best for Eating Like a Local

Mitja Vida (p171) Mouthwatering tapas and vermouth.

El Tossal (p160) No-nonsense Catalan spot with excellent cooking.

5º Pino (p174) Tapas and light fare with outdoor seating near Sarrià.

Best for Architecture

El Asador de Aranda (p173) A beautiful spread of Modernista dining rooms.

Casa Calvet (p138) A stylish restaurant set in an early Gaudí building.

Best Cafes

Copasetic (p135) Vintage-filled cafe.

Café Godot (p160) Friendly and easygoing, with tasty snacks and mains.

Čaj Chai (p72) Teas and lively chatter in Barri Gòtic.

La Nena (p160) Kid-friendly cafe in Gràcia.

Best for Fusion

Can Kenji (p137) Masterful blend of Japanese and Mediterranean cuisine.

Allium (p72) Seasonal organic cuisine with unique twists on Catalan recipes.

Best for Vegetarians

Sésamo (p85) Probably Barcelona's best vegetarian restaurant.

Cereria (p73) Pizzas and galettes in an old-fashioned setting.

Organic (p85) El Raval eatery that lives up to its name.

Rasoterra (p71) Airy vegetarian charmer in Barri Gòtic.

Best for Carnivores

Patagonia Beef & Wine (p137) Feasting on Argentine steaks.

Bilbao (p161) A classic spot for steaks and Spanish reds.

El Asador de Aranda (p173) Roast lamb in a Modernista setting.

Best for Late-Night Eating

Alcoba Azul (p71) Tasty tapas and wine in an atmospheric setting.

Cafè de l'Òpera (p72) Visit for late-night snacks on La Rambla.

Elisabets (p84) Offers late-night dining (till 1am) on Fridays.

Best for Chocolate Lovers

Granja La Pallaresa (p77) One of many chocolate-dispensing cafes on Carrer de Petritxol.

Cacao Sampaka (p144) Chocolate decadence comes in many forms at this L'Eixample shop and cafe.

Museu de la Xocolata (p101) Delve into the world of chocolate, then feast in the cafe.

Best for Brunch

Federal (p192) Excellent brunches and a small roof terrace.

En Aparté (p102) French eatery serving tasty brunch fare on weekends.

Milk (p73) Serves brunch daily (till 4.30pm).

Dos Trece (p87) Fabulous Sunday brunches in El Raval.

Copasetic (p135) Vintage-filled cafe with weekend brunch.

Best for Romantic Dining

La Vinateria dell Call (p73) Flickering candles and medieval walls.

Can Recasens (p118) Romantic spot with market-fresh fare in Poblenou.

Pla (p73) Intimate setting and memorable meals.

Best for Celebrity Chefs

ABaC (p173) Brilliantly inventive menu by Jordi Cruz.

Comerç 24 (p105) One of Carles Abellan's smash hits.

Tickets (p192) Molecular gastronomy in all its glory.

Best for Food & Wine

Viblioteca (p162) Heaven for wine and cheese lovers.

Monvínic (p138) A staggering number of wines on offer.

Onofre (p72) Run by wine lovers, with good tapas to match.

Best for Historic Atmosphere

Can Cortada (p171) Peel back the centuries at this former country estate.

Can Travi Nou (p171) Upscale Catalan cuisine in an 18th-century setting.

Restaurant 7 Portes (p117) Top seafood and art deco elegance.

Best for Lunch Specials

Les Tres a la Cuina (p158) The imaginative menu changes daily.

Cafè de l'Acadèmia (p73) Rich lunch specials and great atmosphere.

Best for Desserts

Caelum (p72) Dine on sweet perfection in the pleasant cafe, or head downstairs for medieval atmosphere.

Granja Petitbo (p137) Sink into a leather armchair and devour a homemade cake at this quaint cafe.

Escribà (p135) A household name in Barcelona for its beautiful pastries and other temptations.

Best for Seafood

Barraca (p117) Sparkling new waterfront restaurant with unique seafood combinations.

Can Majó (p117) Fine seafood in a pleasant outdoor setting.

Can Ros (p117) A family-run Barceloneta classic.

Can Maño (p117) Unfussy place with great, low-price dishes.

Best for Latin American

El Rincón Maya (p135) Real-deal Mexican fare in L'Eixample.

Caravelle (p85) Delectable tacos and other global hits.

Cantina Machito (p161) Dine outside on quesadillas, enchiladas and other Mexican hits.

Best for Italian

Le Cucine Mandarosso (p103) Home-style Italian cooking.

La Bella Napoli (p191) Serves magnificent pizzas.

Best for Galician

Cerveseria Brasseria Gallega (p136) Succulent seafood, loved by neighbourhood regulars.

Botafumeiro (p162) For a decadent seafood feast.

Tapas bar, La Rambla

Drinking & Nightlife

Barcelona is a nightlife-lovers' town, with an enticing spread of candlelit wine bars, old-school taverns, stylish lounges and kaleidoscopic nightclubs where the party continues until daybreak. For something a little more sedate, the city's atmospheric cafes and teahouses make a fine retreat when the skies turn grey.

Bars & Lounges

Barcelona has a dizzying assortment of bars where you can start – or end – the night. The atmosphere varies tremendously – candlelit, mural-covered chambers in the medieval quarter, antique-filled converted storefronts and buzzing Modernista spaces are all part of the scene. Of course, where to go depends as much on the crowd as it does on ambience – here you'll find a quick rundown of the drinking scene by neighbourhood in the city.

Wherever you end up, keep in mind that eating and drinking go hand in hand in Barcelona (as in other parts of Spain), and some of the liveliest bars serve up as much tapas as they do alcohol.

Wine & Cava Bars

A growing number of wine bars scattered around the city provide a showcase for the great produce from Spain and beyond. Vine-minded spots such as Monvínic (p138) serve a huge selection of wines by the glass, with a particular focus on stellar new vintages. A big part of the experience is having a few bites while you drink. Expect sharing plates, platters of cheese and charcuterie, and plenty of tapas.

Cava bars tend to be more about the festive ambience than the actual drinking of *cava*, a sparkling white or rosé, most of

NEED TO KNOW

Opening Hours

➡ **Bars** Typically open around 6pm and close at 2am (3am on weekends).

➡ **Clubs** Open from midnight until 6am, Thursday to Saturday.

➡ **Beach Bars** 10am to around midnight (later on weekends) from April through October.

When to Go

➡ Bars get lively around 11pm or midnight.

➡ Clubs don't get going till around 2am.

Getting In

Cover charges range from nothing to upwards of €20. If you go early you'll often pay less. In most cases the admission price includes your first drink. Bouncers have the last say on dress code and your eligibility to enter. If you're in a big group, break into smaller groups.

Guides for the Latest Nightlife

➡ **Barcelonarocks.com** (www.barcelona rocks.com)

➡ **Clubbingspain.com** (www.clubbing spain.com)

➡ **Barcelona Connect** (www.barcelona connect.com)

➡ **Miniguide** (www.miniguide.es)

➡ **Metropolitan** (www.barcelona-metro politan.com)

➡ **enBarcelona** (www.enbarcelona.com)

Drinking Glossary

Coffee

➡ *cafe con leche:* half coffee, half milk

➡ *cafe solo:* a short black or espresso

➡ *cortado:* a short black with a little milk

Beer

➡ *cerveza:* beer

➡ *caña:* a small draught beer

➡ *tubo:* a large draught beer

➡ *jarra:* a stein of beer (sometimes a pint)

➡ *quinto/tercio:* a 200/300mL bottle

➡ *clara:* a shandy (a beer with lemonade)

Wine

➡ *vino de la casa:* house wine

which is produced in Catalonia's Penedès region. At the more famous *cava* bars you'll have to nudge your way through the garrulous crowds and enjoy your bubbly standing up. Two of the most famous *cava* bars are El Xampanyet (p106) in La Ribera and Can Paixano (p119) in Barceloneta.

Rooftop & Hotel Bars

Barcelona has a handful of rooftop bars that provide an enchanting view over the city. Depending on the neighbourhood, the vista may take in the rooftops of the old city, the curving beachfront or the entire expanse of the city centre with the Collserola Hills and Tibidabo in the distance. Most of these drinking spots are perched atop high-end hotels, but are not solely the domain of visiting foreigners. An increasing number of style-minded *barcelonins* are drawn to these spaces. Late in the evening you'll find a mostly local crowd.

A few top picks:

➡ **Barceló Raval** (p213) Boasts dramatic 360-degree views from its rooftop terrace; its location in Raval makes it a good place to start off the night before heading to nearby nightspots.

➡ **La Isabala** (p213) On the 7th-floor terrace of Hotel 1898, this handsomely designed summertime spot is a peaceful oasis from the Rambla down below.

➡ **Eclipse Lounge** (p216) Not a rooftop bar, but high up nonetheless on the 26th floor of the waterfront hotel W Barcelona, with panoramic views.

➡ **Mirablau** (p175) At the foot of Tibidabo, this open-air spot is a city icon, famous for its unrivalled view over the city.

Beach Bars

During summer small wooden beach bars, affectionately known as *chiringuitos,* open up along the strand, from Barceloneta all the way up to Platja de la Nova Mar Bella. Here you can dip your toes in the sand and nurse a cocktail while watching the city at play against the backdrop of the deep blue Mediterranean. Ambient grooves add to the laid-back environment.

Chiringuitos are also great spots for a snack – particularly the **Guingueta de la Barceloneta** (Map p286; ☺9am-midnight May-Sep) and **Guingueta del Bogatell** (Map p288; ☺9am-10.30pm May-Sep) run by Michelin-starred chef Carles Abellan. The drink

Drinking by Neighbourhood

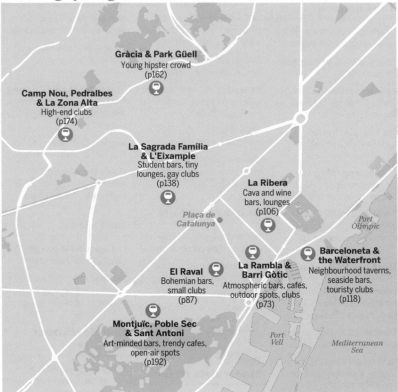

Gràcia & Park Güell
Young hipster crowd
(p162)

Camp Nou, Pedralbes & La Zona Alta
High-end clubs
(p174)

La Sagrada Família & L'Eixample
Student bars, tiny lounges, gay clubs
(p138)

La Ribera
Cava and wine bars, lounges
(p106)

Plaça de Catalunya

Port Olímpic

Barceloneta & the Waterfront
Neighbourhood taverns, seaside bars, touristy clubs
(p118)

El Raval
Bohemian bars, small clubs
(p87)

La Rambla & Barri Gòtic
Atmospheric bars, cafes, outdoor spots, clubs
(p73)

Montjuïc, Poble Sec & Sant Antoni
Art-minded bars, trendy cafes, open-air spots
(p192)

Port Vell

Mediterranean Sea

of choice at either is a refreshing *cava sangria*.

One of the liveliest beachside bars lies northeast of the city on Cavaió beach in Arenys de Mar (accessible from Barcelona by train). **Lasal** (www.lasal.com) hosts top-notch DJs and has a tropical-themed party atmosphere. It opens from mid-May to September.

Clubs

Barcelona's *discotecas* (clubs) are at their best from Thursday to Saturday. Indeed, many open only on these nights. A surprising variety of spots lurk in the old-town labyrinth, ranging from plush former dance halls to grungy subterranean venues that fill to capacity.

Along the waterfront it's another story. At Port Olímpic sun-scorched crowds of visiting yachties mix it up with tourists and a few locals at noisy, back-to-back dance bars right on the waterfront. The best spots are over on La Barceloneta side.

A sprinkling of well-known clubs is spread over the classy parts of town, in L'Eixample and La Zona Alta. As a rule of thumb they attract a beautiful crowd.

Cafes

The cafe scene in Barcelona is incredibly vibrant and makes a great setting for an afternoon pick-me-up. You'll find charming teashops hidden on the narrow lanes of Barri Gòtic, bohemian hang-outs in the Raval, hipster haunts in L'Eixample and Modernista gems on La Rambla. While coffee, tea or perhaps *xocolata calenta* (hot chocolate) are the main attractions, most places also serve snacks, and some serve beer, wine and sometimes cocktails.

Lonely Planet's Top Choices

Ocaña (p73) Stylish spot with a beautifully designed interior.

Ginger (p74) An art deco gem in the Barri Gòtic.

La Caseta del Migdia (p193) An open-air charmer, hidden in the thickets of Montjuïc.

Sor Rita (p74) Join festive crowds in a whimsical Almodovar-esque world.

El Xampanyet (p106) Sip *cava* and munch on tapas in this garrulous icon in El Born.

Dry Martini (p138) Serves perfect martinis and goldfish-bowl-sized gin and tonics.

Best for Wine Lovers

Viblioteca (p162) A small modern space famed for its wine (and cheese) selections.

Monvínic (p138) Boasts a staggering 3000 varieties of wine.

La Vinya del Senyor (p106) Outdoor wine sipping facing Santa Maria del Mar.

La Baignoire (p163) Small, enticing neighbourhood wine bar in Gràcia.

Best for Absinthe

Bar Marsella (p88) Lots of tipplers have sipped at this historic spot, including Hemingway.

Absenta (p119) Colourful and festive spot to have a glass of the 'green fairy' in Barceloneta.

Best for Beer

La Cerveteca (p74) Great microbrews from around the globe (plus cured horsemeat).

Vaso de Oro (p116) Excellent brews go nicely with the tapas.

Best for Vermouth

La Confitería (p88) Fin-de-siècle spot in El Raval that pours a fine house vermouth.

Bodega 1900 (p191) This bistro specialises in tasty vermouth.

Bormuth (p102) Vermouth and tapas make a great combo in this El Born classic.

Mitja Vida (p171) Quaint local eating and drinking spot.

Absenta (p119) Tasty house-made vermouth, in addition to many absinthes.

Best for Cocktails

Dry Martini (p138) Expertly made cocktails in a classy setting.

Juanra Falces (p106) White-jacketed waiters serve up artful elixirs.

Boadas (p88) An iconic drinking den that's been going strong since the 1930s.

Best for Modernista Decor

Bar Muy Buenas (p88) Fanciful Modernista design inside and out.

Casa Almirall (p88) Step back into the 1860s inside this atmospheric drinking den.

London Bar (p89) Former haunt of Picasso and Miró.

Best for Old-World Ambience

Raïm (p162) Old-fashioned tavern with more than a hint of Havana.

Bar Marsella (p88) History lives on in this 1820 watering hole.

Bar Pastís (p89) Atmospheric bar with the warble of French cabaret tunes playing overhead.

Best for Dancing

Marula Cafè (p74) Barri Gòtic favourite for its lively dance floor.

Moog (p89) Small Raval club that draws a fun crowd.

Best for Rock Lovers

Alfa (p163) A rock-loving Gràcia staple.

Magic (p106) Basement club with rock and pop in rotation.

Garaje Hermético (p140) Rollicking good times in a late-night party spot in L'Eixample.

Best Views

La Caseta del Migdia (p193) Great spot for a sundowner.

Mirablau (p175) The whole city stretches out beneath you from the foot of Tibidabo.

Best Beachfront Settings

Santa Marta (p119) Sit at outdoor tables and watch the passing people parade.

CDLC (p119) Come early for a beach-facing outdoor table, stay for dancing.

Best for Funhouse Atmosphere

La Fira (p139) Distorting mirrors, squawking machines and lots of shots.

Bosc de les Fades (p75) Drinking inside a forest-like bar with grotto and trickling fountain.

Best Late Cafes

Cafè de l'Òpera (p72) A 1920s-era spot on La Rambla.

Salterio (p72) Medieval ambience in the Barri Gòtic.

Gay & Lesbian Barcelona

Barcelona has a vibrant gay and lesbian scene, with a fine array of restaurants, bars and clubs in the area known as the 'Gaixample' (a clever conjoining of Gay and L'Eixample), an area about five to six blocks southwest of Passeig de Gràcia around Carrer del Consell de Cent.

Local Attitudes

Despite fierce opposition from the Catholic church, Spain legalised same-sex marriage in 2005. A poll just prior to the legislation found that over 60% of Spaniards favoured the legalisation of same-sex marriage. Gay and lesbian married couples can also adopt children.

As a rule, Barcelona is pretty tolerant and the sight of gay couples arm in arm is generally unlikely to raise eyebrows.

Bars

Befitting a diverse city of its size, the bar scene offers plenty of variety, with stylish cocktail bars, leather bars, bear bars, easygoing pubs and theme bars (with drag shows and other events) all part of the mix.

Clubs

As with all clubs in town, things don't get going until the early morning (around 2am). The bigger and better known clubs like Metro (p193), one of Barcelona's pioneers in the gay club scene, host top-notch DJs, multiple bars, a dark room, drag shows and other amusements. Keep in mind that most of the clubs open only from Thursday to Saturday nights.

The Lesbian Scene

The lesbian bar scene is a little sparse compared to the gay scene, with more places catering to a mixed gay-lesbian crowd (and a few straights thrown in) than an exclusively lesbian clientele. The one place that's proudly lesbian is Aire (p141), which should be a requisite stop for every nightlife-loving lesbian visiting the city. Some nominally straight bars and clubs host periodic lesbian parties. Keep an eye out for party flyers in shops and bars in the Gaixample for the latest.

Special Events

The gay and lesbian community from Barcelona and beyond take centre stage during the annual **Pride Barcelona** (www.pridebarcelona. org). The week-long event takes place in late June and features concerts, campy drag shows, film screenings, art shows and open-air dance parties – complete with lots and lots of foam. It culminates with a festive parade along Carrer de Sepúlveda and ends at the Plaça d'Espanya where the big events are held.

Also of note is the Barcelona International Gay and Lesbian Film Festival (www.barcelonafilmfestival.org) held from mid- to late October, with most screenings at the Filmoteca de Catalunya (p89). Film lovers might also be able to catch a bit of the Sitges Film Festival (sitgesfilmfestival.com), which happens just prior in early October.

Sitges: Catalonia's Gay Capital

Barcelona has a busy gay scene, but Spain's gay capital is the saucily hedonistic Sitges, a major destination on the international gay party circuit. The gay community there takes a leading role in the wild Carnaval celebrations in February/March.

NEED TO KNOW

Gay Organisations

➡ **Casal Lambda** (www.lambda.cat; Carrer de Verdaguer i Callís 10) A gay and lesbian social, cultural and information centre in La Ribera.

➡ Some lesbian groups are to be found at Ca la Dona (p256). It also runs an information line, the **Línia Rosa** (☎900 601601).

Useful Websites

➡ **60by80** (www.60by80.com) An excellent gay travellers' website. Click on Barcelona under Cityguides and take it from there.

➡ **VisitBarcelonaGay.com** (www.visitbarcelonagay.com) A busy listings site for visitors to Barcelona, with everything from fetish sections through to saunas and gay accommodation tips.

➡ **Tillate** (www.tillate.es) Upcoming parties in this nightlife guide to regions around Spain, including Catalonia.

➡ **GaySitges** (www.gaysitges.com) A specific site dedicated to this gay-friendly coastal town.

Lonely Planet's Top Choices

Metro (p193) The city's finest (and longest-running) gay club.

Dietrich Café (p141) Always a fun scene with nightly drag shows.

Hotel Axel (p217) Stylish gay boutique hotel in the heart of Gaixample.

Aire (p141) Barcelona's best lesbian bar, with a fab dance floor.

Best Gay Stays

Room Mate Pau (p217) Stylish but budget-conscious hotel on the edge of Barri Gòtic.

Casa de Billy Barcelona (p217) Gay-friendly B&B with wildly decorated rooms in L'Eixample.

Hotel Axel (p217) Designer rooms, a sauna and a rooftop pool in the heart of the Gaixample.

Best Gay Clubs

Arena Madre (p141) With striptease shows and pumping beats, it's always a fun night at Arena.

Metro (p193) One of Barcelona's top gay clubs with multiple dance floors, dark rooms and shows.

Pervert Club (p141) Electronic beats and a fit young crowd groove to the beat at this mega club.

Best Laid-Back Gay Bars

Mat Bar (p139) Classy Aussie-run space with craft brews and good bar food.

Átame (p139) Join the chatter over drinks early in the night, stay late as things heat up.

La Chapelle (p139) Casual spot for cocktails and a welcoming crowd.

Museum (p193) Lots of kitschy fun to be had at this so-called 'video bar'.

Punto BCN (p139) A two-level bar with a good mix of ages and creeds.

Best Alternative Scene

New Chaps (p140) A leather bar with plenty of erotic intrigue.

Bacon Bear (p140) A man cave retreat for burly folk and their admirers.

Best Mixed Clubs

Arena Classic (p141) Fun, dance-loving crowds of all persuasions flock here.

Teatre Principal (p76) A historic theatre that becomes a late-night dance party for style mavens.

La Terrrazza (p192) Open-air dance parties in the summer up on Montjuïc.

Best Gay-Friendly Beaches

Platja de la Mar Bella (p112) A buzzing beach scene that's clothing optional at the southern tip.

Sitges (p204) Hop on a train to this gay seaside mecca.

Best Gay-Themed Shops

Antinous (p78) Spacious bookstore with cafe in Barri Gòtic.

Cómplices (p78) Mix of lit and grit at this inviting book seller.

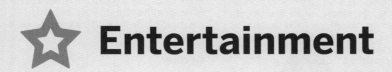

Entertainment

Barcelona teems with stages hosting all manner of entertainment: underground cabaret, comic opera, high drama. Dance companies are thick on the ground and popular local theatre companies, when not touring the rest of Spain, keep folks strapped to their seats.

Live Music

Almost every big international act has passed through Barcelona at some point, more often than not playing at Razzmatazz (p119), Bikini (p175), Sala Apolo (p193)and, increasingly, BARTS (p193), although there is a number of other decent midsize venues. There are also abundant local gigs, in institutions as diverse as CaixaForum (p185), La Pedrera (p131) and L'Ateneu (p76).

Classical Music & Opera

Barcelona is blessed with a fine line-up of theatres for grand performances of classical music, opera and more. The two historic – and iconic – music venues are the Gran Teatre del Liceu (p76) and the Palau de la Música Catalana (p107), while the L'Auditori (p120) is the modern concert hall par excellence and home to the city's orchestra, the OBC.

The main season for classical and opera runs from September to June, while in high summer you might find outdoor festivals or performances around town. Check with the tourist office for details.

Dance

Some fine local contemporary dance companies, along with international visiting companies from time to time, maintain a fairly busy performance program across town. Look for leaflets at Palau de la Virreina (p59) and watch theatre listings. For ballet and other big spectacles, you need to wait for acts to arrive from abroad.

FLAMENCO

Seeing good performances of this essentially Andalucian dance and music is not easy. The few *tablaos* are touristy and often tacky. You can catch flamenco on Friday nights at the Jazz Sí Club (p90); also watch out for big-name performers at the Palau de la Música Catalana (p107). The Festival de Flamenco de Ciutat Vella (http://ciutatflamenco.com) is held in May. A series of concerts can be seen from mid-February to April as part of the De Cajón Festival Flamenco (www.theproject.es).

SARDANA

In Barcelona the best chance you have of seeing people dancing the *sardana* is either at noon on Sunday or 6pm on Saturday in front of La Catedral. They are also performed sometimes in Plaça de Sant Jaume. For more information, contact the **Agrupació Cultural Folklòrica de Barcelona** (☎93 315 14 96; www.acfbarcelona.cat).

Theatre

Most local theatre is performed in Catalan or Spanish, although physical theatre (such as that performed by local group La Fura dels Baus) is popular. The monthly guide *Butxaca* can be picked up at the Palau de la Virreina (p59).

NEED TO KNOW

Tickets

➡ The easiest way to get hold of tickets *(entradas)* for most venues throughout the city is through the Caixa de Catalunya's **Tel-Entrada** (www.telentrada. com) service or **Ticketmaster** (www. ticketmaster.es). Occasionally there are discounted tickets to be had on www.atrapalo.com.

➡ For exhibitions and other free activities, check out www.forfree.cat.

Listings

➡ The Palau de la Virreina (p59) cultural information office has oodles of information on theatre, opera, classical music and more.

➡ The **Guía del Ocio** (www.guiadelociobcn.es, in Spanish; €1, or free with El País newspaper on Fridays) has ample listings for all forms of entertainment.

➡ Good coverage of classical music is to be found on www.classictic.com (in English).

Cinemas

Outdoor cinema screens are set up in summer in the moat of the Castell de Montjuïc, on the beach and in the Fòrum. Foreign films with subtitles and original soundtracks are marked 'VO' *(versió original)* in movie listings.

Football

Football in Barcelona has the aura of religion and for much of the city's population, support of FC Barcelona is an article of faith. But the city has another hardy (if less illustrious) side, RCD Espanyol. FC Barcelona is traditionally associated with the Catalans and even Catalan nationalism, while Espanyol is often identified with Spanish immigrants from other parts of the country.

A match at Barça's Camp Nou (p167) can be breathtaking. If you can't make it to see Barça play, a trip to the multimedia museum with a tour through the locker room and out on the field is a good secondary option.

Cycling

Barcelona's long enticing seafront makes a fine setting for a ride and the bike lane separate from traffic and pedestrians ensures you can get going at a good clip (though you'll have to move slowly at peak times, like on summer weekends). The city itself has over 180km of bike lanes, including lanes along Passeig de Sant Joan, Carrer de Consell de Cent, Avinguda Diagonal and Ronda de Sant Pau/Carrer del Comte d'Urgell, among other major streets. Avid mountain bikers will want to make their way up to the vast Parc de Collserola (p172) with rambling trails on a wooded massif overlooking the city.

Entertainment by Neighbourhood

➡ **La Rambla & Barri Gòtic** This is where you'll find the Gran Teatre del Liceu and the weekly *sardana* dances. (p75)

➡ **El Raval** Great for theatre, jazz and flamenco on Friday nights at the Jazz Sí Club. (p89)

➡ **La Ribera** The eclectic and spectacular Palau de la Música Catalana is here. (p107)

➡ **Montjuïc** This is where you'll find two of the best pop and rock venues, Sala Apolo and BARTS. (p193)

LA FURA DELS BAUS

Keep your eyes peeled for any of the eccentric (if not downright crazed) performances of Barcelona's **La Fura dels Baus** (www.lafura.com) theatre group. It has won worldwide acclaim for its brand of startling, often acrobatic, theatre in which the audience is frequently dragged into the chaos. The company grew out of Barcelona's street-theatre culture in the late 1970s and, although it has grown in technical prowess and received great international acclaim, it has not abandoned the rough-and-ready edge of street performances.

Lonely Planet's Top Choices

Palau de la Música Catalana (p107) This glittering Modernista gem, the city's traditional home for classical and choral music, is a multisensory delight.

Gran Teatre del Liceu (p76) Nineteenth-century style meets cutting-edge acoustics at Barcelona's elegant opera house.

Filmoteca de Catalunya (p89) This cinema and arts centre, recently relocated to the Raval, also comprises a film archive, a bookshop and exhibition space.

Sala Apolo (p193) Characterful old dance hall with a great roster of live acts.

Best for Live Bands

Heliogàbal (p163) A small, quirky little bar where anything goes, from soulful singer-songwriters to pocket opera.

Music Hall (p141) The perfect midsized venue for up-and-coming local and international acts.

Sala Apolo (p193) Cosy booths and a warm red glow give this hugely popular venue something special.

BARTS (p193) The latest contender on the live music circuit, with superb sound and every mod con.

Best for Classical Music

Palau de la Música Catalana (p107) A Modernista fantasy, where the fabulous interior can distract from the finest musician.

Gran Teatre del Liceu (p76) One of Europe's most splendid opera houses, built to impress.

L'Auditori (p120) Fiercely modern concert venue, with a resident orchestra.

L'Ateneu (p76) Elegant old library, hard to enter if you're not a member, unless you catch one of its occasional concerts.

Best for Theatre

Teatre Nacional de Catalunya (p120) A neoclassical building, hosting the best of Catalan theatre.

Teatre Romea (p90) Expect whacky (and not so whacky) versions of modern classics.

Teatreneu (p163) With three different stages, the Teatreneu dares to go where others dare not.

Sala Beckett (p163) With occasional shows in English, it's worth keeping an eye on the programming.

Best for Jazz

Harlem Jazz Club (p75) Not just jazz, but funk, blues, bossa nova and plenty more.

Jazz Sí Club (p90) Small, lively, cramped and never less than fun.

Jamboree (p75) Basement bar that's seen them all under its vaulted ceiling.

Coquette (p107)

Shopping

If your doctor has prescribed an intense round of retail therapy to deal with the blues, then Barcelona is the place. Across Ciutat Vella (Barri Gòtic, El Raval and La Ribera), L'Eixample and Gràcia is spread a thick mantle of boutiques, historic shops, original one-off stores, gourmet corners, wine dens and more designer labels than you can shake your gold card at. You name it, you'll find it here.

Design

Whether you are looking for homewares, gifts or decoration, you'll quickly realise that Barcelona is a style city. This much is clear from its flagship design stores like Vinçon and Cubiña – and even the souvenirs have flair. High-end design shops are best found in L'Eixample and El Born, while arty places are scattered around El Raval, where you'll find, among other things, quirky furniture and homewares with a difference.

Boutique Barcelona

The heart of the Barri Gòtic has always been busy with small-scale merchants, but the area has come crackling to life since the mid-1990s. Some of the most curious old stores, such as purveyors of hats and candles, lurk in the narrow lanes around Plaça de Sant Jaume. The once-seedy Carrer d'Avinyó has become a minor young-fashion boulevard. Antique stores line Carrer de la Palla and Carrer dels Banys Nous.

La Ribera is nothing less than a gourmand's delight. Great old stores and some finger-licking newbies deal in speciality foodstuffs, from coffee and chocolate to roasted nuts. Amid such wonderful aromas, a crop of fashion and design stores caters to the multitude of yuppies in the *barri* (neighbourhood).

Gràcia is also full of quirky little shops. In particular, check out Carrer de Verdi for anything from clothes to bric-a-brac.

El Raval is fantastic for unique boutiques and artists selling their own creations – fashion, prints and curios.

High Street Chains & Department Stores

Everyone knows that across Europe (and further afield), Spain's chains rule the high street. This is the home of the ubiquitous Zara, Mango, Pull and Bear, Bershka, Massimo Dutti, Zara Home (in fact, all owned by one company, Inditex) – and sure enough, you'll find all of them dotted around Barcelona. Women's underwear is stylish and affordable at Oysho and Women's Secret, while UK hits like Topshop and Topman also feature.

Spain's only surviving department store is El Corte Inglés – an enormous fortress-like main branch towers over Plaça de Catalunya. It covers everything from books, music and food, to fashion, jewellery, kids' clothes and toys, technology and homewares. There are smaller branches across town. French chain FNAC is another biggie, selling books, CDs, DVDs, computers and mobile phones.

Vintage Fashion

El Raval is best for vintage fashion. You'll discover old-time stores that are irresistible to browsers, and a colourful array of affordable, mostly second-hand clothes boutiques. The central axis here is Carrer de la Riera Baixa, which plays host to '70s threads and military cast-offs. Carrer dels Tallers is also attracting a growing number of clothing and shoe stores (although CDs remain its core business). Small galleries, designer shops and arty bookstores huddle together along the streets running east of the MACBA towards La Rambla.

Designers

The heart of L'Eixample, bisected by Passeig de Gràcia, is known as the Quadrat d'Or (Golden Sq) and is jammed with all sorts of glittering shops. Passeig de Gràcia is a bit of a who's who of international shopping – you'll find Spain's own high-end designers like Loewe on Passeig de Gràcia, along with Armani, Chanel, Gucci, Stella McCartney and the rest.

PLAN YOUR TRIP SHOPPING

NEED TO KNOW

Where To Go

For high fashion, design, jewellery and department stores, the principal shopping axis starts on Plaça de Catalunya, proceeds up Passeig de Gràcia and turns left into Avinguda Diagonal, along which it extends as far as Plaça de la Reina Maria Cristina.

Sale Time

The winter sales start after Reis (6 January) and, depending on the store, can go on well into February. The summer sales start in July, with stores trying to entice locals to part with one last wad of euros before they flood out of the city on holiday in August. Some shops prolong their sales to the end of August.

Business Hours

➡ In general, shops are open between 9am or 10am and 1.30pm or 2pm and then again from around 4pm or 4.30pm to 8pm or 8.30pm Monday to Friday. Many shops keep the same hours on Saturday, although some don't bother with the evening session.

➡ Large supermarkets, malls and department stores such as El Corte Inglés stay open all day Monday to Saturday, from about 10am to 10pm.

➡ Many fashion boutiques, design stores and the like open from about 10am to 8pm Monday to Saturday.

➡ A few shops open on Sundays and holidays, and the number increases in the run up to key consumer holiday periods.

El Born, particularly Carrer del Rec, is big on cool designers like Isabel Marant, Marni, Chloé and Hoss Intropia, in small, clean-line boutiques. Some Barcelona-based designs are also sold here. This is a great area if you have money to spend and hours to browse.

Markets

Barcelona's food markets are some of the best in Europe – just think of the inviting, glistening, aromatic and voluptuous offerings to be savoured in Mercat de la Boqueria (p81) or **Mercat de Santa**

Caterina (Map p284; Avinguda de Francesc Cambó; underground rail Jaume I) – but every neighbourhood has its own central market, full of seasonal offers.

Several flea markets, like Els Encants Vells (p121), offer opportunities to browse and enjoy the local buzz, and perhaps even find a good bargain.

Shopping Strips

Avinguda del Portal de l'Àngel This broad pedestrian avenue is lined with high-street chains, shoe shops, bookshops and more, and feeds into Carrer dels Boters and Carrer de la Portaferrissa, characterised by stores offering light-hearted costume jewellery and youth-oriented streetwear.

Avinguda Diagonal The boulevard is loaded with international fashion names and design boutiques, suitably interspersed with cafes to allow weary shoppers to take a load off.

Carrer d'Avinyó Once a fairly squalid old city street, Carrer d'Avinyó has morphed into a dynamic young fashion street.

Carrer de la Riera Baixa The place to look for a gaggle of stores flogging preloved threads.

Carrer del Petritxol Best for chocolate shops and art.

Carrer del Consell de Cent The heart of the private art-gallery scene in Barcelona, between Passeig de Gràcia and Carrer de Muntaner.

Carrer del Rec Another threads street, this one-time stream is lined with bright and cool boutiques. Check out Carrer del Bonaire and Carrer de l'Esparteria too. You'll find discount outlets and original local designers.

Carrer dels Banys Nous Along with nearby Carrer de la Palla, this is the place to look for antiques.

Passeig de Gràcia This is the premier shopping boulevard, chic with a capital 'C', but mostly given over to big-name international brands.

Shopping by Neighbourhood

➡ **La Rambla & Barri Gòtic** Excellent for all kinds of retail – boutiques, design and souvenirs. (p76)

➡ **El Raval** Haven for independent stores – vintage fashion and all kinds of original and arty shops – and home to the iconic Mercat de la Boqueria. (p90)

➡ **La Ribera** El Born is the place for cool designer boutiques that sell high-end fashion and excellent food shops for the gourmet traveller. (p107)

➡ **Port Vell & La Barceloneta** This area boasts the monster Maremàgnum shopping mall, and an occasional craft market alongside the port. (p120)

➡ **L'Eixample** High-end heartstoppers, dazzling jewellery and high-street chains find a home along the wealthy streets of L'Eixample. (p141)

➡ **Gràcia** Dotted with fantastic little shops that sell anything from vintage cameras to unique fashion or food. (p164)

➡ **La Zona Alta** This is the city's Beverly Hills, so expect high prices and bijou boutiques. (p175)

SHOPPING MALLS

Barcelona has no shortage of shopping malls. One of the first to arrive was **L'Illa Diagonal** (Map p300; ☑93 444 00 00; www.lilla.com; Avinguda Diagonal 549; ⊗10am-9.30pm Mon-Sat; ⓂMaria Cristina), designed by star Spanish architect Rafael Moneo. The **Centre Comercial Diagonal Mar** (Map p288; ☑902 530300; www.diagonalmar.com; Avinguda Diagonal 3; ⓂEl Maresme Fòrum) by the sea is one of the latest additions.

The city's other emporia include **Centre Comercial de les Glòries** (Map p288; ☑93 486 04 04; www.lesglories.com; Gran Via de les Corts Catalanes 208; ⓂGlòries), in the former Olivetti factory; **Heron City** (☑902 401144; www.heroncitybarcelona.com; Avinguda de Rio de Janeiro 42; ⓂFabra i Puig), just off Avinguda Meridiana, about 4km north of Plaça de les Glòries Catalanes; and the **Centre Comercial Gran Via 2** (☑93 259 05 22; www.granvia2.com; Gran Via de les Corts Catalanes 75; ⓇFGC Ildefons Cerdà) in L'Hospitalet de Llobregat.

Lonely Planet's Top Choices

Vinçon (p141) The Barcelona design icon sells furniture and homewares to die for.

Mercat de la Boqueria (p81) Stock up on budget delicacies amid one of Europe's most vibrant food markets.

Vila Viniteca (p106) Oenophiles unite at this wonderful wine shop.

Coquette (p107) Simple and beautiful designer clothes for women.

Loisaida (p107) Men and women's fashion, antiques and retro vinyl.

Best for Design & Craft

Drap Art (p77) Weird and wonderful recycled art and accessories.

Arlequí Màscares (p107) Hand-made masks to rival any in Venice, the perfect souvenir.

Fantastik (p91) A temple to kitsch, with kooky wonders from all around the world.

Teranyina (p91) The 'Spider's Web', so called for its intricate designs in intricate textiles.

Best for Fashion

Coquette (p107) Offbeat women's clothes designers that share an ethereal elegance.

Holala! Plaza (p91) Today vintage is the new designer, and none has a better selection than Holala!

Loewe (p144) Luxurious luggage for the deep of pocket.

Bagués-Masriera (p145) Exquisite jewellery from a company with a long tradition.

Best Markets

Mercat de Santa Caterina (p99) A colourful alternative to La Boqueria, with fewer crowds and lower prices.

Els Encants Vells (p121) A sprawling flea market in a spanking new building.

El Bulevard dels Antiquaris (p142) A labyrinth of tiny antique shops that merits a morning's browsing.

Best for Souvenirs & Gifts

Vinçon (p141) Though primarily a superstore for smart homewares, Vinçon also has a great range of Barcelona-themed gifts.

Fires, Festes i Tradicions (p77) Gorgeously packed Catalan specialities, from quince jelly to charcuterie.

Born Centre Cultural (p99) The gift shop at this new exhibition space stocks tasteful, well-made souvenirs and books about the city.

Les Topettes (p90) Creams, oils, perfumes and soaps that look every bit as tantalising as they smell.

El Ingenio (p78) Old-time toy and joke shop, with a workshop making the papier-mâché models used in Catalan festivals.

Best for Food & Wine

Casa Gispert (p107) The speciality is roast nuts of every type, but you'll also find chocolate, conserves and olive oils, attractively labelled.

Vila Viniteca (p106) A jaw-dropping cathedral of wines from Catalonia and elsewhere in Spain, tucked away in a Born side street.

Barcelona Reykjavik (p90) The place to come for that organic spelt loaf or buttery croissant.

Caelum (p72) Deliciously wicked sweet treats made by nuns, with a little tea room downstairs.

Explore Barcelona

BARCELONA'S
TOP SIGHTS

Neighbourhoods at a Glance

❶ La Rambla & Barri Gòtic p56

La Rambla, Barcelona's most famous pedestrian strip, is always a hive of activity with buskers and peddlers, tourists and con artists (watch out!) mingling amid the sunlit cafes and shops on the boulevard. The adjoining Barri Gòtic is packed with historical treasures – relics of ancient Rome, 14th-century Gothic churches and atmospheric cobblestone lanes lined with shops, bars and restaurants.

❷ El Raval p79

Although still dicey in parts, El Raval has seen remarkable rejuvenation in recent years, with the addition of cutting-edge museums and cultural centres. Don't miss the Museu d'Art Contemporani de Barcelona, bohemian

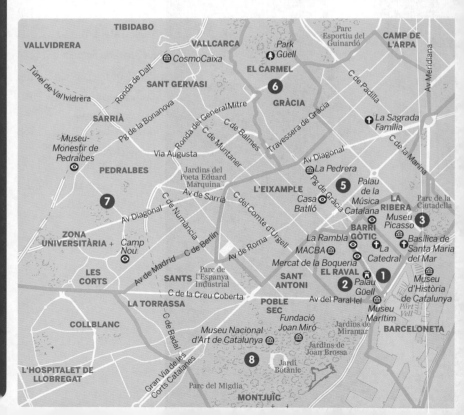

nightlife and the sprawling culinary delights of Mercat de la Boqueria.

③ La Ribera p92

This medieval quarter has a little of everything, from high-end shopping to some of Barcelona's liveliest tapas bars. Key sights include the superb Museu Picasso, the awe-inspiring Gothic Basílica de Santa Maria del Mar and the artfully sculpted Modernista concert hall of Palau de la Música Catalana. For a bit of fresh air, locals head to the manicured gardens of Parc de la Ciutadella.

④ Barceloneta & the Waterfront p109

The formerly industrial waterfront has experienced a dramatic transformation in the last three decades, with sparkling beaches and seaside restaurants, elegant sculptures, a 4.5km-long boardwalk, ultramodern high-

rises and yacht-filled marinas. Your gateway to the Mediterranean is the gridlike neighbourhood of Barceloneta, a former fishing quarter full of traditional seafood eateries.

⑤ La Sagrada Família & L'Eixample p122

The elegant, if traffic-filled, district of L'Eixample is a showcase for Modernista architecture, including Gaudí's unfinished masterpiece, La Sagrada Família. L'Eixample also has a celebrated dining scene, along with high-end boutiques and wildly diverse nightlife: university party spots, gilded cocktail lounges and the buzzing gay club scene of 'Gaixample' are all part of the mix.

⑥ Gràcia & Park Güell p154

Gràcia was an independent town until the 1890s. Its narrow lanes and picturesque plazas still have a village-like feel, and it has long been a magnet to a young, hip, largely international crowd. Here you'll find cafes and bars, vintage shops and a smattering of multicultural eateries. On a hill to the north lies the Modernista storybook of Park Güell, yet another captivating work by Gaudí.

⑦ Camp Nou, Pedralbes & La Zona Alta p165

Several of Barcelona's most sacred sights nestle inside the huge expanse beyond L'Eixample. One is the peaceful monastery of Pedralbes; the other is the great shrine to Catalan football, Camp Nou. Other attractions include the amusement park and great views atop Tibidabo, the wooded trails of Parc de Collserola, and a kid-friendly science museum.

⑧ Montjuïc, Poble Sec & Sant Antoni p177

The hillside overlooking the port has some of the city's finest art collections: the Museu Nacional d'Art de Catalunya, the Fundació Joan Miró and Caixaforum. Other galleries, gardens and an imposing castle form part of the scenery. Just below Montjuïc lies the lively tapas bars and eateries of Poble Sec, while the up-and-coming neighbourhood of Sant Antoni draws the young and hip.

NEIGHBOURHOODS AT A GLANCE

La Rambla & Barri Gòtic

Neighbourhood Top Five

1 Taking in Barcelona's liveliest street scene along **La Rambla** (p58), with its human statues, open-air eateries, flower stalls and saunterers from every corner of the globe.

2 Exploring the hidden nooks and crannies of the magnificent Gothic masterpiece of **La Catedral** (p62).

3 Walking amid the ruins of Roman-era Barcino at the **Museu d'Història de Barcelona** (p65).

4 Ogling the strange and wondrous collections at the **Museu Frederic Marès** (p67).

5 Enjoying an alfresco meal or a drink in the picturesque **Plaça Reial** (p66).

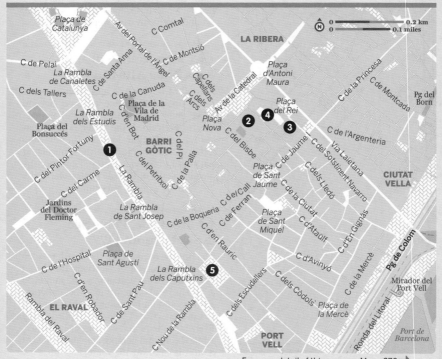

For more detail of this area see Map p276 ➡

Explore: La Rambla & Barri Gòtic

La Rambla is Spain's most talked-about boulevard. It packs a lot of colour into a short walk, with flower stands, historic buildings, a sensory-rich produce market, over-priced beers and tourist tat, and a ceaselessly changing parade of people from all corners of the globe. Lining both sides of La Rambla are a handful of worthwhile attractions – including the Mercat de la Boqueria, Gran Teatre del Liceu and several sizeable galleries.

You could easily spend several days exploring the Barri Gòtic without leaving the medieval streets. In addition to major sights, its tangle of narrow lanes and tranquil plazas conceal some of the city's most atmospheric shops, restaurants, cafes and bars. There are swarms of tourists afoot – as well as some overpriced restaurants best avoided – but Barri Gòtic has plenty of local character as well, and it's full of rewards for the urban explorer.

Wandering without an itinerary is a delight, though you won't want to miss La Catedral and Roman ruins (particularly those in the Museu d'Història de Barcelona). Another highlight is lingering over coffee or an alfresco meal at one of the Barri Gòtic's many outdoor plazas.

By night Barri Gòtic transforms into a collection of bars and clubs – which lay otherwise hidden during the day. The streets around Plaça Reial and Plaça George Orwell (also known as Plaça del Trippy) are good places to bar-hop, though you'll find nightspots all over the neighbourhood.

Local Life

➡ **Folk Dancing** Although it's mostly old-timers dancing the Sardana, a growing number of young folks are enjoying this Catalan dance. Learn a few moves and join in: 6pm on Saturday and noon on Sunday in front of La Catedral (p62).

➡ **Hang-outs** To escape the tourist masses, head to the southeast corner of Barri Gòtic, for microbrews at La Cerveteca (p74), and cocktails and whimsy at Sor Rita (p74). Salterio (p72) is also a much-loved meeting spot.

➡ **Bar-hopping** Plaça Reial, Plaça de George Orwell and the narrow lanes between the two are the best spots to take in the local Gòtic nightlife.

Getting There & Away

➡ **Metro** Key stops near or on La Rambla include Catalunya, Liceu and Drassanes. For Barri Gòtic's east side, Jaume I and Urquinaona are handiest.

➡ **Bus** Airport and night buses arrive and depart from Plaça de Catalunya.

➡ **Taxi** Easiest to catch on La Rambla or Plaça de Catalunya.

Lonely Planet's Top Tip

For the best-value dining, plan to have at least a big meal at lunchtime. Many restaurants in the Barri Gòtic offer three-course meals for €10 to €12, including wine.

 Best Places to Eat

➡ Pla (p73)

➡ La Vinateria dell Call (p73)

➡ Koy Shunka (p73)

➡ Onofre (p72)

➡ Rasoterra (p71)

➡ Cafè de l'Acadèmia (p73)

For reviews, see p71

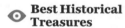 **Best Places to Drink**

➡ Ocaña (p73)

➡ Sor Rita (p74)

➡ Oviso (p74)

➡ La Cerveteca (p74)

➡ L'Ascensor (p74)

➡ Polaroid (p74)

For reviews, see p73

Best Historical Treasures

➡ Temple Romà d'August (p68)

➡ Via Sepulcral Romana (p68)

➡ Sinagoga Major (p68)

➡ Domus Romana (p70)

For reviews, see p68

TOP SIGHT
LA RAMBLA

Barcelona's most famous street is both a tourist magnet and a window into Catalan culture, with cultural centres, theatres and architecturally intriguing buildings lining its sides. Flanked by plane trees, the middle of La Rambla is a broad pedestrian boulevard, packed with souvenir hawkers, buskers, pavement artists and living statues, plus wide-eyed visitors from every corner of the globe.

DON'T MISS...

➡ Palau de la Virreina
➡ Centre d'Art Santa Mònica
➡ Església de Betlem
➡ Palau Moja
➡ Mosaïc de Miró

PRACTICALITIES

➡ Map p276
➡ Ⓜ Catalunya, Liceu or Drassanes

History

La Rambla takes its name from a seasonal stream (*raml* in Arabic) that once ran here. From the early Middle Ages, it was better known as the Cagalell (Stream of Shit) and lay outside the city walls until the 14th century. Monastic buildings were then built and, subsequently, mansions of the well-to-do from the 16th to the early 19th centuries. Unofficially, La Rambla is divided into five sections, which explains why many know it as Las Ramblas.

La Rambla de Canaletes

The section of La Rambla north of Plaça de Catalunya is named after the **Font de Canaletes**, an inconspicuous turn-of-the-20th-century drinking fountain, the water of which supposedly emerges from what were once known as the springs of Canaletes. It used to be said that *barcelonins* 'drank the waters of Les Canaletes'. Nowadays people claim that anyone who drinks from the fountain will return to Barcelona, which is not such a bad prospect. Delirious football fans gather here to celebrate whenever the main home side, FC Barcelona, wins a cup or the league premiership.

A block east along Carrer de la Canuda is Plaça de la Vila de Madrid, with a sunken garden where Roman tombs lie exposed in the Via Sepulcral Romana (p68).

La Rambla dels Estudis

La Rambla dels Estudis, from Carrer de la Canuda running south to Carrer de la Portaferrissa, was formerly home to a twittering bird market, which closed in 2010 after 150 years in operation.

Església de Betlem

Just north of Carrer del Carme, this **church** (☉8.30am-1.30pm & 6-9pm) was constructed in baroque style for the Jesuits in the late 17th and early 18th centuries to replace an earlier church destroyed by fire in 1671. Fire was a bit of a theme for this site: the church was once considered the most splendid of Barcelona's few baroque offerings, but leftist arsonists torched it in 1936.

Palau Moja

Looming over the eastern side of La Rambla, Palau Moja is a neoclassical building dating from the second half of the 18th century. Its classical lines are best appreciated from across La Rambla. Unfortunately, interior access is limited as it houses mostly government offices.

La Rambla de Sant Josep

From Carrer de la Portaferrissa to Placa de la Boqueria, what is officially called La Rambla de Sant Josep (named after a now nonexistent monastery) is lined with flower stalls, which give it the alternative name La Rambla de les Flors. This stretch also contains the scurrilous Museu de l'Eròtica (p70).

Palau de la Virreina

The Palau de la Virreina is a grand 18th-century rococo mansion (with some neoclassical elements) that houses a municipal arts-and-entertainment information and ticket office. More importantly, it's home to the **Centre de la Imatge** (☏93 316 10 00; www.bcn.cat/virreinacentredelaimatge; 99 Palau de la Virreina; ☉noon-8pm Tue-Sun) **FREE**, which has rotating photography exhibits.

Just south of the Palau, in El Raval, is the Mercat de la Boqueria (p81), one of the best-stocked and most colourful produce markets in Europe.

Mosaïc de Miró

At Plaça de la Boqueria, where four side streets meet just north of Liceu metro station, you can walk all over a Miró – the colourful mosaic in the pavement, with one tile signed by the artist. Miró chose this site as it's near the house where he was born on the Passatge del Crèdit. The mosaic's bold colours and vivid swirling forms are instantly recognisable to Miró fans, though plenty of tourists stroll right over it without realising. Near the bottom of the work, there's one tile signed by the artist.

La Rambla dels Caputxins

La Rambla dels Caputxins, named after a now nonexistent monastery, runs from Plaça de la Boqueria to Carrer dels Escudellers. The latter street is named after the potters' guild, founded in the 13th century, the members of which lived and worked here. On the western side of La Rambla is the Gran Teatre del Liceu (p66); to the southeast is the entrance to the palm-shaded Plaça Reial (p66). Below this point La Rambla gets seedier, with the occasional strip club and peep show.

La Rambla de Santa Mònica

The final stretch of La Rambla widens out to approach the Mirador de Colom (p67) overlooking Port Vell. La Rambla here is named after the Convent de Santa Mònica, which once stood on the western flank of the street and has since been converted into the **Centre d'Art Santa Mònica** (☏93 567 11 10; www.artssantamonica.cat; La Rambla de Santa Mònica 7; ☉11am-9pm Tue-Fri, 3-8pm Sat) **FREE**, a cultural centre that mostly exhibits modern multimedia installations.

LA RAMBLA & BARRI GÒTIC LA RAMBLA

DINING & DRINKING ON LA RAMBLA

You can grab ice cream, cold drinks and snack fare on La Rambla, but for something more substantial, skip the chaotic restaurants on the boulevard and try one of these:

➡ Bosc de les Fades (p75) – whimsical drinking spot straight out of *Alice in Wonderland*.

➡ Café de l'Òpera (p72) – elegant art nouveau cafe across from the Gran Teatre del Liceu.

➡ Escribà (p135) – handsome mosaics and tempting window displays lure would-be passersby into this famous patisserie.

➡ Plaça Reial (p66) – for a proper sit-down meal, your best nearby bet is at one of the many restaurants ringing this plaza.

La Rambla saw action during the civil war. In *Homage to Catalonia*, Orwell vividly described the avenue gripped by revolutionary fervour in the early days of the war. 'Down the Ramblas, the wide central artery of the town where crowds of people streamed constantly to and fro, the loud-speakers were bellowing revolutionary songs all day and far into the night...'

La Rambla

A TIMELINE

Look beyond the human statues and tourist-swarmed restaurants, and you'll find a fascinating piece of Barcelona history dating back many centuries.

13th century A serpentine seasonal stream (called ramla in Arabic) runs outside the city walls. As Barcelona grows, the stream will eventually become an open sewer until it's later paved over.

1500–1800 During this early period, La Rambla was dotted with convents and monasteries, including the baroque **Església de Betlem ❶**, completed in the early 1700s.

1835 The city erupts in anticlericism, with riots and the burning of convents. Along La Rambla, many religious assets are destroyed or seized by the state. This paves the way for new developments, including the **Mercat de la Boqueria ❷** in 1840, **Gran Teatre del Liceu ❸** in 1847 and **Plaça Reial ❹** in 1848.

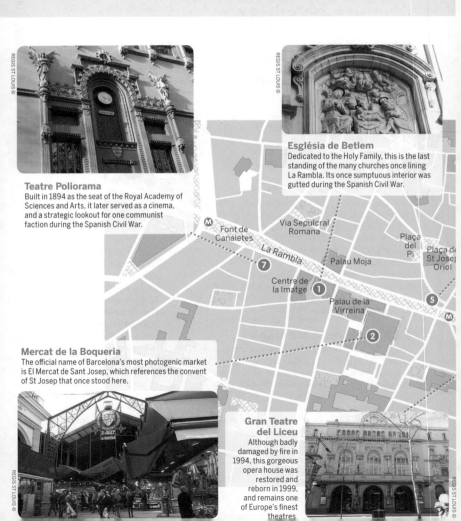

Teatre Poliorama
Built in 1894 as the seat of the Royal Academy of Sciences and Arts, it later served as a cinema, and a strategic lookout for one communist faction during the Spanish Civil War.

Església de Betlem
Dedicated to the Holy Family, this is the last standing of the many churches once lining La Rambla. Its once sumptuous interior was gutted during the Spanish Civil War.

Mercat de la Boqueria
The official name of Barcelona's most photogenic market is El Mercat de Sant Josep, which references the convent of St Josep that once stood here.

Gran Teatre del Liceu
Although badly damaged by fire in 1994, this gorgeous opera house was restored and reborn in 1999, and remains one of Europe's finest theatres

1883 Architect Josep Vilaseca refurbishes the **Casa Bruno Cuadros** ⑤. As Modernisme is sweeping across the city, Vilaseca creates an eclectic work using stained glass, wrought iron, Egyptian imagery and Japanese prints.

1888 Barcelona hosts the Universal Exhibition. The city sees massive urban renewal projects, with the first electric lights coming to La Rambla, and the building of the **Mirador de Colom** ⑥.

1936–39 La Rambla becomes the site of bloody street fighting during the Spanish Civil War. British journalist and author George Orwell, who spends three days holed up in the **Teatre Poliorama** ⑦ during street battles, later describes the tumultuous days in his excellent book, *Homage to Catalonia*.

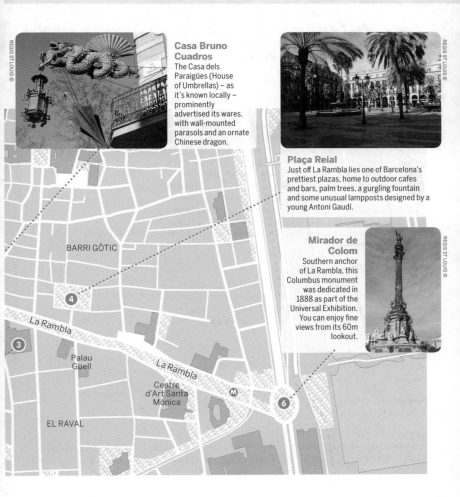

Casa Bruno Cuadros
The Casa dels Paraigües (House of Umbrellas) – as it's known locally – prominently advertised its wares, with wall-mounted parasols and an ornate Chinese dragon.

Plaça Reial
Just off La Rambla lies one of Barcelona's prettiest plazas, home to outdoor cafes and bars, palm trees, a gurgling fountain and some unusual lampposts designed by a young Antoni Gaudí.

Mirador de Colom
Southern anchor of La Rambla, this Columbus monument was dedicated in 1888 as part of the Universal Exhibition. You can enjoy fine views from its 60m lookout.

BARRI GÒTIC

La Rambla

Palau Güell

La Rambla

Centre d'Art Santa Mònica

EL RAVAL

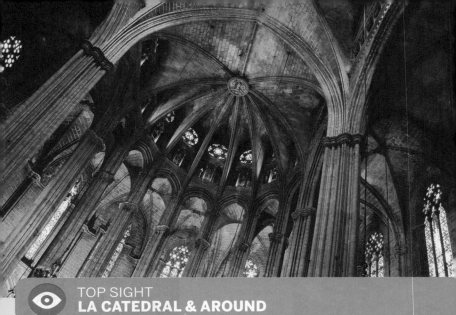

TOP SIGHT
LA CATEDRAL & AROUND

Barcelona's central place of worship presents a magnificent image. The richly decorated main facade, laced with gargoyles and the stone intricacies you would expect of northern European Gothic, sets it quite apart from other churches in Barcelona. The facade was actually added in 1870, although the rest of the building was built between 1298 and 1460. The other facades are sparse in decoration, and the octagonal, flat-roofed towers are a clear reminder that, even here, Catalan Gothic architectural principles prevailed.

The Interior

The interior is a broad, soaring space divided into a central nave and two aisles by lines of elegant, slim pillars. The cathedral was one of the few churches in Barcelona spared by the anarchists in the civil war, so its ornamentation, never overly lavish, is intact.

Coro

In the middle of the central nave is the late-14th-century, exquisitely sculpted timber *coro* (choir stalls). The coats of arms on the stalls belong to members of the Barcelona chapter of the Order of the Golden Fleece. Emperor Carlos V presided over the order's meeting here in 1519.

Crypt

A broad staircase before the main altar leads you down to the crypt, which contains the tomb of Santa Eulàlia, one of Barcelona's two patron saints and more affectionately known as Laia. The reliefs on the alabaster sarcophagus recount some of her tortures and, along

DON'T MISS...

➡ The claustre and its 13 geese
➡ Views from the roof
➡ The crypt
➡ The *coro*

PRACTICALITIES

➡ Map p276
➡ ☎93 342 82 62
➡ www.catedralbcn.org
➡ Plaça de la Seu
➡ admission free, special visit €6, choir admission €2.80
➡ ⏰8am-12.45pm & 5.15-7.30pm Mon-Sat, special visit 1-5pm Mon-Sat, 2-5pm Sun & holidays
➡ Ⓜ Jaume I

the top strip, the removal of her body to its present resting place.

The Roof

For a bird's-eye view (mind the poop) of medieval Barcelona, visit the cathedral's roof and tower by taking the lift (€3) from the Capella de les Animes del Purgatori near the northeast transept.

Claustre

From the southwest transept, exit by the partly Romanesque door (one of the few remnants of the present church's predecessor) to the leafy *claustre* (cloister), with its fountains and flock of 13 geese. The geese supposedly represent the age of Santa Eulàlia at the time of her martyrdom and have, generation after generation, been squawking here since medieval days. They make fine watchdogs! One of the cloister chapels commemorates 930 priests, monks and nuns martyred during the civil war.

In the northwest corner of the cloister is the **Capella de Santa Llúcia**, one of the few reminders of Romanesque Barcelona (although the interior is largely Gothic).

Casa de L'Ardiaca

Upon exiting the Capella de Santa Llúcia, wander across the lane into the 16th-century **Casa de l'Ardiaca** (Archdeacon's House; ☉9am-9pm Mon-Fri, 9am-2pm Sat), which houses the city's archives. Stroll around the supremely serene courtyard, cooled by trees and a fountain; it was renovated by Lluís Domènech i Montaner in 1902, when the building was owned by the lawyers' college. Domènech i Montaner also designed the postal slot, which is adorned with swallows and a tortoise, said to represent the swiftness of truth and the plodding pace of justice. You can get a good glimpse at some stout Roman wall in here. Upstairs, you can look down into the courtyard and across to La Catedral.

Palau Episcopal

Across Carrer del Bisbe is the 17th-century **Palau Episcopal** (Palau del Bisbat; Bishop's Palace). Virtually nothing remains of the original 13th-century structure. The Roman city's northwest gate stood here and you can see the lower segments of the Roman towers that stood on either side of the gate at the base of the Palau Episcopal and Casa de l'Ardiaca. In fact, the lower part of the entire northwest wall of the Casa de l'Ardiaca is of Roman origin – you can also make out part of the first arch of a Roman aqueduct.

VISITING LA CATEDRAL

You may visit La Catedral in one of two ways. In the morning or afternoon, general admission is free, although you have to pay to visit any combination of the choir stalls, chapter house and roof. If you want to visit all three areas, it's better value to go during the so-called 'special visit' between 1pm and 5pm.

In the first chapel on the right from the northwest entrance, the main crucifixion figure above the altar is Sant Crist de Lepant. It is said Don Juan's flagship bore it into battle at Lepanto and that the figure acquired its odd stance by dodging an incoming cannonball. Left from the main entrance is the baptismal font where, according to one story, six North American Indians brought to Europe by Columbus after his first voyage of accidental discovery were bathed in holy water.

◉ SIGHTS

LA RAMBLA
STREET

See p58.

LA CATEDRAL
CHURCH

See p62.

PALAU DEL LLOCTINENT
HISTORIC SITE

Map p276 (Carrer dels Comtes; ☺10am-7pm; MJaume I) FREE This converted 16th-century palace has a peaceful courtyard worth wandering through. Have a look upwards from the main staircase to admire the extraordinary timber *artesonado,* a sculpted ceiling made to seem like the upturned hull of a boat. Temporary exhibitions, usually related in some way to the archives, are often held here. Next to the Plaça del Rei, the *palau* (palace) was built in the 1550s as the residence of the Spanish *lloctinent* (viceroy) of Catalonia and later converted into a convent. From 1853 it housed the Arxiu de la Corona d'Aragón, a unique archive with documents detailing the history of the Crown of Aragón and Catalonia, starting in the 12th century and reaching to the 20th.

MUSEU DIOCESÀ
MUSEUM

Map p276 (Casa de la Pia Almoina; ☎93 315 22 13; www.arqbcn.org; Avinguda de la Catedral 4; adult/child €6/3; ☺10am-2pm & 5-8pm Tue-Sat, 11am-2pm Sun; MJaume I) Next to the cathedral, the Diocesan Museum has a handful of exhibits on Gaudí (including a fascinating documentary on his life and philosophy) on the upper floors. There's also a sparse collection of medieval and romanesque religious art usually supplemented by a temporary exhibition or two. The building itself has fragments of Barcelona's Roman wall, as well as elements from its days as an 11th-century almshouse and its later use as an ecclesiastical residence in the 15th century.

ⓘ MANIC MONDAYS

Many attractions shut their doors on Monday, but there are plenty of exceptions. Following are among the more enticing ones:

➡ Gran Teatre del Liceu (p66)

➡ La Catedral (p62)

➡ Museu de l'Eròtica (p70)

➡ Museu de Cera (p71)

➡ Sinagoga Major (p68)

PLAÇA DE SANT JAUME
SQUARE

Map p276 (MLiceu or Jaume I) In the 2000 or so years since the Romans settled here, the area around this square (often remodelled), which started life as the forum, has been the focus of Barcelona's civic life. This is still the central staging area for Barcelona's traditonal festivals. Facing each other across the square are the Palau de la Generalitat (seat of Catalonia's regional government) on the north side and the *ajuntament* (town hall) to the south. Behind the *ajuntament* rise the awful town hall offices built in the 1970s over Plaça de Sant Miquel. Opposite is a rare 15th-century gem, **Casa Centelles** (Map p276), on the corner of Baixada de Sant Miquel. You can wander into the fine Gothic-Renaissance courtyard if the gates are open.

AJUNTAMENT
ARCHITECTURE

Map p276 (☎93 402 70 00; www.bcn.cat; Plaça de Sant Jaume; ☺10.30am-1.30pm Sun; MLiceu, Jaume I) FREE The *ajuntament,* otherwise known as the Casa de la Ciutat, has been the seat of power for centuries. The Consell de Cent (the city's ruling council) first sat here in the 14th century, but the building has lamentably undergone many changes since the days of Barcelona's Gothic-era splendour.

Only the original, now disused, entrance on Carrer de la Ciutat retains its Gothic ornament. The main 19th-century neoclassical facade on the square is a charmless riposte to the Palau de la Generalitat. Inside, the Saló de Cent is the hall in which the town council once held its plenary sessions. The broad vaulting is pure Catalan Gothic and the *artesonado* (Mudéjar wooden ceiling with interlaced beams leaving a pattern of spaces for decoration) demonstrates fine work. In fact, much of what you see is comparatively recent. The building was badly damaged in a bombardment in 1842 and has been repaired and tampered with repeatedly. The wooden neo-Gothic seating was added at the beginning of the 20th century, as was the grand alabaster *retablo* (retable, or altarpiece) at the back. To the right you enter the small Saló de la Reina Regente, built in 1860, where the *ajuntament* now sits. To the left of the Saló de Cent is the Saló de les Croniques – the murals here recount Catalan exploits in Greece and the Near East in Catalonia's empire-building days.

TOP SIGHT
MUSEU D'HISTÒRIA DE BARCELONA

One of Barcelona's most fascinating museums takes you back to the very foundations of Roman Barcino. You'll stroll amid ruins of the town that flourished here following its founding by Emperor Augustus around 10 BC. Equally impressive is the former palace setting on Plaça del Rei, among the key locations of medieval princely power in Barcelona.

Below ground is a remarkable walk through about 4 sq km of excavated Roman and Visigothic Barcelona. After the display on the typical Roman *domus* (villa), you reach a **public laundry**; outside in the street were containers for people to urinate into, as the urine was used as disinfectant. You pass dyeing shops, a public cold-water bath and shops dedicated to the making of *garum* (a fish sauce enjoyed across the Roman Empire), a 6th-century church and **winemaking stores**.

Ramparts then wind upward, past remains of the patio of a Roman house, the medieval Palau Episcopal (Bishops' Palace) and into two broad vaulted halls with **displays on medieval Barcelona**. The finale is the **Saló del Tinell**, the royal palace banqueting hall and a fine example of Catalan Gothic (built 1359–70). It was here that Fernando and Isabel heard Columbus' first reports of the New World.

DON'T MISS...
➡ Public laundry
➡ Winemaking stores
➡ Salò del Tinell
➡ Displays on medieval Barcelona

PRACTICALITIES
➡ Map p276
➡ 93 256 21 00
➡ www.museu historia.bcn.cat
➡ Plaça del Rei
➡ adult/child €7/free, free 1st Sun of month & 3-8pm Sun
➡ 10am-7pm Tue-Sat, 10am-8pm Sun
➡ Jaume I

PALAU DE LA GENERALITAT   PALACE

Map p276 (www.president.cat; Plaça de Sant Jaume; 2nd & 4th weekend of month; Liceu, Jaume I) Founded in the early 15th century, the Palau de la Generalitat is open on limited occasions only (the second and fourth weekends of the month, plus open-door days). The most impressive of the ceremonial halls is the **Saló de Sant Jordi**, named after St George, the region's patron saint. To see inside, book on the website (unfortunately in Catalan only). Marc Safont designed the original Gothic main entrance on Carrer del Bisbe. The modern main entrance on Plaça de Sant Jaume is a late-Renaissance job with neoclassical leanings. If you wander by in the evening, squint up through the windows into the Saló de Sant Jordi (Hall of St George) and you will get some idea of the sumptuousness of the interior.

If you do get inside, you're in for a treat. Normally you will have to enter from Carrer de Sant Sever. The first rooms you pass through are characterised by low vaulted ceilings. From here you head upstairs to the raised courtyard known as the Pati dels Tarongers, a modest Gothic orangery (opened about once a month for concert performances of the palace's chimes). The 16th-century Sala Daurada i de Sessions, one of the rooms leading off the patio, is a splendid meeting hall lit up by huge chandeliers. Still more imposing is the Renaissance Saló de Sant Jordi, the murals of which were added last century – many an occasion of pomp and circumstance takes place here. Finally, you descend the staircase of the Gothic Pati Central to leave by what was, in the beginning, the building's main entrance.

MUSEU D'IDEES I INVENTS DE BARCELONA   MUSEUM

Map p276 (Museum of Ideas and Inventions; 93 332 79 30; www.mibamuseum.com; Carrer de la Ciutat 7; adult/child €8/6; 10am-2pm & 4-7pm Tue-Fri, 10am-8pm Sat, to 2pm Sun; Jaume I) Although the price is a bit steep for such a small museum, the collection makes for an amusing browse for an hour or so. On display, you'll find both brilliant and bizarre inventions: square egg makers, absorbent pillows for flatulent folks, a chair for inserting suppositories, as well as more useful devices like the Lifestraw (filters contaminants from any drinking source) and gas glasses (adaptive eyecare for any prescription). There's also an exercise bike attached to a vending machine. You select the product, then pedal away; when your calorie output equals the calorie total of the crisps you want, the treat is yours! Don't miss the creatively configured toilets.

PLAÇA DE SANT JOSEP ORIOL   SQUARE

Map p276 (MLiceu) This small plaza flanking the majestic Església de Santa Maria del Pi is one of the prettiest in the Barri Gòtic. Its bars and cafes attract buskers and artists and make it a lively place to hang out. It is surrounded by quaint streets, many dotted with appealing cafes, restaurants and shops.

ESGLÉSIA DE SANTA MARIA DEL PI   CHURCH

Map p276 (admission €5; ⊙10am-7pm Mon-Sat, 4-8pm Sun; MLiceu) This striking 14th-century church is a classic of Catalan Gothic, with an imposing facade, a wide interior and a single nave. The simple decor in the main sanctuary contrasts with the gilded chapels and exquisite stained-glass windows that bathe the interior in ethereal light. The beautiful rose window above its entrance is one of the world's largest. Occasional concerts are staged here (classical guitar, choral groups, chamber orchestras).

The third chapel on the left is dedicated to Sant Josep Oriol, who was parish priest here from 1687 to 1702. The chapel has a map showing the places in the church where he worked numerous miracles (he was canonised in 1909). According to legend, a 10th-century fisherman discovered an image of the Virgin Mary in a *pi* (pine tree) that he was intent on cutting down to build a boat. Struck by the vision, he instead built a little chapel, later to be succeeded by this Gothic church. A pine still grows in the square outside the church.

PLAÇA REIAL   SQUARE

Map p276 (MLiceu) One of the most photogenic squares in Barcelona, the Plaça Reial is a delightful retreat from the traffic and pedestrian mobs on the nearby Rambla. Numerous eateries, bars and nightspots lie beneath the arcades of 19th-century neoclassical buildings, with a buzz of activity at all hours. It was created on the site of a convent, one of several destroyed along La Rambla (the strip was teeming with religious institutions) in the wake of the Spain-wide disentailment laws that stripped the Church of much of its property. The lamp posts by the central fountain are Antoni Gaudí's first known works in the city.

The southern half of the Barri Gòtic is imbued with the memory of Picasso, who lived as a teenager with his family in Carrer de la Mercè, had his first studio in Carrer de la Plata and was a regular visitor to a brothel at Carrer d'Avinyó 27. That experience may have inspired his 1907 painting *Les Demoiselles d'Avignon*.

GRAN TEATRE DEL LICEU   ARCHITECTURE

Map p276 (☑93 485 99 14; www.liceubarcelona.com; La Rambla dels Caputxins 51-59; tour 20/80min €5.50/11.50; ⊙guided tour 10am, short tour 11.30am, noon, 12.30pm & 1pm; MLiceu) If you can't catch a night at the opera, you can still have a look around one of Europe's greatest opera houses, known to locals as the Liceu. Smaller than Milan's La Scala but bigger than Venice's La Fenice, it can seat up to 2300 people in its grand horseshoe auditorium.

Built in 1847, the Liceu launched such Catalan stars as Josep (aka José) Carreras and Montserrat Caballé. Fire virtually destroyed it in 1994, but city authorities were quick to get it back into operation. Carefully reconstructing the 19th-century auditorium and installing the latest in theatre technology, technicians finalised its restoration in

---

ROMAN WALLS

From Plaça del Rei, it's worth taking a detour northeast to see the two best surviving stretches of Barcelona's Roman walls, which once boasted 78 towers (as much a matter of prestige as of defence). **One wall** (Map p276) is on the southwest side of Plaça Ramon de Berenguer Gran, with the **Capella Reial de Santa Àgata** (Map p276) atop. The square itself is dominated by a statue of count-king Ramon de Berenguer Gran done by Josep Llimona in 1880. The **other wall** (Map p276) is a little further south, by the northern end of Carrer del Sotstinent Navarro. The Romans built and reinforced these walls in the 3rd and 4th centuries AD, after the first attacks by Germanic tribes from the north.

TOP SIGHT
MUSEU FREDERIC MARÈS

One of the wildest collections of historical curios lies inside this vast medieval complex, once part of the royal palace of the counts of Barcelona. A rather worn coat of arms on the wall indicates that it was also, for a while, the seat of the Spanish Inquisition in Barcelona.

Frederic Marès i Deulovol (1893–1991) was a rich sculptor, traveller and obsessive collector. He specialised in medieval Spanish **sculpture**, huge quantities of which are displayed in the basement and on the ground and 1st floors – including some lovely polychrome wooden sculptures of the Crucifixion and the Virgin. Among the most eye-catching pieces is a reconstructed Romanesque doorway with four arches, taken from a 13th-century country church in the Aragonese province of Huesca.

The top two floors comprise **'the collector's cabinet'**, a mind-boggling array of knick-knacks: medieval weaponry, finely carved pipes, delicate ladies' fans, intricate 'floral' displays made of seashells, and 19th-century daguerreotypes and photographs. A room that once served as Marès' **study** and library is now crammed with sculptures. The shady courtyard houses a pleasant summer **cafe** (Cafè de l'Estiu), well worth a visit after browsing the collections.

DON'T MISS...

→ Displays from the collector's cabinet
→ Sculptures on the 1st floor
→ Marès' study

PRACTICALITIES

→ Map p276
→ ☑93 256 35 00
→ www.museumares.bcn.es
→ Plaça de Sant Iu 5
→ admission €4.20, after 3pm Sun & 1st Sun of month free
→ ⊙10am-7pm Tue-Sat, 11am-8pm Sun
→ Ⓜ Jaume I

October 1999. You can take a 20-minute guided tour around the main public areas of the theatre or you can join a longer guided tour.

On the 80-minute tour you are taken to the grand foyer, with its thick pillars and sumptuous chandeliers, and then up the marble staircase to the Saló dels Miralls (Hall of Mirrors). These both survived the 1994 fire and the latter was traditionally where theatregoers mingled during intermission. With mirrors, ceiling frescoes, fluted columns and high-and-mighty phrases in praise of the arts, it all exudes a typically neobaroque richness worthy of its 19th-century patrons. You are then led up to the 4th-floor stalls to admire the theatre itself.

The tour also takes in a collection of Modernista art, El Cercle del Liceu, which contains works by Ramon Casas. It is possible to book special tours, one that is similar to the guided tour described but including a half-hour music recital on the Saló dels Miralls, and another tour that penetrates the inner workings of the stage and backstage work areas.

MIRADOR DE COLOM   VIEWPOINT

Map p286 (☑93 302 52 24; Plaça del Portal de la Pau; lift adult/child €4.50/3; ⊙8.30am-8pm; Ⓜ Drassanes) High above the swirl of traffic on the roundabout below, Columbus keeps permanent watch, pointing vaguely out to the Mediterranean. Built for the Universal Exhibition in 1888, the monument allows you to zip up 60m in the lift for bird's-eye views back up La Rambla and across the ports of Barcelona.

It was in Barcelona that Columbus allegedly gave the delighted Catholic monarchs a report of his first discoveries in the Americas after his voyage in 1492. In the 19th century, it was popularly believed here that Columbus was one of Barcelona's most illustrious sons. Some historians still make that claim.

ESGLÉSIA DE SANTS JUST I PASTOR   CHURCH

Map p276 (☑93 301 74 33; www.basilicasantjust.cat; Plaça de Sant Just 5; ⊙11am-2pm & 5-8pm Mon-Sat, 10am-1pm Sun; Ⓜ Liceu or Jaume I) This somewhat neglected, single-nave church, with chapels on either side of the buttressing, was built in 1342 in Catalan

LOCAL KNOWLEDGE

GRAFFITI ARTIST

Across Plaça Nova from La Catedral your eye may be caught by childlike scribblings on the facade of the **Col·legi de Arquitectes** (Architectural College; Map p276). It is, in fact, a giant contribution by Picasso from 1962. The artwork, which represents Mediterranean festivals, was much ridiculed by the local press when it was unveiled.

Gothic style on what is reputedly the site of the oldest parish church in Barcelona. Inside, you can admire some fine stained-glass windows. In front of it, in a pretty little square that was used as a set (a smelly Parisian marketplace) in 2006 for *Perfume: The Story of a Murderer,* is what is claimed to be the city's oldest Gothic fountain.

On the morning of 11 September 1924, Antoni Gaudí was arrested as he attempted to enter the church from this square to attend Mass. In those days of the dictatorship of General Primo de Rivera, it took little to ruffle official feathers, and Gaudí's refusal to speak Spanish to the overbearing Guardia Civil officers who had stopped him earned him the better part of a day in the cells until a friend came to bail him out.

CENTRE D'INTERPRETACIÓ
DEL CALL   HISTORIC SITE

Map p276 (☑93 256 21 22; www.museuhistoria.bcn. cat; Placeta de Manuel Ribé; ⊙11am-2pm Tue-Fri, to 7pm Sat & Sun; ⓂJaume I or Liceu) **FREE** Once a 14th-century house of the Jewish weaver Jucef Bonhiac, this small visitors centre is dedicated to the history of Barcelona's Jewish quarter, El Call. Glass sections in the ground floor allow you to inspect Mr Bonhiac's former wells and storage space. The house, also known as the Casa de l'Alquimista (Alchemist's House), hosts a modest display of Jewish artefacts, including ceramics excavated in the area of El Call, along with explanations and maps of the one-time Jewish quarter.

SINAGOGA MAJOR   SYNAGOGUE

Map p276 (☑93 317 07 90; www.calldebarcelona. org; Carrer de Marlet 5; admission by suggested donation €2.50; ⊙10.30am-6.30pm Mon-Fri, to 2.30pm Sat & Sun; ⓂLiceu) When an Argentine investor bought a run-down electrician's store with an eye to converting it into

central Barcelona's umpteenth bar, he could hardly have known he had stumbled onto the remains of what could be the city's main medieval synagogue (some historians cast doubt on the claim). A guide will explain what is thought to be the significance of the site in various languages.

Fragments of medieval and Roman-era walls remain in the small vaulted space that you enter from the street. Also remaining are tanners' wells installed in the 15th century. The second chamber has been spruced up for use as a synagogue. A remnant of late-Roman-era wall here, given its orientation facing Jerusalem, has led some to speculate that there was a synagogue here even in Roman times. There were four synagogues in the medieval city, but after the pogroms of 1391, this one (assuming it was the Sinagoga Major) was Christianised by the placing of an effigy of St Dominic on the building.

TEMPLE ROMÀ D'AUGUST   RUIN

Map p276 (Carrer del Paradis 10; ⊙10am-2pm Mon, to 7pm Tue-Sun; ⓂJaume I) **FREE** Opposite the southeast end of La Catedral, narrow Carrer del Paradis leads towards Plaça de Sant Jaume. Inside No 10, itself an intriguing building with Gothic and baroque touches, are four columns and the architrave of Barcelona's main Roman temple, dedicated to Caesar Augustus and built to worship his imperial highness in the 1st century AD. You are now standing on the highest point of Roman Barcino, Mont Tàber (a grand total of 16.9m, unlikely to induce altitude sickness). You may well find the door open outside the listed hours. Just pop in.

VIA SEPULCRAL
ROMANA   ARCHAEOLOGICAL SITE

Map p276 (☑93 256 21 00; www.museuhistoria. bcn.cat; Plaça de la Vila de Madrid; adult/child €2/free; ⊙11am-2pm Tue-Fri, to 7pm Sat & Sun; ⓂCatalunya) Along Carrer de la Canuda, a block east of the top end of La Rambla, is a sunken garden where a series of Roman tombs lies exposed. A display in Spanish and Catalan beside the tombs explores burial and funerary rites and customs. A few bits of pottery (including a burial amphora with the skeleton of a three-year-old Roman child) accompany the display. The burial ground stretches along either side of the road that led northwest out of Barcelona's Roman predecessor, Barcino. Roman law forbade burial within city limits and so everyone was generally buried along roads leading out of cities.

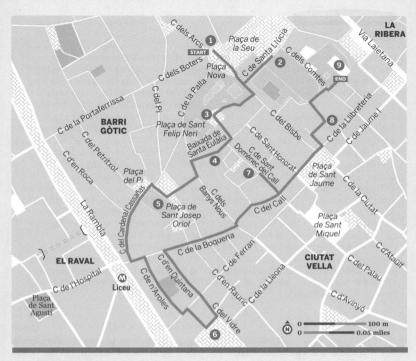

Neighbourhood Walk
Hidden Treasures in the Barri Gòtic

START LA CATEDRAL
END PLAÇA DEL REI
LENGTH 1.5KM; 1½ HOURS

This scenic walk through the Barri Gòtic will take you back in time, from the early days of Roman-era Barcino through to the medieval era.

Before entering the cathedral, have look at **1 three Picasso friezes** on the building facing the square. After noting his signature style, wander through **2 La Catedral** (p62); don't miss the cloister with its flock of 13 geese. Leaving the cathedral, enter the former gates of the ancient fortified city and turn right into **3 Plaça de Sant Felip Neri**. Note the shrapnel-scarred walls of the old church, damaged by pro-Francist bombers in 1939. A plaque commemorates the victims (mostly children) of the bombing.

Head out of the square and turn right. On this narrow lane, you'll spot a small **4 statue of Santa Eulàlia**, one of Barcelona's patron saints who suffered various tortures during her martyrdom. Make your way west to the looming **5 Església de Sant Maria del Pi** (p66), which is famed for its magnificent rose window. Follow the curving road and zigzag down to **6 Plaça Reial** (p66), one of Barcelona's prettiest squares. Flanking the fountain are lamp posts designed by Antoni Gaudí.

Stroll up to Carrer de la Boqueria and turn left on Carrer de Sant Domènec del Call. This leads into the El Call district, once the heart of the medieval Jewish quarter, until the bloody pogrom of 1391. The **7 Sinagoga Major** (p68), one of Europe's oldest, was discovered in 1996. Head across Plaça de Sant Jaume and turn left after Carrer del Bisbe. You'll soon pass the entrance to the remnants of a **8 Roman Temple**, with four columns hidden in a small courtyard. The final stop is **9 Plaça del Rei**, a picturesque plaza where Fernando and Isabel received Columbus following his first New World voyage. The former palace today houses a superb history museum, with significant Roman ruins underground.

LOCAL KNOWLEDGE

EL CALL

One of our favourite places in the Ciutat Vella (Old City) to wander is El Call (pronounced 'kye'), which is the name of the medieval Jewish quarter that flourished here until a tragic pogrom in the 14th century. Today its narrow lanes hide some surprising sites (including an ancient synagogue unearthed in the 1990s and the fragments of a women's bathouse inside the basement of the cafe, Caelum). Some of the old city's most unusual shops are here, selling exquisite antiques, handmade leather products, even kosher wine. Its well-concealed dining rooms and candlelit bars and cafes make a fine destination in the evening.

El Call (which probably derives from the Hebrew word '*kahal*', meaning 'community') is a tiny area, and a little tricky to find. The boundaries are roughly Carrer del Call, Carrer dels Banys Nous, Baixada de Santa Eulàlia and Carrer de Sant Honorat.

Though a handful of Jewish families remained after the bloody pogrom of 1391, the subsequent expulsion of all Jews in the country in the 15th century put an end to the Jewish presence in Barcelona. The Call Menor extended across the modern Carrer de Ferran as far as Baixada de Sant Miquel and Carrer d'en Rauric. The present Església de Sant Jaume on Carrer de Ferran was built on the site of a synagogue.

Even before the pograms of 1391, Jews in Barcelona were not exactly privileged citizens. As in many medieval centres, they were obliged to wear a special identifying mark on their garments and had trouble getting permission to expand their ghetto as El Call's population increased (as many as 4000 people were crammed into the tiny streets of the Call Major).

DOMUS DE SANT HONORAT
ARCHAEOLOGICAL SITE

Map p276 (☑93 256 21 00; www.museuhistoria.bcn.cat; Carrer de la Fruita 2; admission €2; ⊙10am-2pm Sat & Sun; ⓂLiceu) The remains of a Roman *domus* (town house) have been unearthed and opened to the public. The house (and vestiges of three small shops) lay close to the Roman forum and the owners were clearly well off. Apart from getting something of an idea of daily Roman life through these remains, the location also contains six medieval grain silos installed at the time the Jewish quarter, El Call, was located in this area. The whole site is housed in the mid-19th-century Casa Morell. So, in an unusual mix, one gets a glimpse of three distinct periods in history in the same spot.

HEMP MUSEUM GALLERY
MUSEUM

Map p276 (☑93 319 75 39; hempmuseumgallery.com; Carrer Ample 35; admission €7.50; ⊙10am-10pm; ⓂJaume I) The world's largest museum dedicated to all things cannabis opened to much fanfare in 2012 (even Virgin founder Richard Branson was at the opening). Set in the beautifully restored 16th-century Palau Mornau, exhibitions delve into the role the plant has played over the years, with 19th-century medicinal cannabis bottles, pulp film posters and consumer products made from hemp among the displays.

ESGLÉSIA DE LA MERCÈ
CHURCH

Map p276 (Plaça de la Mercè; ⊙10am-1pm & 6-8pm; ⓂDrassanes) Raised in the 1760s on the site of its Gothic predecessor, the baroque Església de la Mercè is home to Barcelona's most celebrated patron saint. It was badly damaged during the civil war. What remains is, however, quite a curiosity. The baroque facade facing the square contrasts with the Renaissance flank along Carrer Ample. Climb the steps behind the altar for a close-up view of the Virgin Mary statue for whom the church is named; it dates from 1361.

MUSEU DE L'ERÒTICA
MUSEUM

Map p276 (Erotica Museum; ☑93 318 98 65; www.erotica-museum.com; La Rambla de Sant Josep 96; admission €9; ⊙10am-midnight; ☜; ⓂLiceu) Observe what naughtiness people have been getting up to since ancient times in this museum, with historical relics such as Indian bas-reliefs showing various aspects of tantric love, 18th-century wood carvings depicting Kama Sutra positions, Japanese porcelain porn and African fornication carvings. Despite the premise, overall it's a rather buttoned-up affair, and probably not worth the steep admission price (despite the free drink).

MUSEU DEL CALÇAT MUSEUM

Map p276 (Footwear Museum; ☑93 301 45 33; Plaça de Sant Felip Neri 5; admission €2.50; ⊙11am-2pm Tue-Sun; ⓂJaume I) This obscure museum is home to everything from Egyptian sandals to dainty ladies' shoes of the 18th century. The museum and cobblers' guild, which has its roots in the city's medieval past, were moved here shortly after the civil war.

MUSEU DE CERA MUSEUM

Map p276 (☑93 317 26 49; www.museocerabcn. com; Passatge de la Banca 7; adult/child €15/9; ⊙10am-10pm daily Jun-Sep, 10am-2pm & 4-8pm Mon-Fri, 11am-2pm & 4.30-9pm Sat Oct-May; ⓂDrassanes) Inside this late-19th-century building, you can stand, sit and lounge about with Frankenstein, Che Guevara and lots of Spanish figures you probably won't recognise. Unintentionally funny, the price tag is steep for often poorly executed representations.

✖ EATING

First things first: skip the strip. La Rambla is fine for people-watching, but no great shakes for the palate. Instead venture off into the streets that wind into the Barri Gòtic and your belly (and wallet) will be eternally grateful. Inside the medieval labyrinth, choices abound. If you had to pinpoint any one area, it would be the eastern half of the *barri* (neighbourhood) near Via Laietana on the narrow streets above the cathedral (around Carrer de les Magdalenes) and between Plaça de Sant Jaume and the waterfront. Here you'll find a huddle of old-time tapas bars as well as innovative newcomers. All are laden with atmosphere.

RASOTERRA VEGETARIAN €

Map p276 (☑93 318 69 26; Carrer del Palau 5; tapas €5-8, lunch specials €7-10; ⊙noon-5pm Tue, to midnight Wed-Sun; ☑; ⓂJaume I) A delightful addition to the Gothic quarter, Rasoterra cooks up first-rate vegetarian dishes in a Zen-like setting with tall ceilings, low-playing jazz and fresh flowers on the tables. The creative, globally influenced menu changes regularly and might feature Vietnamese-style coconut pancakes with tofu and vegetables, beluga lentils with basmati rice, and pear and goat cheese quesadillas. Good vegan and gluten-free options.

ALCOBA AZUL TAPAS, WINE BAR €

Map p276 (Carrer de Sant Domènec del Call 14; tapas €2-7; ⊙4.30pm-2.30am Tue-Fri, to midnight Sat) Peel back the centuries inside this remarkably atmospheric watering hole, with medieval walls, low ceilings, wide plank floors and flickering candles. Grab one of the seats at the tiny bar in front or slide into one of the table booths at the back, where you can enjoy good wines by the glass, satisfying plates of stuffed peppers, salads, *tostas* (sandwiches) and blood sausage with caramelised onions.

CERVECERÍA TALLER DE TAPAS TAPAS €

Map p276 (☑93 481 62 33; www.tallerdetapas. com; Carrer Comtal 28; tapas €4-10; ⊙8.30am-1am Mon-Sat, from noon Sun; ⓂUrquinaona) Amid white stone walls and a beamed ceiling, this buzzing, easygoing place serves a broad selection of tapas as well as changing daily specials like *cochinillo* (roast suckling pig). A smattering of beers from across the globe – Leffe Blond, Guinness, Brahma (Brazil) and Sol (Mexico) – add to the appeal.

It has a few other locations around town, including a well-placed spot with outdoor seating on **Plaça de Sant Josep Oriol** (Map p276; ☑93 301 80 20; Plaça de Sant Josep Oriol 9; ⊙8.30am-1am Mon-Sat, from noon Sun).

BUTIFARRING SANDWICHES €

Map p276 (Carrer del Call 26; sandwiches €4-5; ⊙9am-9pm Mon-Thu, to 11pm Fri & Sat, to 6pm Sun; ☎; ⓂLiceu, Jaume I) Gourmet sausage sandwiches are grilled to perfection at this friendly and appealing new eatery just off Plaça Sant Jaume. You'll find around six different sausages on the menu including seasonal varieties (like calçots in winter), plus homemade sauces, roasted potatoes, Montseny craft beer and chocolate *coulant* (soufflé) for dessert.

LA PLATA TAPAS €

Map p276 (Carrer de la Mercè 28; tapas €2.50-5; ⊙9am-3pm & 6.30-11.30pm Mon-Sat; ⓂJaume I) Tucked away on a narrow lane near the waterfront, La Plata is a humble but well-loved bodega that serves just three plates: *pescadito frito* (small fried fish), *butifarra* (sausage) and tomato salad. Add in the drinkable, affordable wines (€1.10 per glass), and you have the makings of a fine predinner tapas spot.

BEST CAFES

Some of Barcelona's most atmospheric cafes lie hidden in the old cobbled lanes of Barri Gòtic. A round-up of our favourite spots for a pick-me-up.

Salterio (Map p276; Carrer de Sant Domènec del Call 4; ⊙2pm-midnight; MJaume I) A wonderfully photogenic spot tucked down a tiny lane in El Call, Salterio serves refreshing teas, Turkish coffee, authentic mint teas and snacks amid stone walls, incense and ambient Middle Eastern music. If hunger strikes, try the *sardo* (grilled flat-bread covered with pesto, cheese or other toppings).

Čaj Chai (Map p276; ☑93 301 95 92; www.cajchai.com; Carrer de Sant Domènec del Call 12; ⊙3-10pm Mon, 10.30am-10pm Tue-Sun; MJaume I) Inspired by Prague's bohemian tearooms, this bright and buzzing cafe in the heart of the old Jewish quarter is a tea connoisseur's paradise. Čaj Chai stocks more than 100 teas from China, India, Korea, Japan, Nepal, Morocco and beyond. It's a much-loved local haunt.

La Clandestina (Map p276; ☑93 319 05 33; Baixada de Viladecols 2; ⊙9am-10pm Sun-Thu, to midnight Fri & Sat; ☎; MJaume I) Opt for tea, Turkish coffee, mango lassi or a Middle Eastern *narghile* (the most elaborate way to smoke). Like other cafes and bars nearby, Clandestina sports a bohemian ambience with colour-saturated walls and a changing display of local artwork for sale. There's also beer and wine on hand.

Caelum (Map p276; ☑93 302 69 93; www.caelumbarcelona.com; Carrer de la Palla 8; ⊙10.30am-8.30pm Mon-Thu, 10.30am-11.30pm Fri & Sat, 11.30am-9pm Sun; MLiceu) Centuries of heavenly gastronomic tradition from across Spain are concentrated in this exquisite medieval space in the heart of the city. The upstairs cafe is a dainty setting for decadent cakes and pastries, while descending into the underground chamber with its stone walls and flickering candles is like stepping into the Middle Ages.

Cafè de l'Òpera (Map p276; ☑93 317 75 85; www.cafeoperabcn.com; La Rambla 74; ⊙8.30am-2.30am; MLiceu) Opposite the Gran Teatre del Liceu is La Rambla's most intriguing cafe. Operating since 1929, it is pleasant enough for an early evening libation or coffee and croissants. Head upstairs for an elevated seat above the busy boulevard. Can you be tempted by the *cafè de l'Òpera* (coffee with chocolate mousse)?

La Granja (Map p276; ☑93 302 69 75; Carrer dels Banys Nous 4; ⊙9.30am-1.30pm Mon-Sat & 5-9pm daily; MLiceu) This long-running cafe serves up thick, rich cups of chocolate, but it doesn't make its own churros. Buy them a few doors down at **Xurreria** (Map p276; Carrer dels Banys Nous 8; ⊙7am-1.30pm daily & 4-8.30pm Sun) and bring them here for the perfect combo of churros dipped in chocolate.

FORNERIA TIANA
BAKERY €

Map p276 (Carrer Ample 27; sandwiches around €3; ⊙7am-10pm; ☎; MJaume I) Stop at this bright new bakery and cafe for fresh pastries, croissant sandwiches, quiches and other light bites. Friendly staff whip up decent coffees, though there's also wine and other refreshments.

ONOFRE
SPANISH €€

Map p276 (☑93 317 69 37; www.onofre.net; Carrer de les Magdalenes 19; mains €9-14; ⊙10am-4pm & 7.30pm-midnight Mon-Sat; MJaume I) Famed for its wine selections, Onofre is a small, modern eatery (and wine shop and delicatessen) that has a strong local following for its delicious tapas plates, good affordable wines and great-value lunch specials (three-course prix-fixe for €10.75). Among the delectable tapas selections: Italian greens with foie shavings, duck confit, codfish carpaccio, oven-baked prawns, and warm goat cheese salad with ham and anchovies.

ALLIUM
CATALAN, FUSION €€

Map p276 (☑93 302 30 03; Carrer del Call 17; mains €8-16; ⊙noon-4pm Mon-Tue, to 10.30pm Wed-Sat; MLiceu) This inviting newcomer to Barri Gòtic serves beautifully prepared tapas dishes and changing specials (including seafood paella for one). The menu, which changes every two or threee weeks, focuses on seasonal, organic cuisine. Its bright, modern interior sets it apart from other neighbourhood options; it's also open continuously, making it a good bet for those who don't want to wait until 9pm for a meal.

LA VINATERIA DEL CALL   SPANISH €€

Map p276 (☑93 302 60 92; www.lavinateriadel-call.com; Carrer de Sant Domènec del Call 9; small plates €7-12; ⊗7.30pm-1am; Ⓜ Jaume I) In a magical setting in the former Jewish quarter, this tiny jewelbox of a restaurant serves up tasty Iberian dishes including Galician octopus, cider-cooked chorizo and the Catalan *escalivada* (roasted peppers, aubergine and onions) with anchovies. Portions are small and made for sharing, and there's a good and affordable selection of wines.

CAFÈ DE L'ACADÈMIA   CATALAN €€

Map p276 (☑93 319 82 53; Carrer dels Lledó 1; mains €13-19; ⊗1.30-4pm & 8.45-11.30pm Mon-Fri; Ⓜ Jaume I) Expect a mix of traditional dishes with the occasional creative twist. At lunchtime, local *ajuntament* (town hall) office workers pounce on the *menú del día*. In the evening it is rather more romantic, as low lighting emphasises the intimacy of the timber ceiling and wooden decor. On warm days, you can also dine on the pretty square at the front.

CERERÍA   VEGETARIAN €€

Map p276 (☑93 301 85 10; Baixada de Sant Miquel 3; mains €10-16; ⊗7pm-midnight Tue-Sun; 🎅📶; Ⓜ Jaume I) Black-and-white marble floors, a smattering of old wooden tables and ramshackle displays of instruments (most made on-site) lend a certain bohemian charm to this small vegetarian restaurant. The pizzas are delicious, and feature organic ingredients – as do the flavourful galettes, dessert crêpes and bountiful salads. Vegan options too.

MILK   BRUNCH €€

Map p276 (www.milkbarcelona.com; Carrer d'en Gignàs 21; mains €9-12; ⊗9am-2am; 📶; Ⓜ Jaume I) Also known to many as an enticing cocktail spot, the Irish-run Milk's key role for Barcelona night owls is providing morning-after brunches (served till 4.30pm). Avoid direct sunlight and tuck into pancakes, eggs Benedict and other hangover dishes in a cosy lounge-like setting complete with ornate wallpaper, framed prints on the wall and pillow-lined seating.

★ KOY SHUNKA   JAPANESE €€€

Map p276 (☑93 412 79 39; www.koyshunka.com; Carrer de Copons 7; multicourse menus €77-110; ⊗1.30-3pm Tue-Sun & 8.30-11pm Tue-Sat; Ⓜ Urquinaona) Down a narrow lane north of the cathedral, Koy Shunka opens a portal to exquisite dishes from the East – mouth-watering sushi, sashimi, seared Wagyu beef and flavour-rich seaweed salads are served alongside inventive cooked fushion dishes such as steamed clams with sake or tempura of scallops and king prawns with Japanese mushrooms. Don't miss the house speciality of tender *toro* (tuna belly).

Most diners sit at the large wraparound counter, where you can watch the culinary wizardry in action. Set multicourse menus are pricey but well worth it for those seeking a truly extraordinary dining experience.

PLA   FUSION €€€

Map p276 (☑93 412 65 52; www.elpla.cat; Carrer de la Bellafila 5; mains €18-25; ⊗7.30pm-midnight; 📶; Ⓜ Jaume I) One of Gòtic's long-standing favourites, Pla is a stylish, romantically lit medieval dining room where the cooks churn out such temptations as oxtail braised in red wine, seared tuna with oven-roasted peppers, and polenta with seasonal mushrooms. It has a tasting menu for €38 Sunday to Thursday.

DRINKING & NIGHTLIFE

OCAÑA   BAR

Map p276 (☑93 676 48 14; www.ocana.cat; Plaça Reial 13; ⊗5pm-2.30am Mon-Fri, from 11am Sat & Sun; Ⓜ Liceu) Named after a flamboyant artist who once lived on Plaça Reial, Ocaña is a beautifully designed space with fluted columns, stone walls, candlelit chandeliers and plush furnishings. Have a seat on the terrace and watch the passing people parade, or head downstairs to the Moorish-inspired Apotheke bar or the chic lounge a few steps away, where DJs spin for a mix of beauties and bohemians on weekend nights.

MIRILLA   BAR

Map p276 (Carrer de Regomir 16; ⊗6pm-1am Mon-Thu, to 3am Fri & Sat; Ⓜ Jaume I) Mirilla is a great place to stumble upon, with excellent wines by the glass and well-executed cocktails, and there's plenty to munch on when hunger strikes. The ambience hangs somewhere between bohemian and classy, and the crowd is equally eclectic. Friendly multilingual owners.

OVISO
BAR

Map p276 (Carrer d'Arai 5; ⊘10am-2.30am; 🛜; MLiceu) Oviso is a popular budget-friendly restaurant with outdoor tables on the plaza, but shows its true bohemian colours by night, with a mixed crowd, a rock-and-roll vibe and a rustic decorated two-room interior plastered with curious murals – geese taking flight, leaping dolphins and blue peacocks framing the brightly painted concrete walls.

LA CERVETECA
BAR

Map p276 (Carrer de Gignàs 25; ⊘6-11pm Sun-Thu, to midnight Fri & Sat; MJaume I) An unmissable stop for beer lovers, La Cerveteca serves an impressive variety of global craft brews. In addition to scores of bottled brews, there's a frequent rotation of what's on draught. Cheeses, *jamon ibérico* and other charcuterie selections are on hand, including *cecina* (cured horse meat). The standing cask tables (with a few seats at the back) are a fine setting to an early evening pick me up.

SOR RITA
BAR

Map p276 (Carrer de la Mercè 27; ⊘7pm-2.30am; MJaume I) A lover of all things kitsch, Sor Rita is pure eye candy, from its leopard-print wallpaper to its high-heel festooned ceiling, and deliciously irreverent decorations inspired by the films of Almodóvar. It's a fun and festive scene, with special-event nights throughout the week, including tarot readings on Mondays, €5 all-you-can-eat snack buffets on Tuesdays, karaoke Wednesdays and gin specials on Thursdays.

GINGER
COCKTAIL BAR

Map p276 (www.ginger.cat; Carrer de Palma de Sant Just 1; ⊘7.30pm-2.30am Tue-Sat; MJaume I) Tucked away just off peaceful Plaça de Sant Just, Ginger is an art deco–style multilevel drinking den with low lighting, finely crafted cocktails and good ambient sounds (provided by vinyl-spinning DJs some nights). It's a mellow spot, that's great for sipping wine and sampling from the small tapas menu.

CAN FLY
BAR

Map p276 (Baixada de Viladecols 6; ⊘4pm-2am; MJaume I) Overlooking a peaceful little plaza near the edge of the old Roman wall, Can Fly is a friendly lesbian-owned bar that draws a mixed crowd of gay and straight. It's a jovial but mellow spot for a drink, with amber-lighting, graffiti-like wall murals, and budget-friendly cocktails and tapas. Outdoor seating on warm nights.

L'ASCENSOR
BAR

Map p276 (Carrer de la Bellafila 3; ⊘6pm-midnight Mon-Thu, to 3am Fri & Sat; MJaume I) Named after the lift (elevator) doors that serve as the front door, this elegant drinking den with its vaulted brick ceilings, vintage mirrors and marble-topped bar gathers a faithful crowd who comes for old-fashioned cocktails and lively conversation against a soundtrack of up-tempo jazz and funk.

MARULA CAFÈ
BAR

Map p276 (www.marulacafe.com; Carrer dels Escudellers 49; ⊘11pm-5am Wed-Sun; MLiceu) A fantastic funk find in the heart of the Barri Gòtic, Marula will transport you to the 1970s and the best in funk and soul. James Brown fans will think they've died and gone to heaven. It's not, however, a monothematic place and DJs slip in other tunes, from breakbeat to house. Samba and other Brazilian dance sounds also penetrate here.

POLAROID
BAR

Map p276 (Carrer dels Còdols 29; ⊘7pm-2.30am; MDrassanes) For a dash of 1980s nostalgia, Polaroid is a blast from the past with its wall-mounted VHS tapes, old film posters, comic-book-covered tables, action-figure displays and other kitschy decor. Not surprisingly, it draws a fun, unpretentious crowd who comes for cheap *cañas* (draught beer), mojitos and free popcorn.

BOOTLEG
BAR

Map p276 (Carrer dels Lledó 5; ⊘9.30am-2am Mon-Fri, from 6pm Sat; MJaume I) One of a growing number of enticing cafe-bars along this street, tiny Bootleg is a warmly lit, split-level spot with a stylish but unpretentious crowd (equal parts expat and *barcelonin*) that comes for good conversation, fairly priced drinks and snacks, with a soundtrack of ambient electronica.

BARCELONA PIPA CLUB
BAR

Map p276 (📞93 302 47 32; www.bpipaclub.com; Plaça Reial 3; ⊘10am-4am; MLiceu) This pipe-smokers' club is like an apartment, with all sorts of interconnecting rooms and knick-knacks – notably the pipes after which the place is named. Buzz at the door and head two floors up. Note there's no longer any smoking here, though there is occasional live music.

MANCHESTER
BAR

Map p276 (www.manchesterbar.com; Carrer de Milans 5; ☉7pm-2.30am; MLiceu) A drinking den that has undergone several transformations over the years now treats you to the sounds of great Manchester bands, from Joy Division to Oasis, but probably not the Hollies. It has a pleasing rough-and-tumble feel, with tables jammed in every which way.

KARMA
CLUB

Map p276 (✒93 302 56 80; www.karmadisco.com; Plaça Reial 10; ☉midnight-5.30am Tue-Sun; MLiceu) During the week Karma plays good, mainstream indie music, while on weekends the DJs spin anything from rock to disco. A golden oldie in Barcelona, tunnel-shaped Karma is small and becomes quite tightly packed (claustrophobic for some) with a good-natured crowd of locals and out-of-towners.

LA MACARENA
CLUB

Map p276 (✒637 416647; www.macarenaclub.com; Carrer Nou de Sant Francesc 5; ☉midnight-5am; MDrassanes) You simply won't believe this was once a tile-lined Andalucian flamenco musos' bar. Now it is a dark dance space, of the kind where it is possible to sit at the bar, meet people around you and then stand up for a bit of a shake to the DJ's electro and house offerings, all within a couple of square metres.

BOSC DE LES FADES
LOUNGE

Map p276 (Passatage de la Banca 5; ☉11am-1.30am; MDrassanes) The 'Forest of the Faeries' is touristy but offers a whimsical retreat from the busy Ramblas nearby. Lounge chairs and lamplit tables are scattered beneath an indoor forest complete with trickling fountain and grotto. Prices are steep (€8 for a cocktail).

TEATRE PRINCIPAL
CLUB, GAY

Map p276 (✒93 412 31 29; www.teatreprincipalbcn.com; La Rambla 27; admission €10-15; MLiceu) After midnight this historic theatre transforms into a dance club, which attracts a stylish mixed crowd of straight and gay.

⭐ ENTERTAINMENT

HARLEM JAZZ CLUB
JAZZ

Map p276 (✒93 310 07 55; www.harlemjazzclub.es; Carrer de la Comtessa de Sobradiel 8; admission €7-8; ☉8pm-5am Tue-Sat; MDrassanes) This narrow, old-city dive is one of the best spots in town for jazz, as well as funk, Latin, blues and gypsy jazz. It attracts a mixed crowd who maintains a respectful silence during the acts. Most concerts start around 10pm. Get in early if you want a seat in front of the stage.

JAMBOREE
LIVE MUSIC

Map p276 (✒93 319 17 89; www.masimas.com/jamboree; Plaça Reial 17; admission €10-20; ☉8pm-6am; MLiceu) For over half a century, Jamboree has been bringing joy to the jivers of Barcelona, with high-calibre acts featuring jazz trios, blues, Afrobeats, Latin sounds and big-band sounds. Two concerts are held most nights (at 8pm and 10pm), after which Jamboree morphs into a DJ-spinning club at midnight. WTF jam sessions are held Mondays (entrance a mere €5). Buy tickets online to save a few euros.

SIDECAR FACTORY CLUB
LIVE MUSIC

Map p276 (✒93 302 15 86; www.sidecarfactoryclub.com; Plaça Reial 7; admission €8-18; ☉10pm-5am Mon-Sat; MLiceu) With its entrance on Plaça Reial, you can come here for a meal before midnight or a few drinks at ground level (which closes by 3am at the latest), or descend into the red-tinged, brick-vaulted bowels for live music most nights. Just about anything goes here, from UK indie through to country punk, but rock and pop lead the way. Most shows start around 10pm. DJs take over at 12.30am to keep things going.

BLVD
DJ

Map p276 (✒93 301 62 89; www.boulevardcultureclub.es; La Rambla 27; ☉midnight-6am Thu-Sat; MDrassanes) Flanked by striptease bars (in the true spirit of the lower Rambla's old days), this place has undergone countless reincarnations. The culture in this club is what a long line-up of DJs brings to the (turn)table. With three different dance spaces, one of them upstairs, it has a deliciously tacky feel, pumping out anything from 1980s hits to house music (especially on Saturdays in the main room). There's no particular dress code.

EL PARAIGUA
LIVE MUSIC

Map p276 (✒93 302 11 31; www.elparaigua.com; Carrer del Pas de l'Ensenyança 2; ☉10.30am-1am Sun, Tue & Wed, to 2am Thu-Sat; MLiceu) A tiny chocolate box of dark tinted Modernisme, the 'Umbrella' has been serving up drinks since the 1960s. The decor was transferred here from a shop knocked down elsewhere in the district and cobbled back together to create this cosy locale. Take a trip in time from Modernisme to medieval by heading downstairs to the brick and stone basement bar area. Amid 11th-century walls, live bands – funk, soul, rock, blues – hold court on Fridays and Saturdays (from 11.30pm).

L'ATENEU
CLASSICAL MUSIC

Map p276 (📞93 343 21 61; www.ateneubcn/agenda; Carrer de la Canuda 6; admission free to €10; MCatalunya) This historic cultural centre (with roots dating back 150 years) hosts a range of high-brow fare, from classical recitals to film screenings and literary readings.

GRAN TEATRE DEL LICEU
THEATRE, LIVE MUSIC

Map p276 (📞93 485 99 00; www.liceubarcelona.com; La Rambla dels Caputxins 51-59; ⏰box office 1.30-8pm Mon-Fri & 1hr before show Sat & Sun; MLiceu) Barcelona's grand old opera house, restored after fire in 1994, is one of the most technologically advanced theatres in the world. To take up a seat in the grand auditorium, returned to all its 19th-century glory but with the very latest in acoustic accoutrements, is to be transported to another age. Tickets can cost anything from €9 for a cheap seat behind a pillar to €205 for a well-positioned night at the opera.

TEATRE PRINCIPAL
LIVE MUSIC

Map p276 (📞93 412 31 29; www.teatreprincipalbcn.com; La Rambla 27; concerts from €20; MLiceu) Following a €6 million renovation, this historic theatre has been transformed into a lavish concert space and nightclub. It hosts a range of sounds from flamenco to indie rock.

MÚSICA AL MUSEU
CLASSICAL MUSIC

Map p276 (www.masimas.com; Plaça del Rei; admission €10-15; ⏰Feb-Jun; MJaume I) For intense 30-minute sessions of chamber music, visit the Museu d'Història de Barcelona (MUHBA). Concerts are held at 6pm, 7pm and 8pm on Sundays from February to mid-June.

SALA TARANTOS
FLAMENCO

Map p276 (📞93 319 17 89; www.masimas.com/tarantos; Plaça Reial 17; admission €10; ⏰shows 8.30pm, 9.30pm & 10.30pm; MLiceu) Since 1963, this basement locale has been the stage for up-and-coming flamenco groups performing in Barcelona. These days Tarantos has become a mostly tourist-centric

affair, with half-hour shows held three times a night. Still, it's a good introduction to flamenco, and not a bad setting for a drink.

🛍 SHOPPING

A handful of interesting shops dots La Rambla, but the real fun starts inside the labyrinth. Young fashion on Carrer d'Avinyó, a mixed bag on Avinguda del Portal de l'Àngel, some cute old shops on Carrer de la Dagueria and lots of exploring in tight old lanes awaits.

TALLER DE MARIONETAS TRAVI
MARIONETTES

Map p276 (📞93 412 66 92; www.marionetastravi.com; Carrer de n'Amargós 4; ⏰noon-9pm Mon-Sat; MUrquinaona) Opened in the 1970s, this atmospheric shop sells beautifully handcrafted marionettes. Don Quixote, Sancho and other iconic Spanish figures are on hand, as well as unusual works from other parts of the world – including rare Sicilian puppets, and pieces from Myanmar (Burma), Indonesia and other parts.

FORMATGERIA LA SEU
FOOD

Map p276 (📞93 412 65 48; www.formatgerialaseu.com; Carrer de la Dagueria 16; ⏰10am-2pm & 5-8pm Tue-Thu, 10am-3.30pm & 5-8pm Fri & Sat, closed Aug; MJaume I) Dedicated to artisan cheeses from all across Spain, this small shop is run by the oh-so-knowledgeable Katherine McLaughlin and is the antithesis of mass production – she stocks only the best from small-scale farmers and her produce changes regularly.

LA TALENTA
VINTAGE

Map p276 (📞93 412 38 79; latalentabarcelona.com; Carrer dels Còdols 23; ⏰noon-8pm Tue-Sat; MDrassanes) This wonderfully atmospheric shop is a great spot for browsing. La Talenta has an intriguing mix of vintage objects (opera glasses, postcards, furniture, old bicycles suspended from the ceiling), as well as crafty, design-minded items (wooden boxes with images of Barcelona, jewellery and accessories, paper-doll kits, coffeetable books), and original artwork.

B LAB
CLOTHING, ACCESSORIES

Map p276 (📞93 184 38 38; www.b-lab.eu; Carrer Ample 9; ⏰10am-2pm & 4-9pm Mon-Sat; MDrassanes) This creative little boutique for men and women sells beautifully crafted

THE SWEET LIFE

Barcelona has some irresistible temptations for those with a sweet tooth. Chocolate lovers won't want to miss Carrer de Petritxol, which is home to several famous *granjas* (milk bars) that dole out thick cups of hot chocolate, best accompanied by churros. The recommended **Granja La Pallaresa** (Map p276; Carrer de Petritxol 11; ⊘9am-1pm daily & 4-9pm Mon-Sat, 5-9pm Sun; ⓂLiceu) always draws a crowd.

At Christmas specialist pastry stores fill with *turrón*, the traditional holiday temptation. Essentially nougat, it comes in different varieties: softer blocks are *turrón de Valencia* and a harder version is *turrón de Gijón*. You can find the treat year-round at stores such as **Torrons Vicens** (Map p276; Carrer de Petritxol 15; ⓂLiceu), which has been selling its signature sweets since 1775.

Other not-to-be-missed spots include Caelum (p72) and **La Colmena** (Map p276; Plaça de l'Angel 12; ⊘9am-9pm; ⓂJaume I), a pastry shop, selling many delicacies including pine nut encrusted *panellets* (sweet almond cakes), flavoured meringues and feather-light *ensaïmadas* (soft, sweet buns topped with powdered sugar) from Mallorca.

dresses, sneakers, graphic and embroidered T-shirts, chunky jewellery and wooden sunglasses, mostly created by Barcelona designers.

EMPREMTES DE CATALUNYA   HANDICRAFTS

Map p276 (☑93 467 46 60; Carrer dels Banys Nous 11; ⊘10am-8pm Mon-Sat, to 2pm Sun; ⓂLiceu) A celebration of Catalan products, this nicely designed store is a great place to browse for unique gifts. You'll find jewellery with designs inspired by Roman iconography (as well as works that reference Gaudí and Barcelona's Gothic era), plus pottery, wooden toys, silk scarves, notebooks, housewares and more.

ZOEN   ACCESSORIES

Map p276 (☑933 06 96 88; www.zoen.es; Carrer de Sant Domènec del Call 15; ⊘11am-2.30pm & 5-8.30pm Mon-Fri, 4-8.30pm Sat; ⓂLiceu) In the heart of the old Jewish quarter, Zoen is a tiny shop selling finely crafted leather goods made onsite. Handbags, wallets, belts, book covers and satchels are among the one-of-a-kind wares for sale.

SODA   CLOTHING, ACCESSORIES

Map p276 (Carrer d'Avinyó 24; ⓂLiceu) Set on boutique-lined d'Avinyó, Soda is equal parts clothing shop and nightspot. Stop by in the day for stylish dresses, blouses and shoes that draw both a local and foreign hipster crowd. By night, Soda lets down her hair, with a low-lit bar in back where thirsty shopping companions can enjoy a glass or two. Soda also hosts occasional DJ nights where a party atmosphere prevails.

SABATER HERMANOS   BEAUTY

Map p276 (☑93 301 98 32; Plaça de Sant Felip Neri 1; ⊘10.30am-8.30pm; ⓂJaume I) This fragrant little shop sells handcrafted soaps of all sizes. Varieties like fig, cinnamon, grapefruit and chocolate smell good enough to eat, while sandalwood, magnolia, mint, cedar and jasmine add spice to any sink or bathtub.

DRAP ART   ARTS & CRAFTS

Map p276 (☑93 268 48 89; www.drapart.net; Carrer Groc 1; ⊘11am-2pm & 5-8pm Tue-Fri, 6-9pm Sat; ⓂJaume I) A nonprofit arts organisation runs this small store and gallery space, which exhibits wild designs from artists near and far. Works change regularly, but you might find sculptures, jewellery, handbags and other accessories made from recycled products, as well as mixed-media installations.

FIRES, FESTES I TRADICIONS   FOOD, DRINK

Map p276 (☑93 269 12 61; Carrer de la Dagueria 13; ⊘4-8.30pm Mon, 10am-8.30pm Tue-Sat; ⓂJaume I) Whether assembling a picnic or hoping to bring home a few edible momentos, don't miss this little shop, which stocks a wide range of specialities from Catalunya, including jams, sweets, sausages and cheeses.

L'ARCA   VINTAGE, CLOTHING

Map p276 (☑93 302 15 98; www.larca.es; Carrer dels Banys Nous 20; ⊘11am-2pm & 4.30-8.30pm; ⓂLiceu) Step inside this enchanting shop for a glimpse of beautifully crafted apparel from the past, including 18th-century embroidered silk vests, elaborate silk kimonos, and wedding dresses and shawls from the 1920s. Owing to its incredible collection, it has provided clothing for films including *Titanic, Talk to Her* and *Perfume*.

SALA PARÉS
ARTS & CRAFTS

Map p276 (☏93 318 70 20; www.salapares.com; Carrer del Petritxol 5; ⏰4-8pm Mon, 10.30am-2pm & 4-8pm Tue-Sat; MLiceu) In business since 1877, this gallery has maintained its position as one of the city's leading purveyors of Catalan art – with works from the 19th century to the present.

PAPABUBBLE
FOOD

Map p276 (☏93 268 86 25; www.papabubble.com; Carrer Ample 28; ⏰10am-2pm & 4-8.30pm Mon-Fri, 10am-8.30pm Sat; MLiceu) It feels like a step into another era in this candy store, which makes up pots of rainbow-coloured boiled lollies, just like some of us remember from corner-store days as kids. Watch the sticky sweets being made before your eyes.

CERERIA SUBIRÀ
HOMEWARES

Map p276 (☏93 315 26 06; Baixada de la Llibreteria 7; ⏰9.30am-1.30pm & 4-8pm Mon-Fri, 10am-8pm Sat; MJaume I) Even if you're not interested in myriad mounds of colourful wax, pop in just so you've been to the oldest shop in Barcelona. Cereria Subirà has been churning out candles since 1761 and at this address since the 19th century; the interior has a voluptuous, baroque quality.

LA BASILICA GALERIA
JEWELLERY

Map p276 (☏93 304 20 47; www.labasilicagaleria.com; Carrer Sant Sever 7; ⏰noon-3pm & 4.30-8.30pm) A pure wonderland for the senses, La Basilica Galeria is a whimsical jewellery store with artful displays set among crystal- and flower-covered mannequins. In addition to eye-catching necklaces, delicate rings and fairy-tale-esque pendants, you'll find a few original paintings for sale, though there's more artwork a few doors down in Basilica's gallery (and perfume shop).

CÓMPLICES
BOOKS

Map p276 (Carrer de Cervantes 4; ⏰10.30am-8pm Mon-Fri, from noon Sat; MJaume I) One of the most extensive gay and lesbian bookstores in the city has a mix of lowbrow erotica. It's a welcoming place for all ages and orientations.

FC BOTIGA
SOUVENIRS

Map p276 (☏93 269 15 32; Carrer de Jaume I 18; ⏰10am-9pm Mon-Sat; MJaume I) Need a Lionel Messi football shirt, a blue and burgundy ball, or any other football paraphernalia pertaining to what many locals consider the greatest team in the world?

This is a convenient spot to load up without traipsing to the stadium.

ANTINOUS
BOOKS

Map p276 (☏93 301 90 70; www.antinouslibros.com; Carrer de Josep Anselm Clavé 6; ⏰10.30am-2pm & 5-8.30pm Mon-Fri, noon-2pm & 5-8.30pm Sat; MDrassanes) Gay and lesbian travellers may want to browse in this spacious and relaxed gay bookshop, which also has a modest cafe out the back.

HERBORISTERIA DEL REI
BEAUTY

Map p276 (☏93 318 05 12; www.herboristeriadelrei.blogspot.com; Carrer del Vidre 1; ⏰4-8pm Tue-Fri, 10am-8pm Sat; MLiceu) Once patronised by Queen Isabel II, this timeless corner store flogs all sorts of weird and wonderful herbs, spices and medicinal plants. It's been doing so since 1823 and the decor has barely changed since the 1860s. However, some of the products have, and you'll find anything from fragrant soaps to massage oil nowadays. Film director Tom Tykwer shot scenes of *Perfume: The Story of a Murderer* here.

EL INGENIO
NOVELTIES, TOYS

Map p276 (☏93 317 71 38; www.el-ingenio.com; Carrer d'en Rauric 6; ⏰10am-1.30pm & 4.15-8pm Mon-Fri, 10am-2pm & 5-8.30pm Sat; MLiceu) In this whimsical fantasy store you will discover elegant Venetian masks, marionettes, theatrical accessories, flamenco costumes, gorilla heads, yo-yos, kazoos, unicycles and other novelty items. It's a great place to pick up a few gifts for kids back home.

OBACH
ACCESSORIES

Map p276 (☏93 318 40 94; Carrer del Call 2; ⏰10am-1.30pm & 4-8pm Mon-Sat; MLiceu) Since 1924 this store has been purveying all manner of headgear. You'll find Kangol mohair berets, hipsterish short-brimmed hats, fedoras, elegant straw sun hats and a full-colour spectrum of *barrets* (berets).

LA MANUAL ALPARGATERA
SHOES

Map p276 (☏93 301 01 72; lamanualalpargatera.es; Carrer d'Avinyó 7; ⏰9.30am-1.30pm & 4.30-8pm; MLiceu) Everyone from Salvador Dalí to Jean Paul Gaultier has ordered a pair of *espadrilles* (rope-soled canvas shoes or sandals) from this famous store, which is the birthplace of the iconic footware. The shop was founded just after the Spanish Civil War, though the roots of the simple shoe design date back thousands of years.

El Raval

Neighbourhood Top Five

① Shopping and browsing at the buzzing and beautiful **Mercat de la Boqueria** (p81), and eating at one of the lively market bars.

② Exploring the **Antic Hospital de la Santa Creu** (p84) and relaxing with a coffee in its courtyard cafe.

③ Getting to know the art collection at the **MACBA** (p82) and watching the skaters in the front.

④ Having a glass of cloudy absinthe in one of the Raval's **historical bars** (p89).

⑤ Walking around the art-fully restored **Palau Güell** (p83).

For more detail of this area see Map p280 ➡

EL RAVAL

Lonely Planet's Top Tip

For a spot of sun away from the noisy El Raval streets, head for the garden cafe at the Antic Hospital de la Santa Creu (p84).

Best Places to Eat

➡ Bar Pinotxo (p87)

➡ Caravelle (p85)

➡ Mam i Teca (p85)

➡ Suculent (p87)

➡ Elisabets (p84)

For reviews, see p84 ➡

Best Places to Drink

➡ Bar La Concha (p88)

➡ Casa Almirall (p88)

➡ La Confitería (p88)

➡ Negroni (p89)

For reviews, see p88 ➡

Best Gift Shops

➡ Les Topettes (p90)

➡ Fantastik (p91)

➡ Teranyina (p91)

For reviews, see p90 ➡

Explore: El Raval

Long one of the most rough-and-tumble parts of Barcelona, El Raval is now so hip in a grungy, inner-city way that *barcelonins* have even invented a verb for rambling around El Raval: *ravalejar*.

The northern half of El Raval has an almost respectable air about it. Spend a morning wandering around the art shops on the streets around Carrer del Pintor Fortuny, lunching in the colourful Mercat de la Boqueria, and dedicate a few hours to the fascinating Macba. Join the set of people-watchers on the terraces along Rambla del Raval and check out the strip's assortment of bars and the striking cylindrical designer hotel Barceló Raval and its fashionable restaurant.

Night-time is El Raval's forte, and not only because of all the illicit activities taking place under the shroud of darkness. This is where you'll find some of the more eccentric, trendy and ancient bars and clubs. The better part of Universitat de Barcelona's faculties is nearby and fills the bars and clubs along Carrer de Valldonzella and Carrer de Joaquín Costa.

The area between Carrer de l'Hospital and the waterfront – also known as Barri Xino – retains its dodgy flavour of yore. The area around Carrer de Sant Pau remains a haunt of junkies and dealers, and Carrer de Sant Ramon is particularly busy with prostitutes. The national cinema, Filmoteca de Catalunya, has been relocated to the area bounded by the Carrer de Sant Pau and the Carrer de Sant Rafael in an attempt to change the face of this part of town. Despite its slight edginess, you shouldn't miss this part of El Raval – several fine old bars have stood the test of time in these streets.

Local Life

➡ **Market Lunch** Don't miss La Boqueria's food – either queue up and buy some fresh produce and cook it yourself, or sit down at a stall and let the local chefs shower you with Catalan delicacies.

➡ **Vintage Shops** El Raval is the epicentre of Barcelona's fascination with all things vintage – in particular, you'll find plenty of second-hand shops along the pedestrian Carrer de la Riera Baixa.

➡ **Sugar Rush** Locals swear that the best chocolate in town is to be had at Granja M Viader.

Getting There & Away

➡ **Underground Rail** El Raval is encircled by three metro lines. Lines 1, 2 and 3 stop at strategic points around the district, so nothing is far from a metro stop. The Line 3 stop at Liceu is a convenient exit point.

TOP SIGHT
MERCAT DE LA BOQUERIA

One of the greatest sound, smell and colour sensations in Europe is Barcelona's most central produce market, the Mercat de la Boqueria. It spills over with all the rich and varied colour of plentiful fruit and vegetable stands, seemingly limitless varieties of sea critters, cheeses, meat (including the finest Jabugo ham) and sweets.

The Historic Market

According to some chronicles, there has been a market in this place since 1217. As much as it has become a modern-day attraction, this has always been the place where locals have come to shop. Between the 15th and 18th centuries a pig market stood on this spot; it was considered part of a bigger market that extended to the Plaça del Pi. What we now know as La Boqueria didn't come to exist until the 19th century, when the local authorities decided to build a structure that would house fishmongers and butchers, as well as fruit and vegetable sellers. The iron Modernista gate was constructed in 1914. Many of Barcelona's top restaurateurs buy their produce here, although nowadays it's no easy task getting past the seething crowds of tourists to snare the slippery slab of sole, or the tempting piece of *queso de cabra* (goat's cheese).

La Boqueria is dotted with half a dozen or so unassuming places to eat, and eat well, with stallholders opening up at lunchtime. Whether you eat here or you're self-catering, it's worth trying some of Catalonia's gastronomical specialities, such as *bacallà salat* (dried salted cod) that usually comes in an *esqueixada,* a tomato, onion and black olive salad with frisée lettuce; *calçots* (a cross between a leek and an onion), which are chargrilled and the insides eaten as a messy whole; *cargols* (snails), a Catalan staple that is best eaten baked as *cargols a la llauna; peus de porc* (pig's trotters), which are often stewed with snails; or *percebes* (goose-necked barnacles). Much loved across Spain, these look like witch fingers and are eaten with a garlic and parsley sauce.

DON'T MISS...

➤ Digging into local specialities

➤ Buying fresh produce for a beach picnic

PRACTICALITIES

➤ Map p280

➤ 93 318 25 84

➤ www.boqueria.info

➤ La Rambla 91

➤ 8am-8.30pm Mon-Sat, closed Sun

➤ M Liceu

TOP SIGHT
MACBA

The ground and 1st floors of this great white bastion of contemporary art are generally given over to exhibitions from the gallery's own collections. There are some 3000 pieces centred on three periods: post-WWII; around 1968; and the years since the fall of the Berlin Wall in 1989, right up until the present day.

The Collection

Designed by Richard Meier and opened in 1995, MACBA has become the city's foremost contemporary art centre, with captivating exhibitions for serious art lovers. The permanent collection is on the ground floor and dedicates itself to Spanish and Catalan art from the second half of the 20th century, with works by Antoni Tàpies, Joan Brossa and Miquel Barceló, among others, though international artists, such as Paul Klee, Bruce Nauman and John Cage, are also represented.

The gallery is dedicated to temporary visiting exhibitions that are almost always challenging and intriguing. MACBA's 'philosophy' is to do away with the old model of a museum where an artwork is a spectacle and to create a space where art can be viewed critically, so the exhibitions are usually tied in with talks and events. Across the square in front, where the city's skateboarders gather, the renovated 400-year-old Convent dels Àngels houses the **Capella Macba** (Plaça dels Àngels; MUniversitat), where MACBA regularly rotates selections from its permanent collection. The Gothic framework of the one-time convent-church remains intact.

The library and auditorium stage regular concerts, talks and events, all of which are either reasonably priced or free. The extensive art bookshop is fantastic for both stocking up on art and art theory books, as well as quirky gifts and small design objects.

DON'T MISS...

➡ La Capella Macba
➡ The gallery's fascinating temporary exhibitions
➡ Richard Meier's extraordinary building

PRACTICALITIES

➡ Museu d'Art Contemporani de Barcelona
➡ Map p280
➡ 93 412 08 10
➡ www.macba.cat
➡ Plaça dels Àngels 1
➡ adult/concession €10/8
➡ 11am-7.30pm Mon & Wed-Fri, 10am-9pm Sat, 10am-3pm Sun & holidays
➡ MUniversitat

TOP SIGHT
PALAU GÜELL

The extraordinary neo-Gothic mansion, one of the few major buildings of that era raised in the Old City, was finally reopened in its entirety in 2012 after several years of refurbishment. It's a magnificent example of the early days of Antoni Gaudí's fevered architectural imagination, and gives an insight into its maker's prodigious genius.

Gaudí & Güell

Gaudí built the palace just off La Rambla in the late 1880s for his wealthy and faithful patron, the industrialist Eusebi Güell, without whose support it is unlikely he'd have left a fraction of the creative legacy that is now so celebrated, but at the time was viewed with deep suspicion by much of Catalan society. Although a little sombre compared with some of his later whims, the Palau is still a characteristic riot of styles (Gothic, Islamic, art nouveau) and materials. After the civil war the police occupied it and tortured political prisoners in the basement. The building was then abandoned, leading to its long-term disrepair.

The Building

The tour begins on the ground floor, in what was once the coach house, and from there down to the basement, with its squat mushroom-shaped brick pillars; this is where the horses were stabled. Back upstairs you can admire the elaborate wrought iron of the main doors from the splendid vestibule, and the grand staircase lined with sandstone columns. Up another floor are the main hall and its annexes; check out the rosewood coffered ceilings and the gallery behind trellis work, from where the family could spy on their guests as they arrived. Central to the structure of the building is the magnificent music room with a rebuilt organ that is played during opening hours; the choir would sing from the mezzanine up on the other side. Alongside the alcove containing the organ is another that opened out to become the family chapel, with booths to seat nobility and, above them, the servants. The hall is a parabolic pyramid – each wall an arch stretching up three floors and coming together to form a dome, giving a magnificent sense of space in what is a surprisingly narrow building, constructed on a site of just 500 sq metres.

Above this, the main floor, are the family rooms, which are sometimes labyrinthine and dotted with piercings of light, or grand, stained-glass windows. From here the stairs lead up to the attic. This bright, diaphanous space used to house the servants' quarters, but now houses a detailed exhibition on the history and renovation of the building. The roof is a tumult of tiled mosaics and fanciful design in the building's chimney pots. The audio guide, included in the entry price, is worth getting not only for the detailed description of the architecture, but also for the pieces of music and its photographic illustrations of the Güell family's life.

DON'T MISS...

→ The music room
→ The basement stables
→ The tiled chimney pots

PRACTICALITIES

→ Map p280
→ ☎93 472 57 75
→ www.palauguell.cat
→ Carrer Nou de la Rambla 3-5
→ adult/concession €12/8
→ ⏱10am-8pm Tue-Sun
→ Ⓜ Drassanes

EL RAVAL PALAU GÜELL

 SIGHTS

MERCAT DE LA BOQUERIA　　　MARKET
See p81.

MACBA　　　MUSEUM
See p82.

PALAU GÜELL　　　PALACE
See p83.

**CENTRE DE CULTURA
CONTEMPORÀNIA DE
BARCELONA**　　　CULTURAL BUILDING
Map p280 (CCCB; ☑93 306 41 00; www.cccb.org;
Carrer de Montalegre 5; 2 exhibitions adult/child
under 16yr/senior & student €8/free/6, 1 exhibition €6/free/4, free on Sun 3-8pm; ⊙11am-8pm
Tue-Sun; MUniversitat) A complex of auditori-
ums, exhibition spaces and conference halls
opened here in 1994 in what had been an
18th-century hospice, the Casa de la Caritat. The courtyard, with a vast glass wall
on one side, is spectacular. With 4500 sq
metres of exhibition space in four separate
areas, the centre hosts a constantly changing program of exhibitions, film cycles and
other events.

ESGLÉSIA DE SANT PAU DEL CAMP　CHURCH
Map p280 (Carrer de Sant Pau 101; adult/conces-
sion €3/2; ⊙10am-1.30pm & 4-7.30pm Mon-Sat;
MParal·lel) The best example of Romanesque
architecture in the city is the dainty little
cloister of this church. Set in a somewhat
dusty garden, the 12th-century church also
boasts some Visigothic sculptural detail on
the main entrance.

**ANTIC HOSPITAL DE
LA SANTA CREU**　　　HISTORIC BUILDING
Map p280 (Former Hospital of the Holy Cross;
☑93 270 16 21; www.bnc.cat; Carrer de l'Hospital
56; ⊙9am-8pm Mon-Fri, to 2pm Sat; MLiceu)
FREE Behind La Boqueria stands the Antic

LOCAL KNOWLEDGE

LOCAL KNOWLEDGE

Barcelona's best bargain for art lovers
is the **Articket BCN** (www.articketbcn.
org; per person €30), which gives you
entry to six museums for a fraction
of what you'd pay if you bought individual tickets. The six museums are
the MACBA, the CCCB, the Fundació
Antoni Tàpies, Fundació Joan Miró,
the MNAC and the Museu Picasso.

Hospital de la Santa Creu, which was once
the city's main hospital. Begun in 1401, it
functioned until the 1930s, and was considered one of the best in Europe in its
medieval heyday – it is famously the place
where Antoni Gaudí died in 1926. Today it
houses the **Biblioteca de Catalunya**, and
the **Institut d'Estudis Catalans** (Institute
for Catalan Studies). The hospital's Gothic
chapel, **La Capella** (Map p280; ☑93 442 71 71;
www.bcn.cat/lacapella; ⊙noon-2pm & 4-8pm
Tue-Sat, 11am-2pm Sun & holidays; MLiceu)
FREE, shows temporary exhibitions.

Entering from Carrer de l'Hospital,
you find yourself in a peaceful **courtyard
garden** with a cheerful bar-cafe. Off the
garden lies the entrance to the prestigious
Massana conservatorium and, up a sweep
of stairs, the library. Approaching the
complex from Carrer del Carme or down
a narrow lane from Jardins del Doctor
Fleming (the little playground), you arrive
at the entrance to the institute, which was
once the 17th-century Casa de Convalescèn-
cia de Sant Pau. The public can visit the
patio, in the centre of which you'll find a
statue of St Paul. The building (especially
the entrance vestibule) is richly decorated
with ceramics. Situated up on the 1st floor
at the far end is what was once an orange
garden, now named after the Catalan novel-
ist Mercè Rodoreda.

🍴 EATING

**For contrast alone, El Raval is possibly
the most interesting part of the old city.
Timeless classics of Barcelona dining
are scattered across what was long
the old city's poorest *barri*, and since
the late 1990s, battalions of hip new
eateries and artsy restaurants can be
found in the area around the MACBA.
Some of the cheapest eats in town,
full of character, lurk along El Raval's
streets. From Carrer de Sant Pau north
towards Carrer de Pelai, the university
and Ronda de Sant Antoni is where you'll
find most of these haunts.**

ELISABETS　　　CATALAN €
Map p280 (☑93 317 58 26; Carrer d'Elisabets
2-4; mains €8-10; ⊙7.30am-11pm Mon-Thu &
Sat, to 2am Fri, closed Aug; MCatalunya) This
unassuming restaurant is popular for no-
nonsense local fare. The walls are dotted

with old radio sets and the *menú del día* (set menu; €10.85) varies daily. If you prefer *a la carta,* try the *ragú de jabalí* (wild boar stew) and finish with *mel i mató* (a Catalan dessert made from cheese and honey). Those with a post-midnight hunger on Friday nights can probably get a meal here as late as 1am.

SÉSAMO   VEGETARIAN €

Map p280 (☑93 441 64 11; Carrer de Sant Antoni Abat 52; tapas €6; ☺8pm-midnight Tue-Sun; ☑; MSant Antoni) Widely held to be the best veggie restaurant in the city (admittedly not as great an accolade as it might be elsewhere), Sésamo is a cosy, fun place. The menu is mostly tapas, and most people go for the seven-course tapas menu (wine included; €25), but there are a few more substantial dishes. Nice touches include the home-baked bread and cakes.

EL COLECTIVO   CAFE €

Map p280 (☑93 318 63 80; Carrer del Pintor Fortuny 22; bocadillos from €4; ☺9am-9pm Mon-Wed, 9am-midnight Thu, 9am-2am Fri & Sat; ☎; MCatalunya) A relaxed little cafe on a quiet Raval street, El Colectivo makes excellent cake (carrot, pineapple, you name it), creative *bocadillos* (filled rolls) and good coffee. The shop-window seating is perfect for street watching, the decor is simple and minimal with a single row of wooden tables, and there is always good jazz playing in the background. Tapas are served on Thursdays and Fridays.

PLA DELS ÀNGELS   MEDITERRANEAN €

Map p280 (☑93 329 40 47; Carrer de Ferlandina 23; set lunch €6.75-10.30, set dinner €15, mains €8-10; ☺1.30-11.30pm; MUniversitat) Just opposite the MACBA, this is a suitably colourful and lively little bistro with brightly painted walls and tightly squeezed tables in the back room. More space is to be had in the bar area, at the front, though it's not as pretty. The dishes span the Mediterranean, and can be quite quirky, with salads such as mango, tofu, mint and oregano, and pear, chestnut and pine nut soup.

ORGANIC   VEGETARIAN €

Map p280 (Carrer de la Junta de Comerç 11; mains €9.95, menú del día €10.95; ☺noon-midnight; ☑; MLiceu) As you wander into this sprawling vegetarian spot, to the left is the open kitchen, where you choose from a limited range of options that change from

---

REVIVING EL RAVAL

The Filmoteca de Catalunya's relocation to the Raval from the neighbourhood of Sarrià is part of the 'Raval Revival', an ongoing project to set up the neighbourhood as one of Spain's most influential cultural centres. As part of the project, representatives from the MACBA, the Gran Teatre del Liceu, the Centre de Cultura Contemporània de Barcelona, the Biblioteca de Catalunya, Arts Santa Mònica, the Virreina Centre de la Imatge, the Institut d'Estudis Catalans and the Filmoteca de Catalunya meet every three months with the aim of creating a cultural network with the Raval as its nucleus. The idea is that these eight institutions will join forces, showing complementary exhibitions, organising cultural events and collaborating in creative projects.

---

day to day. Servings are generous and imaginative. The salad buffet is copious and desserts are good. The *menú del día* (daily set menu) costs €10.95 plus drinks.

★ MAM I TECA   CATALAN €€

Map p280 (☑93 441 33 35; Carrer de la Lluna 4; mains €9-12; ☺1-4pm & 8pm-midnight Mon, Wed-Fri & Sun, closed Sat lunch; MSant Antoni) A tiny place with half a dozen tables, Mam i Teca is as much a lifestyle choice as a restaurant. Locals drop in and hang about at the bar, and diners are treated to Catalan dishes made with locally sourced products and adhering to Slow Food principles. Try, for example, cod fried in olive oil with garlic and red pepper, or pork ribs with chickpeas.

★ CARAVELLE   INTERNATIONAL €€

Map p280 (☑93 317 98 92; Carrer del Pintor Fortuny 31; mains €10-13; ☺8.30am-6.30pm Mon-Wed, 8.30am-1am Thu, 10.30am-1am Sat, 10.30am-6.30 Sun; MLiceu) A bright little joint, beloved of the hipster element of the Raval and anyone with a discerning palate. Tacos as you've never tasted them (cod, lime alioli and radish; pulled pork with roast corn and avocado), a superior steak sandwich on homemade brioche with pickled celeriac and all manner of soul food. Drinks are every bit as inventive – try the homemade ginger beer or grapefruit soda.

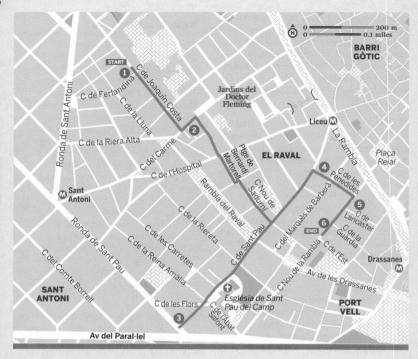

Neighbourhood Walk
Modernista Wining & Dining in El Raval

START CASA ALMIRALL
END LONDON BAR
LENGTH 2KM; 45 MINUTES

Long run by the Almirall family that opened it in the mid-19th century, the corner tavern **1** **Casa Almirall** (p88) on Carrer de Joaquín Costa preserves much of its Modernista decor, especially in the picture windows opening on to the street, and the counter and display cabinet.

You'll recognise similarly sinuous curves as you enter **2** **Bar Muy Buenas** (p88), on Carrer del Carme. Opened as a milk bar in the late 19th century, it retains much of its original decoration. It's a welcoming, cosy spot for a tipple and snacks.

On Carrer de Sant Pau, past the Romanesque church, drop by **3** **La Confitería** (p88), once a barber's shop and then a long-time confectioner's. It was lovingly restored for its reconversion into a bar in 1998. Most of the elements, including facade, bar counter and cabinets, are the real deal.

The **4** **Hotel España** (p214) is known above all for its dining rooms, part of the 1903 design by Domènech i Montaner. The Sala Arnau (Arnau Room) features a magnificent alabaster fireplace designed by Eusebi Arnau. Moderately priced traditional Catalan fare is served.

While wandering around El Raval you should not miss its Modernista star, one of Gaudí's earlier big commissions, **5** **Palau Güell** (p83), a remarkable building recently renovated to perfection. If passing by at night while doing a round of the bars, make a note to return here by day.

A classic of Barcelona nightlife for over a century, the **6** **London Bar** (p89) displays Modernista decor and is run by the family of the waiter who founded it in 1910. In its heyday it stayed open 24 hours and attracted the likes of Pablo Picasso and Joan Miró for countless swift beers.

BAR PINOTXO
TAPAS €€

Map p280 (www.pinotxobar.com; Mercat de la Boqueria; mains €8-15; ⊙6am-4pm Mon-Sat; Liceu) Bar Pinotxo is arguably La Boqueria's, and even Barcelona's, best tapas bar. It sits among the half-dozen or so informal eateries within the market, and the popular owner, Juanito, might serve up chickpeas with a sweet sauce of pine nuts and raisins, a fantastically soft mix of potato and spinach sprinkled with coarse salt, soft baby squid with cannellini beans, or a quivering cube of caramel-sweet pork belly.

BAR CAÑETE
TAPAS €€

Map p280 (☑93 270 34 58; www.barcanete.com; Carrer de la Uniò 17; tapas from €5; Liceu) Part of a trend in creating upmarket versions of traditional bars with food to match. A long, narrow dining room holds an open kitchen along which runs a wooden bar, where diners sit. From here they can point at what they want or order from a long list of classic tapas and *raciones* (full-plate-size tapas serving; literally 'rations'), many of which (such as the mussels with a citric dressing) have a modern twist.

SUCULENT
CATALAN €€

Map p280 (☑93 443 65 79; www.suculent.com; Rambla del Raval 39; mains €11-20; ⊙1-4pm & 8.30-11.30pm Wed-Sun, closed Sun night; Liceu) Michelin-starred chef Carles Abellan (of Comerç 24 fame) adds to his stable with this old-style bistro, which showcases the best of Catalan cuisine. From the cod brandade to the oxtail stew with truffled sweet potato, only the best ingredients are used, so be warned that the prices can mount up a bit, but this is a great place to sample the regional highlights.

DOS TRECE
INTERNATIONAL €€

Map p280 (☑93 301 73 06; www.dostrece.net; Carrer del Carme 40; mains €10-15, menú del día €12; ⊙10am-midnight; Universitat) Lively, sunny and fun, Dos Trece is great for Sunday brunches (beware: the eggs Benedict run out fast), budget lunch deals and late-night bites. The menu ranges from juicy burgers to a more sophisticated rack of lamb, and the bar serves a good array of cocktails. There are a few tables outside, next to the kids' playground.

EN VILLE
FRENCH €€

Map p280 (☑93 302 84 67; www.envillebarcelona. es; Carrer del Doctor Dou 14; menú del día €12.90, mains €14-17; ⊙1-4pm & 8-11.30pm daily, closed dinner Sun & Mon; Universitat) You'll want to come here for the divine decor – the dramatic bouquets, the oil paintings and the antique details all around – as much as the food, though the *menú del día* is good value, and might include a platter of seafood, and ample salads, as well as large glasses of wine. Turning up early for lunch is advised to beat the queues.

RESTAURANT EL CAFETÍ
CATALAN €€

Map p280 (☑93 329 24 19; www.elcafeti.com; Carrer de Sant Rafael 18; mains €12-18, menú del dia €10; ⊙1.30-3.30pm & 8.30-11.30pm Tue-Sun, closed Aug; Liceu) This diminutive eatery is filled with antique furniture and offers traditional local cooking, with one or two unorthodox variations. Paella and other rice dishes dominate. The entrance is down the little Passatge de Bernardí Martorell.

CAN LLUÍS
CATALAN €€

Map p280 (www.restaurantcanlluis.cat; Carrer de la Cera 49; mains €9-19, menú del día €9.80; ⊙Mon-Sat Sep-Jul; Sant Antoni) Three generations have kept this spick and span old-time classic in business since 1929. Beneath the olive-green beams in the back dining room you can see the spot where an anarchist's bomb went off in 1946, killing the then owner. Expect fresh fish and seafood. The *llenguado* (sole) is oven cooked with whisky and raisins.

CASA LEOPOLDO
CATALAN €€€

Map p280 (☑93 441 30 14; www.casaleopoldo. com; Carrer de Sant Rafael 24; mains €19-28; ⊙1.30-3.30pm & 8.30-11pm Tue-Sat, 1.30-3.30pm Sun; Liceu) Hidden down what was a slummy sidestreet of El Raval, Casa Leopoldo has been around for decades and was writer Manuel Vázquez Montalbán's favourite restaurant. Several bright dining areas in this 1929 classic have magnificent tiled walls and exposed beam ceilings. The mostly seafood menu is extensive and there are various fixed-price menus.

🍷 DRINKING & NIGHTLIFE

Bars and clubs have been opening up along the shadowy sidestreets of the Raval for the last two decades, and despite its vestigial edginess, this is

now a great place to go out. You'll find super-trendy places alongside some great old taverns that still thrive – there are joints that have been the hang-outs of the city's bohemia since Picasso's times. The lower end of El Raval has a long history of insalubriousness and the area around Carrer de Sant Pau retains its seedy feel: drug dealers, pickpockets and prostitutes mingle with the streams of nocturnal hedonists. Keep your wits about you if walking around here late at night.

★LA CONFITERÍA   BAR
Map p280 (Carrer de Sant Pau 128; ◎7.30pm-3am Mon-Thu, 1pm-3am Fri-Sun; ⓂParal·lel) This is a trip into the 19th century. Until the 1980s it was a confectioner's shop, and although the original cabinets are now lined with booze, the look of the place has barely changed in its conversion into a laid-back bar. A quiet enough spot for a house *vermut* (€3; add your own soda) in the early evening, it fills with theatregoers and local partiers later at night.

★CASA ALMIRALL   BAR
Map p280 (www.casaalmirall.com; Carrer de Joaquín Costa 33; ◎6pm-2.30am Mon-Thu, 6.30pm-3am Fri, noon-3am Sat, noon-1.30am Sun; ⓂUniversitat) In business since the 1860s, this unchanged corner bar is dark and intriguing, with Modernista decor and a mixed clientele. There are some great original pieces in here, such as the marble counter, and the cast-iron statue of the

---

LOCAL KNOWLEDGE

THE GREEN FAIRY

Bar Marsella (Map p280; Carrer de Sant Pau 65; ◎10pm-2.30am Mon-Wed, 10pm-3am Thu-Sat; ⓂLiceu) has been in business since 1820, and has served the likes of Hemingway, who was known to slump here over an *absenta* (absinthe). The bar still specialises in absinthe, a drink to be treated with respect. Your glass comes with a lump of sugar, a fork and a little bottle of mineral water. Hold the sugar on the fork, over your glass, and drip the water onto the sugar so that it dissolves into the absinthe, which turns yellow. The result should give you a warm glow.

---

muse of the Universal Exposition, held in Barcelona in 1888.

BAR LA CONCHA   BAR, GAY
Map p280 (Carrer de la Guàrdia 14; ◎5pm-3am; ⓂDrassanes) This place is dedicated to the worshipping of the actress Sara Montiel: the walls groan with more than 250 photos of the sultry star. Born in 1928, Montiel bared all on the silver screen in an era that condemned nudity to shameful brazenness – hence '*la concha*' (a word commonly used in the Spanish slang) can be read as a sly salute to the female genitalia. La Concha used to be a largely gay and transvestite haunt, but anyone is welcome and bound to have fun – especially when the drag queens come out to play. Moroccan ownership means you're as likely to see belly dancing nowadays.

GRANJA M VIADER   CAFE
Map p280 (🕿93 318 34 86; www.granjaviader. cat; Carrer d'en Xuclà 6; ◎9am-1.30pm & 5-9pm Mon-Sat; ⓂLiceu) For more than a century, people have flocked down this alley to get to the cups of homemade hot chocolate and whipped cream (ask for a *suís*) ladled out in this classic Catalan-style milk bar-cum-deli. The Viader clan invented Cacaolat, a forerunner of kids' powdered-chocolate beverages. The interior is delightfully vintage and the atmosphere always upbeat.

BAR MUY BUENAS   BAR
Map p280 (Carrer del Carme 63; ◎9am-2.30am Mon-Thu, 9am-3am Fri, 10.30am-3am & 6pm-2am Sun; ⓂLiceu) What sets the Muy Buenas apart is the spectacular Modernista woodwork in its facade and bar area. Aside from this, it's a good spot for a quiet mojito, though it can get pretty lively on Friday and Saturday nights. You may catch a little live music or even a poetry reading, and can nibble on a limited menu of Middle Eastern titbits.

BOADAS   COCKTAIL BAR
Map p276 (www.boadascocktails.com; Carrer dels Tallers 1; ◎noon-2am Mon-Thu, noon-3am Fri & Sat; ⓂCatalunya) One of the city's oldest cocktail bars, Boadas is famed for its daiquiris. Bow-tied waiters have been serving up unique drinkable creations since Miguel Boadas opened it in 1933, in fact Miró and Hemingway both drank here. Miguel was born in Havana, where he was the first barman at the immortal La Floridita.

BAR PASTÍS
BAR

Map p280 (www.barpastis.com; Carrer de Santa Mònica 4; ⊙7.30pm-2am; Ⓜ Drassanes) A French cabaret theme (with lots of Piaf in the background) dominates this tiny, cluttered classic. It's been going, on and off, since the end of WWII. You'll need to be in here before 9pm to have a hope of sitting, getting near the bar or anything much else. On some nights it features live acts, usually performing French *chansons*.

MARMALADE
BAR

Map p280 (www.marmaladebarcelona.com; Carrer de la Riera Alta 4-6; ⊙6.30pm-2.30am Mon-Wed, 10am-2.30am Thu-Sun; Ⓜ Sant Antoni) The golden hues of this backlit bar and restaurant beckon seductively through the glass facade. There are various distinct spaces, decorated in different but equally sumptuous styles, and a pool table next to the bar. Cocktails are big business here, and a selection of them are €5 all night.

LONDON BAR
BAR

Map p280 (Carrer Nou de la Rambla 34-36; ⊙6pm-3am Mon-Thu & Sun, 6pm-3.30am Fri & Sat; Ⓜ Liceu) Open since 1909, this Modernista bar started as a hang-out for circus hands and was later frequented by the likes of Picasso, Miró and Hemingway. Today it fills to the brim with punters at the long front bar and rickety old tables. On occasion, you can attend concerts at the small stage right up the back.

33|45
BAR

Map p280 (Carrer de Joaquín Costa 4; ⊙10am-2.30am daily, from 4pm Mon; Ⓜ Universitat) A super-trendy bar on a street that's not short of them, this place has excellent mojitos – even pink, strawberry ones – and a fashionable crowd. The main area has DJ music and lots of excited noisemaking, while the back room is scattered with sofas and armchairs for a post-dancing slump. On occasional Sundays this is a venue for lunchtime live gigs.

BETTY FORD'S
BAR

Map p280 (www.bettyfords.es; Carrer de Joaquín Costa 56; ⊙5pm-3am; Ⓜ Universitat) This enticing corner bar is one of several good stops along the student-jammed run of Carrer de Joaquín Costa. It puts together some nice cocktails and the place fills with an even mix of locals and foreigners, generally aged not much over 30. There's a decent selection of burgers, too.

EL RAVAL'S HISTORICAL BARS

➠ London Bar
➠ Bar Marsella
➠ La Confitería
➠ Bar Muy Buenas
➠ Casa Almirall

KENTUCKY
BAR

Map p280 (Carrer de l'Arc del Teatre 11; ⊙10pm-4am Wed-Sat; Ⓜ Liceu) Once a haunt of visiting US Navy boys, this exercise in Americana kitsch is the perfect way to finish an evening – if you can squeeze in. All sorts of odd bods from the *barrio* and beyond gather here. An institution in the wee hours, this place often stays open until dawn.

MOOG
CLUB

Map p280 (www.masimas.com/moog; Carrer de l'Arc del Teatre 3; admission €10; ⊙midnight-5am Mon-Thu & Sun, midnight-6am Fri & Sat; Ⓜ Drassanes) This fun and minuscule club is a standing favourite with the downtown crowd. In the main dance area, DJs dish out house, techno and electro, while upstairs you can groove to a nice blend of indie and occasional classic-pop throwbacks.

NEGRONI
COCKTAIL BAR

Map p280 (www.negronicocktailbar.com; Carrer de Joaquín Costa 46; ⊙7pm-2.30am Mon-Thu, 7pm-3am Fri & Sat; Ⓜ Liceu) Good things come in small packages and this dark, teeny cocktail bar confirms the rule. The mostly black decor lures in a largely student set to try out the cocktails, among them, of course, the celebrated Negroni, a Florentine invention with one part Campari, one part gin and one part sweet vermouth.

☆ ENTERTAINMENT

★ FILMOTECA DE CATALUNYA
CINEMA

Map p280 (✆93 567 10 70; www.filmoteca.cat; Plaça de Salvador Seguí 1-9; adult/concession €4/2; ⊙4-10pm Tue-Sun; Ⓜ Liceu) After almost a decade in the planning, the Filmoteca de Catalunya – Catalonia's national cinema – moved into this modern 6000-sq-metre building in 2012. It's a glass, metal and concrete beast that hulks in the midst of the most louche part of the Raval, but the building's interior shouts revival, with light and space, wall-to-wall windows, skylights and glass panels that let the sun in.

In addition to two cinema screens totaling 555 seats, the Filmoteca comprises a film library, a bookshop, a cafe, offices and a dedicated space for exhibitions. This is mainly a film archive space, though, which is being hailed as the marker of a cultural turning point for its new neighbourhood. The Filmoteca's screenings and exhibitions at the time of writing include themes such as 'The Cinema and The Garden', and 'Popular Comedy'.

JAZZ SÍ CLUB   LIVE MUSIC

Map p280 (☑93 329 00 20; www.tallerdemusics. com; Carrer de Requesens 2; admission €4-9, incl drink; ☺8.30-11pm Tue-Sat, 6.30-10pm Sun; MSant Antoni) A cramped little bar run by the Taller de Músics (Musicians' Workshop) serves as the stage for a varied program of jazz jams through to some good flamenco (Friday nights). Thursday night is Cuban night, Tuesday and Sunday are rock, and the rest are devoted to jazz and/or blues sessions. Concerts start around 9pm but the jam sessions can get going earlier.

CANGREJO   GAY

Map p280 (☑93 301 29 78; Carrer de Montserrat 9; ☺11pm-3am Fri & Sat; MDrassanes) This altar to kitsch, a dingy dance hall that has transgressed since the 1920s, is run by the luminous underground cabaret figure of Carmen Mairena and exudes a gorgeously tacky feel, especially with the midnight drag shows on Friday and Saturday. Due to its popularity with tourists, getting in is all but impossible unless you turn up early.

23 ROBADORS   LIVE MUSIC

Map p280 (Carrer d'en Robador 23; admission varies; ☺8pm-3am; MLiceu) On what remains a sleazy Raval street, where a hardy band of streetwalkers, junkies and other misfits hang out in spite of all the work being carried out to gentrify the area, a narrow little bar has made a name for itself with its shows and live music. Jazz is the name of the game, but you'll also find live poetry, flamenco and plenty more.

GIPSY LOU   LIVE MUSIC

Map p280 (www.gipsylou.com; Carrer de Ferlandina 55; ☺7pm-2.30am Sun-Thu, 7pm-3am Sat; MSant Antoni) A louche little bar that packs 'em in for live music from rumba to pop to flamenco, along with occasional storytelling

events, and whatever else Felipe feels like putting on. There are decent bar snacks to keep you going on a long night of pisco sours, the house special.

TEATRE LLANTIOL   THEATRE

Map p280 (☑93 329 90 09; www.llantiol.com; Carrer de la Riereta 7; admission varies; MSant Antoni) At this charming little cafe-theatre, which has a certain scuffed elegance, all sorts of odd stuff, from concerts and theatre to magic shows, is staged. The speciality, though, is stand-up comedy, which is occasionally in English. Check the website for details.

TEATRE ROMEA   THEATRE

Map p280 (☑93 301 55 04; www.teatreromea. com; Carrer de l'Hospital 51; admission varies; ☺box office 4.30pm until start of show Tue-Sun; MLiceu) Just off La Rambla, this 19th-century theatre was resurrected at the end of the 1990s and is one of the city's key stages for quality drama. It usually fills up for a broad range of interesting plays, often classics with a contemporary flavour, in Catalan and Spanish.

🔒 SHOPPING

El Ravel boasts a handful of art galleries around MACBA, along with a burgeoning second-hand and vintage clothes scene on Carrer de la Riera Baixa. Carrer dels Tallers is one of the city's main music strips.

⭐ LES TOPETTES   BEAUTY

Map p280 (www.lestopettes.es; Carrer de Joaquín Costa 33; ☺4-9pm Mon, 11am-2pm & 4-9pm Tue-Sat; MUniversitat) It's a sign of the times that such a chic little temple to soap and perfume can exist in the Raval. Les Topettes' collection has been picked for design as much as the product within, and you'll find gorgeously packaged scents, candles and unguents from Diptyque, Cowshed and L'Artisan Parfumeur, among others.

BARCELONA REYKJAVIK   FOOD

Map p280 (☑93 302 09 21; www.barcelonareykjavik.com; Carrer del Doctor Dou 12; ☺10am-9pm Mon-Sat, 10.30am-8pm Sun; MCatalunya) Bread lovers, rejoice! Good bread can be hard to find in Barcelona, but Reykjavik saves the day. All loaves are made using organic flour –

spelt, wholemeal, mixed cereals and so on – and sourdough yeast, though this does make for fairly high prices. The bakery also produces excellent cakes. Two more shops can be found in the Born and Gràcia.

FANTASTIK
ARTS & CRAFTS

Map p280 (www.fantastik.es; Carrer de Joaquín Costa 62; ⊗11am-2pm & 4-8.30pm Mon-Fri, noon-9pm Sat, closed Sun; MUniversitat) More than 400 products, including a Mexican skull rattle, robot moon explorer from China and recycled plastic zebras from South Africa, are found in this colourful shop, which sources its items from Mexico, India, Bulgaria, Russia, Senegal and 20 other countries. It's a perfect place to buy all the things you don't need but can't live without.

LA PORTORRIQUEÑA
COFFEE

Map p280 (Carrer d'en Xuclà 25; ⊗9am-2pm & 5-8pm Mon-Fri, 9am-2pm Sat; MCatalunya) Coffee beans from around the world, freshly ground before your eyes, has been the winning formula in this store since 1902. It also offers all sorts of chocolate goodies. The street is good for little old-fashioned food boutiques.

HOLALA! PLAZA
FASHION

Map p280 (Plaça de Castella 2; ⊗11am-9pm Mon-Sat; MUniversitat) Backing on to Carrer de Valldonzella, where it boasts an exhibition space (Gallery) for temporary art displays, this Ibiza import is inspired by that island's long established (and somewhat commercialised) hippie tradition. Vintage clothes are the name of the game, along with an eclectic program of exhibitions and activities.

DISCOS CASTELLÓ
MUSIC

Map p280 (Carrer dels Tallers 7; ⊗10am-8.30pm Mon-Sat; MCatalunya) Castelló used to dominate this street of instrument and CD shops, but the recession took its toll and now only this store remains, selling new and second-hand CDs of all types of music from metal to classical, along with a selection of related books and paraphernalia.

TERANYINA
ARTS & CRAFTS

Map p280 (www.teresarosa.com; Carrer del Notariat 10; ⊗11am-3pm & 5-8pm Mon-Fri; MCatalunya) Artist Teresa Rosa Aguayo runs this textile workshop in the heart of the artsy bit of El Raval. You can join courses at the loom, admire some of the rugs and other works that Teresa has created, and, of course, buy them.

La Ribera

Neighbourhood Top Five

1 Admiring the simplicity and beauty of the Gothic **Basílica de Santa Maria del Mar** (p97).

2 Being introduced to the origins of Picasso's genius at the fascinating **Museu Picasso** (p94).

3 Enjoying a show or just the Modernista interior at the **Palau de la Música Catalana** (p98).

4 Taking a stroll or having a picnic at the **Parc de la Ciutadella** (p100).

5 Tucking into tapas at **Bormuth** (p102).

For more detail of this area see Map p284 ➡

Explore: La Ribera

La Ribera is widely used to refer to the entire area covered by the city council's rather long-winded appellation of Sant Pere, Santa Caterina i la Ribera. The gentrified southern half is generally known as El Born, after busy, bar-lined Passeig del Born. Capped at one end by the magnificent Gothic Basílica de Santa Maria del Mar, it runs along to the Born Centre Cultural, in what used to be the neighbourhood's market building. This area should be your first port of call, specifically a stroll down Carrer de Montcada, a street rich in Gothic and baroque mansions as well as some of the city's major museums, the Museu Picasso, along with many art galleries and shops.

Passeig del Born was Barcelona's main square from the 13th to the 18th centuries and still has an air of excitement around it. It's a popular night-time area for locals, especially in summer.

Northwest of Carrer de la Princesa, the area's physiognomy changes. A mess of untidy streets wiggles northwards around the striking modern reincarnation of the Mercat de Santa Caterina and on towards the Modernista Palau de la Música Catalana. North African and South American immigrant communities call this part of La Ribera home. Little by little, some good eating and drinking options have opened up in these narrow, winding streets.

Via Laietana, a rumbling, fuel-fumed thoroughfare, marks the southwest side of La Ribera, while the Parc de la Ciutadella closes off its northeastern flank. The park is a rare green space in central Barcelona, where you can lounge on its stretches of grass, sit by the water at the grand fountain, visit the zoo and, if accompanied by tots, take advantage of its playgrounds.

Local Life

➤ **Market secrets** Locals get their eggs at the Mercat de Santa Caterina (p99), where, in season, stand holders 'flavour' their eggs by stacking them up and placing truffles among them. Soft-boiled, they are divine.

➤ **Catching the rays** Local favourite strip Passeig del Born is perfect for lazy Sunday morning sunbathing on the cafe terraces, as you enjoy a leisurely brunch.

➤ **A slice of culture** Join the largely local clientele for a weekend lunchtime classical concert at the Palau de la Música Catalana (p98).

Getting There & Away

➤ **Metro** Línia 4 goes down the southwest flank of La Ribera, stopping at Urquinaona, Jaume I and Barceloneta. Línia 1 also stops nearby, at Urquinaona and Arc de Triomf (the nearest stop for the Parc de la Ciutadella).

Lonely Planet's Top Tip

Getting around all of Barcelona's museums can be anything but cheap, so take advantage of free Sunday afternoons, when entry into many of the city's museums will cost you zilch!

Best Places to Eat

➡ Casa Delfín (p103)
➡ El Atril (p103)
➡ Comerç 24 (p105)
➡ Bormuth (p102)
➡ En Aparté (p102)

For reviews, see p102 ➡

LA RIBERA

Best Places to Drink

➡ Mudanzas (p106)
➡ La Vinya del Senyor (p106)
➡ Juanra Falces (p106)
➡ Rubí (p106)
➡ Miramelindo (p106)

For reviews, see p106 ➡

Best for Architecture

➡ Basílica de Santa Maria del Mar (p97)
➡ Palau de la Música Catalana (p98)
➡ Carrer de Montcada (p99)

For reviews, see p97 ➡

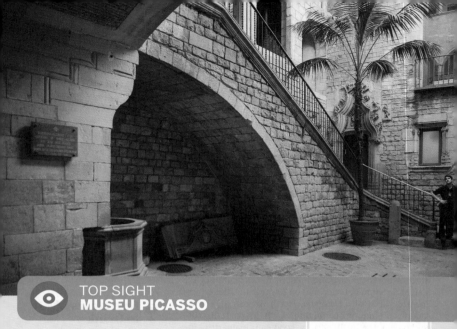

TOP SIGHT
MUSEU PICASSO

The setting alone, in five contiguous medieval stone mansions, makes the Museu Picasso unique. The permanent collection is housed in Palau Aguilar, Palau del Baró de Castellet and Palau Meca, all dating to the 14th century. The 18th-century Casa Mauri, built over medieval remains (even some Roman leftovers have been identified), and the adjacent 14th-century Palau Finestres accommodate temporary exhibitions. The pretty courtyards, galleries and staircases preserved in the first three of these buildings are as delightful as the collection inside.

History of the Museum

Allegedly it was Pablo Picasso himself who proposed the museum's creation, to his friend and personal secretary Jaume Sabartés, a Barcelona native, in 1960. Three years later, the 'Sabartés Collection' was opened, since a museum bearing Picasso's name would have been met with censorship – Picasso's opposition to the Franco regime was well known. The Museu Picasso we see today opened in 1983. It originally held only Sabartés' personal collection of Picasso's art and a handful of works hanging at the Barcelona Museum of Art, but the collection gradually expanded with donations from Salvador Dalí and Sebastià Junyer Vidal, among others, though most artworks were bequeathed by Picasso himself. His widow, Jacqueline Roque, also donated 41 ceramic pieces and the *Woman With Bonnet* painting after Picasso's death.

DON'T MISS...

➜ *Retrato de la Tía Pepa* (Portrait of Aunt Pepa)

➜ *Ciència i caritat* (Science and Charity)

➜ *Terrats de Barcelona* (Roofs of Barcelona)

PRACTICALITIES

➜ Map p284

➜ ☏93 256 30 00

➜ www.museupicasso.bcn.cat

➜ Carrer de Montcada 15-23

➜ adult/child €14/free, temporary exhibitions adult/child €6.50/free, 3-8pm Sun & 1st Sun of month free

➜ ◷9am-7pm daily, until 9.30pm Thu

➜ Ⓜ Jaume I

Sabartés' contribution and years of service are honoured with an entire room devoted to him, including Picasso's famous Blue Period portrait of him wearing a ruff.

The Collection

This collection concentrates on the artist's formative years, yet there is enough material from subsequent periods to give you a thorough impression of the man's versatility and genius. Above all, you come away feeling that Picasso was the true original, always one step ahead of himself (let alone anyone else) in his search for new forms of expression. The collection includes more than 3500 artworks, largely pre-1904, which is apt considering the artist spent his formative creative years in Barcelona.

It is important, however, not to expect a parade of his well-known works, or even works representative of his best-known periods. The holdings at the museum reflect Picasso's years in Barcelona and elsewhere in Spain, and what makes this collection truly impressive – and unique among the many Picasso museums around the world – is the way in which it displays his extraordinary talent at such a young age. Faced with the technical virtuosity of a painting such as *Ciència i caritat* (Science and Charity), for example, it is almost inconceivable that such a work could have been created at the hands of a 15 year old. Some of his self-portraits and the portraits of his parents, which date from 1896, are also evidence of his precocious talent.

Las Meninas through the Prism of Picasso

From 1954 to 1962 Picasso was obsessed with the idea of researching and 'rediscovering' the greats, in particular Velázquez. In 1957 he created a series of renditions of the latter's masterpiece *Las Meninas,* now displayed in rooms 12–14. It is as though Picasso has looked at the original Velázquez painting through a prism reflecting all the styles he had worked through until then, creating his own masterpiece in the process. This is a wonderful opportunity to see *Las Meninas* in its entirety, in this beautiful space.

Ceramics

What is also special about the Museu Picasso is its showcasing of his work in lesser-known mediums. The last rooms contain engravings and some 40 ceramic pieces completed throughout the latter years of his unceasingly creative life. You'll see plates and bowls decorated with simple, single-line drawings of fish, owls and other animal shapes, typical of Picasso's daubing on clay.

GETTING AROUND THE COLLECTION

The permanent collection is located in Palau Aguilar, Palau del Baró de Castellet and Palau Meca. Casa Mauri and the adjacent Palau Finestres host temporary exhibitions.

Though ostensibly aimed at residents, the annual pass is also available to visitors on presentation of ID. The 'Carnet del Museu Picasso' cuts out the need to queue (and queues here can be long, if you haven't booked online ahead of time), and costs a mere €12, or €15 for a family pass. In other words, it's cheaper than a day pass and can be used multiple times within a year of purchase.

LA RIBERA MUSEU PICASSO

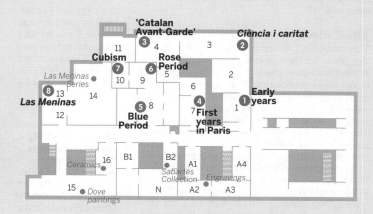

Museum Tour
Museu Picasso

START EARLY YEARS
FINISH LAS MENINAS
LENGTH 1½ HOURS

Rooms 1 and 2 hold sketches and oils from Picasso's **❶ early years** in Málaga and La Coruña – around 1893–95, and lead on to his formative years in Barcelona. *Retrato de la Tía Pepa* (Portrait of Aunt Pepa), done in Málaga in 1896, shows the maturity of his brush strokes and his ability to portray character – at the tender age of 15. As you walk into room 3, you'll see the enormous **❷ Ciència i caritat** (Science and Charity), painted in the same year.

After a period spent in Horta de Sant Joan, Picasso came to Barcelona and joined what was known as the **❸ 'Catalan avant-garde'**, which you'll see in room 4. In rooms 5–7 paintings from **❹ 1900–1901** hang, while room 8 is dedicated to the first significant new stage in his development, the **❺ Blue Period**. *Woman with Bonnet* is an important work from this period, depicting a captive from the Saint-Lazare women's prison and venereal disease hospital, which Picasso visited when in Paris – this also sets up the theme of Picasso's fascination with those inhabiting the down-and-out layers of society. His nocturnal blue-tinted views of *Terrats de Barcelona* (Roofs of Barcelona) and *El foll* (The Madman) are cold and cheerless, yet somehow alive.

These lead to the painting of Benedetta Bianco, from Picasso's **❻ Rose Period** (in room 9), and thence on to **❼ beginnings of cubism**. Though the Museu Picasso is no showcase for his cubist period, it does hold a few examples; check out the *Glass and Tobacco Packet* still-life painting, a beautiful and simple work that marks the beginning of his fascination with still life.

The real highlight of the collection, however, is Picasso's take on Velázquez's **❽ Las Meninas** in rooms 12–14, and a series of interconnecting rooms is devoted to the preparatory sketches, associated works and the painting itself.

TOP SIGHT
BASÍLICA DE SANTA MARIA DEL MAR

At the southwest end of Passeig del Born stands the apse of Barcelona's finest Catalan Gothic church, Santa Maria del Mar (Our Lady of the Sea). Built in the 14th century with record-breaking alacrity for the time (it took just 54 years), the church is remarkable for its architectural harmony and simplicity.

The People's Church

Its construction started in 1329, with Berenguer de Montagut and Ramon Despuig as the architects in charge. During construction the city's porters *(bastaixos)* spent a day each week carrying on their backs the stone required to build the church from royal quarries in Montjuïc. Their memory lives on in reliefs of them in the main doors and stone carvings elsewhere in the church. The walls, the side chapels and the facades were finished by 1350, and the entire structure was completed in 1383.

The Interior

The exterior gives an impression of sternness, and the narrow streets surrounding it are restrictive and claustrophobic. It may come as a (pleasant) surprise then to find a spacious and light interior – the central nave and two flanking aisles separated by slender octagonal pillars give an enormous sense of lateral space.

The interior is almost devoid of imagery of the sort to be found in Barcelona's other large Gothic churches, but Santa Maria was lacking in superfluous decoration even before anarchists gutted it in 1909 and 1936. Keep an eye out for **music recitals**, often baroque and classical.

DON'T MISS...

➡ The church's architects in memorial stone relief

➡ A live-music performance

PRACTICALITIES

➡ Map p284

➡ ☎93 310 23 90

➡ Plaça de Santa Maria del Mar

➡ ⊙9am-1.30pm & 4.30-8.30pm, opens at 10.30am Sun

➡ Ⓜ Jaume I

TOP SIGHT
PALAU DE LA MÚSICA CATALANA

This concert hall is a high point of Barcelona's Modernista architecture, a symphony in tile, brick, sculpted stone and stained glass. Built by Domènech i Montaner between 1905 and 1908 for the Orfeo Català musical society, it was conceived as a temple for the Catalan Renaixença (Renaissance). The *palau* (palace) was built with the help of some of the best Catalan artisans of the time, in the cloister of the former Convent de Sant Francesc, and since 1990 it has undergone several major changes.

The Facade
The *palau,* like a peacock, shows off much of its splendour on the outside. Take in the principal facade with its mosaics, floral capitals and the sculpture cluster representing Catalan popular music.

The Interior
Wander inside the foyer and restaurant areas to admire the spangled, tiled **pillars**. Best of all, however, is the richly colourful **auditorium** upstairs, with its ceiling of blue-and-gold stained glass and shimmering skylight that looks like a giant, crystalline, downward-thrusting nipple. Above a bust of Beethoven on the stage towers a wind-blown sculpture of Wagner's Valkyries (Wagner was top of the Barcelona charts at the time it was created). This can only be savoured on a guided tour or by attending a **performance** – either is highly recommended. Admission is by tour only, and tickets can be bought up to a week in advance by phone or online. Space is limited to a maximum of 55 people.

DON'T MISS...
➡ The principal facade's mosaics and columns
➡ The foyer and pillars in the restaurant
➡ The main auditorium
➡ A performance – day or night

PRACTICALITIES
➡ Map p284
➡ ☎93 295 72 00
➡ www.palau musica.org
➡ Carrer de Sant Francesc de Paula 2
➡ adult/child €17/free
➡ ⏱guided tours 10am-3.30pm daily
➡ Ⓜ Urquinaona

 SIGHTS

MUSEU PICASSO   MUSEUM
See p94.

**BASÍLICA DE SANTA
MARIA DEL MAR**   CHURCH
See p97.

**PALAU DE LA
MÚSICA CATALANA**   ARCHITECTURE
See p98.

CARRER DE MONTCADA   STREET
Map p284 (ⓜJaume I) An early example of town planning, this medieval high street was driven towards the sea from the road that in the 12th century led northeast from the city walls. It was the city's most coveted address for the merchant classes. The bulk of the great mansions that remain today mostly date to the 14th and 15th centuries.

This area was the commercial heartland of medieval Barcelona. Five of the mansions on the east side of the street have been linked to house the Museu Picasso (p94). Across the road, others house what is to become the Museu de Cultures del Món (p102) in 2015. Several other mansions on this street are commercial art galleries where you're welcome to browse. If you promise to drink, you can sip wine or cocktails (both rather expensive) inside the baroque courtyard of the originally medieval **Palau de Dalmases** (Map p284; ☑93 310 06 73; ☉8pm-2am Tue-Sat, 6-10pm Sun; ⓜJaume I) at No 20 while listening to baroque music or operatic snippets (a peek inside isn't allowed without a definitive commitment to consume when you enter!).

At the corner of Carrer dels Corders and the northern end of the street, just beyond the 19th-century Carrer de la Princesa, stands a much-meddled-with Romanesque chapel, the **Capella d'en Marcús** (Map p284), once a wayfarers' stop on the road northeast out of medieval Barcelona.

BORN CENTRE CULTURAL   HISTORIC BUILDING
Map p284 (☑93 256 68 51; www.elborncentrecultural.bcn.cat; Plaça Comercial 12; centre free, exhibition spaces adult/child €6/free; ☉10am-8pm Tue-Sun; ⓜBarceloneta) Launched to great fanfare in 2013, as part of the events held for the tercentenary of the Catalan defeat in the War of the Spanish Succession, this shiny new cultural space is housed in the former Mercat del Born, a handsome 19th-century structure of slatted iron and brick. Excavation in 2001 unearthed remains of whole streets flattened to make way for the much-hated citadel (*ciutadella*) – these are now on show on the exposed subterranean level.

On the ground floor there are panels giving information about the ruins, along with an exhibition space showing items from the period and explaining in greater depth about the events surrounding the destruction of the area. There is also a stark and lofty restaurant serving Catalan cuisine, and a gift shop selling upmarket and high-design souvenirs, along with books about the story of the region.

MERCAT DE SANTA CATERINA   MARKET
Map p284 (☑93 319 17 40; www.mercatsantacaterina.com; Avinguda de Francesc Cambó 16; ☉7.30am-2pm Mon, to 3.30pm Tue, Wed & Sat, to 8.30pm Thu & Fri, closed afternoons Jul & Aug; ☎; ⓜJaume I) Come shopping for your tomatoes at this extraordinary-looking produce market, designed by Enric Miralles and Benedetta Tagliabue to replace its 19th-century predecessor. Finished in 2005, it is distinguished by its kaleidoscopic and undulating roof, held up above the bustling produce stands, restaurants, cafes and bars by twisting slender branches of what look like grey steel trees.

LA RIBERA SIGHTS

PALAU DE LA MÚSICA CATALANA THROUGH THE AGES

The original Modernista creation, now a World Heritage site, did not meet with universal approval in its day. The doyen of Catalan literature, Josep Pla, did not hesitate to condemn it as 'horrible', but few share his sentiments today. Domènech i Montaner himself was also in a huff. He failed to attend the opening ceremony in response to unsettled bills.

The *palau* (palace) was at the centre of a fraud scandal from 2009 to 2012, as its president, Felix Millet, who subsequently resigned, admitted to having siphoned off millions of euros of its funds. He and his partner were ordered to repay the embezzled money to the *palau* in March 2012.

OLD FLAME

Opposite Basílica de Santa Maria del Mar's southern flank, an eternal flame burns brightly over an apparently anonymous sunken square. This is **El Fossar de les Moreres** (The Mulberry Cemetery; Map p284), the site of a Roman cemetery. It's also where Catalan resistance fighters were buried after the siege of Barcelona ended in defeat in September 1714, and for whom the flame burns.

The multicoloured ceramic roof (with a ceiling made of warm, light wood) recalls the Modernista tradition of *trencadís* decoration (a type of mosaic, such as that in Park Güell). Indeed, its curvy design, like a series of Mediterranean rollers, seems to plunge back into an era when Barcelona's architects were limited only by their (vivid) imagination. The market roof bears an uncanny resemblance to that of the Escoles de Gaudí at La Sagrada Família.

The market's 1848 predecessor had been built over the remains of the demolished 15th-century Gothic Monestir de Santa Caterina, a powerful Dominican convent. The **Espai Santa Caterina** (Map p284; ⊙8.30am-2pm Mon-Wed & Sat, to 8pm Thu & Fri) **FREE**, a small section of the church foundations, is glassed over in one corner as an archaeological reminder.

PARC DE LA CIUTADELLA PARK

Map p284 (Passeig de Picasso; MArc de Triomf) **FREE** Come for a stroll, a picnic, a visit to the zoo or to inspect Catalonia's regional parliament, but don't miss a visit to this, the most central green lung in the city. Parc de la Ciutadella is perfect for winding down.

After the War of the Spanish Succession, Felipe V razed a swath of La Ribera to build a huge fortress (La Ciutadella), designed to keep watch over Barcelona. It became a loathed symbol of everything Catalans hated about Madrid and the Bourbon kings, and was later used as a political prison. Only in 1869 did the central government allow its demolition, after which the site was turned into a park and used for the Universal Exhibition of 1888.

The monumental **cascada** (waterfall; Map p284) near the Passeig de Pujades park entrance, created between 1875 and 1881 by

Josep Fontserè with the help of an enthusiastic young Gaudí, is a dramatic combination of statuary, rugged rocks, greenery and thundering water – all of it perfectly artificial. Nearby, you can hire a rowing boat to paddle about in the small lake.

To the southeast, in what might be seen as an exercise in black humour, the fort's former arsenal now houses the **Parlament de Catalunya** (Map p284; www.parlament.cat; ⊙guided tours 10am-1pm Sat, Sun & holidays). You can join free guided tours, in Catalan and Spanish only, on Saturdays and Sundays. The building is open for independent visiting on 11 September from 10am to 7pm. On show to the public are the sweeping Escala d'Honor (Stairway of Honour) and the several solemn halls that lead to the Saló de Sessions, the semicircular auditorium where parliament sits. In the lily pond at the centre of the garden in front of the building is a statue of a seemingly heartbroken woman, *Desconsol* (Distress; 1907), by Josep Llimona.

The Passeig de Picasso side of the park is lined with several buildings constructed for, or just before, the Universal Exhibition. The medieval-looking caprice at the top end is the most engaging. Known as the **Castell dels Tres Dragons** (Castle of the Three Dragons; Map p284), it long housed the Museu de Zoologia, which has since moved to the Fòrum area and is now known as the Museu Blau. Domènech i Montaner put the 'castle's' trimmings on a pioneering steel frame. The coats of arms are all invented and the whole building exudes a teasing, playful air. It was used as a cafe-restaurant during the Universal Exhibition.

To the south is L'Hivernacle, an elaborate greenhouse. Next come the former Museu de Geologia and L'Umbracle, a palm house. On Passeig de Picasso itself is Antoni Tàpies' typically impenetrable **Homenatge a Picasso** (Map p284). Water runs down the panes of a glass box full of bits of old furniture and steel girders.

Northwest of the park, Passeig de Lluís Companys is capped by the Modernista **Arc de Triomf** (Map p284; Passeig de Lluís Companys; MArc de Triomf), designed by Josep Vilaseca as the principal exhibition entrance, with unusual, Islamic-style brickwork. Josep Llimona did the main reliefs. Just what the triumph was eludes us, especially since the exhibition itself was a commercial failure. It is perhaps best thought of as a bricks-and-mortar embodiment of the city's general fin-de-siècle feel-good factor.

ZOO DE BARCELONA   ZOO

Map p284 (☑902 457545; www.zoobarcelona.cat; Parc de la Ciutadella; adult/child €19.90/11.95; ◉10am-5.30pm Nov-Mar, 10am-7pm Apr, May, Sep, Oct, 10am-8pm Jun-Aug; ⊞; MBarceloneta) The zoo is a great day out for kids, with 7500 critters that range from geckos to gorillas, lions and elephants – there are more than 400 species, plus picnic areas dotted all around and a wonderful adventure playground. There are pony rides, a petting zoo and a mini-train meandering through the grounds. A new marine zoo being built on the coast of El Fòrum northeast of the city centre will ease the currently slightly crowded space, although the recession has meant plans are stalled for the time being.

MUSEU DE LA XOCOLATA   MUSEUM

Map p284 (☑93 268 78 78; www.museuxocolata. cat; Carrer del Comerç 36; adult/child under 7yr/ senior & student €5/free/4.25; ◉10am-7pm Mon-Sat, to 3pm Sun & holidays; ☎⊞; MJaume I) Chocoholics have a hard time containing themselves in this museum dedicated to the fundamental foodstuff – particularly when faced with tempting displays of cocoa-based treats in the cafe at the exit. The displays trace the origins of chocolate, its arrival in Europe, and the many myths and images associated with it. Among the informative stuff and machinery used in the production of chocolate are large chocolate models of emblematic buildings such as the Sagrada Família, along with various characters, local and international.

Kids and grown-ups can join tours and occasionally take part in chocolate-making and tasting sessions, especially on weekends. Alongside the Gothic arches of what remains of the convent's one-time cloister is a pleasant cafe-bar, the **Bar del Convent** (open 10am to 9pm Monday to Thursday, 11am to 11pm Friday and Sunday, 1pm to midnight Saturday) – particularly good for people with children. Kids often play football in the cloister grounds, and there are children's books and toys in the cafe itself. You enter at Carrer del Comerç 36.

ARXIU FOTOGRÀFIC
DE BARCELONA   GALLERY

Map p284 (☑93 256 34 20; www.bcn.cat/arxiu/ fotografic; Plaça de Pons i Clerch 2, 2A; ◉10am-7pm Mon-Sat; MJaume I) **FREE** On the 2nd floor of the former Convent de Sant Agustí is the modest exhibition space of this city photo archive. Photos on show are generally related to the city, as the photo collection is principally devoted to that theme, from the late 19th century until the late 20th century.

MUSEU DEL REI DE LA MAGIA   MUSEUM

Map p284 (☑93 318 71 92; www.elreydelamagia. com; Carrer de les Jonqueres 15; admission €3; ◉11am-2pm & 4-8pm Thu-Sun, closed Sun morning Jul & Aug; ⊞; MJaume I) This museum is a timeless curio. It is the scene of magic shows, home to collections of material that hark back to the 19th-century origins of the associated magic shop (p108) at Carrer de la Princesa 11 (which holds everything from old posters and books for learning tricks to magic wands and trick cards) and the place for budding magicians of all ages to enrol in courses. Seeing is believing.

ESGLÉSIA DE SANT
PERE DE LES PUELLES   CHURCH

Map p284 (Plaça de Sant Pere; ◉8.30am-1pm & 5-7.30pm Mon-Sat, 11am-2pm Sun; MArc de Triomf) **FREE** It was around this church that settlement began in La Ribera. In 985 a Muslim raiding force under Al-Mansur attacked Barcelona and largely destroyed what was then a convent, killing or capturing the nuns. It was rebuilt in early medieval times, but not a great deal remains. The church's pre-Romanesque Greek-cross floor plan survives, as do some Corinthian columns, beneath the 12th-century dome and a much-damaged Renaissance vault leading into a side chapel.

MUSEU EUROPEU D'ART MODERN   MUSEUM

Map p284 (MEAM; www.meam.es; Carrer Barra de Ferro 5; adult/child/concession €7/free/5; ◉10am-8pm Tue-Sun; MJaume I) The European Museum of Modern Art opened in the summer of 2011 in the Palau Gomis, a handsome 18th-century mansion around the corner from the Museu Picasso. The art within is strictly representational (the 'Modern' of the name simply means 'contemporary') and is mostly from young Spanish artists, though there are some works from elsewhere in Europe.

CASA LLOTJA DE MAR   ARCHITECTURE

Map p284 (La Llotja; ☑93 547 88 49; www.casa-llotja.com; Passeig d'Isabel II 1; MBarceloneta) The centrepiece of the city's medieval stock exchange (more affectionately known as La Llotja) is the fine Gothic Saló de Contractacions (Transaction Hall), built in the 14th century. Pablo Picasso and Joan Miró attended the art school that was housed in the Saló dels Cònsols from 1849.

These and five other halls were encased in a neoclassical shell in the 18th century. The stock exchange was in action until well into the 20th century and the building remains in the hands of the city's chamber of commerce. Occasionally it opens the doors to the public but the rooms are more generally hired out for events.

MUSEU DE CULTURES DEL MÓN   MUSEUM

Map p284 (www.museuculturesmon.bcn.cat; Carrer de Montcada 12-14; MJaume I) The Palau Nadal and the Palau Marquès de Llió, which once housed the Museu Barbier-Mueller and the Museu Tèxtil respectively, are to reopen to the public as the site of a new museum, the Museum of World Cultures. This will hold exhibits from private and public collections, including many from the Museu Etnològic on Montjuïc. The projected inauguration date is January 2015, although this – as with so many grand projects in Barcelona – will almost certainly prove to be optimistic.

EATING

If you'd mentioned El Born (El Borne in Spanish) in the early 1990s, you wouldn't have raised much interest. Now the area is peppered with bars, dance dives, groovy designer stores and restaurants. You'll find avant-garde chefs playing with fusion and technology cheek by jowl with no-nonsense matrons serving up traditional comfort food, and you'll also find an increasing number of ethnic restaurants.

★BORMUTH   TAPAS €

Map p284 (📞93 310 21 86; Carrer del Rec 31; tapas from €3.50; ⊙5pm-midnight Mon, Tue, noon-1am Wed, Thu & Sun, noon-2.30am Fri, Sat; MJaume I) Opened on the pedestrian Carrer del Rec in 2013, Bormuth has tapped into the vogue for old-school tapas with modern-times service and decor, and serves all the old favourites – *patatas bravas, ensaladilla* (Russian salad), tortilla – along with some less predictable and superbly prepared

numbers (try the chargrilled red pepper with black pudding). The split-level dining room is never less than animated, but there's a more peaceful space with a single long table if you can assemble a group.

EN APARTÉ   FRENCH €

Map p284 (📞93 269 13 35; www.enaparte.es; Carrer Lluis el Piados 2; mains €7-10; ⊙10am-1am Tue-Thu, 10am-2am Fri & Sat, noon-1am Sun; 🔊; MArc de Triomf or Urquinaona) A great low-key place to eat good-quality French food, just off the quiet Plaça de Sant Pere. The restaurant is small but spacious, with sewing-machine tables and vintage details, and floor-to-ceiling windows that bring in some wonderful early-afternoon sunlight.

The lunch menu (€11) is excellent, offering a salad (such as beetroot and apple and walnut), and a quiche or other dish, such as stuffed peppers with a potato gratin. Brunch – including French toast, eggs Benedict and muesli with yoghurt – is served on weekends.

LA LLAVOR DELS ORÍGENS   CATALAN €

Map p284 (📞93 310 75 31; www.lallavordelsorigens.com; Carrer de la Vidrieria 6-8; mains €8-11; ⊙12.30pm-midnight; MJaume I) In this treasure chest of Catalan regional products, the shop shelves groan under the weight of bottles and packets of goodies. It also has a long menu of smallish dishes, such as *sopa de carbassa i castanyes* (pumpkin and chestnut soup) or *mandonguilles amb albergínies* (rissoles with aubergine), that you can mix and match over wine by the glass.

TANTARANTANA   MEDITERRANEAN €

Map p284 (📞93 268 24 10; Carrer d'en Tantarantana 24; mains €7-10; ⊙12.30pm-1am Mon-Sat, closed lunch Mon; MJaume I) Surrounded as it is by the furiously fashionable front-line nuclei of *nueva cocina española* – the new Spanish cuisine – this spot is a refreshing contrast. There is something comforting about the old-style marble-top tables, upon which you can sample simple but well-prepared dishes such as risotto or grilled tuna served with vegetables and ginger. There's also a long list of tapas. It attracts a 30-something crowd who enjoy the outdoor seating in summer.

BAR JOAN   CATALAN €

Map p284 (📞93 310 61 50; Mercat de Santa Caterina; menú del día €11, tapas from €3; ⊙7.30am-2pm Mon, to 3.30pm Tue, Wed & Sat, to 8.30pm

Thu & Fri, closed afternoons Jul & Aug; MJaume I) Along with the popular Cuines de Santa Caterina, there are a couple of bar-eateries in the Mercat de Santa Caterina. Bar Joan is known especially to locals for its *arròs negre* (cuttlefish-ink rice) on Tuesday at lunchtime and paella on Thursdays. It's a simple spot, with only tapas or the *menú del día* (daily set menu), but it's friendly and good value.

BUBÓ
PASTELERÍA €

Map p284 (☑93 268 72 24; www.bubo.es; Carrer de les Caputxes 6 & 10; tapas from €5; ⊙10am-9pm Mon-Thu & Sun, 10am-midnight Fri & Sat; MBarceloneta) Carles Mampel is a wizard of desserts. It is difficult to walk by his bar and pastry shop without being sucked in to try one of his fantasy-laden creations. Try saying no to a mousse of *gianduia* (a dark hazelnut cream) with mango cream, caramelised hazelnuts with spices, and a hazelnut biscuit.

★EL ATRIL
INTERNATIONAL €€

Map p284 (☑93 310 12 20; www.atrilbarcelona.com; Carrer dels Carders 23; mains €11-15; ⊙6pm-midnight Mon, noon-midnight Tue-Thu, noon-1am Fri & Sat, 11.30am-11.30pm Sun; MJaume I) Aussie owner Brenden is influenced by culinary influences from all over the globe, so while you'll see plenty of tapas (the *patatas bravas* are recommended for their homemade sauce), you'll also find kangaroo fillet, salmon and date rolls with mascarpone, chargrilled turkey with fried yucca, and plenty more. If the weather is good or there's no room in the cosy dining room, there are tables outside in a lively square.

CASA DELFÍN
SPANISH €€

Map p284 (☑93 319 50 88; www.tallerdetapas.com; Passeig del Born 36; mains €10-15; ⊙8am-midnight daily, until 1am Fri & Sat; MBarceloneta) One of Barcelona's culinary delights, Casa Delfín is everything you dream of when you think of Catalan (and Mediterranean) cooking. Start with the tangy and sweet *calçots* (a cross between a leek and an onion; February and March only) or salt-strewn *padron* peppers, moving on to grilled sardines speckled with parsley, then tackle the meaty monkfish roasted in white wine and garlic. Or tease some mussels and clams out of their shells while crunching on the Catalan *coca* flatbread – done here to perfection and smeared with tomatoes and olive oil.

For the finale, choose the Eton Mess (the English owner Kate's only tribute to her homeland) – but keep in mind that the long glass of mashed-up cream, meringue and berries will happily sweeten two or three.

EL FORO
ARGENTINIAN €€

Map p284 (☑93 310 10 20; www.restauranteelforo.com; Carrer de la Princesa 53; mains €9-16; ⊙9am-11.30pm Tue-Thu, 10am-12.30am Fri & Sat, 10am-11.30pm Sun; ☎; MArc de Triomf) Friendly El Foro does everything you'd expect an Argentinian restaurant to do – huge slabs of red meat in a variety of cuts, empanadas (small pasties with various fillings), and the inevitable Italian element in the shape of pizzas and pasta dishes. Less predictable are the list of vegetarian dishes (such as vegetable curry with quinoa and coconut milk) and range of salads. It's a sunny, sprawling place with tables on the street, and good for a coffee at any time of day.

CAL PEP
TAPAS €€

Map p284 (☑93 310 79 61; www.calpep.com; Plaça de les Olles 8; mains €12-20; ⊙1-3.45pm & 7.30-11.30pm Tue-Sat, closed Mon lunch & Sat evening, dinner Mon-Fri Sep-Jul; MBarceloneta) It's getting a foot in the door here that's the problem – there can be queues out into the square with people trying to get in. And if you want one of the five tables out the back, you'll need to call ahead. Most people are happy elbowing their way to the bar for some of the tastiest gourmet seafood tapas in town.

Pep recommends *cloïsses amb pernil* (clams and ham) or the *trifàsic* (combo of calamares, whitebait and prawns). The restaurant's other pièce de résistance is a super-smooth *tortilla de patatas* (Spanish omelette) and tuna tartare.

LE CUCINE MANDAROSSO
ITALIAN €

Map p284 (☑93 269 07 80; www.lecucinemandarosso.com; Carrer Verdaguer i Callis 4; mains €12-14, menú del día €11; ⊙1.30-4pm & 9pm-midnight Tue-Sat; MUrquinaona) This is comfort food done to perfection – the menu changes daily, with only a handful of mains to choose from, most of which are pasta, and one or two fish or meat. The antipasti can be vegetables, or fresh cheese, such as the wonderfully creamy *burrata* (fresh cheese made from mozzarella and cream), buffalo-milk mozzarella, or smoked *scamorza* and *provola* cheese.

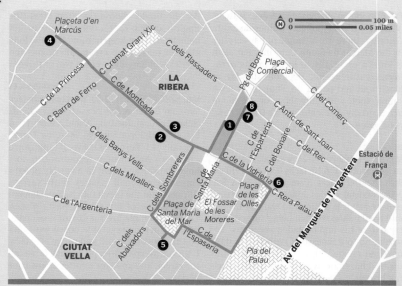

Local Life
Tapas & Bar Hopping in El Born

If there's one place that distils Barcelona's enduring cool to its essence and provides a snapshot of all that's irresistible about this city, it has to be El Born, the tangle of streets surrounding the Basílica de Santa Maria del Mar. Its secret is simple: this is where locals go for an authentic Barcelona night out.

❶ Passeig del Born
Most nights, and indeed most things, in El Born begin along the Passeig del Born, one of the prettiest little boulevards in Europe. It's a place to sit as much as to promenade. It's a graceful setting beneath the trees from which El Born's essential appeal is obvious – thronging people, brilliant bars and architecture that springs from a medieval film set.

❷ Catalan Tapas
Push through the crowd, order a *cava* (sparkling wine) and an assortment of tapas at El Xampanyet (p106), one of the city's best-known *cava* bars, in business since 1929. Star dishes include tangy *boquerons en vinagre* (white anchovies in vinegar) and there's high-quality seafood served from a can in the Catalan way.

❸ Best of Basque
Having taken your first lesson in Barcelona-style tapas it's time to compare it with the

pintxos (Basque tapas of food morsels perched atop pieces of bread) lined up along the bar at **Euskal Etxea** (Map p284; ☎93 343 54 10; Placeta de Montcada 1; tapas from €2; ⊗10am-12.30am daily, until 1am Fri & Sat; ⓂJaume I), a real slice of San Sebastián.

❹ Spain with a Twist
This detour to the northern limits of El Born is worth the walk. At first glance, the tapas at informal **Bar del Pla** (Map p284; ☎93 268 30 03; www.bardelpla.cat; Carrer de Montcada 2; mains from €10; ⊗noon-11pm Tue-Sun, until midnight Fri & Sat; ⓂJaume I) are traditionally Spanish, but the riffs on a theme show an assured touch. Try the ham and roasted-meat croquettes or the marinated salmon, yoghurt and mustard.

❺ Tapas with a View
Back in the heart of El Born, in the shadow of Basílica de Santa Maria del Mar, pastry chef Carles Mampel operates Bubó (p103). If you're not already sated, try the salted

Tapas dishes

cod croquettes at one of the outdoor tables inching onto the lovely square.

❻ Cal Pep
Boisterous Cal Pep (p103) is one of Barcelona's enduring stars. It can be difficult to snaffle a bar stool from which to order gourmet bar snacks such as *cloïsses amb pernil* (clams with ham); if it's full, order a drink and wait. It's always worth it.

❼ El Born's Favourite Bar
El Born Bar (Map p284; ☑93 319 53 33; Passeig del Born 26; ☺10am-2am Mon-Sat, noon-1.30am Sun; MJaume I) effortlessly attracts everyone from cool 30-somethings from all over town to locals who pass judgement on Passeig del Born's passing parade. Its staying power depends on a good selection of beers and spirits and empanadas and other snacks.

❽ The Last Mojito
So many Barcelona nights end with a mojito, and El Born's biggest and best are to be found at **Cactus Bar** (Map p284; www.cactusbar.cat; Passeig del Born 30; ☺9am-3am; MJaume I). The outdoor tables next to Passeig del Born are the perfect way to wind down the night.

Combine a good pasta dish – the *'al forno'* (baked) options are always outstanding with a green salad, and follow up with the homemade cakes. More can be had at **Mandarosso Pastis** (Map p284; ☑93 319 05 02; www.lecucinemandarosso.com; Carrer General Alvarez de Castro 5-7; ☺8.30am-8pm Tue-Sat, 9am-8pm Sun; MUrquinaona), around the corner. The fresh produce is bought daily from the Mercat de Santa Caterina, and the rest is imported from Italy.

CUINES DE SANTA CATERINA
MEDITERRANEAN, ASIAN €€

Map p284 (☑93 268 99 18; www.grupotragaluz.com; Mercat de Santa Caterina; mains €10-14; ☺1-4pm & 8pm-midnight daily, until 1am Fri & Sat; MJaume I) With a contemporary feel and open kitchens, this multifaceted eatery inside the Mercat de Santa Caterina offers all sorts of food. Peck at the sushi bar, tuck into classic rice dishes or go vegetarian. It does some things better than others, so skip the hummus and *tarte Tatin*. A drawback is the speed with which barely finished plates are whisked away from you, but the range of dishes and bustling atmosphere are fun. Reservations aren't taken, so it's first come, first served.

★COMERÇ 24
INTERNATIONAL €€€

Map p284 (☑93 319 21 02; www.carlesabellan.com; Carrer del Comerç 24; mains €24-32; ☺1.30-3.30pm & 8.30-11pm Tue-Sat; MBarceloneta) Michelin-starred chef Carles Abellan playfully reinterprets the traditional (suckling pig 'Hanoi style'), as well as more international classics, such as the bite-sized mini-pizza sashimi with tuna; *melón con jamón*, a *millefeuille* of layered caramelised Iberian ham and thinly sliced melon, or oxtail with cauliflower purée. If your budget will stretch to it, try a little of almost everything with the 'Menú del Gran Festival' (€116).

PASSADÍS DEL PEP
SEAFOOD €€€

Map p284 (☑93 310 10 21; www.passadis.com; Pla del Palau 2; mains €18-23; ☺1.15-3.45pm Mon-Sat; MBarceloneta) There's no sign, but locals know where to head for a seafood feast. They say the restaurant's raw materials are delivered daily from fishing ports along the Catalan coast. There is no menu – what's on offer depends on what the sea has surrendered on the day – but you can count on something along the lines of fresh seafood and/or fish, a bit of *jamón* (cured

LA RIBERA EATING

ham), tomato bread and grilled vegetables. Just head down the long, ill-lit corridor and entrust yourself to its care.

DRINKING & NIGHTLIFE

There are several bars along the Passeig del Born and the web of streets winding off it and around the Basílica de Santa Maria del Mar – the area has an ebullient, party feel.

MUDANZAS
BAR

Map p284 (📞93 319 11 37; Carrer de la Vidrieria 15; ⏰9.30am-2.30am Mon-Fri, 5pm-3am Sat & Sun; 📶; Ⓜ Jaume I) This was one of the first bars to get things into gear in El Born and it still attracts a faithful crowd. It's a straightforward place for a beer, a chat and perhaps a sandwich. Oh, and it has a nice line in rums and malt whisky.

LA VINYA DEL SENYOR
WINE BAR

Map p284 (📞93 310 33 79; www.lavinyadelsenyor. com; Plaça de Santa Maria del Mar 5; ⏰noon-1am Mon-Thu, noon-2am Fri & Sat, noon-midnight Sun; Ⓜ Jaume I) Relax on the *terrassa,* which lies in the shadow of Basílica de Santa Maria del Mar, or crowd inside at the tiny bar. The wine list is as long as *War and Peace* and there's a table upstairs for those who opt to sample by the bottle rather than the glass.

RUBÍ
BAR

Map p284 (📞647 773707; Carrer dels Banys Vells 6; ⏰7.30pm-2.30am; Ⓜ Jaume I) With its boudoir lighting and cheap mojitos, Rubí is where the Born's cognoscenti head for a nightcap – or several. It's a narrow, cosy space – push through to the back where you might just get one of the coveted tables – with superior bar food, from Vietnamese rolls to more traditional selections of cheese and ham.

JUANRA FALCES
COCKTAIL BAR

Map p284 (📞93 310 10 27; Carrer del Rec 24; ⏰8pm-3am, from 10pm Mon & Sun; Ⓜ Jaume I) Transport yourself to a Humphrey Bogart movie in this narrow little bar, formerly (and still, at least among the locals) known as Gimlet. White-jacketed bar staff with all the appropriate aplomb will whip you up a gimlet or any other classic cocktail (around €10) your heart desires.

EL XAMPANYET
WINE BAR

Map p284 (📞93 319 70 03; Carrer de Montcada 22; ⏰noon-3.30pm & 7-11pm Tue-Sat, noon-4pm Sun; Ⓜ Jaume I) Nothing has changed for decades in this, one of the city's best-known *cava* bars. Plant yourself at the bar or seek out a table against the decoratively tiled walls for a glass or three of the cheap house *cava* and an assortment of tapas, such as the tangy *boquerons en vinagre* (fresh anchovies in vinegar).

MIRAMELINDO
BAR

Map p284 (📞93 310 37 27; Passeig del Born 15; ⏰8pm-2.30am; Ⓜ Jaume I) A spacious tavern in a Gothic building, this remains a classic on Passeig del Born for mixed drinks, while soft jazz and soul sounds float overhead. Try for a comfy seat at a table towards the back before it fills to bursting. A couple of similarly barn-sized places line this side of the *passeig.*

MAGIC
CLUB

Map p284 (📞93 310 72 67; www.magic-club.net; Passeig de Picasso 40; ⏰11pm-6am Thu-Sun; Ⓜ Barceloneta) Although it sometimes hosts live acts in its sweaty, smoky basement, it's basically a straightforward, subterranean nightclub offering rock, mainstream dance faves and Spanish pop.

UPIAYWASI
BAR

Map p284 (📞93 268 01 54; www.upiaywasi. com; Carrer d'Allada Vermell 11; ⏰12.30pm-2am Mon-Thu, 11am-3am Fri & Sat, 11am-1am Sun;

MASTERS OF WINE

One of the best wine stores in Barcelona (and Lord knows, there are a few), **Vila Viniteca** (Map p284; 📞902 327777; www.vilaviniteca.es; Carrer dels Agullers 7; ⏰8.30am-8.30pm Mon-Sat; Ⓜ Jaume I) has been searching out the best in local and imported wines since 1932. On a couple of November evenings it organises what has by now become an almost riotous wine-tasting event in Carrer dels Agullers and surrounding lanes, at which cellars from around Spain present their young new wines. At No 9 it has another store devoted to gourmet food products.

Ⓜ Barceloneta) Slide into this dimly lit bar, which crosses a chilled ambience with Latin American music. A mix of sofas and intimate table settings, chandeliers and muted decorative tones lend the place a pleasingly conspiratorial feel. During the day most people will be found out on the terrace.

⭐ ENTERTAINMENT

⭐ PALAU DE LA MÚSICA CATALANA · CLASSICAL MUSIC

Map p284 (📞 93 295 72 00; www.palaumusica. org; Carrer de Sant Francesc de Paula 2; ⊘ box office 9.30am-9pm Mon-Sat; Ⓜ Urquinaona) A feast for the eyes, this Modernista confection is also the city's most traditional venue for classical and choral music, although it has a wide-ranging program, including flamenco, pop and – particularly – jazz. Just being here for a performance is an experience. Sip a preconcert tipple in the foyer, its tiled pillars all a-glitter. Head up the grand stairway to the main auditorium, a whirlpool of Modernista whimsy.

TABLAO NERVIÓN · DANCE

Map p284 (📞 93 315 21 03; www.restaurante nervion.com; Carrer de la Princesa 2; show & set dinner €25-35, show with 1 drink €14; ⊘ shows 8-11pm Thu & Fri; Ⓜ Jaume I) For admittedly tourist-oriented flamenco, this unassuming bar (shows take place in the basement) is cheaper than most, and has good offers. Check the website for details.

🛍 SHOPPING

The former commercial heart of medieval Barcelona is today still home to a cornucopia of old-style specialist food and drink shops, a veritable feast of aroma and atmosphere. They have been joined, since the late 1990s, by a raft of hip little fashion stores.

⭐ CASA GISPERT · FOOD

Map p284 (📞 93 319 75 35; www.casagispert. com; Carrer dels Sombrerers 23; ⊘ 9.30am-2pm & 4-8.30pm Tue-Fri, 10am-2pm & 5-8.30pm Sat; Ⓜ Jaume I) The wonderful, atmospheric and wood-fronted Casa Gispert has been toasting nuts and selling all manner of dried fruit since 1851. Pots and jars piled high on the shelves contain an unending variety of crunchy titbits: some roasted, some honeyed, all of them moreish. Your order is shouted over to the till, along with the price, in a display of old-world accounting.

ARLEQUÍ MÀSCARES · ARTS & CRAFTS

Map p284 (📞 93 268 27 52; www.arlequimask. com; Carrer de la Princesa 7; ⊘ 10.30am-8.30pm Mon-Sat, 10.30am-3pm & 4-7.30pm Sun; Ⓜ Jaume I) A wonderful little oasis of originality, this shop specialises in masks for costume and decoration. Some of the pieces are superb, while stock also includes a beautiful range of decorative boxes in Catalan themes, and some old-style marionettes.

LOISAIDA · CLOTHING, ANTIQUES

Map p284 (📞 93 295 54 92; www.loisaidabcn. com; Carrer dels Flassaders 42; ⊘ 11am-9pm Mon-Sat, 11am-2pm & 4-8pm Sun; Ⓜ Jaume I) A sight in its own right, housed in what was once the coach house and stables for the Royal Mint, Loisaida (from the Spanglish for 'Lower East Side') is a deceptively large emporium of colourful, retro and somewhat preppy clothing for men and women, costume jewellery, music from the 1940s and '50s and some covetable antiques. There is more womenswear and some very cute children's lines a few doors away at **No 32** (Map p284; 📞 93 295 54 92; Carrer dels Flassaders 32; ⊘ 11am-9pm Mon-Sat, 11am-2pm & 4-8pm Sun; Ⓜ Jaume I).

COQUETTE · FASHION

Map p284 (📞 93 295 42 85; www.coquettebcn. com; Carrer del Rec 65; ⊘ 11am-3pm & 5-9pm Mon-Fri, 11.30am-9pm Sat; Ⓜ Barceloneta) With its spare, cut-back and designer look, this fashion store is attractive in its own right. Women can browse through casual, feminine wear by such designers as Humanoid, Vanessa Bruno, UKE and Hoss Intropia, and others, with a further collection nearby at **Carrer de Bonaire 5** (Map p284; 📞 93 310 35 35; Carrer de Bonaire 5; ⊘ 11am-3pm & 5-9pm Mon-Fri, 11.30am-8.30pm Sat; Ⓜ Barceloneta).

OLISOLIVA · FOOD

Map p284 (📞 93 268 14 72; www.olisoliva.com; Mercat de Santa Caterina; ⊘ 9.30am-3pm Mon-Wed & Sat, 9.30am-8pm Fri & Sat; Ⓜ Jaume I) Inside the Mercat de Santa Caterina, this simple, glassed-in store is stacked with olive oils and vinegars from all over Spain. Taste some of the products before deciding. Some of the best olive oils come from southern Spain. The range of vinegars is astounding, also.

EL REI DE LA MÀGIA   SPECIALITY

Map p284 (☑93 319 39 20; www.elreydelamagia.com; Carrer de la Princesa 11; ☺11am-2pm & 5-8pm Mon-Fri, 11am-2pm Sat; ⓂJaume I) For more than 100 years, the people behind this box of tricks have been keeping locals both astounded and amused. Should you decide to stay in Barcelona and make a living as a magician, this is the place to buy levitation brooms, glasses of disappearing milk and decks of magic cards.

NU SABATES   SHOES, ACCESSORIES

Map p284 (☑93 268 03 83; www.nusabates.com; Carrer dels Cotoners 14; ☺11am-9pm Mon-Sat; ⓂJaume I) A couple of modern-day Catalan cobblers have put together some original handmade leather shoes (and a handful of bags and other leather items) in their stylish locale.

CUSTO BARCELONA   FASHION

Map p284 (☑93 268 78 93; www.custo-barcelona.com; Plaça de les Olles 7; ☺10am-9pm Mon-Sat, noon-8pm Sun; ⓂJaume I) The psychedelic decor and casual atmosphere lend this avantgarde Barcelona fashion store a youthful edge. Custo presents daring new women's and men's collections each year on the New York catwalks. The dazzling colours and cut of anything from dinner jackets to hot pants are for the uninhibited. It has five other stores around town.

HOFMANN PASTISSERIA   FOOD

Map p284 (☑93 268 82 21; www.hofmann-bcn.com; Carrer dels Flassaders 44; ☺9am-2pm & 3.30-8pm Mon-Thu, 9am-8.30pm Fri & Sat, 9am-2.30pm Sun; ⓂJaume I) With old timber cabinets, this bite-sized gourmet patisserie, linked to the prestigious Hofmann cooking school, has an air of timelessness. Choose between jars of delicious chocolates, the day's croissants and more dangerous pastries, or an array of cakes and other sweets.

LA BOTIFARRERIA   FOOD

Map p284 (☑93 319 91 23; www.labotifarreria.com; Carrer de Santa Maria 4; ☺8.30am-2.30pm & 5-8.30pm Mon-Fri, 8.30am-3pm Sat; ⓂJaume I) Say it with a sausage! Although this delightful deli sells all sorts of goodies, the mainstay is an astounding variety of handcrafted sausages – the *botifarra*. Not just the regular plain pork variety either – these sausages are stuffed with anything from green pepper and whisky to apple curry.

EL MAGNÍFICO   COFFEE

Map p284 (☑93 319 39 75; www.cafeselmagnifico.com; Carrer de l'Argenteria 64; ☺10am-8pm Mon-Sat; ⓂJaume I) All sorts of coffee has been roasted here since the early 20th century. The variety of coffee (and tea) available is remarkable – and the aromas hit you as you walk in. Across the road, the same people run the exquisite and much newer tea shop **Sans i Sans** (Map p284; ☑93 310 25 18; Carrer de l'Argenteria 59; ⓂJaume I).

🏃 SPORTS & ACTIVITIES

AIRE DE BARCELONA   HAMMAN

Map p284 (☑93 295 57 43; www.airedebarcelona.com; Passeig de Picasso 22; thermal baths & aromatherapy €29; ☺10am-10pm Mon-Wed & Sun, 10am-2am Thu-Sat; ⓂArc de Triomf) With low lighting and relaxing perfumes wafting around you, this basement hammam could be the perfect way to end a day. Hot, warm and cold baths, steam baths and options for various massages, including on a slab of hot marble, make for a delicious hour or so. Book ahead and bring a swimming costume.

Barceloneta & the Waterfront

PORT VELL | LA BARCELONETA | POBLENOU | PORT OLÍMPIC | EL FÒRUM

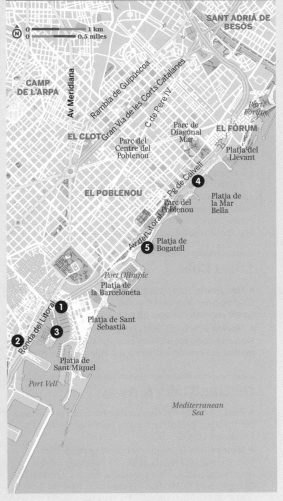

Neighbourhood Top Five

❶ Learning about the Romans, Muslims, feudal lords and civil war free-dom fighters in the proud and interactive **Museu d'Història de Catalunya** (p112); afterwards, head to the rooftop for a meal with panoramic views.

❷ Stepping back in time in the Gothic shipyards of the **Museu Marítim** (p111).

❸ Walking through the eerie shark tunnel inside the massive **l'Aquàrium** (p112).

❹ Frolicking in the sea off the sands of **Platja de la Nova Mar Bella** (p112).

❺ Taking a **bike ride** (p114) along the beachside promenade from Barceloneta to Parc del Fòrum.

For more detail of this area see maps on p286 and p288 ➡

Lonely Planet's Top Tip

If you'd like to explore the sea and the mountains on the same day, take advantage of the Transbordador Aeri, which whisks passengers from Barceloneta up to Montjuïc in a rather vintage-looking cable car. The tower also has a top-end restaurant, a fine destination in its own right.

Best Places to Eat

→ Can Recasens (p118)
→ Barraca (p117)
→ Jai-Ca (p116)
→ Els Pescadors (p118)
→ La Cova Fumada (p116)

For reviews, see p116 →

Best Places to Drink

→ Can Paixano (p119)
→ Absenta (p119)
→ Ké? (p119)
→ Santa Marta (p119)
→ Bar Leo (p119)

For reviews, see p119 →

Best Sights

→ Barceloneta's beaches (p112)
→ Museu Marítim (p111)
→ Museu d'Història de Catalunya (p112)
→ L'Aquàrium (p112)
→ Transbordador Aeri (p113)

For reviews, see p111 →

Explore: Barceloneta & the Waterfront

Barcelona's long, sun-drenched waterfront provides a pleasant escape when you need a break from Gothic lanes and Modernisme. Heading northeast from the old city, you'll soon find yourself amid tempting seafood restaurants and waterfront bars, with a palm-lined promenade taking cyclists, joggers and strollers out to the beaches running some 4km up to Parc del Fòrum.

At the foot of La Rambla, Port Vell draws locals and tourists alike who come to stroll the peaceful pedestrian bridge of Rambla de Mar. This leads out to the shops and restaurants in Maremàgnum mall and the first-rate aquarium next door. Several small parks and plazas provide fine vantage points. Nearby is Barceloneta, an old fishing quarter laid out in the mid-18th century. Festive tapas bars, old-fashioned seafood joints and bohemian drinking spots dot the narrow lanes. Traditional sights are few on the ground here; most visitors come to wander the streets and eat and drink.

Where Barceloneta abuts the water, open-air restaurants offer views out over the promenade and the beaches beyond. On summer days the area fills with sunseekers, making their way to and from the people-packed sands nearby. From here heading north to El Fòrum, it's beaches all the way; rustic shacks called *chiringuitos* dole out music and cocktails on the sands. Tonier outdoor options open year-round, particularly near Port Olímpic.

Inland from these modern artificial beaches lies the up-and-coming neighbourhood of Poblenou, which has its restaurant-lined Rambla. The waterside district ends at El Fòrum, which has a worthwhile new science museum; it's also the setting for outdoor summer concerts and funfairs.

Local Life

→ **Hang-outs** There are many great local haunts full of flowing *cava*, beer and flavourful tapas: Vaso de Oro (p116) and Can Paixano (p119) are long-time favourites.
→ **Markets** Port Vell hosts Port Antic (p121), a small weekend antiques market; near the marina is the craft market of Feria de Artesanía del Palau de Mar (p121).

Getting There & Away

→ **Foot** From the old city, La Rambla and Via Laietana are the main pedestrian access points across busy Ronda del Litoral.
→ **Metro** Go to Drassanes (Línia 3) to reach Port Vell; Barceloneta (Línia 4) has its own stop for the neighbourhood. Línia 4 continues out to Ciutadella Vila Olímpica and El Maresme Fòrum near Parc del Fòrum.

TOP SIGHT
MUSEU MARÍTIM

Venice had its Arsenal and Barcelona the Reials Drassanes (Royal Shipyards), from where Don Juan of Austria's flagship galley was launched to lead a joint Spanish-Venetian fleet into the momentous Battle of Lepanto against the Turks in 1571. These mighty Gothic shipyards are not as extensive as their Venetian counterparts but they're an extraordinary piece of civilian architecture nonetheless. Today the broad arches shelter the Museu Marítim, the city's seafaring-history museum and one of the most fascinating museums in town.

Royal Shipyards

The shipyards were, in their heyday, among the greatest in Europe. Begun in the 13th century and completed by 1378, the long, arched bays (the highest arches reach 13m) once sloped off as slipways directly into the water, which lapped the seaward side of the Drassanes until at least the end of the 18th century. Shipbuilding was later moved to southern Spain, and the Drassanes became a barracks for artillery.

Replica of Don Juan of Austria's Flagship

The centre of the shipyards is dominated by a full-sized replica (made in the 1970s) of Don Juan of Austria's flagship. A clever audiovisual display aboard the vessel brings to life the ghastly existence of the slaves, prisoners and volunteers (!) who, at full steam, could haul this vessel along at 9 knots. They remained chained to their seats, four to an oar, at all times. Here they worked, drank (fresh water was stored below decks, where the infirmary was also located), ate, slept and went to the loo. You could smell a galley like this from miles away.

Exhibitions

Fishing vessels, old navigation charts, models and dioramas of the Barcelona waterfront make up the rest of this engaging museum. Temporary exhibitions are also held (an intriguing show on the history of explorations in Antarctica was held here in 2014). The museum, which has seen major renovations in the past five years, will reopen in its entirety by early 2015. When it reopens, visitors will encounter a greatly expanded collection with multimedia exhibits evoking more of Spain's epic history on the high seas. With a museum ticket, you can also visit the Pailebot de Santa Eulàlia (p113), docked on the waterfront nearby.

Ictíneo

The pleasant museum **cafe** offers courtyard seating and a small assortment of bites, as well as a decent *menú del día* (set-price menu) at lunchtime. Also in the courtyard, you can have a look at a swollen replica of the *Ictíneo,* one of the world's first submarines. It was invented and built in 1858 by Catalan polymath Narcis Monturiol, and was operated by hand-cranked propellers turned by friends of Monturiol who accompanied him on dozens of successful short dives (two hours maximum) in the harbour. He later developed an even larger submarine powered by a combustion engine that allowed it to dive to 30m and remain submerged for seven hours. Despite impressive demonstrations to awestruck crowds he never attracted the interest of the navy, and remains largely forgotten today.

DON'T MISS...

➡ The replica of Don Juan of Austria's flagship
➡ Temporary exhibitions
➡ Ictíneo
➡ The courtyard cafe

PRACTICALITIES

➡ Map p286
➡ 93 342 99 20
➡ www.mmb.cat
➡ Avinguda de les Drassanes
➡ adult/child €5/2, 3-8pm Sun free
➡ 10am-8pm
➡ Drassanes

SIGHTS

Port Vell & La Barceloneta

MUSEU MARÍTIM   MUSEUM
See p111.

L'AQUÀRIUM   AQUARIUM
Map p286 (☎93 221 74 74; www.aquariumbcn.
com; Moll d'Espanya; adult/child €20/15, dive
€300; ☺9.30am-11pm Jul & Aug, to 9pm Sep-Jun;
ⓂDrassanes) It is hard not to shudder at the
sight of a shark gliding above you, displaying its toothy, wide-mouthed grin. But this,
the 80m shark tunnel, is the highlight of one
of Europe's largest aquariums. It has the
world's best Mediterranean collection and
plenty of colourful fish from as far off as the
Red Sea, the Caribbean and the Great Bar-
rier Reef. All up, some 11,000 fish (including
a dozen sharks) of 450 species reside here.

Back in the shark tunnel, which you
reach after passing a series of themed fish
tanks with everything from bream to sea
horses, various species of shark (white tip,
sand tiger, bonnethead, black tip, nurse

and sandbar) flit around you, along with a
host of other critters, from flapping rays to
bloated sunfish. An interactive zone, Plan-
eta Aqua, is host to a family of Antarctic
penguins and a tank of rays that you watch
close up. Divers with a valid dive certificate
may dive in the main tank with the sharks.

MUSEU D'HISTÒRIA DE CATALUNYA   MUSEUM
Map p286 (Museum of Catalonian History; ☎93 225
47 00; www.mhcat.net; Plaça de Pau Vila 3; adult/
child €4.50/3.50, 1st Sun of month free; ☺10am-
7pm Tue & Thu-Sat, to 8pm Wed, to 2.30pm Sun;
ⓂBarceloneta) Inside the **Palau de Mar** (Map
p286), this worthwhile museum takes you
from the Stone Age through to the early
1980s. It is a busy hotchpotch of dioramas,
artefacts, videos, models, documents and interactive bits: all up, an entertaining exploration of 2000 years of Catalan history. See how
the Romans lived, listen to Arab poetry from
the time of the Muslim occupation of the city,
peer into the dwelling of a Dark Ages family
in the Pyrenees, try to mount a knight's horse
or lift a suit of armour.

When you have had enough of all this,
descend into a civil-war air-raid shelter,
watch a video in Catalan on post-Franco

⊙ TOP SIGHT
PLATJAS

A series of pleasant beaches stretches northeast from
the Port Olímpic marina. They are largely artificial, but
this doesn't stop an estimated seven million bathers
from piling in every year!

The southernmost beach, **Platja de la Nova Icària**,
is the busiest. Behind it, across the Avinguda del Litoral
highway, is the Plaça dels Campions, site of the rusting
three-tiered platform used to honour medallists in the
sailing events of the 1992 games.

The next beach is **Platja de Bogatell**. Just in from
the beach is **Cementiri del Poblenou** (Poblenou Cemetery;
☎93 225 16 61; Av d'Icària near Carrer del Taulat; ☺8am-6pm),
created in 1773. The cemetery is full of bombastic family
memorials, but an altogether disquieting touch is the
sculpture El petó de la mort (The Kiss of Death), in which
a winged skeleton kisses a young kneeling lifeless body.

Platja de la Mar Bella (with its brief nudist strip
and sailing school) and **Platja de la Nova Mar Bella**
follow, leading into the new residential and commercial
waterfront strip, the Front Marítim, part of the Diagonal
Mar project in the Fòrum district. It is fronted by the
last of these artificial beaches to be created, **Platja del
Llevant**.

DON'T MISS...

➡ The vibrant bustle
of Platja de la Nova
Icària

➡ The poignant El
petó de la mort sculp-
ture in the Cementiri
del Poblenou

PRACTICALITIES

➡ Map p288
➡ 🚌36 or 41,
ⓂCiutadella Vila
Olímpic, Bogatell,
Llacuna or Selva
de Mar

Catalonia, or head upstairs to the first-rate rooftop restaurant and cafe, 1881 (p118).

The temporary exhibitions are often as interesting as the permanent display. Outside the museum is a string of open-air restaurants serving up seafood dishes.

TRANSBORDADOR AERI   CABLE CAR

Map p286 (www.telefericodebarcelona.com; Passeig Escullera; one way/return €11/16.50; ⊗11am-7pm; ☐17, 39 or 64, MBarceloneta) This cable car strung across the harbour to Montjuïc provides an eagle-eye view of the city. The cabins float between the Torre de Sant Sebastià (in La Barceloneta) and Miramar (Montjuïc), with a midway stop at the Torre de Jaume I in front of the World Trade Center. At the top of the Torre de Sant Sebastià is a restaurant, Torre d'Alta Mar (p117).

PAILEBOT DE SANTA EULÀLIA   SHIP

Map p286 (Moll de la Fusta; adult/child €1/free; ⊗10am-8.30pm Tue-Fri & Sun, 2-8.30pm Sat; MDrassanes) This 1918 three-mast schooner, restored by the Museu Marítim, is moored along the palm-lined Moll de la Fusta. You can see it perfectly well without going aboard, and there's not an awful lot to behold below decks. Admission is free with a paid Museu Marítim ticket. At 10am on Saturdays it sets sail for a three-hour cruise along the coast (adult/child €12/6). Reserve a spot by emailing reserves.mmaritim@diba.cat.

ESGLÉSIA DE SANT
MIQUEL DEL PORT   CHURCH

Map p286 (☑93 221 65 50; Plaça de la Barceloneta; ⊗7am-1.30pm Mon-Fri, 8am-1.30pm Sat; MBarceloneta) Finished in 1755, this sober baroque church was the first building completed in La Barceloneta. Built low so that the cannon in the then Ciutadella fort could fire over it if necessary, it bears images of St Michael (Miquel) and two other saints considered protectors of the Catalan fishing fleet: Sant Elm and Santa Maria de Cerveló. Ferdinand Lesseps, the French engineer who designed the Suez Canal, did a stint as France's consul-general in Barcelona and lived in the house to the right of the church.

FÀBRICA DEL SOL   MUSEUM

Map p286 (☑93 256 44 30; Passeig de Salvat Papasseit 1; ⊗10am-2pm & 4.30-8pm Tue-Fri, 10am-2pm & 4-7pm Sat; MBarceloneta) A relic from the industrial era, this striking Modernista building with its red brick and yellow details today houses an environmental educa-

READING & PLAYING ON THE BEACH

During summer the city sets up several small lending libraries on the beach. These are free for use, and even tourists can take part. You'll find magazines, newspapers and a small foreign-language selection among the Spanish titles. It happens in two places: at **El Centre de la Platja** (Passeig Marítim de la Barceloneta 25; ⊗10am-7pm Tue-Sun Jun-Sep; MCiutadella or Vila Olímpica), located underneath the boardwalk, just up from the Parc de la Barceloneta, and at **l'Espigó de Bac de Roda jetty** (⊗11am-2pm & 3-7pm Mon-Fri Jul-Aug; MPoblenou) near Platja de la Mar Bella.

At the same locations, you can also hire out frisbees, volleyballs and nets, beach racquets and balls and *pétanque* games; for the kiddies, you'll find buckets, spades and watering cans. All you need to hire out the books or gear is your ID.

tion centre, with exhibitions on sustainable energy sources. You can wander around the building (and check out the solar panels on the roof), though all signage is in Catalan or Spanish.

⊙ Poblenou, Port Olímpic & El Fòrum

MUSEU DE LA MÚSICA   MUSEUM

Map p288 (☑93 256 36 50; www.museumusica.bcn.cat; Carrer de Lepant 150; adult/student €5/4, 3-8pm Sun free; ⊗10am-6pm Tue-Sat, to 8pm Sun; MMonumental) Some 500 instruments (less than a third of those held) are on show in this museum, housed on the 2nd floor of the administration building in L'Auditori, the city's main classical-music concert hall.

Instruments range from a 17th-century baroque guitar through to lutes (look out for the many-stringed 1641 archilute from Venice), violins, Japanese kotos, sitars from India, eight organs (some dating from the 18th century), pianos, a varied collection of drums and other percussion instruments from across Spain and beyond, along with all sorts of phonographs and gramophones.

🏃 Cycling Tour
The New Barcelona

START PORT VELL
END PORT VELL
LENGTH 12KM RETURN, 1½ HOURS

This bike tour takes in boardwalks, beaches, sculpture and architecture along Barcelona's ever-changing waterfront. It's a flat and safe ride along a dedicated bike path separate from traffic – though watch out for pedestrians. There are several convenient bike hires nearby, including Biciclot.

With Columbus at your back, make your way northeast along the waterfront. Keep an eye out for the three-mast schooner, **1 Pailebot de Santa Eulàlia**, built in 1918. Another up the road, you'll pass the colourful **2 Barcelona Head** sculpture by famous American pop artist Roy Lichtenstein.

As you make your way along the **3 Marina**, you may have to dismount amid the throng of strollers and open-air restaurants. Hop back on and pedal to the Plaça del Mar, which sports an elegant

sculpture entitled **4 Homenatge als nedadors** (Homage to the Swimmers).

Follow the crowds north, past another well-known sculpture, the **5 Homenatge a la Barceloneta**, which commemorates the old-fashioned shacks that once lined the beach. Cycle another kilometre and you'll pass beneath the copper-hued **6 Peix** sculpture, designed by Frank Gehry.

Next up is **7 Port Olímpic**, which is lined with restaurants and bars. From here you'll pass more **8 beaches**, which fill with sunseekers in summer.

It's another 2.5km or so to the end, where you'll find the **9 Parc del Fòrum**. Dominating this empty plaza is the rather harsh-looking sculpture **10 Fraternitat**, dedicated to hundreds executed here during the Franco years.

The protected bathing area **11 Zona de Banys** is a popular summer attraction for families. Just behind it looms the giant solar panel that powers the area. From here, retrace your journey back to Port Vell.

There are some odd pieces indeed, like the *buccèn,* a snake-head-adorned brass instrument. Much of the documentary and sound material can be enjoyed through audiovisual displays as you proceed. From Tuesday to Sunday at 3.30pm, the museum holds a concert (€15, including museum admission), in which musicians perform on rare instruments held in the collection.

MUSEU DEL DISSENY DE BARCELONA
MUSEUM

Map p288 (☑93 256 68 00; www.museudel disseny.cat; Plaça de les Glòries Catalanes 37; ⓂGlòries) Barcelona's design museum lies inside a new monolithic building with geometric facades and a rather brutalist appearance – unkindly nicknamed *la grapadora* (the stapler) by locals. The museum, expected to open by early 2015, will house a dazzling collection of ceramics, decorative arts and textiles, taken from its old location in the Palau Reial de Pedralbes.

Among the highlights, you'll find Spanish ceramics from the 10th to 20th centuries, including work by Picasso and Miró. Another section will house an eclectic assortment of furnishings, ornaments and knick-knacks dating as far back as the Romanesque period. Exquisite textiles ranging from 4th-century Coptic works to 20th-century local embroidery will segue into clothing dating from the 16th century to the 1930s. There will also be exhibitions devoted to graphic art.

TORRE AGBAR
ARCHITECTURE

Map p288 (www.torreagbar.com; Avinguda Diagonal 225; ⓂGlòries) Barcelona's very own cucumber-shaped tower, Jean Nouvel's luminous Torre Agbar, is among the most daring additions to the skyline since the first towers of La Sagrada Família went up. Completed in 2005, it shimmers at night in shades of midnight blue and lipstick red. At the time of publication, the Hyatt group was in negotiations to purchase the building and transform it into a luxury hotel.

PARC DEL CENTRE DEL POBLENOU
PARK

Map p288 (Avinguda Diagonal; ⊙10am-sunset; ⓂPoblenou) Barcelona is sprinkled with parks whose principal element is cement, and Jean Nouvel's Parc del Centre del Poblenou, with its stylised metal seats and items of statuary, is no exception. However, the park's Gaudí-inspired cement walls are increasingly covered by sprawling bougainvillea and, inside, some 1000 trees of mostly Mediterranean species are complemented by thousands of smaller bushes and plants. Nouvel's idea is that the trees, sustained by local groundwater, will eventually form a natural canopy over the park.

EL FÒRUM
NEIGHBOURHOOD

Map p288 (☑93 356 10 50; ⓂEl Maresme Fòrum) Once an urban wasteland, this area has seen dramatic changes in recent years, with sparkling new buildings, open plazas and waterfront recreation areas. The most striking element is the eerily blue, triangular **Edifici Fòrum** building by Swiss architects Herzog & de Meuron. The facades look like sheer cliff faces, with angular crags cut into them as if by divine laser. Grand strips of mirror create fragmented reflections of the sky. Next door, Josep Lluís Mateo's high-tech **Centre de Convencions Internacional de Barcelona** (CCIB) is a massive work in steel with intriguing contours.

A 300m stroll east from the Edifici Fòrum is the **Zona de Banys**, with kayaks and bikes available for rent, the option to learn diving, and other activities. This tranquil seawater swimming area was won from the sea by the creation of massive cement-block dykes. At its northern end, like a great rectangular sunflower, an enormous photovoltaic panel turns its face up to the sun to power the area with solar energy. Along with another set of solar panels in the form of porticoes, it generates enough electricity for 1000 households. Just behind it spreads **Port Fòrum**, Barcelona's third marina. The area is unified by an undulating esplanade and walkways that are perfect for walking, wheelchair access, bikes and skateboards.

In summer a weekend **amusement park** sets up with all the usual suspects: rides, shooting galleries, snack stands, inflatable castles and dodgem cars. The **Parc de**

LOCAL KNOWLEDGE

BURYING THE PAST

Buried beneath the concrete expanses, bathing zone and marina created in El Fòrum lies the memory of more than 2000 people executed in the fields of Camp de la Bota between 1936 and 1952, most of them under Franco from 1939 onward. To their memory, *Fraternitat* (Brotherhood), a sculpture by Miquel Navarro, stands on Rambla de Prim.

WORTH A DETOUR

EXPLORING CATALAN IMMIGRATION

Dedicated to the history of immigration in Catalonia, the **Museu d'Història de la Immigració de Catalunya** (☑93 381 26 06; www.mhic.net; Carretera de Mataró 124; ☉10am-2pm & 5-8pm Tue-Sat; MVerneda) **FREE** contains a display of photos, text (in Catalan) and various documents and objects that recall the history of immigration to Catalonia from the 19th century on. The star attraction is a wagon of the train (parked outside) known as El Sevillano, which in the 1950s trundled between Andalucía and Catalonia, jammed with migrants on an all-stops trip that often lasted more than 30 hours! There's also a video with images of migrant life decades ago and today. The museum resides in the former country house, Can Serra, which is now surrounded by light industry and ring roads.

Diagonal Mar, designed by Enric Miralles, contains pools, fountains, a didactic botanical walk and sculptures.

MUSEU BLAU   MUSEUM

Map p288 (Blue Museum; ☑93 256 60 02; www.museublau.bcn.cat; Parc del Fòrum; adult/child €6/free; ☉10am-7pm Tue-Sat, to 8pm Sun; MEl Maresme Fòrum) Set inside the futuristic Edifici Fòrum, Museu Blau takes visitors on a journey across the natural world. Multimedia and interactive exhibits explore topics like the history of evolution, the earth's formation and the great scientists who have helped shaped human knowledge. There are also specimens from the animal, plant and mineral kingdoms – plus dinosaur skeletons – all rather dramatically set amid 9000 sq metres of exhibition space.

EATING

Port Vell & La Barceloneta

In the Maremàgnum complex on the Moll d'Espanya you can eat close to the water's edge at a handful of fun, if fairly slapdash, joints. For good food and atmosphere, head around to La Barceloneta, the lanes of which bristle with everything from good-natured, noisy tapas bars to upmarket seafood restaurants. Almost everything shuts on Sunday and Monday evenings.

VASO DE ORO   TAPAS €

Map p286 (Carrer de Balboa 6; tapas €4-12; ☉10am-midnight; MBarceloneta) This narrow bar, which is always packed, gathers a festive, beer-swilling crowd who come for fantastic tapas. Fast-talking, white-jacketed waiters will serve up a few quick quips with your plates of grilled *gambes* (prawns), *foie a la plancha* (grilled liver pâté) or *solomillo* (sirloin) chunks. Want something a little different to drink? Ask for a *flauta cincuenta* – half lager and half dark beer.

JAI-CA   SEAFOOD €

Map p286 (☑93 268 32 65; Carrer de Ginebra 13; tapas €4-7; ☉9am-11.30pm Mon-Sat; MBarceloneta) Jai-Ca is a much-loved eatery that serves up juicy grilled prawns, flavour-rich anchovies, tender octopus, decadent razor clams and other seafood favourites. The *turbio* (Galician white wine), sangria and cold draughts are ideal refreshment after a day on the beach.

LA COVA FUMADA   TAPAS €

Map p286 (☑93 221 40 61; Carrer del Baluard 56; tapas €3.50-7.50; ☉9am-3.20pm Mon-Wed, 9am-3.20pm & 6-8.20pm Thu & Fri, 9am-1.20pm Sat; MBarceloneta) There's no sign and the setting is decidedly downmarket, but this tiny, buzzing family-run tapas spot always packs in a crowd. The secret? Mouthwatering *pulpo* (octopus), *calamar, sardinias* and 15 or so other small plates cooked up to perfection in the small open kitchen near the door. The *bombas* (potato croquettes served with *alioli*) and grilled *carxofes* (artichokes) are good, but everything is amazingly fresh.

EL BEN PLANTAT   INTERNATIONAL €

Map p286 (☑93 624 38 32; Carrer de Sant Carles 21; tapas €4-11; ☉9am-5pm Mon-Wed, to 11.45pm Thu-Fri, 11am-11.45pm Sat, to 7pm Sun; ☑; MBarceloneta) A welcome addition to seafood-centric Barceloneta, El Ben Plantat serves a varied menu of small plates, with excellent vegetarian choices (hummus, guacamole and chips, tofu pâté, veggie burgers). On weekdays you'll also find multicourse lunch specials – mussels with potatoes, homemade felafel, veal stew, vegetable croquettes – good value at €8.

CAN MAÑO
SPANISH €

Map p286 (Carrer del Baluard 12; mains €7-12; ⏰9am-4pm Tue-Sat & 8-11pm Mon-Fri; MBarceloneta) It may look like a dive, but you'll need to be prepared to wait before being squeezed in at a packed table for a raucous night of *raciones* (full-plate-size tapas serving; posted on a board at the back) over a bottle of *turbio*. The seafood is abundant with first-rate squid, shrimp and fish served at rock-bottom prices.

BITÁCORA
TAPAS €

Map p286 (Carrer de Balboa 1; tapas €4-9; ⏰10am-11pm Mon-Fri, to 5pm Sat; MBarceloneta) This youthful little gem is a neighbourhood favourite for its simple but congenial ambience and well-priced tapas plates, which come in ample portions. There's also a small hidden terrace at the back. Top picks: *ceviche de pescado* (fish ceviche), *chipirones* (baby squid) and *gambas a la plancha* (grilled shrimp).

BALUARD BARCELONETA
BAKERY €

Map p286 (Carrer del Baluard 36; pastries €1-2.70; ⏰8am-9pm; MBarceloneta) One of the best bakeries in the city, Baluard serves up warm flaky croissants, perfect baguettes, moist muffins, and a range of tempting pastries and tarts (try one with figs or wild berries).

MAIANS
TAPAS €

Map p286 (☎93 221 10 20; Carrer de Sant Carles 28; tapas €4-7; ⏰1-4pm & 8-11pm Tue-Sat; MBarceloneta) This tiny jovial bar and eatery in Maians serves excellent tapas to a hip, largely neighbourhood crowd. Highlights include the not-to-be-missed *cazón en adobo* (marinated fried dogfish) and *mejillones a la marinera* (mussels in a rich tomato broth) followed by hearty *arròs negre* (paella with cuttlefish).

EL GUINDILLA
CATALAN €€

Map p286 (☎93 221 54 58; Carrer del Baluard 38; lunch specials €9.50; ⏰8am-5pm & 8pm-midnight Mon-Sat; MBarceloneta) In the Mercat de la Barceloneta, this popular new eatery serves tasty lunch specials and draws a tapas-munching and beer-drinking crowd by night. Peruse the market, then grab an outdoor table on the square.

BARRACA
SEAFOOD €€€

Map p286 (☎93 224 12 53; www.barraca-barcelona.com; Passeig Marítim de la Barceloneta 1; mains €19-29; ⏰1pm-midnight; MBarceloneta) Recently opened, this buzzing space has a great location fronting the Mediterranean – a key reference point in the excellent seafood dishes served up here. Start off with a cauldron of chilli-infused clams, cockles and mussels before moving on to the lavish paellas and other rice dishes, which steal the show.

CAN MAJÓ
SEAFOOD €€€

Map p286 (☎93 221 54 55; www.canmajo.es; Carrer del Almirall Aixada 23; mains €16-26; ⏰1-4pm Tue-Sun & 8-11.30pm Tue-Sat; 🚌45, 57, 59, 64 or 157, MBarceloneta) Virtually on the beach, Can Majó has a long and steady reputation for fine seafood, particularly its rice dishes and bountiful *suquets* (fish stews). The bouillabaisse of fish and seafood is succulent. Sit outside (there are heat lamps in winter) and admire the beach goers.

RESTAURANT 7 PORTES
SEAFOOD €€€

Map p286 (☎93 319 30 33; www.7portes.com; Passeig d'Isabel II 14; mains €16-32; ⏰1pm-1am; MBarceloneta) Founded in 1836 as a cafe and converted into a restaurant in 1929, 7 Portes is a classic. It exudes an old-world atmosphere with its wood panelling, tiles, mirrors and plaques naming some of the famous – such as Orson Welles – who have passed through. Paella is the speciality, or go for the surfeit of seafood in the *gran plat de marisc* (literally 'big plate of seafood').

TORRE D'ALTA MAR
MEDITERRANEAN €€€

Map p286 (☎93 221 00 07; www.torredealtamar.com; Torre de Sant Sebastià, Passeig de Joan Borbó 88; mains around €35; ⏰1-3.30pm Tue-Sat & 8-11.30pm daily; 🚌17, 39, 57 or 64, MBarceloneta) Head 75m skyward to the top of the Torre de Sant Sebastià and take a ringside seat for magnificent waterfront views while dining on seafood. Menu hits include prawn risotto, grilled sea bass and sirloin with zucchini flower tempura. Prices are steep and would seem poor value apart from the fine vistas.

CAN ROS
SEAFOOD €€€

Map p286 (☎93 221 45 79; Carrer del Almirall Aixada 7; mains €16-28; ⏰1-4.30pm & 7-11pm Tue-Sun; 🚌45, 57, 59, 64 or 157, MBarceloneta) The fifth generation is now at the controls of this immutable seafood favourite, which first opened in 1911. In a restaurant where the decor is a reminder of simpler times, there's a straightforward guiding principle: serve juicy fresh fish cooked with a light touch. Can Ros also does a rich *arròs a la marinera* (seafood rice), *fideuà* (similar to paella, but using vermicelli noodles as the base) with squid and mussels, and a grilled fish and seafood platter.

1881
SPANISH €€€

Map p286 (📞93 221 00 50; www.sagardi.com; Plaça de Pau Vila 3; mains €14-28; ⊘10am-midnight Tue-Sun; 🛜; ⓂBarceloneta) On the top floor of the Museu d'Història de Catalunya, 1881 serves excellent seafood plates to lovely views over the waterfront. Feel free to send away the unordered bread baskets and hors d'oeuvres, as these will be added to your bill. You can also stop in for coffee at the small cafe attached.

✕ Poblenou, Port Olímpic & El Fòrum

The Port Olímpic marina is lined on two sides by dozens of restaurants and tapas bars, popular in spring and summer but mostly underwhelming. A more upmarket series of places huddles at the northeast end of Platja de la Barceloneta – it's hard to beat the sand, sea and palm-tree backdrop. Otherwise, the search for culinary curios will take you behind the scenes in El Poblenou, where a few nuggets glitter.

EL TÍO CHÉ
SNACKS €

Map p288 (Rambla del Poblenou 44; snacks €2-4; ⊘10am-10pm; ⓂPoblenou) First opened back in 1912 (in El Born), this local icon is famed for its *horchata,* a sweet and refreshing if somewhat grainy drink made of tigernut milk. Some love it, others less so, though you can also opt for sandwiches, ice cream and other homemade beverages.

⭐CAN RECASENS
CATALAN €€

Map p288 (📞93 300 81 23; Rambla del Poblenou 102; mains €6-14; ⊘9pm-1am Mon-Sat & 1-4pm Sat; ⓂPoblenou) One of Poblenou's most romantic settings, Can Recasens hides a warren of warmly lit rooms full of oil paintings, flickering candles, fairy lights and baskets of fruit. The food is outstanding, with a mix of salads, fondues, smoked meats, cheeses, and open-faced sandwiches piled high with delicacies like wild mushrooms and brie, *escalivada* (grilled vegetables) and gruyère, and spicy chorizo.

ELS PESCADORS
SEAFOOD €€€

Map p288 (📞93 225 20 18; www.elspescadors.com; Plaça de Prim 1; mains €18-34; ⊘1-3.45pm & 8-11.30pm; ⓂPoblenou) Set on a picturesque square lined with low houses and *bella ombre* trees long ago imported from South America, this quaint family restaurant continues to serve some of the city's great grilled fish and seafood-and-rice dishes. There are three dining areas inside: two quite modern, while the main one preserves its old tavern flavour. On warm nights, though, try for a table outside.

EL CANGREJO LOCO
SEAFOOD €€€

Map p288 (📞93 221 05 33; www.elcangrejoloco.com; Moll de Gregal 29-30; mains €15-28, menú del día €26; ⊘1-4pm & 8pm-midnight; ⓂCiutadella Vila Olímpica) Of the hive of eating activity along the docks of Port Olímpic, the 'Mad Crab' is among the best. Fish standards, such as sea bass and monkfish, are served in various guises and melt in the mouth. For utter decadence, there's a seafood platter, which has lobster, prawns, razor clams, crayfish and other delights.

XIRINGUITO D'ESCRIBÀ
SEAFOOD €€€

Map p288 (📞93 221 07 29; www.xiringuito escriba.com; Ronda del Litoral 42; mains €15-32; ⊘1-4.30pm year-round, 8pm-midnight Thu-Sat Apr-Sep; ⓂLlacuna) The clan that brought you Escribà sweets and pastries also operates one of Barcelona's most popular waterfront seafood eateries. This is one of the few places where one person can order from a selection of paella and *fideuà* (normally reserved for a minimum of two people). You can also choose from a selection of Escribà pastries for dessert – worth the trip alone.

DRINKING & NIGHTLIFE

🍷 Port Vell & La Barceloneta

The northeastern end of the beach on the Barceloneta waterfront near Port Olímpic is a pleasant corner of evening chic that takes on a balmy, almost Caribbean air in the warmer months. A selection of restaurant-lounges and trendy bar-clubs vies for your attention. Several other attractive options are scattered about away from this core of night-time entertainment.

CAN PAIXANO
WINE BAR

Map p286 (☎93 310 08 39; Carrer de la Reina Cristina 7; tapas €3-6; ⊙9am-10.30pm Mon-Sat; ⓂBarceloneta) This lofty old champagne bar has long been run on a winning formula. The standard poison is bubbly rosé in elegant little glasses, combined with bite-sized *bocadillos* (filled rolls). This place is jammed to the rafters, and elbowing your way to the bar to ask harried staff for menu items can be a titanic struggle.

ABSENTA
BAR

Map p286 (Carrer de Sant Carles 36; ⊙7pm-2am Wed-Thu, from 1pm Sat & Sun; ⓂBarceloneta) Decorated with old paintings, vintage lamps and curious sculpture, this whimsical and creative drinking den takes its liquor seriously. Stop in for the house-made vermouth or for more bite try one of the many absinthes on hand. Absenta gathers a hipsterish but easygoing crowd.

KÉ?
BAR

Map p286 (Carrer del Baluard 54; ⊙noon-2am; ⓂBarceloneta) An eclectic and happy crowd hangs about this small bohemian bar run by a friendly Dutchman. Pull up a padded 'keg chair' or grab a seat on one of the worn lounges at the back and join in the animated conversation wafting out over the street. Outdoor seating in summer, just a few steps from Barceloneta's market.

BAR LEO
BAR

Map p286 (Carrer de Sant Carles 34; ⊙noon-9.30pm; ⓂBarceloneta) Bar Leo is a hole-in-the-wall drinking spot plastered with images of late Andalucian singer and heart-throb Bambino, and a jukebox mostly dedicated to flamenco. For a youthful, almost entirely *barcelonin* crowd, Bar Leo is it! It's liveliest on weekends.

OPIUM MAR
CLUB

Map p286 (☎902 267486; www.opiummar.com; Passeig Marítim de la Barceloneta 34; admission €10-20; ⊙8pm-6am; ⓂCiutadella Vila Olímpica) This seaside dance place has a spacious dance floor that attracts a mostly North American crowd. It only begins to fill from about 3am and is best in summer, when you can spill onto a terrace overlooking the beach. The beachside outdoor section works as a chilled restaurant-cafe.

CDLC
LOUNGE

Map p286 (www.cdlcbarcelona.com; Passeig Marítim de la Barceloneta 32; ⊙noon-4am; ⓂCiutadella Vila Olímpica) Seize the night by the scruff at the Carpe Diem Lounge Club, where you can lounge in Asian-inspired surrounds. Ideal for a slow warm-up before heading to the nearby clubs. You can come for the food (quite good, but pricey) or wait until about midnight, when they roll up the tables and the DJs and dancers take full control.

SANTA MARTA
BAR

Map p286 (Carrer de Guitert 60; ⊙9.30am-midnight; 🚌45, 57, 59 or 157, ⓂBarceloneta) This chilled bar just back from the beach attracts a garrulous mix of locals and expats, who come for light meals, beers and prime people-watching at one of the outdoor tables near the boardwalk. It has some tempting food too: a mix of local and Italian items, with a range of satisfying sandwiches.

📍 Poblenou, Port Olímpic & El Fòrum

Several options present themselves along the coast. The line-up of raucous bars along the marina at Port Olímpic is one. More chilled are the beach bars. In deepest Poblenou you'll find a small but appealing selection of nightspots, attracting mostly locals.

BHARMA
BAR

Map p288 (www.bharma.com; Carrer de Pere IV 93; ⊙8am-5pm Mon-Fri & 6pm-3am Fri & Sat; ⓂLlacuna) Located in Barcelona's Poblenou district, Bharma is a wildly configured bar that pays homage to the American TV series, *Lost*. Its stone-lined interior is reminiscent of the bunker-like 'hatch', save for the tail end of a plane wreck imbedded in one wall. In the bathroom, you'll hear the eerie racket of 'the smoke monster', and there is of course Bharma Initiative beer, an (almost) exact duplication of the Dharma logo.

☆ ENTERTAINMENT

RAZZMATAZZ
LIVE MUSIC

Map p288 (☎93 320 82 00; www.salarazzmatazz. com; Carrer de Pamplona 88; admission €12-32; ⊙midnight-3.30am Thu, to 5.30am Fri & Sat; ⓂMarina, Bogatell) Bands from far and wide occasionally create scenes of near hysteria in this, one of the city's classic live-music and clubbing venues. Bands can appear throughout the week (check the website), with different start times. On weekends the live music then gives way to club sounds.

Five different clubs in one huge post-industrial space attract people of all dance persuasions and ages. The main space, the Razz Club, is a haven for the latest international rock and indie acts. The Loft does house and electro, while the Pop Bar offers anything from garage to soul. The Lolita room is the land of house, hip-hop and dubstep, and upstairs in the Rex Room guys and girls sweat it out to experimental sounds.

SHÔKO
DJ

Map p286 (www.shoko.biz; Passeig Marítim de la Barceloneta 36; ☻noon-3am Tue-Sun; Ⓜ️Ciutadella Vila Olímpica) This stylish restaurant, club and beachfront bar brings in a touch of the Far East via potted bamboo, Japanese electro and Asian-Med fusion cuisine. As the food is cleared away, Shôko transforms into a deep-grooving nightspot with DJs spinning for the beautiful crowd. The open-sided beachfront lounge is a popular spot for a sundowner.

CATWALK
CLUB

Map p286 (☎93 224 07 40; www.clubcatwalk. net; Carrer de Ramon Trias Fargas 2-4; admission €15-18; ☻11pm-6am Thu-Sun; Ⓜ️Ciutadella Vila Olímpica) A well-dressed crowd piles in here for good house music, occasionally mellowed down with more body-hugging electro, R&B, hip-hop and funk. Alternatively, you can sink into a fat lounge for a quiet tipple and whisper. Popular local DJ Raúl Orellana leads the way most nights.

TEATRE NACIONAL
DE CATALUNYA
PERFORMING ARTS

Map p288 (☎93 306 57 00; www.tnc.cat; Plaça de les Arts 1; admission €12-30; ☻box office 3-8pm Wed-Fri, 3-9.30pm Sat, 3-6pm Sun & 1hr before show; Ⓜ️Glòries or Monumental) Ricard Bofill's ultraneoclassical theatre, with its bright, airy foyer, hosts a wide range of performances, including dramas, comedies, musicals and dance performances. Some shows are free.

L'AUDITORI
CLASSICAL MUSIC

Map p288 (☎93 247 93 00; www.auditori.org; Carrer de Lepant 150; admission €10-51; ☻box office 5-9pm Tue-Fri, 10am-1pm & 5-9pm Sat; Ⓜ️Monumental) Barcelona's modern home for serious music lovers, L'Auditori puts on plenty of orchestral, chamber, religious and other mu-

sic. The ultramodern building (designed by Rafael Moneo) is home to the Orquestra Simfònica de Barcelona i Nacional de Catalunya.

MONASTERIO
LIVE MUSIC

Map p286 (☎93 319 19 88; Passeig d'Isabel II 4; ☻9pm-2.30am; Ⓜ️Barceloneta) Wander downstairs to the brick vaults of this jamming basement music den. There's a little of everything, currently jazz on Sunday nights, *forró* (music from northeastern Brazil) on Wednesdays, blues on Thursdays, and eclectic fare (usually rock) on Fridays and Saturdays.

YELMO CINES ICÀRIA
CINEMA

Map p288 (☎902 220922; www.yelmocines.es; Carrer de Salvador Espriú 61; Ⓜ️Ciutadella Vila Olímpica) This vast cinema complex screens movies in the original language on 15 screens, making for plenty of choice. Aside from the screens, you'll find several cheerful eateries, bars and the like.

🛍 SHOPPING

Aside from several weekend markets and the mall mayhem of Maremàgnum, there aren't many shopping options along the waterfront.

MAREMÀGNUM
MALL

Map p286 (www.maremagnum.es; Moll d'Espanya 5; ☻10am-10pm; Ⓜ️Drassanes) Created out of largely abandoned docks, this buzzing shopping centre, with its bars, restaurants and cinemas, is pleasant enough for a stroll virtually in the middle of the old harbour. The usual labels are on hand, including the Spanish chain Mango, mega-retailer H&M and eye-catching fashions from Barcelona-based Desigual. Football fans will be drawn to the paraphernalia at FC Botiga. It's particularly popular on Sundays when most other stores in the city remain shuttered.

BESTIARI
BOOKS, HANDICRAFTS

Map p286 (Plaça de Pau Vila 3; ☻10am-7pm Tue-Sat, to 2.30pm Sun; Ⓜ️Barceloneta) On the ground floor of the Museu d'Història de Catalunya, this nicely stocked shop sells books in English, Spanish and Catalan for all ages, plus you'll find lots of Catalan-themed gift ideas: CDs, T-shirts, umbrellas, messenger bags, chess sets, mugs and toys (along the lines of the build-your-own Gothic or Gaudí structures).

WATERFRONT MARKETS

On weekends Port Vell springs to life with a handful of markets selling a mix of antiques and contemporary art and crafts at key points along the waterfront.

At the base of La Rambla, the small **Port Antic** (Map p286; Plaça del Portal de la Pau; ☺10am-8pm Sat & Sun; ⓂDrassanes) market is a requisite stop for strollers and antique hunters. Here you'll find old photographs, frames, oil paintings, records, shawls, cameras, vintage toys and other odds and ends.

Near the Palau de Mar, you'll find **Feria de Artesanía del Palau de Mar** (Map p286; Moll del Dipòsit; ☺11am-8pm Sat & Sun; ⓂBarceloneta), with artisans selling a range of crafty items, including jewellery, graphic T-shirts, handwoven hats, fragrant candles and soaps, scarves and decorative items. In July and August the market runs daily.

Take a stroll along the pedestrian-only Rambla de Mar to reach the weekend art fair **Mercado de Pintores** (Map p286; Passeig d'Ítaca; ☺10am-8pm Sat & Sun; ⓂDrassanes), with a broad selection of paintings both collectable and rather forgettable.

MERCAT DE LA BARCELONETA MARKET

Map p286 (☏93 221 64 71; www.mercatdelabarceloneta.com; Plaça de la Font 1; ☺7am-3pm Mon-Thu & Sat, 7am-8pm Fri; ⓂBarceloneta) Set in a modern glass and steel building fronting a long plaza in the heart of Barceloneta, this airy market has the usual array of fresh veg and seafood stalls, as well as several places where you can enjoy a sit-down meal. El Guindilla (p117) deserves special mention for its good-value lunch specials and outdoor seating on the plaza.

ELS ENCANTS VELLS MARKET

Map p288 (Fira de Bellcaire; ☏93 246 30 30; www.encantsbcn.com; Plaça de les Glòries Catalanes; ☺8am-8pm Mon, Wed, Fri & Sat; ⓂGlòries) In a gleaming open-sided complex near Plaça de les Glòries Catalanes, the 'Old Charms' flea market is the biggest of its kind in Barcelona. Over 500 vendors ply their wares beneath massive mirror-like panels. It's all here, from antique furniture through to second-hand clothes. A lot of it is junk, but occasionally you'll stumble across a *ganga* (bargain). The most interesting time to be here is from 8am to 9.30am on Monday, Wednesday and Friday, when the public auctions take place.

🏃 SPORTS & ACTIVITIES

If gazing at the deep blue Mediterranean leaves you yearning for something a bit more immersive, there are plenty of ways to experience the life aquatic from joining a harbour cruise to trying your hand at stand-up paddleboarding.

BOARDRIDERS BARCELONETA WATER SPORTS

Map p286 (☏93 221 44 91; Carrer de la Drassana 10; ☺10am-8pm Mon-Sat, from 11am Sun; ⓂBarceloneta) Facing the seafront, Boardriders rents out surfboards (per hour/half-day €12/25), stand-up paddleboards (per hour/half-day €15/30) and wetsuits. It also sells gear.

ORSOM CRUISE

Map p286 (☏93 441 05 37; www.barcelona-orsom.com; Moll de les Drassanes; adult/child €16.50/11; ☺Apr-Oct; ⓂDrassanes) Aboard a large catamaran, Orsom makes the 90-minute journey to Port Olímpic and back. There are three departures per day (four on weekends in July and August), and the last is a jazz cruise, around sunset. There's also five daily, 50-minute speedboat tours (adult/child €12.50/11).

BC NAVAL TOURS BOAT TOUR

Map p286 (☏93 795 85 68; www.barcelonanavaltours.com; Moll de las Drassanes; cruise 40/80min €7.50/12; ⓂDrassanes) One of several companies running boat cruises from the dock near Mirador de Colom. The 75-minute catamaran tour takes you out past Barceloneta and up to Port Olímpic and back. If you just want a peek at the area around the port, you can opt for the 40-minute excursion to the breakwater and back. Both run throughout the day.

CLUB NATACIÓ ATLÈTIC-BARCELONA SWIMMING

Map p286 (www.cnab.cat; Plaça del Mar; day pass adult/child €12.20/7.10; ☺7am-11pm Mon-Sat, 8am-8pm Sun; ☒17, 39, 57 or 64, ⓂBarceloneta) This club has one indoor and two outdoor pools. Of the latter, one is heated for lap swimming in winter. Admission includes use of the gym and private beach access.

La Sagrada Família & L'Eixample

L'ESQUERRA DE L'EIXAMPLE | LA DRETA DE L'EIXAMPLE

Neighbourhood Top Five

1 Seeing history being made at **La Sagrada Família** (p124).

2 Witnessing ground-breaking architecture at **La Pedrera** (p131).

3 Marvelling at the almost-alive, swirling interior of the **Casa Batlló** (p130).

4 Deciphering contemporary art at the fascinating **Fundació Antoni Tàpies** (p129).

5 Admiring a lesser-known masterpiece of Modernisme at the **Recinte Modernista de Sant Pau** (p133).

For more detail of this area see maps on p290 and p294 ▶

Explore: L'Eixample

L'Eixample's grid of streets is home to most of the city's most expensive shops and hotels, and range of restaurants and bars. This is where you'll find most Modernista architecture, most spectacularly along Passeig de Gràcia, where you'll find Gaudí's La Pedrera and the Manzana de la Discordia, which comprises three Modernista gems by the three top architects of the period.

Eating is at the high end, while drinking and nightlife are student- and gay-oriented. The obvious streets to start on are Passeig de Gràcia (with a line-up of international names) and the appealing, parallel, tree-lined Rambla de Catalunya. La Dreta (the Right) de L'Eixample, stretching from Passeig de Gràcia to Passeig de Sant Joan and beyond, contains much sought-after real estate. Beyond, it takes on a dowdy feel, even around La Sagrada Família. L'Esquerra (the Left) de L'Eixample, running southwest from Passeig de Gràcia, changes character several times. The whole area between Carrer d'Aribau, Passeig de Sant Joan, Avinguda Diagonal and the Ronda de Sant Pere has been known since the early 20th century as the Quadrat d'Or (Golden Square) thanks to its extravagant architecture and grand houses. The area is now home to high-end shops selling a wide range, from teak furniture to designer clothes, gourmet nibbles and shoes.

At night L'Esquerra de L'Eixample has its own flavour. From Thursday to Saturday, Carrer d'Aribau becomes a busy nightlife axis, with a range of bars north of Carrer de Mallorca (and spilling north over Avinguda Diagonal). Closer to the Universitat is the heart of the 'Gaixample', a cluster of gay and gay-friendly bars and clubs in an area bounded by Carrer de Balmes and Carrer de Muntaner.

Local Life

→ **Student life** The presence of the Universitat de Barcelona (p131) makes for a line of unpretentious hang-outs nearby on the Carrer d'Enric Granados.

→ **Coffee with a view** Take a lift to the very top of El Corte Inglés (p144) for a cafe with a great view.

→ **Say it with flowers** Walking round the Flores Navarro (p142), a cathedral to colourful plant life, is quite a trip at 4am.

Getting There & Away

→ **Metro** Four metro lines criss-cross L'Eixample, three stopping at Passeig de Gràcia for the Manzana de la Discordia. Línia 3 stops at Diagonal for La Pedrera, while Línies 2 and 5 stop at Sagrada Família.

→ **Train** FGC lines from Plaça de Catalunya take you one stop to Provença, in the heart of L'Eixample.

 Best Places to Eat

→ Tapas 24 (p137)
→ Can Kenji (p137)
→ Cinc Sentits (p136)
→ Cata 1.81 (p136)
→ Cerveseria Catalana (p134)

For reviews, see p134 →

 Best Places to Drink

→ Dry Martini (p138)
→ Monvínic (p138)
→ Milano (p138)
→ Les Gens Que J'Aime (p140)

For reviews, see p138 →

 Best Places to Shop

→ Vinçon (p141)
→ Flores Navarro (p142)
→ El Bulevard dels Antiquaris (p142)
→ Joan Múrria (p142)

For reviews, see p141 →

LA SAGRADA FAMÍLIA & L'EIXAMPLE

TOP SIGHT
LA SAGRADA FAMÍLIA

If you have time for only one sightseeing outing, this should be it. La Sagrada Família inspires awe by its sheer verticality, and, in the manner of the medieval cathedrals it emulates, it's still under construction after more than 100 years. When completed, the highest tower will be more than half as high again as those that stand today.

A Holy Mission

The Temple Expiatori de la Sagrada Família (Expiatory Temple of the Holy Family) was Antoni Gaudí's all-consuming obsession. Given the commission by a conservative society that wished to build a temple as atonement for the city's sins of modernity, Gaudí saw its completion as his holy mission. As funds dried up, he contributed his own, and in the last years of his life he was never shy of pleading with anyone he thought a likely donor.

Gaudí devised a temple 95m long and 60m wide, able to seat 13,000 people, with a central tower 170m high above the transept (representing Christ) and another 17 of 100m or more. The 12 along the three facades represent the Apostles, while the remaining five represent the Virgin Mary and the four evangelists. With his characteristic dislike for straight lines (there were none in nature, he said), Gaudí gave his towers swelling outlines inspired by the weird peaks of the holy mountain Montserrat outside Barcelona, and encrusted them with a tangle of sculpture that seems an outgrowth of the stone.

At Gaudí's death, only the crypt, the apse walls, one portal and one tower had been finished. Three more towers were added by 1930, completing the northeast (Nativity) facade. In 1936 anarchists burned and smashed the interior, including workshops, plans and models.

DON'T MISS...

➡ The apse, the extraordinary pillars and stained glass
➡ Nativity Facade
➡ Passion Facade
➡ Museu Gaudí

PRACTICALITIES

➡ Map p294
➡ ☎93 207 30 31
➡ www.sagrada familia.cat
➡ Carrer de Mallorca 401
➡ adult/child under 11yr/senior & student €14.80/free/12.80
➡ ◷9am-8pm Apr-Sep, to 6pm Oct-Mar
➡ Ⓜ Sagrada Família

Work began again in 1952, but controversy has always clouded progress. Opponents of the continuation of the project claim that the computer models based on what little of Gaudí's plans survived the anarchists' ire have led to the creation of a monster that has little to do with Gaudí's plans and style. It is a debate that appears to have little hope of resolution. Like or hate what is being done, the fascination it awakens is undeniable.

Guesses on when construction might be complete range from the 2020s to the 2040s. Even before reaching that point, some of the oldest parts of the church, especially the apse, have required restoration work.

The Interior & the Apse

Inside, work on roofing over the church was completed in 2010. The roof is held up by a forest of extraordinary angled pillars. As the pillars soar towards the ceiling, they sprout a web of supporting branches, creating the effect of a forest canopy. The tree image is in no way fortuitous – Gaudí envisaged such an effect. Everything was thought through, including the shape and placement of windows to create the mottled effect one would see with sunlight pouring through the branches of a thick forest.

The pillars are made from four different types of stone. They vary in colour and load-bearing strength, from the soft Montjuïc stone pillars along the lateral aisles through to granite, dark grey basalt and finally burgundy-tinged Iranian porphyry for the key columns at the intersection of the nave and transept. The stained glass, divided in shades of red, blue, green and ochre, creates a hypnotic, magical atmosphere when the sun hits the windows. Tribunes built high above the aisles can host two choirs: the main tribune up to 1300 people and the children's tribune up to 300.

Nativity Facade

The Nativity Facade is the artistic pinnacle of the building, mostly created under Gaudí's personal supervision. You can climb high up inside some of the four towers by a combination of lifts and narrow spiral staircases – a vertiginous experience. Do not climb the stairs if you have cardiac or respiratory problems. The towers are destined to hold tubular bells capable of playing complex music at great volume. Their upper parts are decorated with mosaics spelling out *'Sanctus, Sanctus, Sanctus, Hosanna in Excelsis, Amen, Alleluia'*. Asked why he lavished so much care on the tops of the spires, which no one would see from close up, Gaudí answered: 'The angels will see them.'

A HIDDEN PORTRAIT

Careful observation of the Passion Facade will reveal a special tribute from sculptor Josep Subirachs to Gaudí. The central sculptural group (below Christ crucified) shows, from right to left, Christ bearing his cross, Veronica displaying the cloth with Christ's bloody image, a pair of soldiers and, watching it all, a man called the evangelist. Subirachs used a rare photo of Gaudí, taken a couple of years before his death, as the model for the evangelist's face.

Unfinished it may be, but La Sagrada Família attracts around 2.8 million visitors a year and is the most visited monument in Spain. The most significant tourist in recent times was Pope Benedict XVI, who consecrated the church in a huge ceremony in November 2010.

La Sagrada Família

A TIMELINE

1882 Francesc del Villar is commissioned to construct a neo-Gothic church.

1883 Antoni Gaudí takes over as chief architect, and plans a far more ambitious church to hold 13,000 faithful.

1926 Death of Gaudí; work continues under Domènec Sugrañes. Much of the apse ❶ and Nativity Facade ❷ is complete.

1930 Bell towers ❸ of the Nativity Facade completed.

1936 Construction is interrupted by Spanish Civil War; anarchists destroy Gaudí's plans.

1939-40 Architect Francesc de Paula Quintana i Vidal restores the crypt and meticulously reassembles many of Gaudí's lost models, some of which can be seen in the museum ❹.

1976 Completion of Passion Facade ❺.

1986-2006 Sculptor Josep Subirachs adds sculptural details to the Passion Facade including the panels telling the story of Christ's last days, amid much criticism for employing a style far removed from what was thought typical of Gaudí.

2000 Central nave vault ❻ completed.

2010 Church completely roofed over; Pope Benedict XVI consecrates the church; work begins on a high-speed rail tunnel that will pass beneath the church's Glory Facade ❼.

2020-40 Projected completion date.

TOP TIPS

» **Light** The best light through the stained-glass windows of the Passion Facade bursts through into the heart of the church in the late afternoon.

» **Time** Visit at opening time on week-days to avoid the worst of the crowds.

» **Views** Head up the Nativity Facade bell towers for the views, as long queues generally await at the Passion Facade towers.

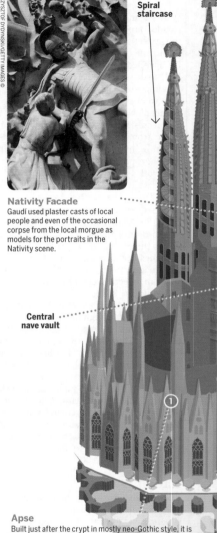

Spiral staircase

Nativity Facade
Gaudí used plaster casts of local people and even of the occasional corpse from the local morgue as models for the portraits in the Nativity scene.

Central nave vault

Apse
Built just after the crypt in mostly neo-Gothic style, it is capped by pinnacles that show a hint of the genius that Gaudí would later deploy in the rest of the church.

KRZYSZTOF DYDYNSKI/GETTY IMAGES ©

CALLE MONTES/GETTY IMAGES ©

Bell towers
The towers (eight completed) of the three facades represent the 12 Apostles. Lifts whisk visitors up one tower of the Nativity and Passion Facades (the latter gets longer queues) for fine views.

③

Completed church
Along with the Glory Facade and its four towers, six other towers remain to be completed. They will represent the four Evangelists, the Virgin Mary and, soaring above them all over the transept, a 170m colossus symbolising Christ.

Glory Facade
This will be the most fanciful facade of all, with a narthex boasting 16 hyperboloid lanterns topped by cones that will look something like an organ made of melting ice cream.

⑦

⑥

Museu Gaudí
Jammed with old photos, drawings and restored plaster models that bring Gaudí's ambitions to life, the museum also houses an extraordinarily complex plumb-line device he used to calculate his constructions.

⑤

④

Escoles de Gaudí

Crypt
e first completed
art of the church,
the crypt is in
rgely neo-Gothic
style and lies
der the transept.
udí's burial place
here can be seen
from the Museu
Gaudí.

Passion Facade
See the story of Christ's last days from Last Supper to burial in an S-shaped sequence from bottom to top of the facade. Check out the cryptogram in which the numbers always add up to 33, Christ's age at his death.

Three sections of the portal represent, from left to right, Hope, Charity and Faith. Among the forest of sculpture on the Charity portal you can see, low down, the manger surrounded by an ox, an ass, the shepherds and kings, and angel musicians. Some 30 different species of plant from around Catalonia are reproduced here, and the faces of the many figures are taken from plaster casts done of local people and the occasional one made from corpses in the local morgue.

Directly above the blue stained-glass window is the archangel Gabriel's Annunciation to Mary. At the top is a green cypress tree, a refuge in a storm for the white doves of peace dotted over it. The mosaic work at the pinnacle of the towers is made from Murano glass, from Venice.

To the right of the facade is the curious Claustre del Roser, a Gothic style minicloister tacked on to the outside of the church (rather than the classic square enclosure of the great Gothic church monasteries). Once inside, look back to the intricately decorated entrance. On the lower right-hand side you'll notice the sculpture of a reptilian devil handing a terrorist a bomb. Barcelona was regularly rocked by political violence, and bombings were frequent in the decades prior to the civil war. The sculpture is one of several on the 'temptations of men and women'.

Passion Facade

The southwest Passion Facade, on the theme of Christ's last days and death, was built between 1954 and 1978 based on surviving drawings by Gaudí, with four towers and a large, sculpture-bedecked portal. The sculptor, Josep Subirachs, worked on its decoration from 1986 to 2006. He did not attempt to imitate Gaudí, rather, producing angular, controversial images of his own. The main series of sculptures, on three levels, are in an S-shaped sequence, starting with the Last Supper at the bottom left and ending with Christ's burial at the top right. Decorative work on the Passion Facade continues even today, as construction of the Glory Facade moves ahead.

To the right, in front of the Passion Facade, the Escoles de Gaudí is one of his simpler gems. Gaudí built this as a children's school, creating an original, undulating roof of brick that continues to charm architects to this day. Inside is a recreation of Gaudí's modest office as it was when he died, and explanations of the geometric patterns and plans at the heart of his building techniques.

Glory Facade

The Glory Facade is under construction and will, like the others, be crowned by four towers – the total of 12 representing the Twelve Apostles. Gaudí wanted it to be the most magnificent facade of the church. Inside will be the narthex, a kind of foyer made up of 16 'lanterns', a series of hyperboloid forms topped by cones. Further decoration will make the whole building a microcosmic symbol of the Christian church, with Christ represented by a massive 170m central tower above the transept, and the five remaining planned towers symbolising the Virgin Mary and the four evangelists.

Museu Gaudí

Open the same times as the church, the Museu Gaudí, below ground level, includes interesting material on Gaudí's life and other works, as well as models and photos of La Sagrada Família. You can see a good example of his plumb-line models that showed him the stresses and strains he could get away with in construction. A side hall towards the eastern end of the museum leads to a viewing point above the simple crypt in which the genius is buried. The crypt, where Mass is now held, can also be visited from the Carrer de Mallorca side of the church.

◉ SIGHTS

◉ L'Esquerra de L'Eixample

CASA BATLLÓ · ARCHITECTURE
See p130.

FUNDACIÓ ANTONI TÀPIES · GALLERY
Map p290 (☑93 487 03 15; www.fundaciota-pies.org; Carrer d'Aragó 255; adult/concession €7/5.60; ◷10am-7pm Tue-Sun; ⓂPasseig de Grà-cia) The Fundació Antoni Tàpies is both a pioneering Modernista building (completed in 1885) and the major collection of leading 20th-century Catalan artist Antoni Tàpies. A man known for his esoteric work, Tàpies died in February 2012, aged 88; he left be-hind a powerful range of paintings and a foundation intended to promote contempor-ary artists.

The building, designed by Domènech i Montaner for the publishing house Edito-rial Montaner i Simón (run by a cousin of the architect), combines a brick-covered iron frame with Islamic-inspired decora-tion. Tàpies crowned it with the meander-ings of his own mind, a work called *Núvol i Cadira* (Cloud and Chair) that spirals above the building like a storm.

Although it's difficult to understand the art of Antoni Tàpies, it's worth seeing the one-hour documentary on his life, on the top floor, to understand his influences, method and the course of his interesting life. In his work, Tàpies expressed a number of themes, such as left-wing politics and humanitar-ianism; the practices of Zen meditation and its relationship between nature and insight; incarnation as seen in Christian faith; and art as alchemy or magic.

He launched the Fundació in 1984 to promote contemporary art, donating a large part of his own work. The collection spans the arc of Tàpies' creations (with more than 800 works) and contributions from other contemporary artists. In the main exhibition area (level 1, upstairs) you can see an ever-changing selection of around 20 of Tàpies's works, from early self-portraits of the 1940s to grand items like *Jersei Negre* (Black Jumper; 2008). Level 2 hosts a small space for temporary exhibi-tions. Rotating exhibitions take place in the basement levels.

CASA LLEÓ MORERA · ARCHITECTURE
Map p290 (☑93 676 27 33; www.casalleomorera.com; Passeig de Gràcia 35; adult/concession/child under 12yr €15/13.50/free; ◷guided tour in English 10am Mon-Sat; ⓂPasseig de Gràcia) Domènech i Montaner's 1905 contribution to the Manzana de la Discordia, with Mod-ernista carving outside and a bright, tiled lobby in which floral motifs predominate, is perhaps the least odd-looking of the three main buildings on the block. In 2014 part of the building was opened to the public (by guided tour only), so you can appreciate the 1st floor, giddy with swirling sculptures, rich mosaics and whimsical decor.

CASA AMATLLER · ARCHITECTURE
Map p290 (☑93 487 72 17; www.amatller.org; Pas-seig de Gràcia 41; tour €10; ◷tour Sat; ⓂPasseig de Gràcia) FREE One of Puig i Cadafalch's most striking bits of Modernista fantasy, Casa Amatller combines Gothic window frames with a stepped gable borrowed from Dutch urban architecture. But the busts and reliefs of dragons, knights and other characters dripping off the main facade are pure caprice. The pillared foyer and stair-case lit by stained glass are like the inside of some romantic castle. The building was ren-ovated in 1900 for the chocolate baron and philanthropist Antoni Amatller (1851–1910) and it will one day open partly to the public. Renovation – still continuing at the time of research – will see the 1st (main) floor con-verted into a museum, while the 2nd floor will house the Institut Amatller d'Art His-panic (Amatller Institute of Hispanic Art).

For now, you can wander into the foyer, admire the staircase and lift, and head through the shop to see the latest tempo-rary exhibition out the back. Depending on the state of renovation, it is also possible to join a 1½-hour guided tour of the 1st floor, with its early-20th-century furniture and decor intact, and Amatller's photo studio. These are generally held on Saturdays; check the website for details.

Amatller was a keen traveller and photo-grapher (his absorbing shots of turn-of-the-20th-century Morocco are occasionally on show). The tour also includes a tasting of Amatller chocolates in the original kitchen.

PALAU ROBERT · EXHIBITION
Map p290 (☑93 238 40 00; www.gencat.cat/palaurobert; Passeig de Gràcia 107; ◷10am-8pm Mon-Sat, to 2.30pm Sun; ⓂDiagonal) FREE Catalonia's regional tourist office, which

TOP SIGHT
CASA BATLLÓ

This is Gaudí at his hallucinatory best: one of the strangest residential buildings in Europe. The facade, sprinkled with bits of blue, mauve and green tiles and studded with wave-shaped window frames and balconies, rises to an uneven blue-tiled roof with a solitary tower. Casa Batlló and neighbouring Casa Amatller (p129) and Casa Lleó Morera (p129) were all renovated between 1898 and 1906, and together demonstrate Modernisme's eclecticism.

Locals know Casa Batlló as the *casa dels ossos* (house of bones) or *casa del drac* (house of the dragon). The balconies look like the bony jaws of some strange beast and the roof represents Sant Jordi (St George) and the dragon. Even the roof was built to represent the shape of an animal's back, with shiny scales. Before going inside, take a look at the pavement. Each paving piece carries stylised images of an octopus and a starfish, designs Gaudí originally cooked up for Casa Batlló. The Manzana de la Discordia is still known by its Spanish name to preserve a pun on *manzana*, which means 'block' and 'apple'. In Greek mythology, the original Apple of Discord was tossed onto Mt Olympus by Eris (Discord), with orders that it be given to the most beautiful goddess, sparking jealousies that were the catalyst for the Trojan War.

DON'T MISS...

➡ The facade and balconies
➡ The swirling interior
➡ The dragon-back roof

PRACTICALITIES

➡ Map p290
➡ ☎93 216 03 06
➡ www.casabatllo.es
➡ Passeig de Gràcia 43
➡ adult/concession/child under 7yr €21.50/€18.50/free
➡ ⏰9am-9pm
➡ Ⓜ Passeig de Gràcia

holds a huge range of books and leaflets, also serves as an exhibition space, mostly for those with Catalan themes. In summer concerts are occasionally held in the peaceful gardens at the back of this fine building or in its main hall.

FUNDACIÓN FRANCISCO GODIA GALLERY
Map p290 (☎93 272 31 80; www.fundacionfgodia.org; Carrer de la Diputació 250; adult/child under 6yr/student €6/free/3; ⏰10am-8pm Mon & Wed-Sat, 10am-3pm Sun; Ⓜ Passeig de Gràcia) Francisco Godia (1921–90), head of one of Barcelona's great establishment families, liked fast cars (he came sixth in the 1956 Grand Prix season driving Maserati) and fine art. An intriguing mix of medieval art, ceramics and modern paintings make up this varied private collection. Housed in Casa Garriga Nogués, this is a stunning, carefully restored Modernista residence originally built for a rich banking family by Enric Sagnier in 1902–05.

The ground floor is given over to a display of Godia's driving trophies (and goggles) and a video on his feats behind the wheel, as well as occasional temporary exhibitions.

The art is up the languidly curvaceous marble stairway on the 1st floor and organised along roughly chronological lines across 17 rooms. The first five are given over mostly to Romanesque and Gothic wooden sculptures. Some of these are especially arresting because of their well-preserved colouring. The early-14th-century wood cut of Joseph of Armithea (room 1), with its bright red, pyjama-like outfit, is a case in point. Jaume Huguet is represented in room 5 by *Santa Maria Magdalena,* a bright, Gothic representation of Mary Magdalene dressed in red ermine.

Room 6 is a long and overwhelming rococo room with aqua-green walls and a selection of Godia's extensive ceramics collection, with pieces from all the historic porcelain production centres in Spain (including Manises in Valencia and Talavera de la Reina in Castilla-La Mancha). Admire the fine Modernista stained-glass windows in room 8.

Godia's interests ranged from the Neapolitan baroque painter Luca Giordano to Catalan Modernisme and Valencia's Joaquim Sorolla. Room 17 has works by Modernista and Noucentista painters, like Ramon Casas and Santiago Rusiñol. There's even a modest Miró.

MUSEU DEL MODERNISME CATALÀ MUSEUM

Map p290 (☎93 272 28 96; www.mmcat.cat; Carrer de Balmes 48; adult/concession €10/8.50; ⊙10am-8pm Mon-Sat, to 2pm Sun; ⓂPasseig de Gràcia) Housed in a Modernista building, the ground floor seems like a big Modernista furniture showroom. Several items by Antoni Gaudí, including chairs from Casa Batlló and a mirror from Casa Calvet, are supplemented by items by his lesser-known contemporaries, including some typically whimsical, mock medieval pieces by Puig i Cadafalch. The basement, showing off Modernista traits like mosaic-coated pillars, bare brick vaults and metal columns, is lined with Modernista art, including paintings by Ramon Casas and Santiago Rusiñol, and statues by Josep Llimona and Eusebi Arnau.

MUSEU DEL PERFUM MUSEUM

Map p290 (☎93 216 01 21; www.museudelperfum.com; Passeig de Gràcia 39; adult/child €5/3; ⊙10.30am-2pm & 4.30-8pm Mon-Fri, 11am-2pm Sat; ⓂPasseig de Gràcia) Housed in the back of the Regia (p145) perfume store, this museum contains everything from ancient Egyptian and Roman (the latter mostly from the 1st to 3rd centuries AD) scent receptacles to classic eau de cologne bottles – all in all, some 5000 bottles of infinite shapes, sizes and histories. You can admire anything from ancient bronze Etruscan tweezers to little early-19th-century potpourris made of fine Sèvres porcelain. Also on show are old catalogues and advertising posters.

UNIVERSITAT DE BARCELONA ARCHITECTURE

Map p290 (☎93 402 11 00; www.ub.edu; Gran Via de les Corts Catalanes 585; ⊙9am-9pm Mon-Fri; ⓂUniversitat) Although a university was first set up on what is now La Rambla in the 16th century, the present, glorious mix of (neo) Romanesque, Gothic, Islamic and Mudéjar architecture is a caprice of the 19th century (built 1863–82). Wander into the main hall, up the grand staircase and around the various leafy cloisters, or take a stroll in the rear gardens. On the 1st floor, the main hall for big occasions is the Mudéjar-style Paranimfo.

MUSEU I CENTRE D'ESTUDIS DE L'ESPORT DR MELCIOR COLET MUSEUM

Map p290 (☎93 419 22 32; Carrer de Buenos Aires 56-58; ⊙9am-2pm Mon-Fri; ⓂHospital Clínic) **FREE** Puig i Cadafalch's Casa Company (1911) looks like an odd Tyrolean country

---

TOP SIGHT
LA PEDRERA

This undulating beast is another madcap Gaudí masterpiece, built from 1905 to 1910 as a combined apartment and office block. Formally called Casa Milà after the businessman who commissioned it, it is better known as La Pedrera (the Quarry) because of its uneven grey stone facade.

Pere Milà had married the older – and far richer – Roser Guardiola, the widow of Josep Guardiola, and clearly knew how to spend his new wife's money. Milà was one of the city's first car owners and Gaudí built parking space into this building, itself a first. When commissioned to design this apartment building, Gaudí wanted to top anything else done in L'Eixample.

The Fundació Caixa Catalunya has opened the top-floor apartment, attic and roof, together called the Espai Gaudí (Gaudí Space), to visitors. The roof is the most extraordinary element, with its chimney pots looking like multicoloured medieval knights. Gaudí wanted to put a tall statue of the Virgin up here too: when the Milà family said no, fearing it might make the building a target for anarchists, Gaudí resigned from the project in disgust.

One floor below the roof is a modest museum dedicated to Gaudí's work. The next floor down is the apartment (El Pis de la Pedrera).

DON'T MISS...

➡ The marvellous roof
➡ The apartment
➡ The stone facade

PRACTICALITIES

➡ Casa Milà
➡ Map p294
➡ ☎93 484 59 00
➡ www.lapedrera.com
➡ Carrer de Provença 261-265
➡ adult/student/child €16.50/14.85/8.25
➡ ⊙9am-8pm Mar-Oct, to 6.30pm Nov-Feb
➡ ⓂDiagonal

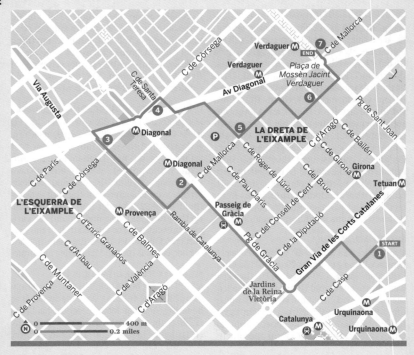

Neighbourhood Walk
More Modernisme in L'Eixample

START CASA CALVET
END CASA MACAYA
LENGTH 4KM; 1 HOUR

Gaudí's most conventional contribution to L'Eixample is ① **Casa Calvet**, built in 1900. Inspired by baroque, the noble ashlar facade is broken up by protruding wrought-iron balconies. Inside, the main attraction is the staircase, which you can admire if you eat in the swanky restaurant.

② **Casa Enric Batlló** was completed in 1896 by Josep Vilaseca (1848–1910), The brickwork facade is especially graceful when lit up at night.

Puig i Cadafalch let his imagination loose on ③ **Casa Serra** (1903–08), a neo-Gothic whimsy that is home to government offices. With its central tower topped by a witch's hat, grandly decorated upper-floor windows and tiled roof, it must have been a strange house to live in!

④ **Casa Comalatis**, built in 1911 by Salvador Valeri (1873–1954), is similarly striking. Note Gaudí's obvious influence on the main facade, with its wavy roof and bulging balconies. Head around the back to Carrer de Còrsega to see a more playful facade, with its windows stacked like cards.

Completed in 1912, ⑤ **Casa Thomas** was one of Domènech i Montaner's earlier efforts – the ceramic details are a trademark and the massive ground-level wrought-iron decoration (and protection?) is magnificent. Wander inside to the Cubiña design store to admire his interior work.

⑥ **Casa Llopis i Bofill** is an interesting block of flats designed by Antoni Gallissà (1861–1903) in 1902. The graffiti-covered facade is particularly striking to the visitor's eye. The use of elaborate parabolic arches on the ground floor is a clear Modernista touch, as are the wrought-iron balconies.

Puig i Cadafalch's ⑦ **Casa Macaya** (1901) has a wonderful courtyard and features the typical playful, pseudo-Gothic decoration that characterises many of the architect's projects. It belongs to La Caixa bank and is occasionally used for temporary exhibitions, when visitors are permitted to enter.

house and is marvellously out of place. A collection of photos, documents and sports memorabilia stretches over two floors – from an incongruous 1930s pair of skis and boots to the skull-decorated swimming costume of a champion Catalan water-polo player. A curio on the ground floor is the replica of a stone commemoration in Latin of Lucius Minicius Natal, a Barcelona boy who won a *quadriga* (four-horse chariot) race at the 227th Olympic Games...in AD 129.

CASA GOLFERICHS ARCHITECTURE

Map p290 (☑93 323 77 90; www.golferichs.org; Gran Via de les Corts Catalanes 491; ⊙5.30-9.30pm Mon-Sat; ⓜRocafort) **FREE** This quirky mansion is an oddity of another era on one of the city's busiest boulevards. Its owner, businessman Macari Golferichs, wanted a Modernista villa and he got one. Brick, ceramics and timber are the main building elements of the house, which displays a distinctly Gothic flavour. It came close to demolition in the 1970s but was saved by the town hall and converted into a cultural centre. Opening times can vary depending on temporary exhibitions and other cultural activities.

⊙ La Dreta de L'Eixample

LA SAGRADA FAMÍLIA CHURCH
See p124.

LA PEDRERA ARCHITECTURE
See p131.

RECINTE MODERNISTA
DE SANT PAU ARCHITECTURE

(☑93 553 78 01; www.santpaubarcelona.org; Carrer de Cartagena 167; adult/concession/child €8/5.60/free; ⊙10am-6.30pm Mon-Sat, to 2.30pm Sun; ⓜHospital de Sant Pau) Domènech i Montaner outdid himself as architect and philanthropist with the Modernista Hospital de la Santa Creu i de Sant Pau, redubbed in 2014 the 'Recinte Modernista'. It was long considered one of the city's most important hospitals, and only recently repurposed, its various spaces becoming cultural centres, offices and something of a monument.

Domènech i Montaner wanted to create an environment that would also cheer up patients. Among artists who contributed statuary, ceramics and artwork was the prolific Eusebi Arnau. The hospital facilities have been transferred to a new complex

PLATJA DE L'EIXAMPLE

In a hidden garden inside a typical Eixample block is an old water tower and an urban 'beach', the **Platja de l'Eixample** (Map p294; ☑93 291 62 60; Carrer de Roger de Llúria 56; admission €1.55; ⊙10am-8pm Mon-Sat; 10am-3pm Sun Jun-Aug only). In reality, this is a knee-height swimming pool, perfect for little ones, and surrounded by sand.

on the premises, freeing up the century-old structures, which are being restored to their former glory in a plan to convert the complex into an international centre on the Mediterranean. There are guided tours (€14/9.80) in a variety of languages, upon request.

FUNDACIÓ SUÑOL GALLERY

Map p294 (☑93 496 10 32; www.fundaciosunol.org; Passeig de Gràcia 98; adult/concession/child €4/2/free; ⊙11am-2pm & 4-8pm Mon-Fri, 4-8pm Sat; ⓜDiagonal) Rotating exhibitions of portions of this private collection of mostly 20th-century art (some 1200 works in total) offer anything from Man Ray's photography to sculptures by Alberto Giacometti. Over two floors, you are most likely to run into Spanish artists, anyone from Picasso to Jaume Plensa, along with a sprinkling of others from abroad. It makes a refreshing pause between the crush of crowded Modernista monuments on this boulevard. Indeed, you get an interesting side view of one of them, La Pedrera, from out the back.

PALAU DEL BARÓ QUADRAS ARCHITECTURE

Map p294 (☑93 467 80 00; Avinguda Diagonal 373; ⊙8am-8pm Mon-Fri; ⓜDiagonal) **FREE** Puig i Cadafalch designed Palau del Baró Quadras (built 1902–06) in an exuberant Gothic-inspired style. The main facade is its most intriguing, with a soaring, glassed-in gallery. Take a closer look at the gargoyles and reliefs – the pair of toothy fish and the sword-wielding knight clearly have the same artistic signature as the architect behind Casa Amatller. Decor inside is eclectic, but dominated by Middle Eastern and East Asian themes. The *palau* no longer houses the Casa Asia cultural centre, which means much of it is now closed to the public. However you can visit the ground floor.

ℹ MODERNISME UNPACKED

Travellers interested in running the gamut of L'Eixample's Modernista gems should consider the **Ruta del Modernisme** (www.rutadelmodernisme. com; €12) pack. It includes a guide (in various languages) and discounted entry prices to major Modernista sights.

CASA DE LES PUNXES   ARCHITECTURE

Map p294 (Casa Terrades; Avinguda Diagonal 420; M Diagonal) Puig i Cadafalch's Casa Terrades is better known as the Casa de les Punxes (House of Spikes) because of its pointed turrets. This apartment block, completed in 1905, looks like a fairy-tale castle and has the singular attribute of being the only fully detached building in L'Eixample.

MUSEU EGIPCI   MUSEUM

Map p294 (☎93 488 01 88; www.museuegipci. com; Carrer de València 284; adult/senior & student €11/8; ⊙10am-8pm Mon-Sat, to 2pm Sun; M Passeig de Gràcia) Hotel magnate Jordi Clos has spent much of his life collecting ancient Egyptian artefacts, brought together in this private museum. It's divided into different thematic areas and boasts an interesting variety of exhibits. There are statuary, funereal implements, jewellery, ceramics, and even a bed made of wood and leather. In the basement is an exhibition area and library, displaying volumes including original editions of works by Carter, the Egyptologist who led the Tutankhamen excavations. On the rooftop terrace is a pleasant cafe.

ESGLÉSIA DE LA PURÍSSIMA CONCEPCIÓ I ASSUMPCIÓ DE NOSTRA SENYORA   CHURCH

Map p294 (☎93 457 65 52; Carrer de Roger de Llúria 70; ⊙7.30am-1pm & 5-9pm; M Passeig de Gràcia) One hardly expects to run into a medieval church on the grid-pattern streets of the late-19th-century city extension, yet that is just what this is. Transferred stone by stone from the old centre in 1871–88, this 14th-century church has a pretty 16th-century cloister with a peaceful garden. Behind is a Romanesque-Gothic bell tower (11th to 16th century), moved from another old town church that didn't survive, Església de Sant Miquel. This is one of a handful of such old churches shifted willy-nilly from their original locations to L'Eixample.

PALAU MONTANER   ARCHITECTURE

Map p294 (☎93 317 76 52; www.rutadelmodern-isme.com; Carrer de Mallorca 278; adult/child & senior €6/3; M Passeig de Gràcia) Interesting on the outside and made all the more enticing by its gardens, this creation by Domènech i Montaner is spectacular on the inside. Completed in 1896, its central feature is a grand staircase beneath a broad, ornamental skylight. The interior is laden with sculptures (some by Eusebi Arnau), mosaics and fine woodwork. It is currently only open, by guided tour, to groups by prior arrangement.

ESGLÉSIA DE LES SALESES   CHURCH

Map p294 (Passeig de Sant Joan; ⊙5-9pm Mon-Fri; M Tetuan) A singular neo-Gothic effort, this church is interesting because it was designed by Joan Martorell i Montells (1833–1906), Gaudí's architecture professor. Raised in 1878–85 with an adjacent convent (badly damaged in the civil war and now a school), it offers hints of what was to come with Modernisme, with his use of brick, mosaics and sober stained glass.

✗ EATING

Most of this huge area's many restaurants are concentrated in the Quadrat d'Or between Carrer de Pau Claris and Carrer de Muntaner, Avinguda Diagonal and Gran Via de les Corts Catalanes. There is no shortage of perfectly acceptable bar-restaurants (often with street-side tables) that offer reasonable *menús del día* (daily set menus) and stock-standard dishes *a la carta*. In among these places are sprinkled with real finds, offering both local and international cuisine.

✗ L'Esquerra de L'Eixample

★ CERVESERIA CATALANA   TAPAS €

Map p290 (☎93 216 03 68; Carrer de Mallorca 236; tapas €4-11; ⊙9.30am-1.30am; M Passeig de Gràcia) The 'Catalan Brewery' is good for breakfast, lunch and dinner. Come for a morning coffee and croissant, or wait until lunch to enjoy the tapas and *montaditos* (canapés). You can sit at the bar, on the pavement terrace or in the restaurant at the back. The hot tapas, salads and other snacks draws a well-dressed crowd of locals and outsiders.

COPASETIC
CAFE

Map p290 (✆93 532 76 66; www.copaseticbarcelona.com; Carrer de la Diputació 55; mains €8-12; ⏱7pm-midnight Mon, noon-midnight Tue & Wed, noon-1am Thu, noon-3am Fri, 10.30am-3am Sat, 10.30am-6pm Sun; MRocafort) A friendly new cafe, decked out with retro furniture. The menu holds plenty for everyone, whether your thing is eggs Benedict, wild-berry tartlets or a juicy burger. There are lots of vegetarian, gluten-free and organic options, and superb brunches on weekends. Wednesday night is ladies' night, with cheap cocktails.

FASTVÍNIC
CAFE €

Map p290 (✆93 487 32 41; www.fastvinic.com; Carrer de la Diputació 251; sandwiches €4.25-12; ⏱noon-midnight Mon-Sat; MPasseig de Gracia) 🍃 A project in sustainability all round, this is Slow Food done fast, with ingredients, wine and building materials all sourced from Catalonia. Designed by Alfons Tost, there are air-purifying plants, energy-efficient LED lighting, and a water and food recycling system. It's all sandwiches on the menu, with some wonderful choices of roast beef, mustard and honey, or more adventurous crunchy suckling pig, banana chutney and coriander; there is also a self-service wine machine with quality Spanish choices. The interior is sleek and calm, with classical music accompanying your food. There are large tables for groups and smaller niches for quieter affairs. A word of warning: don't sit at the table right between the sliding door and the food recycling machine or you'll be subjected to hot/cold draughts and food blitzing.

ESCRIBÀ
DESSERTS €

Map p302 (✆93 454 75 35; www.escriba.es; Gran Via de les Corts Catalanes 546; pastries from €2; ⏱8.30am-3pm & 5-9.30pm Mon-Fri, 8.30am-8.30pm Sat & Sun; MUrgell) Antoni Escribà carries forward a family tradition (since 1906) of melting *barcelonins'* hearts with remarkable pastries and criminal chocolate creations. Try the Easter *bunyols de xocolata* (little round pastry balls filled with chocolate cream). Escribà has another branch in a Modernista setting at **La Rambla de Sant Josep 83** (www.escriba.es; La Rambla de Sant Josep 83; ⏱8.30am-9pm; MLiceu).

CREMERIA TOSCANA
GELATERIA €

Map p290 (✆93 539 38 25; www.cremeria-toscana.es; Carrer de Muntaner 161; ice cream from €2.80; ⏱1pm-midnight Tue-Sun; MHospital Clínic) Yes, you can stumble across quite reasonable ice cream in Barcelona, but close your eyes and imagine yourself across the Mediterranean with the real ice-cream wizards. Creamy *stracciatella* and wavy *nocciola* and myriad other flavours await at the most authentic gelato outlet in town. Buy a cone or a tub.

MAURI
PASTELERÍA €

Map p290 (✆93 215 10 20; www.pasteleriasmauri.com; Rambla de Catalunya 102; pastries from €3.40; ⏱8am-midnight Mon-Sat, 9am-4pm Sun; MDiagonal) Ever since it opened in 1929, this pastry shop has had its regular customers salivating over the endless range of sweets, chocolate croissants and gourmet delicatessen items.

CRUSTO
CAFE €

Map p290 (✆93 487 05 51; www.crusto.es; Carrer de València 246; pastry from €3; ⏱7.30am-9pm Mon-Sat; MPasseig de Gràcia) A French-inspired bakery and pastry shop, its wonderful perfume of freshly baked bread, baguettes, croissants and pastries will be enough to convince you that it's worth pulling up a stool here for a long and tasty breakfast.

AMALTEA
VEGETARIAN €

Map p290 (www.amalteaygovinda.com; Carrer de la Diputació 164; mains €5-9; ⏱1-4pm & 8-11.30pm Mon-Sat; 🍴; MUrgell) The ceiling fresco of blue sky sets the scene in this popular vegetarian eatery. The *menú del día* (€10.70) offers a series of dishes that change frequently with the seasons. At night, the set two-course dinner (€15) offers good value. The homemade desserts are tempting. The place is something of an alternative lifestyle centre, with yoga, t'ai chi and belly-dancing classes.

EL RINCÓN MAYA
MEXICAN €

Map p290 (✆93 451 39 46; Carrer de València 183; mains €6-9.50; ⏱9-11.30pm Mon, 1.30-4pm & 8.30-11.30pm Tue-Sat; MPasseig de Gràcia) Getting a seat in this Mexican eatery can be a trial. The setting is warm, modest and simple. The pocket-sized serves of nachos, guacamole and fajitas all burst with flavour. You'll also discover lesser-known items like *tacos de pibil* (pork tacos) and *tinga*, little pasta pockets of chicken. There are also more substantial dishes. The owner-chef spent much of his life in the restaurant business in Mexico City.

A CASA PORTUGUESA
CAFE €€

Map p290 (✆93 226 25 77; www.acasaportuguesa.com; Carrer d'Aragó 111; mains €12-18; ⏱1pm-1am Mon-Sat, 1-8pm Sun; MRocafort) An attractive, colourful space where you can try Barcelona's best Portuguese custard tarts, *pastéis de Belém*, but you can also sample the vast variety of food from the region, much of it chargrilled meat and fish. In addition, there is well over 150 different Portuguese wines, and a *menú del día* offering typical dishes.

CATA 1.81
TAPAS €€

Map p290 (☎93 323 68 18; www.cata181.com; Carrer de València 181; tapas €6-8; ☺7pm-midnight Mon-Sat; ⓂPasseig de Gràcia) A beautifully designed venue (with lots of small lights, some trapped in birdcages), this is the place to come for fine wines and dainty gourmet dishes like *raviolis amb bacallà* (salt-cod dumplings) or *truita de patates i tòfona negre* (thick potato tortilla with a delicate trace of black truffle). The best option is to choose from one of several tasting-menu options ranging from €29 to €45.

TAKTIKA BERRI
BASQUE, TAPAS €€

Map p290 (☎93 453 47 59; Carrer de València 169; tapas from €3; ☺1-4pm & 8.30-11pm Mon-Fri, 1-4pm Sat; ⓂHospital Clínic) Get in early because the bar teems with punters from far and wide, anxious to wrap their mouths around some of the best Basque tapas in town. The hot morsels are all snapped up as soon as they arrive from the kitchen, so keep your eyes peeled. The seated dining area out the back is also good. In the evening, it's all over by about 10.30pm.

ALBA GRANADOS
SPANISH, MEDITERRANEAN €€

Map p290 (☎93 454 61 16; www.albagranados. cat; Carrer d'Enric Granados 34; mains €14-28; ☺1-4pm & 8pm-midnight; ⒺFGC Provença) In summer ask for one of the romantic tables on the 1st-floor balcony. Overlooking the trees, it is a unique spot, with little traffic. Inside, the ground- and 1st-floor dining areas are huge, featuring exposed brick and dark parquet. The menu offers a little of everything but the best dishes revolve around meat, such as *solomillo a la mantequilla de trufa con tarrina de patata y beicon* (sirloin in truffle butter, potato and bacon terrine).

CERVESERIA BRASSERIA GALLEGA
TAPAS €€

Map p290 (☎93 439 41 28; Carrer de Casanova 238; mains €8.50-19; ☺1.30-3.30pm & 8.30-11.30pm Mon-Sat, closed Aug; ⓂHospital Clínic) You could walk right by this modest establishment without giving it a second glance. If you did, you'd notice it was chock-full of locals immersed in animated banter and surrounded by plates of abundant Galician classics. The fresh *pulpo a la gallega* (spicy octopus chunks with potatoes) as starter confirms this place is a cut above the competition. Waiters have little time for loitering, but always a quick quip. The setting is simple, the meat dishes succulent and the *fideuà* (similar to paella but with vermicelli noodles as the base) full of seafood flavour.

LA BODEGUETA PROVENÇA
TAPAS €€

Map p290 (☎93 215 17 25; Carrer de Provença 233; mains €11-25; ☺8am-4pm & 8-11.30pm; ⓂDiagonal) The 'Little Wine Cellar' offers classic tapas presented with a touch of class, from *calamares a la andaluza* (lightly battered squid rings) to *cecina* (dried cured veal meat). The house speciality is *ous estrellats* (literally 'smashed eggs') – a mix of scrambled egg white, egg yolk, potato and then ingredients ranging from foie gras to *morcilla* (black pudding). Wash it all down with a good Ribera del Duero or *caña* (little glass) of beer. Staff can be a bit curt.

KOYUKI
JAPANESE €€

Map p290 (☎93 237 84 90; Carrer de Còrsega 242; mains €15-20; ☺1-3.30pm & 8-11pm Tue-Sat, 8-11pm Sun; ⓂDiagonal) This unassuming basement Japanese diner is one of those rough-edged diamonds that it pays to revisit. Sit at a long table and order from the cheesy menu complete with pictures courtesy of the Japanese owner – you won't be disappointed. The variety of *sashimi moriawase* is generous and constantly fresh. The *tempura udon* is a particularly hearty noodle option.

★CINC SENTITS
INTERNATIONAL €€€

Map p290 (☎93 323 94 90; www.cincsentits. com; Carrer d'Aribau 58; tasting menus €65-109; ☺1.30-3pm & 8.30-10pm Tue-Sat; ⓂPasseig de Gràcia) Enter the realm of the 'Five Senses' to indulge in a jaw-dropping tasting menu (there is no à la carte, although dishes can be tweaked to suit diners' requests), consisting of a series of small, experimental dishes. A key is the use of fresh local produce, such as fish landed on the Costa Brava and top-quality suckling pig from Extremadura, along with the kind of creative genius that has earned chef Jordi Artal a Michelin star.

SPEAKEASY
INTERNATIONAL €€€

Map p290 (☎93 217 50 80; www.javierdelasmuelas.com; Carrer d'Aribau 162-166; mains €19-28; ☺1-4pm & 8pm-midnight Mon-Fri, 8pm-midnight

Sat, closed Aug; MDiagonal) This clandestine restaurant lurks behind the Dry Martini (p138) bar. You will be shown a door through the open kitchen area to the 'storeroom', lined with hundreds of bottles of backlit, quality tipples. Dark decorative tones, a few works of art, low lighting, light jazz music and smooth service complete the setting. The menu has tempting options like the wild mushroom ravioli with langoustine or venison with puréed sweet potato.

✕ La Dreta de L'Eixample

★ TAPAS 24
TAPAS €€

Map p294 (✆93 488 09 77; www.carlesabellan.com; Carrer de la Diputació 269; tapas €4-9; ⊙9am-midnight Mon-Sat; MPasseig de Gràcia) Carles Abellan, master of Comerç 24 in La Ribera, runs this basement tapas haven known for its gourmet versions of old faves. Specials include the *bikini* (toasted ham and cheese sandwich – here the ham is cured and the truffle makes all the difference) and *arròs negre de sípia* (squid-ink black rice). The McFoie-Burger is fantastic and, for dessert, choose *xocolata amb pa, sal i oli* (balls of chocolate in olive oil with a touch of salt and wafer). You can't book but it's worth the wait.

CAN KENJI
JAPANESE €€

Map p294 (✆93 476 18 23; www.cankenji.com; Carrer del Rosselló 325; mains €8-14; ⊙1-3.30pm & 8.30-11pm Mon-Sat; MVerdaguer) If you want to go Japanese in Barcelona, this is the place. The chef of this understated little *izakaya* (the Japanese version of a tavern) gets his ingredients fresh from the city's markets, with traditional Japanese recipes receiving a Mediterranean touch, so you'll get things like sardine tempura with an aubergine, miso and anchovy puree, or *tataki* (lightly grilled meat) of *bonito* (tuna) with *salmorejo* (a Córdoban cold tomato and bread soup). This is fusion at its very best.

GRANJA PETITBO
MEDITERRANEAN €€

Map p294 (✆93 265 65 03; www.granjapetitbo.com; Passeig de Sant Joan 82; sandwiches €5-6, menú del día €12.90; ⊙8.30am-10pm Mon-Wed, 8.30am-midnight Thu, 8.30am-1am Fri, 10am-1am Sat, 10am-5pm Sun; ☎; MGirona) High ceilings, battered leather armchairs and dramatic flower arrangements set the tone in this sunny little corner cafe, beloved of local hipsters and young families, who up until now have been ill-served in this part of town. As well as an all-day parade of homemade cakes, freshly squeezed juices and superior coffee, there's a brunch menu on weekends, and a *menú del día* during the week.

CASA AMALIA
CATALAN €€

Map p294 (✆93 458 94 58; Passatge del Mercat 4-6; mains €8-17; ⊙1-3.30pm & 9-10.30pm Tue-Sat, 1-3.30pm Sun; MGirona) This very local restaurant is popular for its hearty Catalan cooking that uses fresh produce, mainly sourced from the busy market next door. On Thursdays during winter it offers the mountain classic, *escudella*. Otherwise, you might try light variations on local cuisine, such as the *bacallà al allioli de poma* (cod in an apple-based aioli sauce). The three-course *menú del día* is exceptional lunchtime value at €12.

PATAGONIA BEEF & WINE
SOUTH AMERICAN €€

Map p294 (✆93 304 37 35; www.patagoniabw.com; Gran Via de les Corts Catalanes 660; mains €18-25; ⊙1.30-4pm & 8-11.30pm; MPasseig de Gràcia) This stylish restaurant does exactly what it says on the tin – which is offer an Argentinian meat-fest. Start with empanadas (small pies filled with various meats), then you might want to skip the *achuras* (offal) and head for a hearty meat main, such as a juicy beef *medallón con salsa de colmenillas* (a medallion in a morel sauce) or such classics as the juicy *bife de chorizo* (sirloin strip) or Brazilian *picanha* (rump). You can choose from one of five side dishes to accompany your pound of flesh.

CASA ALFONSO
SPANISH €€

Map p294 (✆93 301 97 83; www.casaalfonso.com; Carrer de Roger de Llúria 6; tapas from €4, mains €18-28; ⊙8am-1am Mon-Sat; MUrquinaona) In business since 1934, Casa Alfonso is perfect for a morning coffee or a tapas stop at the long marble bar. Festooned with old photos, posters and swinging hams, it attracts a faithful local clientele at all hours for its *flautas* (thin custom-made baguettes with your choice of filling), hams, cheeses and homemade desserts, but there are also more substantial dishes, mostly involving huge hunks of grilled meat. Consider rounding off with an *alfonsito* (miniature Irish coffee).

DE TAPA MADRE
CATALAN €€

Map p294 (✆93 459 31 34; www.detapamadre.cat; Carrer de Mallorca 301; tapas from €4; ⊙8am-midnight Mon-Fri, 10am-midnight Sat, noon-midnight Sun; MVerdaguer) A chatty atmosphere greets you from the bar the moment you swing open the door. A few tiny tables line the window, but head upstairs for more space in the gallery, which hovers above the array of tapas on the bar below, or go deeper inside past the bench with the ham legs. The *arròs caldós amb llagostins* (a hearty rice dish with king prawns) is delicious.

EMBAT
MEDITERRANEAN €€

Map p294 (☎93 458 08 55; www.restaurantembat. es; Carrer de Mallorca 304; mains €10-24; ⏱1.30-3.30pm & 9-11pm Tue-Sat; Ⓜ Girona) Enthusiastic young chefs turn out beautifully presented dishes in this basement eatery. Indulge perhaps in *raviolis de pollo amb bacon i calabassó* (chicken ravioli in a sauce of finely chopped bacon, courgette and other vegetables) followed by *lluç amb pa amb tomàquet, carxofes i maionesa de peres* (a thick cut of hake on tomato-drenched bread, dressed with artichoke slices and a pear mayonnaise).

ALKÍMIA
CATALAN €€€

(☎93 207 61 15; www.alkimia.cat; Carrer de l'Indústria 79; mains €18-29; ⏱1.30-3.30pm & 8-11pm Mon-Fri; Ⓜ Sagrada Família) Jordi Vilà, a culinary alchemist, serves up refined Catalan dishes with a twist in this elegant, white-walled locale well off the tourist trail. Dishes such as his *arròs de nyora i safrà amb escamarlans de la costa* (saffron and sweet-chilli rice with crayfish) earned Vilà his first Michelin star. He presents a series of set menus from €68 to €130.

CASA CALVET
CATALAN €€€

Map p294 (☎93 412 40 12; www.casacalvet.es; Carrer de Casp 48; mains €26-31; ⏱1-3.30pm & 8.30-11pm Mon-Sat; Ⓜ Urquinaona) An early Gaudí masterpiece loaded with his trademark curvy features now houses a swish restaurant (just to the right of the building's main entrance). Dress up and ask for an *taula cabina* (wooden booth). You could opt for sole and lobster on mashed leeks, with balsamic vinegar and Pedro Ximénez reduction, and artichoke chips. It has tasting menus for up to €70, and a lunch menu for €34.

DRINKING & NIGHTLIFE

Much of middle-class L'Eixample is dead at night, but several streets are exceptions. Noisy Carrer de Balmes is lined with a **rowdy adolescent set. More interesting is the cluster of locales lining Carrer d'Aribau between Avinguda Diagonal and Carrer de Mallorca. They range from quiet cocktail bars to '60s retro joints. Few get going much before midnight and are generally closed or dead from Sunday to Wednesday. Lower down, on and around Carrer del Consell de Cent and Carrer de la Diputació, is the heart of the Gaixample, with several gay bars and clubs.**

🍸 L'Esquerra de L'Eixample

★DRY MARTINI
BAR

Map p290 (☎93 217 50 72; www.javierdelasmuelas.com; Carrer d'Aribau 162-166; ⏱1pm-2.30am Mon-Thu, 6pm-3am Fri & Sat; Ⓜ Diagonal) Waiters with a discreetly knowing smile will attend to your cocktail needs here. The house drink is a safe bet. The gin and tonic comes in an enormous mug-sized glass – a couple of these and you're well on the way. Out the back is a restaurant, Speakeasy (p136).

MONVÍNIC
WINE BAR

Map p290 (☎932 72 61 87; www.monvinic.com; Carrer de la Diputació 249; ⏱wine bar 1.30-11pm Mon-Sat; Ⓜ Passeig de Gracia) Proclaimed as 'possibly the best wine bar in the world' by the *Wall Street Journal,* and apparently considered unmissable by El Bulli's sommelier, Monvínic is an ode to wine loving. The interactive wine list sits on the bar for you to browse on a digital tablet and boasts more than 3000 varieties. But that's not to say that it's for connoiseurs only; enthusiasts can also come here to taste wine by the glass – there are 60 selections. You can search by origin, year or grape, from a vast range.

Prices start at €3.50 for a glass of Albariño, and go up – and you can order by the bottle, too. There is an emphasis on affordability, but if you want to splash out, there are fantastic vintage wines. Feel free to talk to one of the six sommeliers who work on the list. At the back is the restaurant (open 1.30pm to 3.30pm and 8.30pm to 10.30pm Monday to Saturday) that specialises in Mediterranean cuisine, with ingredients sourced locally from Catalan farmers.

MILANO
COCKTAIL BAR

Map p290 (☎93 112 71 50; www.camparimilano. com; Ronda de la Universitat 35; ⏱noon-3am;

Catalunya) You don't quite know what to expect when heading downstairs into this cocktail den. Then you are confronted by its vastness and the happily imbibing crowds ensconced at tables or perched at the broad, curving bar to the right.

COSMO
CAFE

Map p290 (www.galeriacosmo.com; Carrer d'Enric Granados 3; 10am-10pm Mon-Thu, 10am-midnight Fri & Sat, 11am-10pm Sun; Universitat) This groovy space – with psychedelic colouring in the tables and bar stools, high white walls out the back for exhibitions and events, a nice selection of teas, pastries and snacks, all set on a pleasant pedestrian strip just behind the university – is perfect for a morning session on your laptop or a civilised evening tipple while admiring the art.

CITY HALL
CLUB

Map p290 (652 176272; www.cityhallbarcelona. com; Rambla de Catalunya 2-4; admission €15 (incl 1 drink); 12.30-5am Mon-Thu, to 6am Fri & Sat; Catalunya) A corridor leads to the dance floor of this place, located in a former theatre. House and other electric sounds dominate, including a rather forward-sounding session of cutting-edge funk called Get Funkd! on Tuesdays. Wednesday night is electro-house, while different guest DJs pop up on Thursdays. Out the back from the dance floor is a soothing terrace.

MAT BAR
GAY

Map p290 (93 453 77 22; www.matbar.es; Carrer de Consell de Cent 245; 5pm-2am Tue-Thu & Sun, until 3am Fri & Sat; Universitat) A high-design gay bar run by two Aussies, with a retro sporting theme (antique racquets and so on adorn the walls) and some superior bar food, along with craft beers. Those hoping for handbag house and go-go boys will be disappointed – while it gets animated at night, Mat is still a very civilised affair.

LA FIRA
BAR

Map p290 (682 323 714; Carrer de Provença 171; admission €5 (incl 1 drink); 11pm-5am Fri & Sat; FGC Provença) A designer bar with a difference. Wander in past distorting mirrors and ancient fairground attractions from Germany. Put in coins and listen to hens squawk. Speaking of squawking, the music swings wildly from whiffs of house through '90s hits to Spanish pop classics. You can spend the earlier part of the night trying some of the bar's shots – it claims to

THE GAIXAMPLE

The area just above Gran Via de les Corts Catalanes and to the left of Rambla de Catalunya is popularly known as the 'Gaixample', for its proliferation of gay bars and restaurants. We include some of the best here, such as Mat Bar (p139), Átame (p139), Arena Classic (p141) and Aire (p141) (this last one for the ladies), but note that some old favourites are also to be found in adjoining neighbourhoods, such as Metro (p193) in Sant Antoni.

have 500 varieties (but we haven't counted them up).

ÁTAME
GAY

Map p290 (93 454 92 73; Carrer del Consell de Cent 257; 10pm-2.30am; Universitat) Cool for a coffee in the early evening, Átame (Tie Me Up) heats up later in the night when the gay crowd comes out to play. There is usually a raunchy show on Friday nights and a happy hour on Thursdays.

CAFÉ SAN TELMO
BAR

Map p290 (93 439 17 09; www.cafesantelmo. com; Carrer de Buenos Aires 60; 9am-2.30pm Mon-Fri, 9am-3.30pm Sat & Sun; Diagonal) This narrow bar has an appealingly busy feel, with big windows along Carrer de Casanova revealing the crowds and traffic of nearby Avinguda Diagonal. Perch at the bar for a couple of afternoon drinks while you ponder the evening ahead (some of the area's key bars and clubs are just over the other side of Avinguda Diagonal).

LA CHAPELLE
GAY

Map p290 (93 453 30 76; Carrer de Muntaner 67; 4pm-2.30am; Universitat) A typical, long, narrow Eixample bar with white-tiled walls like a 1930s hospital, it houses a plethora of crucifixes and niches that far outdo what you'd find in any other 'chapel'. This is a relaxed gay meeting place that welcomes all comers. No need for six-pack bellies here.

PUNTO BCN
GAY

Map p290 (93 487 83 42; www.arenadisco.com; Carrer de Muntaner 63-65; 6pm-3am; Universitat) With a big bar over two levels and a crowd ranging from their 20s to their 40s and beyond, this place fills to bursting on

Friday and Saturday nights. It's a friendly early stop on a gay night out, and you can shoot a round of pool if you feel so inclined.

QUILOMBO   BAR
Map p290 (☑93 439 54 06; Carrer d'Aribau 149; ◷9.30pm-2.30am Tue-Sat; ☒FGC Provença) Some formulas just work, and this place has been working since the 1970s. Set up a few guitars in the back room, which you pack with tables and chairs, add some cheapish pre-prepared mojitos and plastic tubs of nuts, and let the punters do the rest. They pour in, creating plenty of *quilombo* (fuss).

ASTORIA   CLUB
Map p290 (☑93 414 47 99; www.astoriabarcelona. com; Carrer de París 193-197; ◷9pm-2.30am Wed, Thu & Sun, to 3am Fri & Sat; ☒Diagonal) **FREE** Reds, roses and yellows dominate the colour scheme in this wonderful former cinema. Barcelona's beautiful people, from a broad range of ages, gather to drink around the central bar, dance a little and eye one another up. Some come earlier for a bite. At 9pm from Thursday to Saturday there is a 'Circus Cabaret' show with dinner (around €40).

PREMIER   BAR
Map p290 (☑93 532 16 50; www.barpremier. com; Carrer de Provença 236; ◷6pm-2.30am Mon-Thu, 7am-3am Fri & Sat; ☒FGC Provença) A little cross-pollination has happened in this funky French-run wine bar. The rather short wine list is mostly French – or you can opt for a Moritz beer or a mojito. Hug the bar, sink into a lounge or hide up on the mezzanine. Later in the evening, a DJ adds to the ambience.

BACON BEAR   GAY
Map p290 (☑93 451 00 00; Carrer de Casanova 64; ◷6pm-2.30am Mon-Thu, 6pm-3am Fri & Sat, 6pm-2.30am Sun; ☒Urgell) Every bear needs a cave to go to, and this is a rather friendly one. It's really just a big bar for burly gay folk. On weekends the music cranks up enough for a bit of bear-hugging twirl.

DACKSY   GAY
Map p290 (☑93 451 29 25; Carrer del Consell de Cent 247; ◷1pm-2am Sun-Thu, to 3am Fri & Sat; ☒Universitat) Eye-candy bartenders know their stuff when it comes to mixing, shaking and/or stirring their way to your heart with a fine selection of cocktails in this chilled lounge in the heart of the Gaixam-

ple action. It makes a perfect start to the evening, or a nice way to finish off if clubbing is not on the night's agenda.

PLATA BAR   BAR
Map p290 (☑93 452 46 36; Carrer del Consell de Cent 235; ◷6pm-2.30am; ☒Universitat) A summer seat on the corner terrace of this wide-open bar attracts a lot of lads hopping the area's gay bars in the course of an evening. Inside, metallic horse-saddle stools are lined up at the bar and high tables, the music drifts through modes of dance and trance, and waiters whip up drinks from behind a couple of candelabras on the bar.

🍷 La Dreta de L'Eixample

CAFÈ DEL CENTRE   CAFE
Map p294 (☑93 488 11 01; Carrer de Girona 69; ◷9am-11pm Mon-Fri, 11am-11pm; ☒Girona) Step back a century in this cafe, in business since 1873. The wooden bar extends down the right side as you enter, fronted by a slew of marble-topped tables and dark timber chairs. It exudes an almost melancholy air by day but gets busy at night.

LES GENS QUE J'AIME   BAR
Map p294 (☑93 215 68 79; www.lesgensquejaime. com; Carrer de València 286; ◷6pm-2.30am Sun-Thu, 7pm-3am Fri & Sat; ☒Passeig de Gràcia) This intimate basement relic of the 1960s follows a deceptively simple formula: chilled jazz music in the background, minimal lighting from an assortment of flea-market lamps and a cosy, cramped scattering of red velvet-backed lounges around tiny dark tables.

GARAJE HERMÉTICO   BAR
Map p294 (☑670 253318; Avinguda Diagonal 440; ◷11pm-4am; ☒Diagonal) It's a pool-playing, rock and roll kinda world in this popular late-night haunt, where those without disco desire but in search of one (or two) more drinkies converge when most of the other bars in Barcelona have closed. It's a no-nonsense place and full of beans after 3am.

NEW CHAPS   GAY
Map p294 (☑93 215 53 65; www.newchaps.com; Avinguda Diagonal 365; ◷7pm-3am Sun-Thu, to 3.30am Fri & Sat; ☒Diagonal) Leather lovers get in some close-quarters inspection on the dance floor and more, especially in

the dark room, downstairs past the fairly dark loos in the vaulted cellars. It's a classic handlebar-moustache gay-porn kinda place.

 ENTERTAINMENT

MÉLIÈS CINEMES
CINEMA

Map p290 (☎93 451 00 51; www.cinesmelies.net; Carrer de Villarroel 102; tickets €4-7; MUrgell) A cosy cinema with two screens, the Méliès specialises in the best of recent releases from Hollywood and Europe.

MUSIC HALL
CONCERT VENUE

Map p290 (☎652 176272; www.musichall.es; Rambla de Catalunya 2-4; admission varies; ☺7.30pm-midnight; MCatalunya) The early-evening incarnation of City Hall, this former theatre is a perfect size and shape for live music, holding a crowd of around 500. The acoustics are also great and the layout means everyone gets a good view of the stage.

ARENA CLASSIC
CLUB

Map p290 (☎93 487 83 42; www.arenadisco.com; Carrer de la Diputació 233; admission Fri/Sat €6/12; ☺2.30am-6.30am Fri & Sat; MPasseig de Gràcia) It attracts a mixed gay crowd that tends not to get too wild. The dominant sound is handbag, and the vibe joyfully cheesy.

ARENA MADRE
GAY

Map p290 (☎93 487 83 42; www.grupoarena.com; Carrer de Balmes 32; admission Sun-Fri €6, Sat €12; ☺12.30am-5am Sun-Thu, until 5.30am Fri & Sat; MPasseig de Gràcia) Popular with a hot young crowd, Arena Madre is one of the top clubs in town for boys seeking boys. Keep an eye out for the striptease shows on Mondays and drag queens on Wednesdays, along with the usual combination of disco and Latin music to get those butts moving. Heteros are welcome but a minority.

PERVERT CLUB
GAY

Map p294 (☎93 453 05 10; Ronda de Sant Pere 19-21; admission €12, incl 1 drink; ☺midnight-6am Sat; MUrquinaona) With pink laser lights and dense crowds of fit young lads, this is one of the big dance-club locations on a Saturday night. Electronic music dominates the dance nights here and, in spite of the 6am finish, for many this is only the start of the 'evening'. You need to look your gorgeous best to get in past the selective doormen.

AIRE
LESBIAN

Map p290 (☎93 487 83 42; www.arenadisco.com; Carrer de València 236; admission free Thu, €5 Fri, €6 Sat; ☺11pm-2.30am Thu-Sat; MPasseig de Gràcia) A popular locale for lesbians, the dance floor is spacious and there is usually a DJ in command of the tunes, which range from hits of the '80s and '90s to techno. As a rule, only male friends of the girls are allowed entry, although in practise the crowd tends to be fairly mixed. Things can heat up on Thursday nights with live music.

MEDITERRÁNEO
LIVE MUSIC

Map p290 (☎678 211253; www.elmedi.net; Carrer de Balmes 129; ☺11pm-3am; MDiagonal) This studenty jam joint is a great hang-out that attracts a mostly casual student set. Order a beer, enjoy the free nuts and chat at one of the tiny tables while waiting for the next act to tune up at the back. Sometimes the young performers are surprisingly good.

DIETRICH CAFÉ
CABARET

Map p290 (☎93 451 77 07; Carrer del Consell de Cent 255; ☺10.30pm-3am; MUniversitat) It's show time at 1am, with at least one drag-queen gala each night in this cabaret-style locale dedicated to Marlene Dietrich. Soft house is the main musical motif and the place has an interior garden. In between performances, go-go boys heat up the ambience.

TEATRE TÍVOLI
THEATRE

Map p294 (☎902 332211; www.grupbalana.com; Carrer de Casp 8; admission varies; ☺box office 5pm-30min after beginning of show; MCatalunya) A grand old theatre with three storeys of boxes and a generous stage, the Tívoli has a fairly rapid turnover of drama and musicals, with pieces often not staying on for more than a couple of weeks.

 SHOPPING

Most of the city's classy shopping spreads across the heart of L'Eixample, in particular along Passeig de Gràcia, Rambla de Catalunya and adjacent streets. All about are dotted an array of speciality stores.

VINÇON
HOMEWARES

Map p294 (☎93 215 60 50; www.vincon.com; Passeig de Gràcia 96; ☺10am-8.30pm Mon-Fri, 10.30am-9pm Sat; MDiagonal) An icon of the Barcelona design scene, Vinçon has the slickest furniture and household goods (particularly lighting), both local and imported. Not surprising, really, since the building, raised in 1899, belonged to the Modernista artist Ramon Casas. Head upstairs to the furniture area – from the windows and terrace you get side views of La Pedrera.

FLORES NAVARRO
FLOWERS

Map p294 (☑93 457 40 99; www.floristeri-asnavarro.com; Carrer de València 320; ⊗24hr; ⓂDiagonal) You never know when you might need flowers. What better way to follow up the first night of a new romance than with a bunch of roses? No problem, because this florist never closes!

JOAN MÚRRIA
FOOD

Map p294 (☑93 215 57 89; www.murria.cat; Carrer de Roger de Llúria 85; ⊗9am-2pm & 5-9pm Tue-Thu, 9am-9pm Fri, 10am-2pm & 5-9pm Sat; ⓂPasseig de Gràcia) Ramon Casas designed the century-old Modernista shop-front advertisements featured at this culinary temple. For a century the gluttonous have trembled at this altar of speciality food goods from around Catalonia and beyond.

EL BULEVARD DELS ANTIQUARIS
ANTIQUES

Map p290 (☑93 215 44 99; www.bulevarddelsan-tiquaris.com; Passeig de Gràcia 55; ⊗9am-6pm Mon-Thu, 9am-2pm Fri & Sat; ⓂPasseig de Gràcia) More than 70 stores (most are open from 11am to 2pm and 5pm to 8.30pm) are gathered under one roof (on the floor above the more general Bulevard Rosa arcade) to offer the most varied selection of collector's pieces, ranging from old porcelain dolls through to fine crystal, from Asian antique furniture to old French goods, and from African and other ethnic art to jewellery.

CASA DEL LLIBRE
BOOKS

Map p294 (☑902 026 407; www.casadellibro.com; Passeig de Gràcia 62; ⊗9.30am-9.30pm Mon-Sat; ⓂPasseig de Gràcia) With branches elsewhere in Spain, the 'Home of the Book' is a well-stocked general bookshop with reasonable sections devoted to literature in English, French and other languages, as well as a good number of guidebooks. Check the website for Spanish literature if the shop is a walk too far.

COME IN
BOOKS

Map p290 (☑93 453 12 04; www.libreriainglesa.com; Carrer de Balmes 129; ⊗9.30am-8.30pm Mon-Fri, 9.30am-2pm & 4-8pm Sat; ⓂDiagonal) English teachers, those wanting the latest

🏃 Local Life
Shopping in the Quadrat d'Or

While visitors to L'Eixample do the sights, locals go shopping in the Quadrat d'Or, the grid of streets either side of Passeig de Gràcia. This is Barcelona at its most fashion- and design-conscious, which also describes a large proportion of L'Eixample's residents. All the big names are here, alongside boutiques of local designers who capture the essence of Barcelona cool.

❶ Designer Barcelona
It has a reputation as the essence of innovative Catalan design and the frame within which Spanish design evolves, but Vinçon (p141) has its roots in L'Eixample and is a neighbourhood icon. Pamper your aesthetic senses with a journey through its household wares.

❷ The New Wave
You could spend an entire day along Passeig de Gràcia but detour for a moment to **Lurdes Bergada** (☑93 218 48 51; www.lurdesbergada.es; Rambla de Catalunya 112; ⊗10.30am-8.30pm Mon-Sat; ⓂDiagonal), a boutique run by mother-and-son designer team Lurdes Bergada and Syngman Cucala. The classy men's and women's fashions use natural fibres and have attracted a cult following.

❸ A Pastry Stop
Time for a break. And few pastry shops have such a long-established pedigree as Mauri (p135). The plush interior is capped by an ornate fresco dating back to Mauri's first days in 1929. Its croissants and feather-light ensaïmadas (sweet buns) are near perfect.

❹ Modernista Jewellery
This is more than just any old jewellery store. The boys from Bagués-Masriera (p145) have been chipping away at precious stones and moulding metal since the 19th century, and many of the classic pieces here have a flighty, Modernista influence. Bagués backs it up with service that can be haughty, but owes much to old-school courtesies.

QUIM ROSER/ALAMY ©

Vinçon (p141)

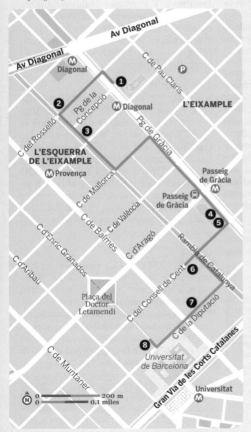

5 Luxury Luggage

While bags and suitcases in every conceivable colour of buttersoft leather are the mainstay at Loewe (p144), there is also a range of clothing for men and women, along with some stunning – and stunningly priced – accessories. The shop itself is worth a visit, housed in the Casa Lleó Morera (p129), and with some interior details by Domènech i Montaner.

6 Say It With Chocolate

A sleek and modern temple to the brown stuff, Cacao Sampaka (p144) doubles as a shop and cafe and is the perfect place to stock up with gifts to take back home. Select from every conceivable flavour (rosemary, anyone? Curry?), either in bar form or as individual choccies to fill your own elegant little gift box.

7 Fine Wines

For superior souvenirs in liquid form, head to the state-of-the-art Monvínic (p138), a veritable palace of wine with some 3000 wines in its cellar, including some extremely rare finds. Try before you buy in the wine bar, and ask them to make you up a gift box for someone special back home.

8 Chill Down

Cosmo (p139) is a bright, white cavernous space, dotted with colour from the exhibitions that adorn its high walls. It has a nice selection of teas, cakes and snacks. Set on a pleasant pedestrian strip, it's perfect for an evening tipple outside or in.

thrillers in English and learners of Shakespeare's tongue will all find something to awaken their curiosity in this, one of the city's main English-language bookshops. There are even a few odds and ends in other languages.

LAIE
BOOKS

Map p294 (☑93 318 17 39; www.laie.es/pauclaris; Carrer de Pau Claris 85; ⊙9am-9pm Mon-Fri, 10am-9pm Sat; MCatalunya, Urquinaona) Laie has novels and books on architecture, art and film in English, French, Spanish and Catalan. Better still, it has a great upstairs cafe where you can examine your latest purchases or browse through the newspapers provided for customers in true Central European style.

CACAO SAMPAKA
FOOD

Map p290 (☑93 272 08 33; www.cacaosampaka.com; Carrer del Consell de Cent 292; ⊙9am-9pm Mon-Sat; MPasseig de Gràcia) Chocoholics will be convinced they have died and passed on to a better place. Load up in the shop or head for the bar out the back where you can have a classic *xocolata* (hot chocolate) and munch on exquisite chocolate cakes, tarts, ice cream, sweets and sandwiches.

NORMA COMICS
BOOKS

Map p294 (☑93 244 84 23; www.normacomics.com; Passeig de Sant Joan 7-9; ⊙10.30am-8.30pm Mon-Sat; MArc de Triomf) With a huge range of comics, both Spanish and international, this is Spain's biggest dealer – everything from Tintin to some of the weirdest sci-fi and sex comics can be found here. Also on show are model superheroes and other characters produced by fevered imaginations. Kids from nine to 99 can be seen snapping up items to add to their collections.

EL CORTE INGLÉS
DEPARTMENT STORE

Map p294 (☑93 306 38 00; www.elcorteingles.es; Plaça de Catalunya 14; ⊙9.30am-9.30pm Mon-

Sat; MCatalunya) This is now the city's only department store, with everything you'd expect, from computers to cushions, and high fashion to homewares, and famous for its decent customer service (not always the case in Spain). The top floor is occupied by a so-so restaurant with fabulous city views. El Corte Inglés has other branches, including at **Portal de l'Àngel 19-21** (Map p276; MCatalunya), **Avinguda Diagonal 617** (Map p298; MMaria Cristina) and **Avinguda Diagonal 471-473** (Map p290; MHospital Clínic), near Plaça de Francesc Macià.

CUBIÑA
HOMEWARES

Map p294 (☑93 476 57 21; www.cubinya.es; Carrer de Mallorca 291; ⊙10am-2pm & 4.30-8.30pm Mon-Sat; MVerdaguer) Even if interior design doesn't ring your bell, it's worth a visit to this extensive temple to furniture, lamps and just about any home accessory your heart might desire just to see this Domènech i Montaner building. Admire the enormous and whimsical wrought-iron decoration at street level before heading inside to marvel at the ceiling, timber work, brick columns and windows. Oh, and don't forget the furniture.

ADOLFO DOMÍNGUEZ
FASHION

Map p294 (☑93 487 41 70; www.adolfodominguez.es; Passeig de Gràcia 32; ⊙10am-9pm Mon-Sat; MPasseig de Gràcia) One of the stars of Spanish prêt-à-porter, this label produces classic men's and women's garments from quality materials. Encompassing anything from regal party gowns to kids' outfits (that might have you thinking of British aristocracy), the broad range generally oozes a conservative air, with elegant cuts that make no concessions to rebellious urban ideals.

LOEWE
FASHION

Map p290 (☑93 216 04 00; www.loewe.com; Passeig de Gràcia 35; ⊙10am-8.30pm Mon-Sat; MPasseig de Gràcia) Loewe is one of Spain's leading and oldest fashion stores, founded in 1846. It specialises in luxury leather (shoes, accessories and travel bags), and also has lines in perfume, sunglasses, cuff links, silk scarves and jewellery. This branch opened in 1943 in the Modernista Casa Lleó Morera.

PURIFICACIÓN GARCÍA
FASHION

Map p290 (☑93 496 13 36; www.purificaciongarcia.es; Carrer de Provença 292; ⊙10am-8.30pm Mon-Sat; MPasseig de Gràcia) Ms García has

---

ⓘ SHOPPING OUT OF HOURS

Got the munchies at 1am? Forgot to buy the paper from your local kiosk? Need something on a Sunday? **Open-Cor** (Map p290; www.opencor.es; Carrer de Còrsega 241; ⊙8am-2am daily; MEntença) is your friend, open 18 hours a day, 365 days a year, selling useful items like snacks, chocolate bars, magazines and newspapers.

AN OUTLET OUTING

For the ultimate discount fashion overdose, head out of town for some outlet shopping at **La Roca Village** (☎93 842 39 39; www.larocavillage.com; ◷10am-9pm Mon-Sat, until 10pm Jun-Sep). Here, a village has been given over to consumer madness. At a long line of Spanish and international fashion boutiques you'll find clothes, shoes, accessories and designer homewares at (they claim) up to 60% off normal retail prices.

To get here, follow the AP-7 tollway north from Barcelona, take exit 12 (marked Cardedeu) and follow the signs for 'Centre Comercial'. The **Sagalés bus company** (☎902 130014; www.sagales.com) organises shuttles from Plaça de Catalunya (return €10.80 if bought online 24 hours in advance, 40 minutes, 12 daily Monday to Saturday). Alternatively, take a slower bus from the same company from Fabra i Puig metro station (each way €4, four departures Monday to Friday, three in August) or a *rodalies* train to Granollers and pick up the shuttle (Monday to Friday only) or a taxi there.

an enormous spread of offerings over two floors. Her collections are breathtaking as much for their breadth as anything else. You'll find all kinds of clothing, from women's cardigans to men's ties, as well as light summer dresses and jeans.

BAGUÉS-MASRIERA — JEWELLERY

Map p290 (☎93 216 01 74; www.masriera.es; Passeig de Gràcia 41; ◷10am-8.30pm Mon-Fri, 11am-8pm Sat; ⓜPasseig de Gràcia) This jewellery store, in business since the 19th century, is in thematic harmony with its location in the Modernista Casa Amatller. Some of the classic pieces of jewellery to come out of the Bagués clan's workshops have an equally playful, Modernista bent.

REGIA — PERFUME

Map p290 (☎93 216 01 21; www.regia.es; Passeig de Gràcia 39; ◷9.30am-8.30pm Mon-Fri, 10.30am-8.30pm Sat; ⓜPasseig de Gràcia) Reputed to be one of the best perfume stores in the city, and in business since 1928, Regia stocks all the name brands and also has a private perfume museum (p131) out the back. Aside from the range of perfumes, Regia sells all sorts of creams, lotions and colognes. It also has its own line of bath products.

CAMPER — SHOES

Map p290 (☎93 215 63 90; www.camper.com; Carrer de València 249; ◷10am-8pm Mon-Sat; ⓜPasseig de Gràcia) What started as a modest Mallorcan family business (the island has a long shoemaking tradition) has, over the decades, and particularly with the success of the 'bowling shoe' in the '90s, become the Clarks of Spain. The shoes, from the eminently sensible to the stylishly fashionable, are known for solid reliability and are sold all over the world. It now has shops all over Barcelona.

🏃 SPORTS & ACTIVITIES

ANTILLA BCN ESCUELA DE BAILE — DANCE COURSE

Map p290 (☎93 451 45 64; www.antillasalsa.com; Carrer d'Aragó 141; 10 1hr classes €100; ◷8-11pm Tue-Fri; ⓜUrgell) The best *salsateca* in town, this is the place to come for Cuban *son,* merengue, salsa and a whole lot more. If you don't know how to dance to any of this, you may feel a little silly (as a guy) but women will probably get free lessons. The guys can come back at another time and pay for classes.

BABYLON IDIOMAS — LANGUAGE COURSE

Map p294 (☎93 467 36 36; www.babylon-idiomas.com; Carrer del Bruc 65; ◷8.30am-6pm Mon-Fri; ⓜGirona) This small school offers a high degree of flexibility – you can study for a week or enlist for a half-year intensive course in Spanish. The big selling point is class size, with a maximum of eight students per class. A week of tuition (20 hours) costs €160.

BARCELONA WALKING TOURS — WALKING TOUR

Map p290 (☎93 285 38 34; www.barcelonaturisme.com; Plaça de Catalunya 17-S; ⓜCatalunya) The Oficina d'Informació de Turisme de Barcelona organises walking tours. One explores the **Barri Gòtic** (adult/child €15.50/free; ◷in English 9.30am daily); another follows in the footsteps of **Picasso** (adult/child €21.50/7; ◷in English 3pm Tue, Thu & Sat) and winds up at the Museu Picasso, entry to which is included in the price, and a third takes in the main jewels of **Modernisme** (adult/child €15.50/free; ◷in English 4pm Fri). Also offered is a **gourmet tour** (adult/child €21.50/7; ◷in English 10am Fri & Sat) of purveyors of fine foodstuffs; it includes a couple of chances to taste some of the products.

Antoni Gaudí & Modernisme

Barcelona's architectural gift to the world was Modernisme, a flamboyant Catalan creation that erupted in the late 19th century. Modernisme was personified by the visionary work of Antoni Gaudí, a giant in the world of architecture. Imaginative creations by Gaudí and his contemporaries have filled Barcelona with dozens of masterpieces.

A Blank Canvas

In the 1850s a rapidly growing city fuelled by industrialisation meant notoriously crowded conditions in the narrow streets of the Ciutat Vella, Barcelona's old quarter. It was time to break down the medieval walls and dramatically expand the city. In 1869 the architect Ildefons Cerdà was chosen to design a new district, which would be called L'Eixample (the Enlargement).

He drew wide boulevards on a gridlike layout, and envisioned neighbourhoods with plenty of green space – an objective that city planners unfortunately overruled amid the rampant land speculation of the day. With a blank slate before them, and abundant interest from upper-class residents eager to custom design a new home, architects were much in demand. What developers could not have predicted was the calibre of those architects.

Antoni Gaudí

Leading the way was Antoni Gaudí. Born in Reus to a long line of coppersmiths, Gaudí was initially trained in metalwork. In childhood he suffered from poor health, including rheumatism, and became an early adopter of a vegetarian diet. He was not a promising student. In 1878, when he obtained his architecture degree, the school's headmaster was reputed to have said, 'Who knows if we have given a diploma to a nutcase or a genius. Time will tell.'

The Book of Nature

As a young man, what most delighted Gaudí was being outdoors, and he became fascinated by the plants, animals and geology beyond his door. This deep admiration for the natural world would heavily influence his designs. 'This tree is my teacher,' he once said. 'Everything comes from the book of nature.' Throughout his work, he sought to emulate the harmony he observed in the natural world, eschewing the straight line and favouring curvaceous forms and more organic shapes.

The spiral of a nautilus shell can be seen in staircases and ceiling details, tight buds of flowers in chimney pots and roof ornamentation, while undulating arches evoke a cavern, overlapping roof tiles mimic the scales of an armadillo and flowing walls resemble waves on the sea. Tree branches, spider webs, stalactites, honeycombs, starfish, mushrooms, beetle wings and many other elements from nature – all were part of the Gaudían vernacular.

1. Stained-glass ceiling at the Palau de la Música Catalana (p98)
2. Interior of La Sagrada Família (p124)

GAUDÍ OFF THE BEATEN TRACK

Gaudí, like any freelancer, was busy all over town. While his main patron was Eusebi Güell and his big projects were bankrolled by the wealthy bourgeoisie, he also took on smaller jobs. One example is the **Casa Vicens** (p158), a remarkable home with Moorish and Eastern motifs. Another is the **Col·legi de les Teresianes** (p170), for which he created an unusual brick facade, topped with castle-like merlons.

Gaudí fanatics might also want to reach **Bellesguard** (p169), whose castle-like appearance is reinforced by heavy stonework, generous wrought iron and a tall spire. Gaudí also worked in some characteristically playful mosaic and colourful tiles.

Gaudí's Creations

The architect's work is an earthy appeal to sinewy movement, but often with a dreamlike or surreal quality. The private apartment house Casa Batlló is a fine example in which all appears a riot of the unnaturally natural – or the naturally unnatural. Not only are straight lines eliminated, but the lines between real and unreal, sober and dream-drunk, good sense and play are all blurred. Depending on how you look at the facade, you might see St George (one of Barcelona's patron saints) defeating a dragon, a magnificent and shimmering fish (a symbol of Mediterranean peoples), or elements of an effusive Carnaval parade.

Gaudí seems to have particularly enjoyed himself with rooftops. At Palau Güell he created all sorts of fantastical, multicoloured tile figures as chimney pots, resembling oversized budlike trees that seem straight out of *Alice in Wonderland* – or perhaps Dr Seuss.

La Sagrada Família

Gaudí's masterpiece was La Sagrada Família (begun in 1882), and in it you can see the culminating vision of many ideas developed over the years. Its massive scale evokes the grandeur

1. Park Güell (p156) 2. Ceiling in Casa Batlló (p130)

of Catalonia's Gothic cathedrals, while organic elements foreground its harmony with nature.

The church is rife with symbols that tangibly express Gaudí's Catholic faith through architecture: 18 bell towers symbolise Jesus, the Virgin Mary, the four evangelists and the 12 apostles. Three facades cover Jesus' life, death and resurrection. Even its location: the Nativity Facade faces east where the sun rises; the Passion Facade depicting Christ's death faces west where the sun sets.

Domènech i Montaner

Although overshadowed by Gaudí, Lluís Domènech i Montaner (1849–1923) was one of the great masters of Modernisme. He was a widely travelled man of prodigious intellect, with knowledge in everything from mineralogy to medieval heraldry, and he was an architectural professor, a prolific writer and a nationalist politician.

The question of Catalan identity and how to create a national architecture consumed Domènech i Montaner, who designed more than a dozen large-scale works in his lifetime.

The exuberant, steel-framed Palau de la Música Catalana is one of his masterpieces. Adorning the facade are elaborate Gothic-style windows, floral designs (Domènech i Montaner also studied botany) and sculptures depicting characters from Catalan folklore and the music world as well as everyday citizens of Barcelona. Inside, the hall leaves visitors dazzled with its delicate floral-covered colonnades, radiant stained-glass walls and ceiling, and a rolling, sculpture-packed proscenium that references the epics of musical lore.

His other great masterpiece is the Hospital de la Santa Creu i de Sant Pau, with sparkling mosaics on the facade and a stained-glass skylight which fills the vestibule with golden light (like Matisse, Domènech i Montaner believed in the therapeutic powers of colour).

Puig i Cadafalch

Like Domènech i Montaner, Josep Puig i Cadafalch (1867–1956) was a polymath; he was an archaeologist, an expert in Romanesque art and one of Catalonia's most prolific architects. As a politician – and later president of the Mancomunitat de Catalunya (Commonwealth of Catalonia) – he was instrumental in shaping the Catalan nationalist movement.

One of his many Modernista gems is the Casa Amatller, a rather dramatic contrast to Gaudí's Casa Batlló next door. Here the straight line is very much in evidence, as is the foreign influence (the gables are borrowed from the Dutch). Blended with playful Gothic-style sculpture, Puig i Cadafalch has designed a house of startling beauty and invention.

Another pivotal work by Puig i Cadafalch was the Casa Martí (better known as Els Quatre Gats), at Carrer de Montsió 3. It was one of Barcelona's first Modernista-style buildings (from 1896), with Gothic window details and whimsical wrought-iron sculpture.

Materials & Decorations

Modernista architects relied on the skills of artisans that have now been all but relegated to history. There were no concrete pours (contrary to what is being done at La Sagrada Família today). Stone, unclad brick, exposed iron and steel frames, and copious use of stained glass and ceramics in decoration, were all features of the new style – and indeed it is often in the decor that Modernisme is at its most flamboyant.

The craftsmen required for these tasks were the heirs of the guild masters and had absorbed centuries of know-how about just what could and could not be done with these materials. Forged iron and steel were newcomers to the scene, but the approach to learning how they could be used was not dissimilar to that adopted for more traditional materials. Gaudí, in particular, relied on these old skills and even ran schools in La Sagrada Família workshops to keep them alive.

1. Hospital de la Santa Creu i de Sant Pau (Recinte Modernista de Sant Pau; p133) 2. La Pedrera (p131) 3. Tile mosaic, Park Güell (p156)

Exploring Modernisme

Barcelona is home to dozens of Modernista masterpieces, making for some tough decisions when it comes to deciding what to see. The following are two suggested half-day itineraries of the major highlights, though the very ambitious could combine these for a packed day of architectural gazing.

A MORNING OF MODERNISME

Start the day off with pastries and coffee at the Modernista gem **Escribà ❶**. From there walk a few blocks south and down Carrer Nou de Rambla to visit the **Palau Güell ❷**, one of

Gaudí's early masterpieces. Afterwards take the metro up to Passeig de Gràcia and have a look at the so-called Manzana de la Discordia – **Casa Batlló**, **Casa Amatller ❸** and Casa Lleó Morera – deciding for yourself who among Gaudí, Puig i Cadafalch and Domènech i Montaner has created the most successful work of art. Afterwards, stroll up Passeig de Gràcia, a true architectural showcase, and end your tour at Gaudí's **La Pedrera ❹** (Casa Milà). Don't miss the sentinel-like chimney pots on the roof – and the great view over the city.

La Sagrada Família

Still over a decade from completion, the magnificent basilica is an ever-changing work in progress. The beautifully sculpted Nativity Facade, with its rich symbolism, is a masterpiece unto itself.

GRÀCIA

SANT GERVASI

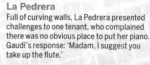

Park Güell

Gaudí's imagination runs wild here, with fairy-tale-like gatehouses, tilting tree-like columns, organic rock-strewn passageways and one much photographed lizard.

La Pedrera

Full of curving walls, La Pedrera presented challenges to one tenant, who complained there was no obvious place to put her piano. Gaudí's response: 'Madam, I suggest you take up the flute.'

AN AFTERNOON OF MODERNISME

Start the tour at **La Sagrada Família** ❺ where you can gaze upon one of the world's most dynamic ecclesiastical designs. Afterwards, make your way up to **Park Güell** ❻ for an afternoon stroll through the eye-catching park. If time allows, pay a visit to the Casa-Museu Gaudí in the park. Next head back down to the Ciutat Vella for a guided tour (or perhaps attend a concert) inside the luminescent **Palau de la Música Catalana** ❼. Afterwards, stroll over to **Els Quatre Gats** ❽ for a drink (or a meal) inside a whimsical building designed by Puig i Cadafalch.

TOP TIPS

» Go first thing in the morning or late in the day to beat the crowds at Gaudí sites.

» Buy La Sagrada Família tickets online to avoid long queues.

» La Pedrera also hosts rooftop evening concerts in the summer.

Palau de la Música Catalana
The sculptural facade is packed with folk symbols, with an open-armed nymph, a peasant, a fisherman, and other types gathered below a sword-bearing St George.

LA RIBERA

Escribà
This magnificent pastry shop has a stunning art nouveau exterior. Note the swirling mosaics and stained glass, key elements of Modernista design.

L'EIXAMPLE

Passeig de Gràcia

❼

❽

BARRI GÒTIC

La Rambla

❸

❶

❷

Palau Güell
There are many unusual features in this early work by Antoni Gaudí, including the massive entry doors, which allowed carriages to be driven right into the house.

Els Quatre Gats
From 1897 to 1903, this was the hang-out for avant-garde artists of the day. A young Picasso had his first exhibition here in 1900.

Casa Batlló & Casa Amatller
These two side-by-side buildings show how wildly different the Modernistas ranged in their inspirations. Puig i Cadafalch references Gothic Dutch architecture, while Gaudí's is a shimmering tile-covered fantasy.

Gràcia & Park Güell

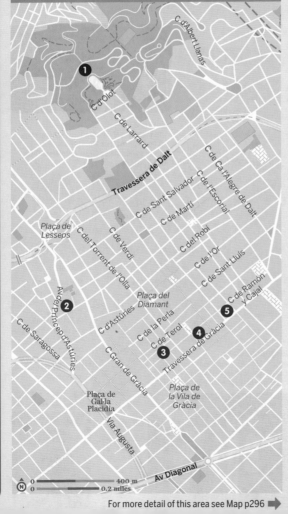

Neighbourhood Top Five

1 Getting lost along the winding paths of **Park Güell** (p156) and exploring its more-natural-than-nature sculptures, mosaics and columns, then resurfacing on one of the park's sunny plazas.

2 Checking out the swirling patterns of the facade of **Casa Vicens** (p158), Gaudí's first commission.

3 Wandering around and taking in the sun on one of **Gràcia's many squares** (p159).

4 Getting high on chocolate with the locals at **La Nena** (p160).

5 Taking in a local band or even some live poetry at **Heliogàbal** (p163).

For more detail of this area see Map p296 ➡

Explore: Gràcia & Park Güell

Once a separate village north of L'Eixample, and an industrial district famous for its republican and liberal ideas, Gràcia was incorporated into the city of Barcelona in 1897, much to the disgust of the locals. The neighbourhood retains its distinct character today, with a boho feel that varies between chic and downtrodden, and a demographic that includes young families and students.

You know you are in Gràcia when you hit the maze of crowded narrow streets and lanes that characterise it. The heart of the neighbourhood is bounded by Carrer de Còrsega and Avinguda Diagonal in the south, Via Augusta and Avinguda del Príncep d'Astúries to the west, Carrer de Sardenya to the east and Travessera de Dalt to the north.

Start the day in Gràcia by exploring Park Güell and move down to the centre of the neighbourhood. If you walk from the park, cut across the traffic-choked Travessera de Dalt and go down Carrer de Verdi, where you will find wonderful cafes, bars and shops; Plaça del Sol, a raucous square populated by cool bars and (often loud) drunks; Plaça de la Vila de Gràcia (formerly Plaça de Rius i Taulet), dotted with cafes and restaurants; Plaça de la Revolució de Setembre de 1868, a family-friendly square with a playground and ice-cream parlour; and the tree-lined Plaça de la Virreina, a particularly lovely square with cafes, shops and a chilled-out feel. On Plaça de Rovira i Trias you can sit on a bench next to a statue of Antoni Rovira, Ildefons Cerdà's rival in the competition to design L'Eixample in the late 19th century. Rovira's design has been laid out in the pavement, so you can judge his merits for yourself.

Local Life

→ **Markets** Locals get their fresh produce from Mercat de la Llibertat (p158), the neighbourhood's emblematic larder – queue up and sample some wonderful food.

→ **Independent stores** Wander up Carrer de Verdi for an insight into what Gràcia does best. Independent boutiques and food shops abound on this tree-lined little street.

→ **Old-time bars** Gràcia still has plenty of tapas bars that have been around forever, such as El Roure (p160).

Getting There & Away

→ **Underground Rail** Metro Línia 3 (Fontana stop) leaves you halfway up Carrer Gran de Gràcia and close to a network of busy squares. To enter Gràcia from the other side, take Línia 4 to Joanic.

→ **On Foot** Strolling up Passeig de Gràcia from Plaça de Catalunya is a wonderful way to reach the neighbourhood, but it does take around 40 minutes.

Lonely Planet's Top Tip

A wonderful way to take in Gràcia's atmosphere is from a cafe or restaurant on one of its many squares. Arrive after dusk and watch as the place comes to life in the post-work hours.

GRÀCIA & PARK GÜELL

Best Places to Eat

→ Botafumeiro (p162)
→ Les Tres a la Cuina (p158)
→ Sol i Lluna (p160)
→ El Tossal (p160)

For reviews, see p158

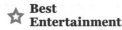
Best Places to Drink

→ Viblioteca (p162)
→ Raïm (p162)
→ El Roure (p160)

For reviews, see p162

Best Entertainment

→ Heliogàbal (p163)
→ Verdi (p163)
→ Sala Beckett (p163)

For reviews, see p163 →

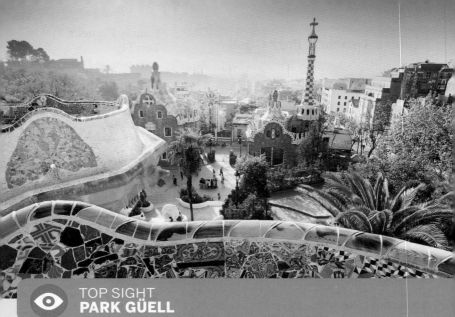

TOP SIGHT
PARK GÜELL

Park Güell – north of Gràcia and about 4km from Plaça de Catalunya – is where Gaudí turned his hand to landscape gardening. It's a strange, enchanting place where this iconic Modernista's passion for natural forms really took flight, to the point where the artificial almost seems more natural than the natural.

A City Park

Park Güell originated in 1900, when Count Eusebi Güell bought the tree-covered hillside of El Carmel (then outside Barcelona) and hired Gaudí to create a miniature city of houses for the wealthy, surrounded by landscaped grounds. The project was a commercial flop and was abandoned in 1914 – but not before Gaudí had created, in his inimitable manner, steps, a plaza, two gatehouses and 3km of roads and walks. In 1922 the city bought the estate for use as a public park. The park became a Unesco World Heritage site in 2004. The idea was based on the English 'garden cities', much admired by Güell, hence the spelling of 'Park'.

Just inside the main entrance on Carrer d'Olot, immediately recognisable by the two Hansel-and-Gretel gatehouses, is the park's newly refurbished Centre d'Interpretació, in the Pavelló de Consergeria, which is a typically curvaceous former porter's home that hosts a display on Gaudí's building methods and the history of the park. There are nice views from the top floor.

Sala Hipóstila (The Doric Temple)

The steps up from the entrance, guarded by a mosaic dragon/lizard (a copy of which you can buy in many central

DON'T MISS...

➡ Learning about Gaudí's building methods at the Centre d'Interpretació
➡ The Sala Hipóstila's stone forest
➡ The life of the artist at Casa-Museu Gaudí
➡ The undulating tiled bench with a view right across the city

PRACTICALITIES

➡ ☎93 409 18 31
➡ www.parkguell.cat
➡ Carrer d'Olot 7
➡ adult/child €7/4.50
➡ ⊙8am-9.30pm daily
➡ 🚌24 or 32, Ⓜ Lesseps or Vallcarca

souvenir shops), lead to the Sala Hipóstila (aka the Doric Temple). This forest of 88 stone columns – some leaning like mighty trees bent by the weight of time – was originally intended as a market. To the left curves a gallery, with twisted stonework columns and roof that give the effect of a cloister beneath tree roots – a motif repeated in several places in the park. On top of the Sala Hipóstila is a broad open space. Its centrepiece is the Banc de Trencadís, a tiled bench curving sinuously around its perimeter, which was designed by one of Gaudí's closest colleagues, architect Josep Maria Jujol (1879–1949). With Gaudí, however, there is always more than meets the eye. This giant platform was designed as a kind of catchment area for rainwater washing down the hillside. The water is filtered through a layer of stone and sand, and it drains down through the columns to an underground cistern.

Casa-Museu Gaudí

The spired house above and to the right of the entrance is the Casa-Museu Gaudí, where Gaudí lived for almost the last 20 years of his life (1906–26). It contains furniture he designed (including items that once lived in La Pedrera, Casa Batlló and Casa Calvet) along with other memorabilia. The house was built in 1904 by Francesc Berenguer i Mestres as a prototype for the 60 or so houses that were originally planned here.

Much of the park is still wooded, but it's laced with pathways. The best views are from the cross-topped Turó del Calvari in the southwest corner.

GETTING THERE

The walk from metro stop Lesseps is signposted. From the Vallcarca stop, the walk is marginally shorter and the uphill trek eased by escalators. Bus 24 drops you at an entrance near the top of the park.

The park is extremely popular (it gets an estimated 4 million visitors a year, about 86% of them tourists) and in 2013 an entrance fee was imposed on the central area containing most of its attractions. Access is limited to a certain number of people every half-hour, and it's wise to book ahead online.

◉ SIGHTS

PARK GÜELL　　　　　　　　　　PARK
See p156.

MERCAT DE LA LLIBERTAT　　　MARKET
Map p296 (☎93 217 09 95; www.mercatllibertat. com; Plaça de la Llibertat 27; ⊗8am-8pm Mon-Fri, 8am-3pm Sat; ⛽FGC Gràcia) **FREE** Built in the 1870s, the 'Market of Liberty' was covered over in 1893 in typically fizzy Modernista style, employing generous whirls of wrought iron. It got a considerable facelift in 2009 and has lost some of its aged charm, but the market remains emblematic of the Gràcia district: full of life and all kinds of fresh produce. The man behind the 1893 remake was Francesc Berenguer i Mestres (1866–1914), Gaudí's long-time assistant.

FUNDACIÓ FOTO COLECTANIA　　GALLERY
Map p296 (☎93 217 16 26; www.colectania.es; Carrer de Julián Romea 6; adult/child €3/free; ⊗10am-2pm & 4-8pm Mon-Sat, closed Aug; ⛽FGC Gràcia) Photography lovers should swing by here to see the latest exhibition; they change over about three times a year. When you reach what seems like offices, head through to the back on the ground floor, where two floors of exhibition space await. The exhibits may come from the foundation's own collection of Spanish and Portuguese snappers from the 1950s onwards, but more likely will be temporary exhibitions.

CASA VICENS　　　　　　　ARCHITECTURE
(Carrer de les Carolines 22; ⛽FGC Plaça Molina) The angular, turreted 1888 Casa Vicens was one of Gaudí's first commissions. Tucked away west of Gràcia's main drag, the richly detailed facade of this private house is awash with ceramic colour and shape. The house was up for sale at the time of writing, but rumour had it that an Andorran bank had placed an offer and was planning to open it to the public.

As was frequently the case, Gaudí sought inspiration from the past, in this case the rich heritage of building in the Mudéjar-style brick, typical in those parts of Spain reconquered from the Muslims. Mudéjar architecture was created by those Arabs and Berbers allowed to remain in Spain after the Christian conquests.

✖ EATING

Spread across this busy quarter are all sorts of enticing options, from simple tapas bars to top-class seafood. Gràcia is loaded with Middle Eastern and other ethnic restaurants, many of which are upbeat and good value. Several classic Catalan taverns tick along nicely with a strong local following. There's little of interest, however, around Park Güell.

★LES TRES A LA CUINA　　INTERNATIONAL €
Map p296 (☎93 105 49 47; Carrer de Sant Lluis 35; menú del día €9, brunch menú €10; ⊗10am-6pm Mon-Fri, 11.30am-4.30pm Sat & Sun; ⓜJoanic) Colourful, Instagrammable food that tastes superb and uses ingredients you won't find in most other restaurants around town. The menu changes daily but you can choose from the likes of chicken with apricots, prunes and tamarind sauce, or quinoa salad with baked fennel and avocado, and finish up with pistachio and lemon drizzle cake. All this prepared with love and Slow Food principles for an unbeatable price. There are few tables, so arrive early.

ENVALIRA　　　　　　　　CATALAN €
Map p296 (☎93 218 58 13; Plaça del Sol 13; mains €8-12; ⊗noon-4.30pm & 9pm-midnight Tue-Sat, noon-4.30pm Sun; ⓜFontana) You might not notice the modest entrance to this delicious relic, surrounded as it is by cool hang-outs, Lebanese eateries and grunge bars. Head for the 1950s time-warp dining room out the back. Serious waiters deliver all sorts of seafood and rice dishes to your table, from *arròs a la milanesa* (savoury rice with chicken, pork and a light cheese gratin) to a *bullit de lluç* (slice of white hake boiled with herb-laced rice and a handful of clams).

LOCAL KNOWLEDGE

GAUDÍ EXPERIÈNCIA

Opened in 2012, the 'Gaudí Experience' is a fun-filled Disney-style look at the life and work of Barcelona's favourite son, just a stone's throw from Park Güell. There are models of his buildings and achingly modern interactive exhibits and touchscreens, but the highlight is the stomach-churning 4D presentation in its tiny screening room. Not recommended for the frail or children aged under six years.

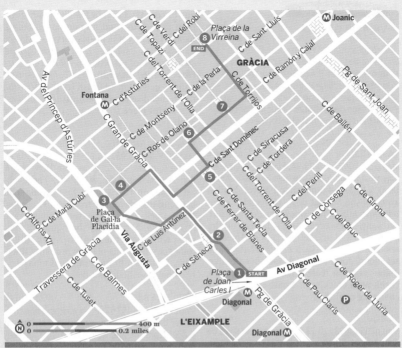

🏃 Neighbourhood Walk
The Squares of Gràcia

START PLAÇA DE JOAN CARLES I
END PLAÇA DE LA VERREINA
LENGTH 1.9KM; 50 MINUTES

The obelisk at **1 Plaça de Joan Carles I** honours Spain's present king for stifling an attempted coup d'état in February 1981, six years after Franco's death. Under the dictatorship, the avenue that passes through the square was known as Avenida de Francisco Franco. To *barcelonins* it was simply 'La Diagonal'. That name stuck. Where Carrer Gran de Gràcia leads you into Gràcia proper, a grand Modernista edifice now turned hotel, **2 Casa Fuster** (p219), rises in all its glory.

3 Plaça de Gal·la Placidia recalls the brief sojourn of the Roman empress-to-be Galla Placidia, captive and wife of the Visigothic chief Athaulf in the 5th century AD. She had been hauled across from Italy, where she hastily returned upon her captor-husband's death. **4 Plaça de la Llibertat** (Liberty Sq) is home to the bustling Modernista produce market of the same name. It was designed by one of Gaudí's colleagues, Francesc Berenguer, who was busy

in this part of town despite never having been awarded a diploma as an architect.

Popular **5 Plaça de la Vila de Gràcia** was, until a few years ago, named after the mayor under whom Gràcia was absorbed by Barcelona, Francesc Rius i Taulet. It is fronted by the local town hall (designed by Berenguer). At its heart stands the Torre del Rellotge (Clock Tower), long a symbol of Republican agitation. Possibly the rowdiest of Gràcia's squares, **6 Plaça del Sol** (Sun Sq) is lined with bars and eateries and comes to life on long summer nights. The square was the scene of summary executions after an uprising in 1870. During the 1936–39 civil war, an air-raid shelter was installed.

7 Plaça de la Revolució de Setembre de 1868 is a popular meeting point, with its cafe terraces and playground. Terraces adorn pedestrianised **8 Plaça de la Virreina**, notable for its shady trees and presided over by the 17th-century Església de Sant Joan. It was largely destroyed by anarchists during the unrest of the Setmana Tràgica (Tragic Week) of 1909. Rebuilt by Berenguer, it was damaged again during the civil war.

VILA DE GRÀCIA

Gràcia's busiest square, the Plaça de la Vila de Gràcia, was, until a few years ago, known as Plaça de Rius i Taulet, and you'll still hear that name appear occasionally. Some locals refer to it as the Plaça del Rellotge ('Clock') for the tall clock tower that stands there.

LA PUBILLA
CATALAN €

Map p296 (☑93 218 29 94; Plaça de la Llibertat 23; mains €8-12; ☻8.30am-5pm Mon-Sat; ⓂFontana) A little neighbourhood secret, hidden away by the Mercat de la Llibertat, La Pubilla specialises in *'esmorzars de forquilla'* (literally, 'fork breakfasts'), hearty affairs beloved of the market workers and nearby residents. There's also a *menú del día* (daily set menu) for €14, which includes Catalan dishes such as baked cod, or roast pork cheek with chickpeas. Arrive early for any chance of a table.

EL ROURE
TAPAS €

Map p296 (☑93 218 73 87; Carrer de la Riera de Sant Miquel 51; tapas from €3.50; ☻7am-1am Mon-Sat; ⓂFontana) This old-time locals' bar is what Hemingway meant by a 'clean, well-lighted place'. Sidle up to the bar or pull up a little wooden chair and tuck into good-value tapas from the bar, washed down by a few cold Estrellas. The *bunyols de bacallà* are delightful battered balls of cod that demand to be gobbled up. The place is full to bursting most of the time.

LA NENA
CAFE €

Map p296 (☑93 285 14 76; Carrer de Ramon i Cajal 36; snacks from €3; ☻9am-10.30pm; ⊞; ⓂFontana) A French team has created this delightfully chaotic space for indulging in cups of *suïssos* (rich hot chocolate) served with a plate of heavy homemade whipped cream and *melindros* (spongy sweet biscuits), fine desserts and even a few savoury dishes (including crêpes). The place is strewn with books and the area out the back is designed to keep kids busy, with toys, books and a blackboard with chalk, making it an ideal family rest stop.

EL GLOP
CATALAN €

Map p296 (☑93 213 70 58; www.tavernaelglop.com; Carrer de Sant Lluís 24; mains €8-12; ☻1pm-1am; ⓂJoanic) This raucous eatery is decked out in country Catalan fashion, with gingham tablecloths and no-nonsense, slap-up meals. The secret is hearty serves of simple dishes, such as *bistec a la brasa* (grilled steak), perhaps preceded by *albergínies farcides* (stuffed aubergines) or *calçots* (spring onions) in winter. To finish try the *tocinillo*, a caramel dessert. Open until 1am, El Glop is a useful place to have up your sleeve for a late bite.

NOU CANDANCHÚ
TAPAS €

Map p296 (☑93 237 73 62; Plaça de la Vila de Gràcia 9; mains €7-10; ☻7am-1am Mon, Wed & Sun, 7am-3am Fri & Sat; ⓂFontana) The liveliest locale on the square, Nou Candanchú is a long-time favourite for various reasons. Many flock to its sunny terrace just for a few drinks. Accompany the liquid refreshment with one of the giant *entrepans* (filled rolls) for which this place is famous. Otherwise, it offers a limited range of tapas and reasonable grilled-meat dishes.

★EL TOSSAL
SPANISH €€

Map p296 (☑93 457 63 82; www.eltossalbcn.com; Carrer de Tordera 12; mains €10-16; ☻1.30-4pm & 8.30-11pm Tue-Sat; ⓂJoanic) A proper old-fashioned, no-frills Catalan restaurant, of the sort in which Gràcia excels, with tables arrayed around a central bar area and into a low-ceilinged dining annexe. The speciality is game and similarly hearty fare – the oxtail stew is excellent, as is the duck magret with caramelised onions and a port reduction, and there is a short but well-chosen list of suitably robust wines.

SOL I LLUNA
FRENCH €€

Map p296 (☑93 237 10 52; Carrer de Verdi 50; mains €10.50-16.50; ☻7.30-11pm Mon-Fri, 1-4pm & 7.30pm-midnight Sat & Sun; ⓂFontana) Bright and sunny by day, softly lit at night, Sol i Lluna is a peaceful, elegant place that has as its distinguishing feature a giant wooden hippo (frequently topped with a small child) in the window. The food is mostly French, but draws in influences from around the globe, such as the 'lasagne' of ratatouille with goat's cheese or the vegetarian Puy lentil 'meatballs'.

CAFÉ GODOT
INTERNATIONAL €€

Map p296 (☑93 368 20 36; www.cafegodot.com; Carrer de Sant Domènec 19; mains €8-12; ☻10am-1am Mon-Fri, 11am-2am Sat & Sun; ⓂFontana) Managing to combine spacious, stylish and friendly (especially if you have kids in tow),

Godot is a relaxing place for a long lunch or Sunday brunch, with a mouthwatering list of snacks and more substantial bistro dishes, from a roast beef and horseradish sandwich to duck confit with lentils and spinach. There's plenty for vegetarians, too.

O'GRÀCIA!
MEDITERRANEAN €€

Map p296 (www.ogracia.es; Plaça de la Revolució de Setembre de 1868 15; mains €10-12; ⊙1.30-3.30pm & 8-10.30pm Tue-Sat, 1.30-3.30pm Sun; ⓂFontana) This is an especially popular lunch option, with the *menú del día* good value at €12.90. The *arròs negre de sepia* (black rice with cuttlefish) makes a good first course, followed by a limited set of meat and fish options with vegetable sides. Serves are decent, presentation is careful and service is attentive. There's a more elaborate menu at night for €17.

CANTINA MACHITO
MEXICAN €€

Map p296 (☑93 217 34 14; www.cantinamachito.com; Carrer de Torrijos 47; mains €12-14; ⊙11am-2am; ⓂFontana or Joanic) On the leafy Torrijos street, the colourful Machito – which seems devoted to the image of Frida Kahlo – gets busy with locals, and the outside tables are a great place to eat and drink until late. You'll find all the standard Mexican delights like quesadillas, tacos, enchiladas and so on, and some wonderfully refreshing iced water flavoured with honey and lime, mint and fruit.

BILBAO
SPANISH €€

Map p296 (☑93 458 96 24; Carrer del Perill 33; mains €16-22; ⊙1-4pm & 9-11pm Mon-Sat; ⓂDiagonal) It doesn't look much from the outside, but Bilbao is a timeless classic, where reservations for dinner are imperative. The back dining room, with bottle-lined walls, stout timber tables and a yellow light evocative of a country tavern, will appeal to carnivores especially, although some fish dishes are also on offer. Consider opting for a *chuletón* (T-bone steak), accompanied with a good Spanish red wine.

CAL BOTER
CATALAN €€

Map p296 (☑93 458 84 62; www.restaurantcalboter.com; Carrer de Tordera 62; mains €8-15; ⊙1-4pm & 9pm-midnight Tue-Sat, 1-4pm Sun & Mon; ⓂJoanic) Families and noisy groups of pals are drawn to this classic eatery for *cargols a la llauna* (snails sautéed in a tin dish), *filet de bou a la crema de foie* (a thick clump of tender beef drowned in an orange and foie gras sauce), and other Catalan specialities, including curious *mar i muntanya* (sea and mountain) combinations like *bolets i gambes* (mushrooms and prawns). The *menú del día* (lunch Tuesday to Friday) comes in at a good-humoured €10.

LA PANXA DEL BISBE
TAPAS €€

Map p296 (☑93 213 70 49; Carrer de Rabassa 37; mains €12-15; ⊙1.30-3.30pm & 8.30pm-midnight Tue-Sat; ⓂJoanic) With low lighting and a hip, young feel, the 'Bishop's Belly' is a great place to indulge in some creative gourmet tapas, washed down with a fine wine, like the Albariño white from Galicia, for a surprisingly modest outlay.

HIMALI
NEPALESE €€

Map p296 (☑93 285 15 68; Carrer de Milà i Fontanals 60; mains €10-11; ⊙1-4pm & 8pm-midnight Tue-Sun; ⓂJoanic) Spacious and simple, with gruff service and paper placemats, this is a great spot for Nepalese chow and vegetarian dishes. A vegetarian set dinner menu costs €14.95; the meatier version is €16.95. Carnivores can also opt for mixed grills with rice and naan, or *kukhurako fila* (roast chicken in walnut sauce).

LA LLAR DE FOC
CATALAN €€

Map p296 (☑93 284 10 25; www.lallardefoc.com; Carrer de Ramón i Cajal 13; mains €8-12; ⊙1-5pm & 8pm-midnight Tue-Sat, 1-5pm Sun; ⓂFontana) For a hearty sit-down meal, with fresh, simple Catalan food at rock-bottom prices, 'The Fireplace' is hard to beat. At lunch, it has a €9.80 *menú del día*. You could start with a gazpacho or *empanadita* (big slice of tuna pie), followed by chicken in a mild curry sauce or *costelles* (ribs) and *escalivada* (grilled red peppers and aubergines, served with an olive oil, salt and garlic dressing). Go for flan for dessert, as the ice creams are on a stick.

IPAR-TXOKO
BASQUE €€€

Map p296 (☑93 218 19 54; www.ipar-txoko.com; Carrer de Mozart 22; mains €20-25; ⊙1-3.30pm & 9-10.30pm Mon-Sat, closed Mon evening & Aug; ⓂDiagonal) Inside this Basque eatery the atmosphere is warm and traditional. Hefty wooden beams hold up the Catalan vaulted ceiling, and the bar (with tapas available) has a garish green-columned front. Getxo-born Mikel turns out traditional cooking from northern Spain, including a sumptuous *chuletón* (T-bone steak for two – look at the size of that thing) or a less gargantuan *tortilla de bacalao* (a thick salt-cod omelette). Then there are curiosities like *kokotxas de merluza,* heart-shaped cuts from the hake's throat. The wine list is daunting but Mikel is on hand to explain everything – in English, too.

CON GRACIA
FUSION €€€

Map p296 (☑93 238 02 01; www.congracia.es; Carrer de Martínez de la Rosa 8; set menu €59; ⏰7-11pm Tue-Sat; Ⓜ Diagonal) This teeny hideaway (seating about 20 in total) is a hive of originality, producing delicately balanced Mediterranean cuisine with Asian touches. On offer is a regularly changing surprise tasting menu or the set 'traditional' one, which includes such items as *sopa de foie y miso con aceite de trufa blanca* (miso and foie gras soup with white truffle oil) and a nice Chilean sea bass. At lunch, only groups are accepted. Book ahead.

BOTAFUMEIRO
SEAFOOD €€€

Map p296 (☑93 218 42 30; www.botafumeiro.es; Carrer Gran de Gràcia 81; mains €16-28; ⏰noon-1am; Ⓜ Fontana) It is hard not to mention this classic temple of Galician shellfish and other briny delights, long a magnet for VIPs visiting Barcelona. You can bring the price down by sharing a few *medias raciones* (large tapas plates) to taste a range of marine offerings or a *safata especial del Mar Cantàbric* (seafood platter) between two. Try the *percebes,* the strangely twisted goose barnacles harvested along Galicia's north Atlantic coast, which many Spaniards consider the ultimate seafood delicacy.

ROIG ROBÍ
CATALAN €€€

Map p296 (☑93 218 92 22; www.roigrobi.com; Carrer de Sèneca 20; mains €18-30; ⏰1.30-4pm & 8.30-11.30pm Mon-Sat, closed Sat lunchtime; Ⓜ Diagonal) This is an altar to refined traditional cooking. Try the *textures de carxofes amb vieires a la plantxa* (artichokes with grilled scallops) for the delicate scent of artichoke wafting over the prized shellfish. The restaurant also does several seafood-and-rice dishes and offers half portions for those with less of an appetite.

TIBET
CATALAN €€€

(☑93 284 50 45; Carrer de Ramiro de Maetzu 34; mains €15-25; ⏰2-3.30pm & 9-11pm Mon, Wed-Sat, 2-3.30pm Sun; ☐24 or 39, Ⓜ Alfons X) This Catalan restaurant, nestled in a semi-rustic setting not far from Park Güell, has as much to do with Tibet as this author does with Outer Mongolia. For 50 years it has been sizzling meat on the grill and dishing up snails, one of the house specialities.

DRINKING & NIGHTLIFE

Gràcia is a quirky place. In many ways it's its own world, with the mix of rowdy young beer swillers and beaming young parents that fill its bars and cafes.

VIBLIOTECA
WINE BAR

Map p296 (☑93 284 42 02; www.viblioteca.com; Carrer de Vallfogona 12; ⏰7pm-1am; Ⓜ Fontana) If the smell of ripe cheese doesn't rock your boat, this is not the place for you – a glass cabinet piled high with the stuff assaults your olfactory nerves as you walk into this small, white, cleverly designed space. The real speciality at Viblioteca, however, is wine, and you can choose from 150 mostly local labels, many of them available by the glass.

RAÏM
BAR

Map p296 (Carrer del Progrés 48; ⏰7pm-2.30am; Ⓜ Diagonal) The walls in Raïm are alive with black-and-white photos of Cubans and Cuba. Tired old wooden chairs of another epoch huddle around marble tables, while grand old wood-framed mirrors hang from the walls. They just don't make old Spanish taverns like this anymore.

LA CIGALE
BAR

Map p296 (☑93 457 58 23; Carrer de Tordera 50; ⏰6pm-2.30am Tue-Thu & Mon, 6pm-3am Fri & Sat; Ⓜ Joanic) A very civilised place for a cocktail (or, in summer, two for €8 if you order before 10pm) and to hear some poetry readings. Prop up the zinc bar, sink into a second-hand lounge chair around a teeny table or head upstairs. Music is chilled, conversation lively, and you're likely to see Charlie Chaplin in action on the silent flat-screen TV. You can also snack on wok-fried dishes.

LE JOURNAL
BAR

Map p296 (☑93 368 41 37; Carrer de Francisco Giner 36; ⏰6pm-2.30am Sun-Thu, 6pm-3am Fri & Sat; Ⓜ Fontana) Students love the conspiratorial basement air of this narrow bar, whose walls and ceiling are plastered with newspapers (hence the name). Read the headlines of yesteryear while reclining in an old lounge. For a slightly more intimate feel, head upstairs to the rear gallery. It's a smokers' paradise.

LA BAIGNOIRE
BAR

Map p296 (☑93 284 39 67; Carrer de Verdi 6; ☺7pm-2am Mon-Sat, 7pm-1am Sun; MFontana) This inviting, tiny wine bar is always packed. Grab a stool and high table and order fine wines by the glass (beer and cocktails available too). It's perfect before and after a movie at the nearby Verdi cinema.

BAR CANIGÓ
BAR

Map p296 (☑93 213 30 49; Carrer de Verdi 2; ☺10am-2am Mon-Thu, to 3am Fri & Sat; MFontana) Especially welcoming in winter, this corner bar overlooking Plaça de la Revolució de Setembre de 1868 is an animated spot to simply sip on an Estrella beer around rickety old marble-top tables, as people have done here for decades. There's also a pool table.

ALFA
BAR

Map p296 (☑93 415 18 24; www.alfabar.cat; Carrer Gran de Gràcia 36; ☺8pm-3.30am Tue-Sat; MDiagonal) Fans of good old-fashioned rock love this unchanging bar-cum-minidisco, a Gràcia classic. Records hang from the ceiling as if to remind you that most of the music comes from the pre-CD era, '60s to '80s and the occasional later intruder. Take up a stool for a drink and chat or head for the no-frills dance area just beyond. There's another bar right up the back.

MUSICAL MARIA
BAR

Map p296 (☑93 501 04 60; Carrer de Maria 5; ☺9pm-3am; MDiagonal) Even the music hasn't changed since this place got going in the late 1970s. Those longing for rock 'n' roll crowd into this animated bar, listen to old hits and knock back beers. Out the back there's a pool table and the bar serves pretty much all the variants of the local Estrella Damm brew.

SOL SOLER
BAR

Map p296 (☑93 172 99 75; Plaça del Sol 21-22; ☺11am-2.30am; MFontana) A pleasant place with old tile floors, wood panelling and little marble tables perfect for an early beer or glass of red and a chat. Drop by earlier in the day for wi-fi (available to 6.30pm) and, if hunger strikes, order in some bar snacks (the chicken wings are delicious).

EL SABOR
BAR

Map p296 (☑654 849975; Carrer de Francisco Giner 32; ☺10pm-3am Tue-Sun; MDiagonal) Ruled since 1992 by the charismatic Havana-born Angelito is this home of *ron y son* (rum and sound). A mixed crowd of Cubans and fans of the Caribbean island come to drink mojitos and shake their stuff in this diminutive, good-humoured hang-out.

☆ ENTERTAINMENT

HELIOGÀBAL
LIVE MUSIC

Map p296 (www.heliogabal.com; Carrer de Ramón i Cajal 80; ☺9.30pm-3am Wed-Sat; MJoanic) This compact bar is a veritable hive of cultural activity where you never quite know what to expect. Aside from art exhibitions and poetry readings, you will be pleasantly surprised by the eclectic live-music program. Jazz groups are often followed by open jam sessions, and experimental music of all colours gets a run. While many performers are local, international acts also get a look in.

SALA BECKETT
THEATRE

Map p296 (☑93 284 53 12; www.salabeckett.com; Carrer de Ca l'Alegre de Dalt 55; ☺box office 10am-2pm & 4-8pm Mon-Fri & 1hr before start of show; MJoanic) One of the city's principal alternative theatres, the Sala Beckett is a smallish space that does not shy away from challenging theatre, contemporary or otherwise, and usually a heterodox mix of local productions and foreign drama.

VERDI
CINEMA

Map p296 (☑93 238 79 90; www.cines-verdi.com; Carrer de Verdi 32; MFontana) A popular original-language movie house in the heart of Gràcia, handy to lots of local eateries and bars for pre- and post-film enjoyment.

VERDI PARK
CINEMA

Map p296 (☑93 238 79 90; www.cines-verdi.com; Carrer de Torrijos 49; MFontana) Sister to the Verdi cinema, the Verdi Park is an art-house cinema.

TEATRENEU
THEATRE

Map p296 (☑93 285 37 12; www.teatreneu.com; Carrer de Terol 26; ☺box office 1hr before show; MFontana or Joanic) This lively theatre (with a bustling, rambling downstairs bar facing the street) dares to fool around with all sorts of material, from monologues to social comedy. Aside from the main theatre, two cafe-style spaces serve as more intimate stage settings for small-scale productions. Films are also shown.

 ## SHOPPING

A wander along the narrow lanes of Gràcia turns up all sorts of surprises, mostly tiny enterprises producing a variety of pretty garments and trinkets. These places tend to come and go, so you never quite know what you might turn up. Carrer de Verdi has plenty of interesting threads shops.

NOSTÀLGIC
PHOTOGRAPHY

Map p296 (☑93 368 57 57; www.nostalgic.es; Carrer de Goya 18; ☺5-8.30pm Mon, 11am-2.30pm & 5-8.30pm Tue-Sat; ⓜFontana) A beautiful space with exposed brick walls and wooden furniture specialising in all kinds of modern and vintage photography equipment – you'll find camera bags and tripods for the digital snappers, and the inevitable collection of Lomo cameras, with their quirky variations. There is also a decent collection of photography books to buy or browse.

HIBERNIAN
BOOKS

Map p296 (☑93 217 47 96; www.hibernian-books.com; Carrer de Montseny 17; ☺4-8.30pm Mon, 10.30am-8.30pm Tue-Sat; ⓜFontana) The biggest second-hand English bookshop in Barcelona stocks thousands of titles covering all sorts of subjects, from cookery to children's classics. There is a smaller collection of new books in English, too.

MUSHI MUSHI
FASHION

Map p296 (☑93 292 29 74; www.mushimushicollection.com; Carrer de Bonavista 12; ☺4.30-8.30pm Mon, 11am-3pm & 4.30-8.30pm Tue-Sat; ⓜFontana) A gorgeous little fashion boutique in an area that's not short of them, Mushi Mushi specialises in quirky but elegant women's fashion and accessories. It stocks labels that include Des Petits Hauts, Sessùn, Custommade and lesser known French labels. The collection changes frequently, with only a few of each item being stocked, so a return visit can pay off.

ÉRASE UNA VEZ
FASHION

Map p296 (☑697 805409; www.eraseunavez.info; Carrer de Goya 7; ☺11am-2pm Mon, 11am-2pm & 5-9pm Tue-Sat; ⓜFontana) 'Once Upon a Time' is the name of this fanciful boutique, which brings out the princess in you. It offers ethereal, delicate women's clothes, almost exclusively evening wear, as well as wedding dresses. Local designers such as Llamazares y de Delgado and Zazo & Brull are behind these sometimes sumptuous creations.

BODEGA BONAVISTA
WINE

Map p296 (☑93 218 81 99; Carrer de Bonavista 10; ☺10am-2.30pm & 5-9pm Mon-Fri, noon-3pm & 6-9pm Sat, noon-3pm Sun; ⓜFontana) An excellent little neighbourhood wine shop that endeavours to seek out great wines at reasonable prices. The stock is mostly from Catalonia and elsewhere in Spain, but there's also a good selection from France. The Bonavista also acts as a deli, and there are some especially good cheeses.

 ## SPORTS & ACTIVITIES

AQUA URBAN SPA
DAY SPA

Map p296 (☑93 238 41 60; www.aqua-urbanspa.com; Carrer Gran de Gràcia 7; 90min session from €51; ☺9am-9pm Mon-Sat; ⓜDiagonal) With sessions for anything from stress to tired legs (helpful for diehard sightseers), this spa offers smallish pool and shower areas, along with steam baths, Roman-style baths and a series of beauty treatment options.

FLOTARIUM
FLOTARIUM

Map p296 (☑93 217 36 37; www.flotarium.com; Plaça de Narcís Oller 3; 1hr session €35; ☺10am-10pm; ⓜDiagonal) Be suspended in zero gravity and feel the stress ebb away. Each flotarium, like a little space capsule with water, is in a private room, with shower, towels and shampoo, and Epsom salts that allow you to float as if in the Dead Sea.

Camp Nou, Pedralbes & La Zona Alta

SANT GERVASI | TIBIDABO | SARRIÀ | LES CORTS | CAMP NOU | PEDRALBES | ZONA UNIVERSITÀRIA

Neighbourhood Top Five

1 Reliving the great moments of one of the world's legendary football teams at the multimedia museum of **Camp Nou** (p167). Or, better yet, seeing a game live.

2 Walking the 14th-century cloister and gazing at exquisite murals at peaceful **Museu-Monestir de Pedralbes** (p168).

3 Getting a taste of the Amazon, and travelling through earth's evolution at warp speed, at **Cosmocaixa** (p170).

4 Gazing upon imposing **Bellesguard** (p169), Gaudí's medieval-like masterpiece, only recently opened to the public.

5 Travelling by tram and funicular railway up to **Tibidabo** (p172) for its lovely views and old-fashioned amusement park.

For more detail of this area see maps on p298 and p300 ➡

Lonely Planet's Top Tip

To make the most of the neighbourhood, try to visit on a weekend. Saturday and Sunday are the only days when you can peek inside the Pavellons Güell (with guided visits in English offered twice daily) at Palau Reial de Pedralbes. The weekend is also the best time to catch the tram up to Tibidabo.

Best Places to Eat

➡ Ajoblanco (p173)

➡ Vivanda (p173)

➡ Via Veneto (p173)

➡ ABaC (p173)

➡ Hofmann (p173)

For reviews, see p173 ➡

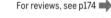 Best Places to Drink

➡ Dõ Bar (p174)

➡ Mirablau (p175)

➡ Berlin (p174)

➡ Marcel (p174)

For reviews, see p174 ➡

Best Parks & Gardens

➡ Parc de Collserola (p172)

➡ Jardins del Laberint d'Horta (p171)

➡ Jardins del Palau de Pedralbes (p169)

➡ Parc de la Creueta del Coll (p169)

For reviews, see p169 ➡

Explore: Camp Nou, Pedralbes & La Zona Alta

This vast area, which runs north of L'Eixample and west of Gràcia, includes some intriguing sites, although football and fun parks aside, few people make the journey north. Framing the north end of 'the High Zone' lies the Collserola hills, which are a major draw for outdoor enthusiasts.

Nearby Tibidabo marks the city's highest point, and its old-fashioned amusement park and fine views are the big attraction. Getting here is half the fun – you can take an old tram past Modernista mansions, then a steeply inclined funicular railway to reach the top.

The upscale neighbourhood of Pedralbes has a mix of peaceful streets and manicured gardens hidden off the busy thoroughfares. Standouts include an atmospheric monastery, elegant gardens (the Jardins del Palau de Pedralbes) and a little-visited Gaudí site (Pavellons Güell).

Just south of Pedralbes is Camp Nou, the enshrined playing field of FC Barcelona, one of the world's best football teams. To the northeast lies Sarrià, a small, quaint neighbourhood of brick streets, tiny plazas and medieval buildings, with a lively collection of shops, restaurants and bars. For an authentic and charming side of Barcelona, relatively untouristed, this is the place to come.

Local Life

➡ **Outdoors** Going for a run or a mountain-bike ride in the vast reserve of Parc de Collserola (p172).

➡ **Nightlife** Having a few drinks in the bars near Carrer de Muntaner, followed by late-night dancing in Otto Zutz (p175) and other nearby clubs.

➡ **Village days** Wondering through the picturesque narrow lanes of Sarrià, stopping for cakes at Foix de Sarrià (p173), tapas at Bar Tomàs (p173) and a great meal at Vivanda (p173).

Getting There & Away

➡ **Metro** Línia 3 will get you to the Jardins del Laberint d'Horta (Mundet) and Camp Nou and Palau Reial de Pedralbes (Palau Reial).

➡ **Train** FGC trains are handy for getting close to sights in and around Tibidabo and Parc del Collserola.

➡ **Tram** Outside Avinguda Tibidabo station, the *tramvia blau* runs to Plaça del Doctor Andreu, where you can catch an onward funicular up to Tibidabo.

➡ **Funicular** Two funicular railways provide hilltop access: the funicular del Tibidabo runs between Plaça del Doctor Andreu and Plaça del Doctor Tibidabo. The funicular de Vallvidrera runs between Peu del Funicular and Vallvidrera Superior.

TOP SIGHT
CAMP NOU

Among Barcelona's most-visited sites is the massive stadium of Camp Nou (which means New Field in Catalan), home to the legendary FC Barcelona. Attending a match amid the roar of the crowds is an unforgettable experience, but if you can't make a game, don't miss the high-tech museum, with its multimedia exhibits, and a self-guided tour of the stadium.

Museu del Futbol Club Barcelona

The **museum** (Map p298; ☑93 496 36 00; www.fcbarcelona.es; Carrer d'Aristides Maillol; adult/child €8.50/6.80; ☉10am-8pm Mon-Sat, to 2.30pm Sun & holidays mid-Apr–mid-Oct, 10am-6.30pm Mon-Sat, 10am-2.30pm Sun & holidays mid-Oct–mid-Apr; underground rail Collblanc), renovated in 2010, provides a high-tech view into the club. Giant touch screens allow interactive exploring, delving into the club's history, its social commitment and connection to Catalan identity as well as indepth stats of on-the-field action. Sound installations include the club's anthem (which you can hear in many languages, including Hindi) and match-day sounds from the stadium.

The best bits of the museum itself are the photo section, the goal videos and the views over the stadium. You can admire the (in at least one case literally) golden boots of great goal scorers of the past and learn about the greats who have played for Barça over the years, including Maradona, Ronaldinho, Kubala and many others.

The Stadium

Gazing out across Camp Nou is an experience in itself. The stadium, built in 1957 and enlarged for the 1982 World Cup, is one of the world's biggest, holding 99,000 people. The club has a world-record membership of 173,000.

The self-guided tour of the stadium takes in the team's dressing rooms, heads out through the tunnel, onto the pitch and winds up in the presidential box. You'll also get to visit the television studio, the press room and the commentary boxes. Set aside about 2½ hours for the whole visit.

Getting Tickets

Tickets to FC Barcelona matches are available at Camp Nou, online (through FC Barcelona's official website) as well as through various city locations. Tourist offices sell them – the branch at Plaça de Catalunya (p255) is a centrally located option – as do FC Botiga stores. Tickets can cost anything from €35 to upwards of €200, depending on the seat and match. On match day the ticket windows open weekdays from 9am until half time, on Saturdays from 10am until half time; on Sundays they open two hours before kick off through half time. Usually tickets are not available for matches against Real Madrid. If you attend a game, go early so you'll have ample time to find your seat (this stadium is massive) and soak up the atmosphere.

You will almost definitely find scalpers lurking near the ticket windows. They are often club members and can sometimes get you in at a significant reduction. Don't pay until you are safely seated.

DON'T MISS...

➡ Hearing the rousing Barça anthem sung before FC Barcelona takes the field

➡ The museum's footage of the team's best goals

➡ A self-guided tour of the stadium

PRACTICALITIES

➡ Map p298

➡ ☑902 189900

➡ www.fcbarcelona.com

➡ Carrer d'Aristides Maillol

➡ adult/child €23/17

➡ ☉10am-7.30pm Mon-Sat, to 2.30pm Sun

➡ ⓜPalau Reial

CAMP NOU, PEDRALBES & LA ZONA ALTA CAMP NOU

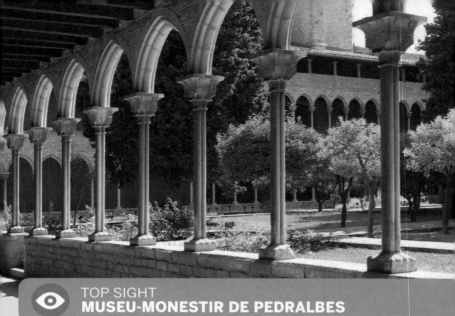

TOP SIGHT
MUSEU-MONESTIR DE PEDRALBES

Now a museum of monastic life, this peaceful convent is full of architectural treasures and provides a fascinating glimpse into centuries past. Perched at the top of busy Avinguda de Pedralbes in what was once unpeopled countryside, the monastery remains a divinely quiet corner of Barcelona. Adjoining the monastery is the sober church, an excellent example of Catalan Gothic.

The Cloister & Chapel

The architectural highlight is the large, elegant, three-storey cloister, a jewel of Catalan Gothic, built in the early 14th century. Following its course to the right, stop at the first chapel, the Capella de Sant Miquel, the **murals** of which were done in 1346 by Ferrer Bassá, one of Catalonia's earliest documented painters. A few steps on is the ornamental grave of Queen Elisenda, who founded the convent. It is curious, as it is divided in two: the side in the cloister shows her dressed as a penitent widow, while the other part, an alabaster masterpiece inside the adjacent church, shows her dressed as queen.

The Refectory & Dormidor

As you head around the ground floor of the cloister, you can peer into the restored refectory, kitchen, stables, stores and a reconstruction of the infirmary – all giving a good idea of convent life. Eating in the refectory must not have been a whole lot of fun, judging by the **enscriptions** around the walls exhorting *Silentium* (Silence) and *Audi Tacens* (Listen and Keep Quiet). Upstairs is a grand hall that was once the *dormidor* (sleeping quarters). It was lined by tiny night cells but they were long ago removed. Today a modest collection of the monastery's art and furniture grace this space.

DON'T MISS...

➡ Ferrer Bassá's murals

➡ The three-storey Gothic cloister

➡ The refectory's admonishing enscriptions

PRACTICALITIES

➡ Map p298

➡ 93 256 34 34

➡ www.bcn.cat/monestirpedralbes

➡ Baixada del Monestir 9

➡ adult/child €7/5, free 3-8pm Sun

➡ 10am-5pm Tue-Fri, to 7pm Sat, to 8pm Sun

➡ 22, 63, 64 or 75, FGC Reina Elisenda

◉ SIGHTS

CAMP NOU   STADIUM
See p167.

**MUSEU-MONESTIR DE
PEDRALBES**   MONASTERY
See p168.

JARDINS DEL PALAU DE PEDRALBES   PARK
Map p298 (Avinguda Diagonal 686; ☺10am-8pm
Apr-Oct, to 6pm Nov-Mar; MPalau Reial) FREE
A few steps from busy Avinguda Diagonal lies this small enchanting green space.
Sculptures, fountains, citrus trees, bamboo
groves, fragrant eucalyptus, towering cypresses and bougainvillea-covered nooks
lie scattered along the paths criss-crossing
these peaceful gardens.

Among the little-known treasures here
are a vine-covered parabolic pergola and
a gurgling fountain of Hercules, both designed by Antoni Gaudí. At the north end
of the park is the **Palau Reial de Pedralbes**, an early-20th-century building
that belonged to the family of Eusebi Güell
(Gaudí's patron) until they handed it over
to the city in 1926 to serve as a royal residence. Among its guests have been King
Alfonso XIII, the president of Catalonia
and General Franco. The *palau* (palace) is
currently closed to the public; until 2014 it
housed several museums, which have since
moved to Poblenou, and now compose the
Museu del Disseny de Barcelona.

PAVELLONS GÜELL   ARCHITECTURE
Map p298 (☎93 317 76 52; Avinguda de Pedralbes 7;
guided tour adult/child €6/3; ☺Sat & Sun) A short
stroll from the Jardins del Palau de Pedralbes
are the stables and porter's lodge designed by
Gaudí for the Finca Güell, as the Güell estate

here was called. Known also as the Pavellons Güell, they were built in the mid-1880s,
when Gaudí was strongly impressed by Islamic architecture. You can peer inside on
guided visits, with English-language tours at
10.15am and 12.15pm on weekends. Outside
visiting hours, there is nothing to stop you
admiring Gaudí's fantastical wrought-iron
dragon gate from the exterior.

BELLESGUARD   ARCHITECTURE
Map p298 (☎93 250 40 93; www.bellesguardgaudi.
com; Carrer de Bellesguard 16; admission €7;
☺10am-7pm Mon-Sat Apr-Oct, 10am-3pm Mon-Sat
Nov-Mar; ⓇFGC Avinguda Tibidabo) This Gaudí
masterpiece was recently rescued from ob-
scurity, and opened to the public in 2013.
Built between 1900 and 1909, this private
residence (still owned by the original Guil-
era family) has a castle-like appearance with
crenellated walls of stone and brick, narrow
stained-glass windows, elaborate ironwork
and a soaring turret mounted by a Gaudian
cross. It's a fascinating work that combines
both Gothic and Modernista elements.

Guided tours in English (€16 per person) happen daily at 11am and include the
interior of the building; otherwise visits
are limited to the grounds – its gardens
and stables, but do include an audioguide
that gives historical background. The other
downside: it's a long walk to a train station,
though many buses pass near (including
bus 22 and bus 58 from Plaça de Catalunya).

PARC DE LA CREUETA DEL COLL   PARK
(☎93 413 24 00; Passeig de la Mare de Déu del
Coll 77; ☺10am-sunset; ♿; MPenitents) Not
far from Park Güell, this refreshing public
park has a pleasant, meandering, splashing
pool. The pool, along with swings, showers
and snack bar, makes a relaxing family

A WANDER THROUGH OLD SARRIÀ

Hugging the left flank of thundering Via Augusta, the old centre of Sarrià is a largely
pedestrianised haven of peace. Probably founded in the 13th century and only
incorporated into Barcelona in 1921, ancient Sarrià is formed around sinuous
Carrer Major de Sarrià, today a mix of old and new, with a sprinkling of shops and
restaurants. At its top end is pretty **Plaça de Sarrià** (from where Passeig de la Reina
Elisenda de Montcada leads west to the medieval Museu-Monestir de Pedralbes),
where you'll want to check out Foix De Sarrià (p173), an exclusive pastry shop. As you
wander downhill, duck off into **Plaça del Consell de la Vila**, **Plaça de Sant Vicenç
de Sarrià** and Carrer de Rocaberti, at the end of which is the **Monestir de Santa
Isabel** (Map p298), with its neo-Gothic cloister. Built in 1886 to house Clarissan nuns,
whose order had first set up in El Raval in the 16th century, it was abandoned during
the civil war and used as an air-raid shelter.

TOP SIGHT
COSMOCAIXA

Kids (and kids at heart) are fascinated by displays here and the museum has become one of the city's most popular attractions. The single greatest highlight is the re-creation of over 1 sq km of a chunk of flooded **Amazon rainforest** (Bosc Inundat). More than 100 species of Amazon flora and fauna (including anacondas, colourful poisonous frogs and caymans) prosper in this unique, living diorama in which you can even watch a tropical downpour. In another original section, the Mur Geològic, seven great chunks of rock (90 tonnes in all) have been assembled to create a **Geological Wall**.

Also worthwhile, are the 3D shows in the **Planetari** (Planetarium), which are screened several times a day. Shows typically run for 35 minutes and cost €4; headsets provide commentary in English and other languages.

These and other displays on the lower 5th floor (the bulk of the museum is underground) cover many fascinating areas of science, from fossils to physics, and from the alphabet to outer space.

Outside, there's a nice stroll through the extensive Plaça de la Ciència, with the modest garden of flourishing Mediterranean flora.

DON'T MISS...

➡ A tropical storm in the Amazon
➡ The Geological Wall
➡ The Planetarium

PRACTICALITIES

➡ Museu de la Ciència
➡ Map p298
➡ 📞93 212 60 50
➡ www.fundacio.lacaixa.es
➡ Carrer de Isaac Newton 26
➡ adult/child €4/free
➡ 🕙10am-8pm Tue-Sun
➡ 🚌60, 🚇FGC Avinguda Tibidabo

stop on hot summer days and is strictly a local affair. The park area is open all year; only the lake-pool closes outside summer.

The park is set inside a deep crater left by long years of stone quarrying. On one side of it, an enormous cement sculpture, *Elogio del Agua* (Eulogy to Water) by Eduardo Chillida, is suspended. You can wander the trails around the high part of this hill-park and enjoy views of the city and Tibidabo. From the Penitents metro station, it's a 15-minute walk. Enter from Carrer Mare de Déu del Coll.

OBSERVATORI FABRA   OBSERVATORY
Map p298 (📞93 431 21 39; www.fabra.cat; Carretera del Observatori; admission €10; 🚇FGC Avinguda Tibidabo then 🚋tramvia blau) Inaugurated in 1904, this Modernista observatory is still a functioning scientific foundation. It can be visited on certain evenings to allow people to observe the stars through its grand old telescope. Visits, generally in Catalan or Spanish (Castilian) have to be booked. From mid-June to mid-September an option is to join in for the nightly **Sopars amb Estrelles** (Dinner under the Stars; 📞93 327 01 21; www.soparsambestrelles.com). You

dine outside, tour the building, peer into the telescope and get a lecture (in Catalan) on the heavens. The evening starts at 8.30pm and costs €70 per person. The easiest way here is by taxi.

COL·LEGI DE LES TERESIANES   ARCHITECTURE
Map p298 (📞93 212 33 54; Carrer de Ganduxer 85-105; 🚇FGC Tres Torres) This striking work by Gaudí has exposed brick pillars and steep catenary arches, each of which is unique. It was built in 1889 for the Order of St Teresa.

EATING

Some of the grandest kitchens in the city are scattered across La Zona Alta, from Tibidabo across Sant Gervasi (as far down as Avinguda Diagonal, west of Gràcia) to Pedralbes. Plenty of places of all cuisines and qualities abound, often tucked away in quiet, unassuming residential streets far from anything of interest to tourists. Eating in La Zona Alta can be both a culinary and, with a couple of notable exceptions, a genuinely local experience.

✖ Sant Gervasi

MITJA VIDA
TAPAS €

Map p300 (Carrer de Brusi 39; tapas €2-6; ⊙6-11pm Mon-Thu, noon-4pm & 6-11pm Fri & Sat, noon-4pm Sun; 🚇FGC Sant Gervasi) A fun, youthful mostly local crowd gathers around the stainless-steel tapas bar of tiny Mitja Vida. It's a jovial eating and drinking spot, with flavourful servings of anchovies, calamares, smoked herring, cheeses and *mojama* (salt-cured tuna). The drink of choice is house-made vermouth.

COMAXURROS
CHURROS €

Map p298 (Carrer de Muntaner 562; churros from €2; ⊙9am-1.30pm & 4-8.30pm Tue-Fri, 9am-2pm & 5-8.30pm Sat & Sun; 🚇FGC El Putxet) At this eye-catching little cafe, brought to you by Barcelona's famous *pastelería* Canals, the humble churro receives a dramatic make-over: it's fried in olive oil to crispy (healthier) perfection and served with unique fillings and toppings (pistachio, strawberry sauce, dark chocolate). You'll even find savoury

churros – with cheese, mushrooms and *jamón ibérico* (Iberian ham) among other delicacies.

LIADÍSIMO
CAFE €

Map p300 (Carrer de Guillem Tell 23-25; mains €5-8; ⊙7.30am-9.30pm Mon-Fri, 8.30am-9.30pm Sat; 🚇St Gervasi or Molina) This enticing cafe has an art-loving soul with changing artwork adorning the walls, whimsical light fixtures and a backdrop of films playing silently against a back wall. There's also a lush garden, which is a relaxing retreat to enjoy the juices and smoothies, sweet or savoury crêpes, pastas, grilled sandwiches and decent coffees.

FLASH FLASH
SPANISH €

Map p300 (☏93 237 09 90; Carrer de la Granada del Penedès 25; mains €7-12; ⊙1pm-1.30am; 🚇FGC Gràcia) Decorated with black-and-white murals and all-white interior, Flash Flash has a fun and kitschy pop-art aesthetic that harks back to its opening in 1969. Fluffy tortillas are the speciality, with more than 50 varieties, as well as massive bunless hamburgers.

WORTH A DETOUR

JARDINS DEL LABERINT D'HORTA

Laid out in the twilight years of the 18th century by Antoni Desvalls, Marquès d'Alfarras i de Llupià, this carefully manicured **park** (☏93 413 24 00; Passeig del Castanyers 1; adult/student €2.23/1.42, free Wed & Sun; ⊙10am-sunset; 🚼; 🚇Mundet) remained a private family idyll until the 1970s, when it was opened to the public. Many a fine party and theatrical performance was held here over the years, but it now serves as a kind of museum-park.

The gardens take their name from a maze in their centre, but other paths take you past a pleasant artificial lake (estany), waterfalls, a neoclassical pavilion and a false cemetery. The last is inspired by 19th-century romanticism, characterised by an obsession with a swooning, anaemic (some might say silly) vision of death.

The labyrinth, in the middle of these cool gardens (somehow odd in this environment, with modern apartments and ring roads nearby), can be surprisingly frustrating! This is a good one for kids.

Scenes of the film adaptation of Patrick Süsskind's novel *Perfume* were shot in the gardens.

To reach the gardens, take the right exit upstairs at Mundet metro station; on emerging, turn right and then left along the main road (with football fields on your left) and then the first left uphill to the gardens (about 10 minutes).

Also in the area are two exceptional restaurants.

Can Cortada (☏93 427 23 15; www.gruptravi.com; Avinguda de l'Estatut de Catalunya; mains €13-27; ⊙1.30-4pm & 8.30-11.30pm; 🚇Mundet), set on an 11th-century estate (complete with the remains of a defensive tower), serves up traditional Catalan fare. Try for a table in the former cellars or on the garden terrace.

Can Travi Nou (☏93 428 03 01; www.gruptravi.com; Carrer Jorge Manrique; mains €18-28; ⊙1-4pm daily & 8.30-11pm Mon-Sat; 🚇Montbau) is an expansive 18th-century mansion with several dining areas that stretch out across two floors. The warm colours, grandfather clock and wholesome, rustic air make for a magical setting for a Catalan splurge.

WORTH A DETOUR

TIBIDABO: GARDENS OF EARTHLY DELIGHTS

Framing the north end of the city, the forest-covered mountain of Tibidabo, which tops out at 512m, is the highest peak in Serra de Collserola. Aside from the superb views from the top, the highlights of Tibidabo include an 8000-hectare park, an old-fashioned amusement park, a telecommunications tower with viewing platform and a looming church that's visible from many parts of the city. Tibidabo gets its name from the devil, who, trying to tempt Christ, took him to a high place and said, in Latin: 'Haec omnia tibi dabo si cadens adoraberis me' ('All this I will give you if you fall down and worship me').

To reach the church and amusement park, take an FGC train to Avinguda Tibidabo. Outside Avinguda Tibidabo station, hop on the tramvia blau, which runs past fancy Modernista mansions to Plaça del Doctor Andreu (one way €4.20, 15 minutes, every 15 or 30 minutes 10am to 8pm daily late June to early September, 10am to 6pm Saturday, Sunday and holidays early September to late June). From Plaça del Doctor Andreu the Tibidabo funicular railway climbs to the top of the hill (return €7.70, five minutes). Departures start around 10am and continue until shortly after the Parc d'Atraccions' closing time.

An alternative is bus T2A, the 'Tibibús', from Plaça de Catalunya to Plaça de Tibidabo (€3, 30 minutes, every 30 to 50 minutes on Saturday, Sunday and holidays year-round and hourly from 10.15am Monday to Friday late June to early September).

For Parc de Collserola, take an FGC train to Baixador de Vallvidrera. Or you can stop one station earlier at Peu del Funicular and ride to the top via funicular railway. Bus 111 runs between Tibidabo and Vallvidrera (passing in front of the Torre de Collserola).

Parc de Collserola

Barcelonins needing an escape from the city without heading too far into the countryside seek out the vast **Parc de Collserola** (Map p298; ☑93 280 35 52; www.parcnaturalcollserola.cat; Carretera de l'Església 92; ⊙Centre d'Informació 9.30am-3pm, Can Coll 9.30am-3pm Sun & holidays, closed Jul & Aug; ☒FGC Peu del Funicular, funicular Baixador de Vallvidrera) in the hills. It is a great place to hike and bike and bristles with eateries and snack bars. Pick up a map from the Centre d'Informació.

Aside from nature, the main point of interest is the **Museu-Casa Verdaguer**, 100m from the info centre and a short walk from the train station. Catalonia's revered writer Jacint Verdaguer lived in this late-18th-century country house before his death on 10 July 1902. Beyond, the park has other minor highlights, including a smattering of country chapels, the ragged ruins of the 14th-century Castellciuro castle in the west, various lookout points and, to the north, the 15th-century Can Coll, a grand farmhouse.

Temple del Sagrat Cor

The **Temple del Sagrat Cor** (Church of the Sacred Heart; ☑93 417 56 86; Plaça de Tibidabo; admission free, lift €2; ⊙7am-8pm, lift 10am-8pm) **FREE**, looming above the top funicular station, is meant to be Barcelona's answer to Paris' Sacré-Cœur. The church, built from 1902 to 1961 in a mix of styles with some Modernista influence, is certainly as visible as its Parisian namesake, and even more vilified by aesthetes. It's actually two churches, one on top of the other. The top one is surmounted by a giant statue of Christ and has a lift to take you to the roof for the panoramic views.

Parc d'Atraccions

The reason most barcelonins come to Tibidabo is for some thrills in this **funfair** (☑93 211 79 42; www.tibidabo.cat; Plaça de Tibidabo 3-4; adult/child €29/10.30; ⊙closed Jan & Feb), close to the top funicular station. Here you'll find high-speed rides and high-tech 4D cinema, as well as old-fashioned attractions, including an old steam train and the Museu d'Autòmats, with its collection of automated puppets. Check the website for opening times.

Torre de Collserola

Sir Norman Foster designed the 288m-high **Torre de Collserola** (Map p298; ☑93 406 93 54; www.torredecollserola.com; Carretera de Vallvidrera al Tibidabo; adult/child €6/4; ⊙noon-2pm & 3.30-8pm Wed-Sun Jul & Aug, noon-2pm & 3.15-6pm Sat, Sun & holidays Sep-Jun, closed Jan & Feb; ☒111, Funicular de Vallvidrera) telecommunications tower, which was completed in 1992. The visitors' observation area, 115m up, offers magnificent views.

AJOBLANCO TAPAS €€

Map p300 (☎93 667 87 66; Carrer de Tuset 20; sharing plates €8-20; ⊙noon-3am; 🚇FGC Gràcia) New in 2014, this beautifully designed space serves up a mix of classic and creative tapas plates that go nicely with the imaginative cocktail menu. Sip the house vermouth while feasting on oxtail tacos, jumbo prawns with avocado and cherry tomato, or arugula salad with goat cheese, strawberries and toasted almonds.

VIA VENETO CATALAN €€€

Map p300 (☎93 200 72 44; www.viavenetorestaurant.com; Carrer de Ganduxer 10; mains €29-40; ⊙1-3.30pm Mon-Fri & 7.30-11.30pm Mon-Sat, closed Aug; 🚇FGC La Bonanova) Dalí used to regularly waltz into this high-society eatery after it opened in 1967. The vaguely art deco setting (note the oval mirrors), orange-rose tablecloths, leather chairs and fine cutlery may cater to more conservative souls, but the painter was here for the kitchen exploits. Catalan dishes dominate, with delicacies such as roast rack of baby lamb or chargrilled sea bass with black rice and razor clams.

HOFMANN MEDITERRANEAN €€€

Map p300 (☎93 218 71 65; www.hofmann-bcn.com; Carrer de la Granada del Penedès 14-16; mains €24-37; ⊙1.30-3.30pm & 9-11.30pm Mon-Fri; 🚇FGC Gràcia) What's cooking here are the trainee chefs, helped along by their instructors. Dishes are generally elegant renditions of classic Mediterranean food, followed by such delicious desserts that some people prefer a starter and two sweets, skipping the main course altogether.

Tibidabo

ABAC CATALAN €€€

Map p298 (☎93 319 66 00; www.abacbarcelona.com; Av del Tibidabo 1; mains €42-72, tasting menu €135-155; ⊙1.30-4pm & 8.30-11pm Tue-Sat) Led by celebrated chef Jordi Cruz, ABaC offers one of Barcelona's most memorable dining experiences (and also one of its priciest). Expect creative, mouthwatering perfection in dishes such as sea urchin curry with lime, Guinea fowl with Norway lobster, and roasted seabass with artichokes and oysters.

LA BALSA MEDITERRANEAN €€€

Map p298 (☎93 211 50 48; www.labalsarestaurant.com; Carrer de la Infanta Isabel 4; mains €17-27; ⊙1.30-3.30pm Tue-Sun & 8.30-11pm Tue-Sat, in Aug dinner only; 🚇FGC Avinguda Tibidabo) With its grand ceiling and the scented gardens that surround the main terrace dining area, La Balsa is one of the city's top dining experiences. The menu changes frequently and is a mix of traditional Catalan and off-centre inventiveness. Lounge over a cocktail at the bar before being ushered to your table.

EL ASADOR DE ARANDA SPANISH €€€

Map p298 (☎93 417 01 15; www.asadordearanda.com; Av del Tibidabo 31; mains €20-22; ⊙1-4pm daily & 8-11pm Mon-Sat; 🚇Av Tibidabo) A great place for a meal after visiting Tibidabo, El Asador de Aranda is set in a striking art nouveau building, complete with stained-glass windows, Moorish-style brick arches and elaborate ceilings. You'll find a fine assortment of tapas plates for sharing, though the speciality is the meat (roast lamb, spare ribs, beef), beautifully prepared in a wood oven.

Sarrià

BAR TOMÀS TAPAS €

Map p298 (☎93 203 10 77; Carrer Major de Sarrià 49; tapas €3-5; ⊙noon-4pm & 6-10pm Mon-Sat; 🚇FGC Sarrià) Many *barcelonins* have long claimed that Bar Tomàs is the best place in the city for *patatas bravas* (potato chunks in a slightly spicy tomato sauce), prepared here with a variation on the traditional sauce. The place is a rough-edged bar, but that doesn't stop the well-off citizens of Sarrià piling in, particularly for lunch on weekends.

FOIX DE SARRIÀ PASTELERÍA €

Map p298 (☎93 203 04 73; www.foixdesarria.com; Plaça de Sarrià 12-13; desserts €2-5; ⊙8am-8pm; 🚇FGC Reina Elisenda) Since 1886 this exclusive pastry shop has been selling the most exquisite cakes and sweets. You can take them away or head out the back to sip tea, coffee or hot chocolate while sampling the little cakes and other wizardry.

VIVANDA CATALAN €€

Map p298 (☎93 203 19 18; www.vivanda.cat; Carrer Major de Sarrià 134; sharing plates €9-15; ⊙1.30-3.30pm Tue-Sun, 9-11pm Tue-Sat; 🚇FGC Reina Elisenda) With a menu designed by celebrated Catalan chef Jordi Vilà, diners are in for a treat at this Sarrià classic. The changing menu showcases seasonal fare (recent selections include eggs with truffles, rice with cuttlefish, and artichokes with romesco sauce). One of Vivanda's best features is the garden-like terrace hidden behind the restaurant. With heat lamps, it's open year-round – blankets and hot broth are distributed to diners in winter.

5° PINO
CATALAN €€

Map p298 (Quinto Pino; ☎93 252 22 81; http://quintopino.es; Passeig de la Bonanova 98; mains €9-12; ☺8.30am-1.30am Mon-Fri, from 10am Sat & Sun; ☒FGC Sarrià) While exploring Sarrià, it's worth detouring a few blocks east to this charming cafe and restaurant, which is a favourite local spot for tasty sandwiches, salads, tortillas, tapas and drinks. It's on a busy road, though the outdoor, tree-shaded terrace is still a pleasant spot for a bite. The playground next door adds to the appeal for parents with kids in tow.

SANTANA
CATALAN €€

Map p298 (☎93 280 36 06; Carrer Major de Sarrià 97; mains €10-17; ☺1-4pm daily, 8-11pm Mon-Sat; ☒FGC Reina Elisenda) Next door to Sarrià's pretty 18th-century church (Sant Vicenç de Sarrià), Santana is an elegant spot for dining on sharing plates of seared tuna, chargrilled asparagus with romesco sauce, creative salads and steak tartar. Three-course lunch specials, including wine, cost €14.

✕ Les Corts & Camp Nou

BANGKOK CAFE
THAI €€

Map p298 (☎93 339 32 69; Carrer d'Evarist Arnús 65; mains €9-14; ☺8-11pm daily & 1.30-3.30pm Fri-Sun, closed mid-Jul–mid-Sep; Ⓜ Plaça del Centre) If you're craving Thai cuisine, it's well worth making the trip out to Bangkok Cafe, which serves up delectable papaya salad, steamed dumplings, crispy prawns, red curries and other classics, with more spice than you'll find in most Catalan eateries. It's a small place with an open kitchen, Formica tables and bustling crowds, but the excellent dishes for the decent prices are unbeatable.

🍷 DRINKING & NIGHTLIFE

North of Avinguda Diagonal, the *pijos* (cashed-up mamma's boys and papa's girls) are in charge. Whether you sample the bars around Carrer de Marià Cubí (and surrounding streets) or try the clubs around Carrer d'Aribau or Tibidabo, **expect to be confronted by perma-tanned Audi- and 4WD-driving folks in designer threads. What do you care? The eye candy more than compensates for the snobbery.**

🍷 Sant Gervasi

CAFE TURÓ
CAFE

Map p300 (Carrer del Tenor Viñas 1; ☺8am-midnight; ☒FGC Muntaner) This pleasant cafe on the edge of Turó Parc is reminiscent of a Parisian-style cafe, with year-round seating on the footpath at the front – ideal for catching a bit of sun. There's a good selection of bistro plates and tapas.

DÔ BAR
BAR

Map p300 (☎93 209 18 88; www.do-bcn.com; Carrer de Santaló 30; ☺7pm-1am Mon-Sat; ☒FGC Muntaner) This neighbourhood charmer has a warm and inviting interior, where friends gather over tall wooden tables to enjoy excellent gin and tonics, wines by the glass, craft beer and satisfying small plates (anchovies, mussels, tacos, charcuterie). On warm nights, arrive early for one of the terrace tables out the front.

MARCEL
BAR

Map p300 (☎93 209 89 48; Carrer de Santaló 42; ☺7am-1am Mon-Thu, to 2am Fri & Sat, to 11pm Sun; ☒FGC Muntaner) A classic meeting place, Marcel has a homey, old-world feel, with a timber bar, black-and-white floor tiles and high windows. It offers a few snacks and tapas as well. Space is somewhat limited and customers inevitably spill out onto the footpath, where there are also a few tables.

BERLIN
BAR

Map p300 (Carrer de Muntaner 240; ☺10am-2am Mon-Thu, to 3am Fri & Sat; Ⓜ Diagonal or Hospital Clínic) This elegant corner bar offers views over Avinguda Diagonal. There is a cluster of tables outside on the ground floor and designer lounges downstairs. Service can be harried, but the location is excellent for starting an uptown night. All ages and creeds snuggle in and many kick on to nearby clubs afterwards.

THE END
BAR

Map p300 (☎61 762 50 98; Carrer de l'Avenir 50; ☺11pm-2am Tue & Wed, to 3am Thu-Sat; ☒FGC Muntaner) The End starts in quiet fashion with patrons gathered around its low tables lined up on one side of the rear bar area. Two backlit bars also keep the drinks coming to this spot of good-looking 20- and 30-somethings. After 1am the music takes off and punters rev up for an outing to nearby clubs.

SUTTON CLUB   CLUB
Map p300 (www.thesuttonclub.com; Carrer de Tuset 13; admission €15; ⊗midnight-5am Wed-Thu, midnight-6am Fri & Sat, 10.30pm-4am Sun; MDiagonal) A classic disco with mainstream sounds on the dance floor, some hopping house in a side bar and a fair spread of eye candy, this place inevitably attracts just about everyone pouring in and out of the nearby bars at some stage of the evening. The main dance floor is akin to a writhing bear pit. The people are mostly beautiful and the bouncers can be tough.

🍷 Tibidabo & Sarrià

MIRABLAU   BAR
Map p298 (Plaça del Doctor Andreu; ⊗11am-4.30am; ℝAvinguda Tibidabo then ℝtramvia blau) Gaze out over the entire city from this privileged balcony restaurant on the way up to Tibidabo. Wander downstairs to join the folk in the tiny dance space. In summer you can step out onto the even smaller terrace for a breather.

CAFFÈ SAN MARCO   CAFE
Map p298 (⌨93 280 29 73; Carrer de Pedro de la Creu 15; ⊗9am-9.30pm; ℝFGC Reina Elisenda) For one of the best coffees you're likely to have, it is hard to beat this place. It boasts a charming atmosphere where you can settle in to read the paper or simply watch passersby.

🍸 Pedralbes & Zona Universitària

LIZARRAN   BAR
Map p298 (Carrer de Can Bruixa 6; ⊗8am-midnight Sun-Thu, to 2am Fri & Sat; MLes Corts) This is a fine pre- or post-game drinking spot if you're catching an FC Barça game at Camp Nou. The beer is plentiful and cheap, there's a decent tapas selection, and on warm days you can sit on the pleasant terrace at the front. From here it's about a 15-minute walk to the stadium.

⭐ ENTERTAINMENT

LUZ DE GAS   CLUB
Map p300 (⌨93 209 77 11; www.luzdegas.com; Carrer de Muntaner 246; admission up to €20; ⊗Wed-Sun; ⬚6, 7, 15, 27, 32, 33, 34, 58 or 64, MDiagonal) Several nights a week this club, set in a grand former theatre, stages concerts ranging through rock, soul, salsa, jazz and pop. From about 2am, the place turns into a club that attracts a well-dressed crowd with varying musical tastes, depending on the night.

BIKINI   CLUB
Map p300 (⌨93 322 08 00; www.bikinibcn.com; Av Diagonal 547; admission €10-20; ⊗midnight-6am Thu-Sat; ⬚6, 7, 33, 34, 63, 67 or 68, MEntença) This grand old star of the Barcelona nightlife scene has been keeping the beat since the darkest days of Franco. Every possible kind of music gets a run, from Latin and Brazilian beats to 1980s disco, depending on the night and the space you choose.

OTTO ZUTZ   CLUB
Map p300 (www.ottozutz.com; Carrer de Lincoln 15; admission €10-15; ⊗midnight-6am Tue-Sat; ℝFGC Gràcia) Beautiful people only need apply for entry to this three-floor dance den. Shake it all up to house on the ground floor, or head upstairs for funk and soul. DJs come from the Ibiza rave mould and the top floor is for VIPs (although at some ill-defined point in the evening the barriers all seem to come down).

SALA BECOOL   CLUB
Map p300 (⌨93 362 04 13; www.salabecool.com; Plaça de Joan Llongueras 5; admission €10-15; ⊗midnight-6am Thu-Sun; ⬚27, 32, 59, 66, 67 or 68) Electro is the leitmotif in this middle-sized dance place dominated by a single giant mirror ball at the stage end, where earlier in the night you might catch a concert (from 9pm). The secondary Redrum space runs at a slower pace, with indie music to the fore.

🛍 SHOPPING

Although many of Barcelona's better-off folks descend from the 'High Zone' to L'Eixample to shop, there are still plenty of trendy little boutiques scattered around La Zona Alta.

DEATH BY CHOCOLATE

Spain has been importing cocoa from its Latin American colonies since the 16th century and, ever since, the pastry makers of Barcelona have been doing it the greatest justice. The city's love affair with chocolate is exemplified in the existence of a museum dedicated to the stuff. Traditional purveyors of fine chocolates have long operated alongside *granjas* (milk bars) and other similar outlets for sipping cups of the thick hot stuff. Since the 1980s they have been joined by a slew of chocolatiers whose creativity seems to know no bounds. Chocoholics should seek out the following:

Oriol Balaguer (Map p300; ☑93 201 18 46; www.oriolbalaguer.com; Plaça de Sant Gregori Taumaturg 2; ⊙10am-2pm & 5-9pm Mon-Sat; ℝFGC La Bonanova)

Pastisseria Natcha (Map p300; ☑93 430 10 70; www.natcha.cat; Avinguda de Sarrià 45; ⊙8am-9pm; ℳHospital Clínic)

Foix de Sarrià (Map p298; Plaça de Sarrià 12; ⊙8am-8pm)

Chocolat Factory (Map p298; www.chocolatfactory.com; Carrer de Balmes 391; ⊙10am-2pm & 5-8.30pm Mon-Sat; ℝFGC El Putxet)

FC BOTIGA
SOUVENIRS

(☑93 492 31 11; http://shop.fcbarcelona.com; Carrer de Arístides Maillol; ⊙10am-7pm Mon-Sat; ℳCollblanc) Here you will find footballs, shirts, scarves, socks, wallets, bags, sneakers, iPhone covers – pretty much anything you can think of, all featuring Barça's insignia.

TOMATES FRITOS
FASHION

Map p300 (Carrer del Tenor Viñas 7; ⊙10.30am-8.30pm Mon-Fri, 10.30am-3pm & 5-8.30pm Sat; ℝFGC Muntaner) One of a growing number of boutiques along this street, Tomates Fritos is an obligatory stop for design-minded window shoppers, and carries a trove of unique wears. The cache of global designers includes denim by Seven Jeans, handbags by Liebeskind, knits by Le Mont St Michel and beautifully tailored tops by Scotch & Soda.

MERCAT DE GALVANY
MARKET

Map p300 (Carrer de Santaló 65; ⊙7am-2pm Mon-Sat; ℝFGC Muntaner) Opened in the 1920s, Galvany is one of the city's most attractive markets, with a brick facade and glass- and cast-iron interior. Stop by for the usual assortment of bakery items, fresh produce and deli items, plus craft beers from Beer Corner.

🏃 SPORTS & ACTIVITIES

CAMP NOU
SPECTATOR SPORT

Map p298 (☑902 189900; www.fcbarcelona.com; Carrer d'Aristides Maillol; tickets €20-265; ⊙box ofice 10am-7.45pm Mon-Sat, to 2.15pm Sun, 11am to kick-off on match days; ℳPalau Reial or Collblanc) Seeing an FC Barcelona football match inside massive Camp Nou stadium is an experience that is not to be missed. You can purchase tickets at the stadium box office, at tourist offices and online.

ESPAI BOISA
COOKING COURSE

Map p290 (☑93 192 60 21; http://espaiboisa.com; Ptge Lluís Pellicer 8; 3hr class €70) 🍃 Run by a young, multilingual Venezuelan-Catalan couple, this first-rate outfit offers three-hour cooking courses for both lunch and dinner. They emphasise organic, seasonal ingredients from local producers outside of Barcelona – put to good use in preparing five courses, including paella (at lunch), a range of tapas dishes and *crema Catalana* (Catalan version of crème brulée). The best part is eating your creations, served up with generous glasses of organic Catalan wine, or sangria on warm summer nights.

RITUELS D'ORIENT
SPA

Map p300 (☑93 419 14 72; www.rituelsdorient.com; Carrer de Loreto 50; baths only €28; ⊙1-9pm Sun-Wed, to 10pm Thu-Sat; ℳHospital Clínic) True to name, Rituels d'Orient offers a setting that resembles a Moroccan fantasy with its dark woods, window grills, candle lighting and ancient-looking stone walls. It's a fine setting for luxuriating in hammams and indulging in massages, body scrubs and other treatments.

Montjuïc, Poble Sec & Sant Antoni

MONTJUÏC | EL POBLE SEC | SANT ANTONI | SANTS

Neighbourhood Top Five

❶ Dedicating a day to the world's most important collection of early-medieval art in the Romanesque art section of the **Museu Nacional d'Art de Catalunya** (p179), and exploring the stunning Gothic art, plus two fascinating private collections.

❷ Admiring the beauty of Josep Lluís Sert's **Fundació Joan Miró** (p184) that houses the work of Barcelona's best-known 20th-century artist.

❸ Taking in the **Caixa-Forum** (p185), one of the city's best art spaces, which showcases the bank's extensive global collection.

❹ Watching the colours and water come alive in the evening display of **Font Màgica** (p186).

❺ Getting inside a **cable car** (p189) and watching Montjuïc from the air.

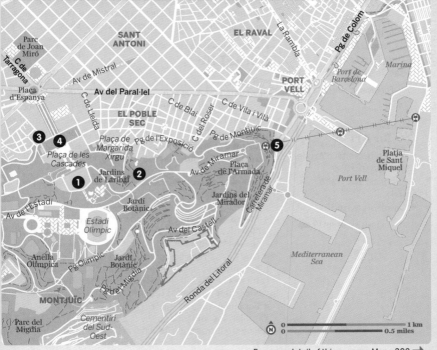

For more detail of this area see Map p302 ➡

Lonely Planet's Top Tip

The Arqueoticket is a special pass, available at tourist offices and participating museums for €13, that allows entry into the Museu d'Arqueologia de Catalunya (MAC) (p187), the Museu Egipci (p134), the Museu Marítim (p111) and the Museu d'Història de Barcelona (p65).

Best Places to Eat

➡ Tickets (p192)

➡ Quimet i Quimet (p191)

➡ Xemei (p191)

➡ Federal (p192)

➡ Barramón (p191)

For reviews, see p191

Best Places to Drink

➡ La Caseta del Migdia (p193)

➡ La Terrrazza (p192)

➡ Tinta Roja (p193)

➡ Bar Calders (p193)

For reviews, see p192 ➡

Best for Art

➡ Museu Nacional d'Art de Catalunya (p179)

➡ Fundació Joan Miró (p184)

➡ CaixaForum (p185)

For reviews, see p179 ➡

Explore: Montjuïc, Poble Sec & Sant Antoni

Montjuïc is home to two of the city's finest art collections in the MNAC and the Fundació Joan Miró, and several lesser museums, various parks and gardens, curious sights like the Poble Espanyol, the sinister Castell de Montjuïc and the beautiful remake of Mies van der Rohe's 1929 German pavilion. The bulk of the 1992 Olympic installations are also here. Come at night and witness the spectacle of the Font Màgica and a handful of busy theatres and nightclubs. You can approach the hill from Plaça d'Espanya on foot and via a series of escalators to the MNAC; alternatively, and spectacularly, you can get a cable-car from Barceloneta and take in the views. Another opportunity for a cable-car ride is from Estació Parc Montjuïc to the castle. Otherwise, explore on foot, along the numerous paths that zigzag through gardens and skirt the various sights.

The swirling traffic roundabout of Plaça d'Espanya marks the boundary between Montjuïc and the barri (neighbourhood) of Sants, an area worth seeing if you are keen on witnessing the everyday life of residential, tourist-free Barcelona.

Sloping down the north face of Montjuïc is the tight warren of working-class Poble Sec. Though short on sights, it hides various interesting bars and restaurants. Avinguda del Paral·lel was, until the 1960s, the centre of Barcelona nightlife, crammed with theatres and cabarets, and a handful of theatres and cinemas survive, one of which, the Sala Apolo, managed to convert itself into a club.

Local Life

➡ **Hang-outs** For tapas, head for Carrer de Blai, a street lined with tables belonging to the numerous little tapas bars that stretch along this pedestrian artery of Poble Sec.

➡ **Nightlife** Catch a burlesque show at the Sala Apolo (p193) or a concert at new venue, BARTS (p193).

➡ **Greenery** Join the locals on a stroll through the gardens of Montjuïc and catch all that art on the way.

Getting There & Away

➡ **Metro** Metro Línia 3 runs down Avinguda Paral·lel, which divides Poble Sec from Sant Antoni. The closest stops to Montjuïc are Espanya, Poble Sec and Paral·lel.

➡ **Bus** Bus 55 runs across town via Plaça de Catalunya to terminate at the Estació Parc Montjuïc funicular station. The bus 150 (Parc de Montjuïc) line does a circle trip from Plaça d'Espanya to Castell de Montjuïc.

➡ **Funicular** Take the metro (Línia 2 or 3) to the Paral·lel stop and pick up the funicular railway, part of the metro fare system, to Estació Parc Montjuïc.

From across the city, the flamboyant neobaroque silhouette of the Palau Nacional can be seen on the slopes of Montjuïc. Built for the 1929 World Exhibition and restored in 2005, it houses a vast collection of mostly Catalan art spanning the early Middle Ages to the early 20th century. The high point is the collection of extraordinary Romanesque frescoes.

The Romanesque Masterpieces

The Romanesque art section is considered the most important concentration of early medieval art in the world. Rescued from neglected country churches across northern Catalonia in the early 20th century, the collection consists of 21 frescoes, woodcarvings and painted altar frontals (low-relief wooden panels that were the forerunners of the elaborate altarpieces that adorned later churches). The insides of several churches have been re-created and the frescoes – in some cases fragmentary, in others extraordinarily complete and alive with colour – have been placed as they were when in situ.

The first of the two most-striking frescoes, in Sala 7, is a magnificent image of Christ in Majesty done around 1123. Based on the text of the Apocalypse, we see Christ enthroned with the world at his feet. He holds a book open with the words *Ego Sum Lux Mundi* (I am the Light of the World) and is surrounded by the four Evangelists. The images were taken from the apse of the Església de Sant Climent de Taüll in northwest Catalonia. Also in Sala 7 are frescoes done around the same time in the nearby Església de Santa Maria de Taüll. This time the central image taken

DON'T MISS...

➡ The Romanesque pieces

➡ Gothic artworks

➡ The paintings of the Cambó Bequest and Thyssen-Bornemisza collections

➡ Modernista furniture and decoration

PRACTICALITIES

➡ Map p302

➡ ☎93 622 03 76

➡ www.museu nacional.cat

➡ Mirador del Palau Nacional

➡ adult/senior & child under 16yr/student €12/free/€8.40, 1st Sun of month free

➡ ☉10am-8pm Tue-Sat, to 3pm Sun, library 10am-6pm Mon-Fri

➡ Ⓜ Espanya

THE FRESCO STRIPPERS

The Stefanoni brothers, Italian art restorers, brought the secrets of *strappo* (stripping of frescoes from walls) to Catalonia in the early 1900s. The Stefanoni would cover frescoes with a sheet of fabric, stuck on with a glue made of cartilage. When dry, this allowed the image to be stripped off the wall and rolled up. For three years the Stefanoni roamed the Pyrenean countryside, stripping churches and chapels and sending the rolls back to Barcelona, where they were eventually put back up on walls and inside purpose-built church apses to reflect how they had appeared in situ.

The museum's displays account for little more than 20% of its holdings. The rest is kept in storerooms that can be visited on a guided tour (€8.40, call ahead to arrange). Since the displays themselves already represent an enormous chunk to absorb in a day, a separate day should be set aside for visiting the reserves.

from the apse is of the Virgin Mary and Christ Child. These images were not mere decoration but tools of instruction in the basics of Christian faith for the local population – try to set yourself in the mind of the average medieval citizen: illiterate, ignorant, fearful and in most cases eking out a subsistence living. These images transmitted the basic personalities and tenets of the faith and were accepted at face value by most.

The Gothic Collection

Opposite the Romanesque collection on the ground floor is the museum's Gothic art section. In these halls you can see Catalan Gothic painting and works from other Spanish and Mediterranean regions. Look out especially for the work of Bernat Martorell in Sala 25 and Jaume Huguet in Sala 26. Among Martorell's works figure images of the martyrdom of St Vincent and St Llúcia. Huguet's *Consagració de Sant Agustí,* in which St Augustine is depicted as a bishop, is dazzling in its detail.

The Cambò Bequest & the Thyssen-Bornemisza Collection

As the Gothic collection draws to a close, you pass through two separate and equally eclectic private collections. The Cambò Bequest by Francesc Cambó spans the history of European painting between the 14th century and the beginning of the 19th century, and the Thyssen-Bornemisza collection presents a selection of European painting and sculpture produced between the 13th and the 18th centuries on loan to the MNAC by the Museo Thyssen-Bornemisza in Madrid. The Thyssen-Bornemisza collection's highlight is Fra Angelico's *Madonna of Humility,* whereas the Cambò Bequest holds wonderful works by masters Veronese, Titian and Canaletto, particularly. Cranach, Titian, El Greco, Rubens and even Gainsborough also feature, but the collection's finale is examples of work by Francisco de Goya.

Modern Catalan Art

Up on the next floor, the collection turns to modern art, mainly but not exclusively Catalan. At the time of writing, this collection was being rearranged thematically (Modernisme, Noucentisme, civil war and so on), but it is worth looking out for Modernista painters Ramon Casas and Santiago Rusiñol, as well as the recently deceased Antoni Tàpies.

Also on show are items of Modernista furniture and decoration, which include a mural by Ramon Casas (the artist and Pere Romeu on a tandem bicycle) that once adorned the legendary bar and restaurant Els Quatre Gats.

MUSEU NACIONAL D'ART DE CATALUNYA

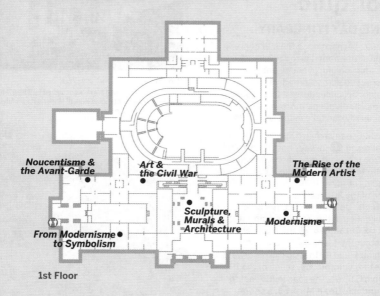

**Noucentisme &
the Avant-Garde**

**Art &
the Civil War**

**The Rise of the
Modern Artist**

**Sculpture,
Murals &
Architecture**

Modernisme

**From Modernisme
to Symbolism**

1st Floor

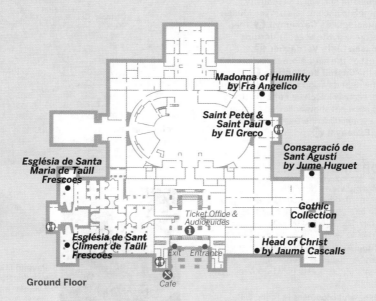

**Madonna of Humility
by Fra Angelico**

**Saint Peter &
Saint Paul
by El Greco**

**Consagració de
Sant Agustí
by Jume Huguet**

**Església de Santa
Maria de Taüll
Frescoes**

**Gothic
Collection**

Ticket Office &
Audioguides

**Església de Sant
Climent de Taüll
Frescoes**

Exit   Entrance

**Head of Christ
by Jaume Cascalls**

Ground Floor

Cafe

Montjuïc

A ONE-DAY ITINERARY

Montjuïc, perhaps once the site of pre-Roman settlements, is today a hilltop green lung looking over city and sea. Interspersed across varied gardens are major art collections, a fortress, an Olympic stadium and more. A solid one-day itinerary can take in the key spots.

Alight at Espanya metro stop and make for CaixaForum ❶, always host to three or four free top-class exhibitions. The nearby Pavelló Mies van der Rohe ❷ is an intriguing study in 1920s futurist housing by one of the 20th century's greatest architects. Uphill, the Romanesque art collection in the Museu Nacional d'Art de Catalunya ❸ is a must, and its restaurant is a pleasant lunch stop. Escalators lead further up the hill towards the Estadi Olímpic ❹, scene of the 1992 Olympic Games. The road leads east to the Fundació Joan Miró ❺, a shrine to the master surrealist's creativity. Contemplate ancient relics in the Museu d'Arqueologia de Catalunya ❻, then have a break in the peaceful Jardins de Mossèn Cinto Verdaguer ❼, the prettiest on the hill, before taking the cable car to the Castell de Montjuïc ❽. If you pick the right day, you can round off with the gorgeously kitsch La Font Màgica ❾ sound and light show, followed by drinks and dancing in an open-air nightspot in Poble Espanyol ❿.

TOP TIPS

» **Moving views** Ride the Transbordador Aeri from Barceloneta for a bird's eye approach to Montjuïc. Or take the Teleféric de Montjuïc cable car to the Castell for more aerial views.

» **Summer fun** The Castell de Montjuïc features outdoor summer cinema and concerts (see http://sala montjuic.org).

» **Beautiful bloomers** Bursting with colour and serenity, the Jardins de Mossèn Cinto Verdaguer are exquisitely laid out with bulbs, especially tulips, and aquatic flowers.

CaixaForum
This former factory and barracks designed by Josep Puig i Cadafalch is an outstanding work of Modernista architecture; like a Lego fantasy in brick.

Piscines Bernat Picornell

Olympic Needle

Poble Espanyol
Amid the rich variety of traditional Spanish architecture created in replica for the 1929 Barcelona World Exhibition, browse the art on show in the Fundació Fran Daurel.

Pavelló Mies van der Rohe
Admire the inventiveness of the great German architect Ludwig Mies van der Rohe in this recreation of his avant garde German pavillion for the 1929 World Exhibition.

La Font Màgica
Take a summer evening to behold the Magic Fountain come to life in a unique 15-minute sound and light performance, when the water glows like a cauldron of colour.

PAUL BIRIS/GETTY IMAGES ©

Museu Nacional d'Art de Catalunya
Make a beeline for the Romanesque art selection and the 12th-century polychrome image of Christ in majesty, which was recovered from the apse of a country chapel in northwest Catalonia.

Fundació Joan Miró
Take in some of Joan Miró's giant canvases, and discover little-known works from his early years in the Sala Joan Prats and Sala Pilar Juncosa.

⑨

③

Museu Etnològic

⑥

Teatre Grec

⑤

④
Estadi Olímpic

Museu Olímpic i de l'Esport

Jardí Botànic

⑦

⑧

Jardins de Mossèn Cinto Verdaguer

Castell de Montjuïc
Enjoy the sweeping views of the sea and city from atop this 17th-century fortress, once a political prison and long a symbol of oppression.

Museu d'Arqueologia de Catalunya
Seek out the Roman mosaic depicting the Three Graces, one of the most beautiful items in this museum, which was dedicated to the ancient past of Catalonia and neighbouring parts of Spain.

CULTURA TRAVEL/QUIM ROSER/GETTY IMAGES ©

TOP SIGHT
FUNDACIÓ JOAN MIRÓ

Joan Miró, the city's best-known 20th-century artistic progeny, bequeathed this art foundation to his home town in 1971. Its light-filled buildings, designed by close friend and architect Josep Lluís Sert (who also built Miró's Mallorca studios), are crammed with seminal works, from Miró's earliest timid sketches to paintings from his last years.

Sert's Temple to Miró's Art

Sert's shimmering white temple to one of Spain's artistic luminaries is considered one of the world's most outstanding museum buildings. The architect designed it after spending many of Franco's dictatorship years in the USA as the head of the School of Design at Harvard University. The foundation rests amid the greenery of the mountains and holds the greatest single collection of the artist's work, containing around 220 of his paintings, 180 sculptures, some textiles and more than 8000 drawings spanning his entire life. Only a small portion is ever on display.

The Collection

The exhibits give a broad impression of Miró's artistic development. The first couple of rooms (11 and 12) hold various works, including a giant tapestry in his trademark primary colours. Room 13, a basement space called Espai 13, leads you downstairs to a small room for temporary exhibitions.

Next (oddly enough) comes room 16, the Sala Joan Prats, with works spanning the early years until 1931, entitled The Early Years and Paris and Surrealism. Here, you can see how the young Miró moved away, under surrealist influence, from his relative realism (for instance his 1917 painting *Ermita de Sant Joan d'Horta*) towards his own unique style that uses primary colours and morphed shapes symbolising the moon, the female form and birds.

This theme is continued upstairs in room 17, the Sala Pilar Juncosa (named after his wife), which covers the years 1932–55, his surrealist years. Rooms 18 and 19 contain masterworks of the years 1956–83, and room 20 a series of paintings done on paper. Room 21 hosts a selection of the private Katsuka collection of Miró works from 1914 to the 1970s. Room 22 rounds off the permanent exhibition with some major paintings and bronzes from the 1960s and 1970s. On the way here, you will see *Mercury Fountain* by Alexander Calder, a rebuilt work that was originally created for the 1937 Paris Fair.

The basement rooms 14 and 15, together labelled Homenatge a Joan Miró (Homage to Joan Miró), are dedicated to photos of the artist, with a 15-minute video on his life and a series of works from some of his contemporaries, like Henry Moore, Antoni Tàpies, Eduardo Chillida, Yves Tanguy, Fernand Léger and others.

The museum library contains Miró's personal book collection.

The Garden

Outside on the eastern flank of the museum is the Jardí de les Esculturas, a small garden with various pieces of modern sculpture (it is also a wi-fi zone). The green areas surrounding the museum, together with the garden, are perfect for a picnic in the shade, after a hard day's sightseeing.

DON'T MISS...

➡ Sert's architectural design
➡ Masterworks in rooms 18 and 19
➡ Miro's move to Surrealism, room 16
➡ The sculpture garden

PRACTICALITIES

➡ Map p302
➡ ☏93 443 94 70
➡ www.fundacio miro-bcn.org
➡ Parc de Montjuïc
➡ adult/child €11/free
➡ ⏱10am-8pm Tue-Sat, to 9.30pm Thu, to 2.30pm Sun & holidays
➡ ▣55, 150, funicular Paral·lel

◉ SIGHTS

**MUSEU NACIONAL
D'ART DE CATALUNYA (MNAC)**   MUSEUM
See p179.

FUNDACIÓ JOAN MIRÓ   MUSEUM
See p184.

CAIXAFORUM   GALLERY
Map p302 (☑93 476 86 00; www.fundacio.la
caixa.es; Avinguda de Francesc Ferrer i Guàrdia
6-8; adult/student & child €4/free, 1st Sun of
month free; ☉10am-8pm Mon-Fri, to 9pm Sat &
Sun; ℙ; ⓂEspanya) The Caixa building society prides itself on its involvement in (and
ownership of) art, in particular all that is
contemporary. Its premier art expo space
in Barcelona hosts part of the bank's extensive collection from around the globe. The
setting is a completely renovated former
factory, the Fàbrica Casaramona, an outstanding Modernista brick structure designed by Puig i Cadafalch. From 1940 to
1993 it housed the First Squadron of the
police cavalry unit – 120 horses in all.

Now it is home to a major exhibition
space. On occasion portions of La Caixa's
own collection of 800 works of modern and
contemporary art go on display, but more
often than not major international exhibitions are the key draw.

In the courtyard where the police horses
used to drink is a steel tree designed by the
Japanese architect Arata Isozaki. Musical
recitals are sometimes held in the museum,
especially in the warmer months.

CASTELL DE MONTJUÏC   FORTRESS, GARDENS
Map p302 (☑93 256 44 45; www.bcn.cat/castell-
demontjuic; Carretera de Montjuïc 66; adult/con-
cession/child €5/3/free, free Sun pm & 1st Sun of
month; ☉10am-8pm; ☐150, Telefèric de Montjuïc,
Castell de Montjuïc) This forbidding *castell*
(castle or fort) dominates the southeastern
heights of Montjuïc and enjoys command-
ing views over the Mediterranean. It dates,
in its present form, from the late 17th and
18th centuries. For most of its dark history,
it has been used to watch over the city and
as a political prison and killing ground.

Anarchists were executed here around
the end of the 19th century, fascists during
the civil war and Republicans after it – most
notoriously Lluís Companys in 1940. The
castle is surrounded by a network of ditches
and walls (from which its strategic position
over the city and port become clear).

Until 2009 the castle was home to a
somewhat fusty old military museum,
closed since the Ministry of Defence
handed the fortress over to the city after
protracted negotiations, although it is currently undergoing renovations and will be
used as exhibition space. The artillery that
once stood in the central courtyard has
been removed, but some of the seaward big
guns remain in place.

In 2014 parts of the castle previously
closed to the public – such as the tower and
the dungeons – were opened, and an entrance fee was applied. A large part of the
castle will now function as exhibition space,
although the finer details had yet to be
ironed out at the time of writing. The cur-
rent exhibition explains something of the
history of the place as well as detailing plans
for its future. Perhaps when all this is done,
the tombstones (some dating to the 11th century) from the one-time Jewish cemetery on
Montjuïc will get a more imaginative exhibition space than the drab room once set aside
for them in the military museum.

The views from the castle and the surrounding area looking over the sea, port
and city below are the best part of making the trip here. Around the seaward foot
of the castle is an airy walking track, the
Camí del Mar, which offers breezy views of
the city and sea.

From the **Jardins del Mirador**, opposite
the Mirador (Telefèric) station, you have
fine views over the port of Barcelona. A little further downhill, the **Jardins de Joan
Brossa** (Map p302; ☉10am-sunset; cable car Telefèric de Montjuïc, Mirador) FREE are charming,
landscaped gardens on the site of a former
amusement park near **Plaça de la Sardana**
(Map p302). These gardens contain many
Mediterranean species, from cypresses to
pines and a few palms. There are swings
and things, thematic walking trails and
some good city views.

MUSEU OLÍMPIC I DE L'ESPORT   MUSEUM
Map p302 (☑93 292 53 79; www.mu-
seuolimpicbcn.com; Avinguda de l'Estadi 60;
adult/student €5.10/3.20; ☉10am-8pm Tue-
Sat, 10am-2.30pm Sun; ☐55, 150) The Museu
Olímpic i de L'Esport is an information-
packed interactive museum dedicated
to the history of sport and the Olympic
Games. After picking up tickets, you wander down a ramp that snakes below ground
level and is lined with displays on the history of sport, starting with the ancients.

WORTH A DETOUR

COLÒNIA GÜELL

Apart from La Sagrada Família, Gaudí's last big project was the creation of a utopian textile workers' complex for his magnate patron Eusebi Güell outside Barcelona at Santa Coloma de Cervelló. Gaudí's main role was to erect the colony's church, **Colònia Güell** (☎93 630 58 07; www.gaudicoloniaguell.org; Carrer de Claudi Güell; adult/student €7/5.50; ⏱10am-7pm Mon-Fri, to 3pm Sat & Sun). Work began in 1908 but the idea fizzled eight years later and Gaudí only finished the crypt, which still serves as a working church.

This structure is a key to understanding what the master had in mind for his magnum opus, La Sagrada Família. The mostly brick-clad columns that support the ribbed vaults in the ceiling are inclined at all angles in much the way you might expect trees in a forest to lean. That effect was deliberate, but also grounded in physics. Gaudí worked out the angles so that their load would be transmitted from the ceiling to the earth without the help of extra buttressing. Similar thinking lay behind his plans for La Sagrada Família, whose Gothic-inspired structure would tower above any medieval building, without requiring a single buttress. Gaudí's hand is visible down to the wavy design of the pews. The primary colours in the curvaceous plant-shaped stained-glass windows are another reminder of the era in which the crypt was built.

Near the church spread the cute brick houses designed for the factory workers and still inhabited today. A short stroll away, the 23 factory buildings of a Modernista industrial complex, idle since the 1970s, were brought back to life in the early 2000s, with shops and businesses moving into the renovated complex.

In a five-room display with audiovisual and interactive material, the history and life of the industrial colony and the story of Gaudí's church are told in colourful fashion.

FONT MÀGICA   FOUNTAIN

Map p302 (☎93 316 10 00; Avinguda de la Reina Maria Cristina; ⏱every 30min 7-9pm Fri & Sat Oct-Apr, 9.30-11pm Thu-Sun May-Sep; Ⓜ Espanya) A huge fountain that crowns the long sweep of the Avinguda de la Reina Maria Cristina to the grand facade of the Palau Nacional, Font Màgica is a unique performance in which the water can look like seething fireworks or a mystical cauldron of colour.

It is wonderful that an idea that was cooked up for the 1929 World Exposition has, since the 1992 Olympics, again become a magnet. With a flourish, the 'Magic Fountain' erupts into a feast of musical, backlit aquatic life. On hot summer evenings especially, this 15-minute spectacle (repeated several times throughout the evening) mesmerises onlookers. On the last evening of the Festes de la Mercè in September, a particularly spectacular display includes fireworks.

**PAVELLÓ MIES VAN
DER ROHE**   ARCHITECTURE

Map p302 (☎93 423 40 16; www.miesbcn.com; Avinguda de Francesc Ferrer i Guàrdia 7; adult/child €5/free; ⏱10am-8pm; Ⓜ Espanya) The Pavelló Mies van der Rohe is not only a work of breathtaking beauty and simplicity, it is a highly influential building em-blematic of the modern movement. The structure has been the subject of many studies and interpretations, and it has inspired several generations of architects.

Designed in 1929 by Ludwig Mies van der Rohe (1886–1969) as the Pavelló Alemany (German Pavilion) for the World Exhibition, it was removed after the show and reconstructed only in 1980, after the building had been consistently referred to as one of the key works of modern architecture. The Pavelló was built using glass, steel and marble, reflecting Mies van der Rohe's originality in the use of materials – he admired their visual rigour and precision, and their embodiment of modernity. Mies van der Rohe also designed the Barcelona Chair for the pavilion, an iconic piece of furniture that can be seen in design-conscious spaces across the world today. Watch out for the graceful copy of a statue of *Alba* (Dawn) by Berlin sculptor Georg Kolbe (1877–1947) in one of the exterior areas.

There is a free English guided tour on Saturdays at 10am.

POBLE ESPANYOL   CULTURAL CENTRE

Map p302 (www.poble-espanyol.com; Avinguda de Francesc Ferrer i Guàrdia 13; adult/child €11/6.25; ⏱9am-8pm Mon, to midnight Tue-Thu & Sun, to 3am Fri, to 4am Sat; 🚌13, 23, 150,

Espanya) Welcome to Spain! All of it! This 'Spanish Village' is both a cheesy souvenir hunters' haunt and an intriguing scrapbook of Spanish architecture built for the Spanish crafts section of the 1929 World Exhibition. You can meander from Andalucía to the Balearic Islands in the space of a couple of hours, visiting surprisingly good copies of Spain's characteristic buildings.

You enter from beneath a towered medieval gate from Ávila. Inside, to the right, is an information office with free maps. Straight ahead from the gate is the Plaza Mayor (Town Sq), surrounded with mainly Castilian and Aragonese buildings. It is sometimes the scene of summer concerts. Elsewhere you'll find an Andalucian *barrio,* a Basque street, Galician and Catalan quarters, and even a Dominican monastery (at the eastern end). The buildings house dozens of restaurants, cafes, bars, craft shops and workshops (for glass artists and other artisans), and some souvenir stores.

Spare some time for the **Fundació Fran Daurel** (www.fundaciofrandaurel.com; Avinguda Francesc Ferrer i Guàrdia 13; ⊙10am-7pm) **FREE**, an eclectic collection of 300 works of art including sculptures, prints, ceramics and tapestries by modern artists ranging from Picasso and Miró to more contemporary figures, including Miquel Barceló. The foundation also has a sculpture garden, boasting 27 pieces, nearby within the grounds of Poble Espanyol (look for the Montblanc gate). Frequent temporary exhibitions broaden the offerings further.

At night the restaurants, bars and especially the discos become a lively corner of Barcelona's nightlife.

Children's groups can participate in the Joc del Sarró. Accompanied by adults, the kids go around the *poble* seeking the answers to various mysteries outlined in a kit distributed to each group. Languages catered for include English.

ESTADI OLÍMPIC LLUÍS COMPANYS
STADIUM
Map p302 (☎93 426 20 89; Avinguda de l'Estadi; ⊙10am-8pm; ☐150) **FREE** The Estadi Olímpic was the main stadium of Barcelona's Olympic Games. If you saw the Olympics on TV, the 65,000-capacity stadium may seem surprisingly small. So might the Olympic flame holder into which an archer spectacularly fired a flaming arrow during the opening ceremony. The stadium was opened in 1929 and restored for 1992.

MUSEU D'ARQUEOLOGIA DE CATALUNYA
MUSEUM
Map p302 (MAC; ☎93 423 21 49; www.mac.cat; Passeig de Santa Madrona 39-41; adult/student €4.50/3.50; ⊙9.30am-7pm Tue-Sat, 10am-2.30pm Sun; MPoble Sec) This archaeology museum, housed in what was the Graphic Arts palace during the 1929 World Exhibition, covers Catalonia and cultures from elsewhere in Spain. Items range from copies of pre-Neanderthal skulls to lovely Carthaginian necklaces and jewel-studded Visigothic crosses.

There's good material on the Balearic Islands (rooms X to XIII) and Empúries (Emporion, the Greek and Roman city on the Costa Brava; rooms XIV and XVII). The Roman finds upstairs were mostly dug up in and around Barcelona. The most beautiful piece is a mosaic depicting Les Tres Gràcies (The Three Graces), unearthed near Plaça de Sant Jaume in the 18th century. Another is of Bellerophon and the Chimera. In the final room, dedicated to the dying centuries of the Roman world, a beautiful golden disk depicting Medusa stands out. The museum has been renovated slowly over recent years, and the displays are now updated with a more modern design and interactive displays.

MUSEU ETNOLÒGIC
MUSEUM
Map p302 (www.museuetnologic.bcn.cat; Passeig de Santa Madrona 16-22; ☐55) Barcelona's ethnology museum presents a curious permanent collection that explores how various societies have worked down the centuries, as seen through collections of all sorts of objects. The entire museum was closed at the time of writing for major refurbishments. Check the website for reopening date.

Prior to the refurbishment, the museum started with a general look at ethnology in an introductory section, Orígens (Origins). Thereafter, collections covered the Pyrenees

MONTJUÏC, POBLE SEC & SANT ANTONI SIGHTS

ⓘ ARQUEOTICKET

The Arqueoticket is a special pass, available at tourist offices and participating museums for €13, that allows entry into the Museu d'Arqueologia de Catalunya (MAC) (p187), the Museu Egipci (p134), the Museu Marítim (p111) and the Museu d'Història de Barcelona (p65).

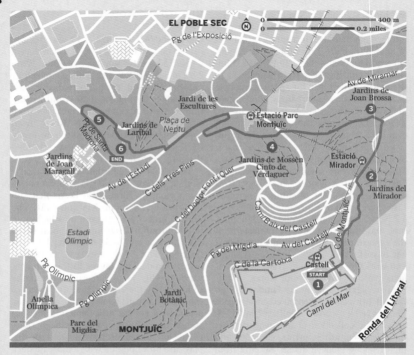

Neighbourhood Walk
Views & Gardens on Montjuïc

START CASTELL DE MONTJUÏC
END CENTRE GESTOR DEL PARC DE MONTJUÏC
LENGTH 2KM; 45 MINUTES

Long synonymous with oppression, the dark history of ❶ **Castell de Montjuïc** (p185) is today overshadowed by the fine views it commands over the city and sea. The ride up on the Telefèric is the perfect way to get there.

A short stroll down the road or the parallel Camí del Mar pedestrian trail leads to another fine viewpoint over the city and sea, the ❷ **Jardins del Mirador** (p185). Take the weight off on the park benches or pick up a snack.

Further downhill is the multitiered ❸ **Jardins de Joan Brossa** (p185). The entrance is on the left just beyond Plaça de la Sardana, with the sculpture of people engaged in the classic Catalan folk dance. More fine city views can be had from among the many Mediterranean trees and plants.

Exiting the Jardins de Joan Brossa at the other (west) side, you cross Camí Baix del Castell to the painstakingly laid-out ❹ **Jardins de Mossèn Cinto de Verdaguer** (p190). This is a beautiful setting for a slow meander among tulip beds and water lilies.

Dropping away behind the Fundació Joan Miró, the ❺ **Jardins de Laribal** are a combination of terraced gardens linked by paths and stairways. The pretty sculpted watercourses along some of the stairways were inspired by Granada's Muslim-era palace of El Alhambra.

Finally, revive yourself with a snack at the cafe in the ❻ **Centre Gestor del Parc de Montjuïc**.

region in Catalonia (including traditional instruments and archive images of traditional dances) and Salamanca in central Spain, looking at a now largely extinct rural society. Further collections explored other regions around the world, but these are to be ceded to the new Museu de Cultures del Món, which will open in the Born in 2015. The museum typically displays only a fraction of its collections at a time, showcasing a number of countries at different intervals, including for temporary exhibitions.

JARDÍ BOTÀNIC
GARDENS

Map p302 (www.jardibotanic.bcn.cat; Carrer del Doctor Font i Quer 2; adult/child €3.50/free; ◉10am-7pm; ◻55, 150) This botanical garden is dedicated to Mediterranean flora and has a collection of some 40,000 plants and 1500 species that thrive in areas with a climate similar to that of the Mediterranean, such as the Eastern Mediterranean, Spain (including the Balearic and Canary Islands), North Africa, Australia, California, Chile and South Africa.

The garden is a work in progress and the plan is to reach 4000 species.

CEMENTIRI DEL SUD-OEST
CEMETERY

Map p302 (☎93 484 19 70; www.cbsa.cat; Carrer de la Mare de Déu de Port 56-58; ◉8am-6pm; ◻9, 21) **FREE** On the hill to the south of the Anella Olímpica stretches this huge cemetery, the Cementiri del Sud-Oest (or 'Cementiri Nou'), which extends down the southern side of the hill. Opened in 1883, it's an odd combination of elaborate architect-designed tombs for rich families and small niches for the rest. It includes the graves of numerous Catalan artists and politicians, and, at the entrance, the Col·lecció de Carrosses Fúnebres.

Among the big names are Joan Miró, Carmen Amaya (the flamenco dance star from La Barceloneta), Jacint Verdaguer (the 19th-century priest and poet to whom the rebirth of Catalan literature is attributed), Francesc Macià and Lluís Companys (nationalist presidents of Catalonia; Companys was executed by Franco's henchmen in the Castell de Montjuïc in 1940), Ildefons Cerdà (who designed L'Eixample) and Joan Gamper (the founder of the FC Barcelona football team, aka Hans Gamper). Many victims of Franco's postwar revenge were buried in unmarked graves here – the last of them in 1974. Both buses 9 and 21 stop around 10 minutes' walk away – the cemetery is easy to spot.

> ### ⓘ MAR I MUNTANYA SEA & MOUNTAIN
>
> The quickest way from the beach to the mountain is via the **Transbordador Aeri** (Map p302; www.telefericodebarcelona.com; Av de Miramar, Jardins de Miramar; one way/return €11/16.50; ◉11am-7pm; ◻50 & 153), the cable car that runs between Torre de Sant Sebastiá in La Barceloneta and the Miramar stop on Montjuïc (from mid-June to mid-September only). From Estació Parc Montjuïc, the Telefèric de Montjuïc cable car carries you to the Castell de Montjuïc via the Mirador (a lookout point).

COL·LECCIÓ DE CARROSSES FÚNEBRES
MUSEUM

(☎93 484 19 99; www.cbsa.cat; Carrer de la Mare de Déu de Port 56-58; ◉10am-2pm Wed-Sun; ◻9, 21) **FREE** If late-18th-century to mid-20th-century hearses (complete with period-dressed dummies) are your thing, then this collection, set at the entrance to the Cementiri del Sud-Oest, is probably the city's weirdest sight, a place to contemplate the pomp and circumstance of people's last earthly ride. The funeral company claims it is the biggest museum of its kind in the world. The collection incorporates funeral carriages spanning 90 years, four of them with horses and accompanying walkers in powdered wigs and tricorn hats, as well as a metallic Buick hearse and a couple of earlier motorised hearses.

MUHBA REFUGI 307
HISTORIC SITE

Map p302 (☎93 256 21 22; www.museuhistoria.bcn.cat; Carrer Nou de la Rambla 169; admission incl tour adult/child under 7yr €3.40/free; ◉tours 10.30am, 11.30am & 2.30pm Sun; ⓂParal·lel) Part of the Museu d'Història de Barcelona (MUHBA), this is a shelter that dates back to the days of the Spanish Civil War. Barcelona was the city most heavily bombed from the air during the Spanish Civil War and had more than 1300 air-raid shelters. Local citizens started digging this one under a fold of Montjuïc in March 1937.

In the course of the next two years, the web of tunnels was slowly extended to 200m, with a theoretical capacity for 2000 people. People were not allowed to sleep overnight in the shelter – when raids were not being carried out work continued on its extension. Vaulted to displace the weight above the shelter to the clay brick walls (clay is porous, which allowed the bricks to absorb the shock waves of falling bombs without cracking), the tunnels were narrow and winding. Coated in lime to seal out humidity and whitewashed to relieve the sense of claustrophobia, they became a second home for many El Poble Sec folks.

When the civil war ended, Franco had some extensions made because he considered the option of entering WWII on Hitler's side. When he decided not to join the war, this and other shelters were largely abandoned. In the tough years of famine and rationing during the 1940s and 1950s, families from Granada took up residence here rather than in the shacks springing up all over the area, as poor migrants arrived from southern Spain. Later on, an enterprising fellow grew mushrooms here for sale on the black market.

The half-hour tours (in Catalan or Spanish; book ahead for English or French) explain all this and more.

JARDINS DE MOSSÈN
CINTO DE VERDAGUER   GARDENS
Map p302 (www.bcn.cat/parcsijardins; ☉10am-sunset; ☐55,150) **FREE** Near the Estació Parc Montjuïc funicular/Telefèric station are the ornamental Jardins de Mossèn Cinto de Verdaguer. These sloping, verdant gardens are home to various kinds of bulbs and aquatic plants. Many of the former (some 80,000) have to be replanted each year. They include tulips, narcissus, crocus, varieties of dahlia and more. The aquatic plants include lotus and water lilies.

JARDINS DE MOSSÈN
COSTA I LLOBERA   GARDENS
Map p302 (www.bcn.cat/parcsijardins; Carretera de Miramar 1; ☉10am-sunset; cable car Transbordador Aeri, Miramar) **FREE** Towards the foot of the part of Montjuïc below the castle, above the thundering traffic of the main road to Tarragona, the Jardins de Mossèn Costa i Llobera have a good collection of tropical and desert plants – including a veritable forest of cacti.

PLAÇA D'ESPANYA
& AROUND   SQUARE, NEIGHBOURHOOD
Map p302 (Ⓜ️Espanya) The whirling roundabout of Plaça d'Espanya, distinguished by its so-called Venetian towers (because they

are vaguely reminiscent of the belltower in Venice's St Mark's Square), was built for the 1929 World Exhibition and is the junction of several major thoroughfares.

It is flanked on its northern side by the facade of the former Les Arenes bullring. Built in 1900 and once one of three bullrings in the city, it was recently converted into a shopping and leisure centre by Lord Richard Rogers. There are good views of the city from its 4th-floor rooftop terrace.

Behind the bullring is the **Parc de Joan Miró** (Map p302; Carrer de Tarragona), created in the 1980s – worth a quick detour for Miró's phallic sculpture **Dona i Ocell** (Map p302) (Woman and Bird) in the western corner. Locals know the park (which apart from the Miró is a dispiriting affair) as the Parc de l'Escorxador (Abattoir Park), after the slaughterhouse that once stood here – unsurprisingly given the proximity to the bullring.

A couple of blocks west and just south of Estació Sants is **Parc d'Espanya Industrial** (Map p302; Carrer de Sant Antoni, Sants; ☉10am-sunset; underground rail Sants Estació). With its ponds, little waterfalls, green spaces, trees, children's swings, bar, and the odd towers that look for all the world like sci-fi prison-camp searchlight towers, it is a strange park indeed.

✖️ EATING

Montjuïc is largely bereft of notable eating options, for the obvious reason that it is mostly parks and gardens. In gruff old El Poble Sec, however, you'll turn up all sorts of priceless nuggets, from historic taverns offering Catalan classics to a handful of smart, new-wave eateries, while Sant Antoni is the place for new cafe openings. The pickings in Sants are slimmer, but there are still some worthy exceptions.

✖️ Montjuïc

MIRAMAR   MEDITERRANEAN, ASIAN €€
Map p302 (☎93 443 66 27; www.club-miramar.es; Carretera de Miramar 40; mains €16-23, lunchtime 3-course fixed menu €19.50; ☉1-4pm & 9pm-midnight Tue-Sat, 1-4pm Sun; ☐D20) With several terraces and a cool designer main dining area, this restaurant's key draw is

the views it offers over Barcelona's waterfront. Hovering just above the Transbordador Aeri cable-car station, you can linger over a coffee or tuck into an elegant meal with a creative Catalan and Mediterranean slant, or opt for an extensive Asian menu.

✗ El Poble Sec

LA BELLA NAPOLI   PIZZA €
Map p302 (☑93 442 50 56; Carrer de Margarit 14; pizzas €8-15; ⊗1.30-4pm & 8.30pm-midnight; ⓂParal·lel) There are pizza joints all over Barcelona. And then there's the real thing: the way they make it in Naples. This place even *feels* like Naples. The waiters are mostly from across the Med and have that cheeky southern Italian approach to food, customers and everything else. The pizzas are good, ranging from the simple margherita to a heavenly black-truffle number.

BARRAMÓN   CANARIAN €
Map p302 (☑93 442 30 80; www.barramon.es; Carrer de Blai 28; mains €9-11; ⊗7-11.30pm Mon-Thu, 1pm-midnight Fri-Sun; ⓂParal·lel) On the lively Carrer de Blai, Barramón is a great little bar that serves Canarian food and is a bit rock and roll at the same time. Try the *ropa vieja* (an infinitely more flavoursome version of its Cuban cousin), a wonderful stew of chickpeas and shredded pork; *papas arrugadas* (baked new potatoes with a spicy sauce); and *almogrote* (cured cheese topped with olive oil, garlic and red pepper).

TAVERNA CAN MARGARIT   CATALAN €
Map p302 (☑93 177 07 40; Carrer de la Concòrdia 21; mains €8-12; ⊗9-11.30pm Mon-Sat; ⓂPoble Sec) For decades this former wine store has been dishing out dinner to often raucous groups. Traditional Catalan cooking is the name of the game. Surrounded by aged wine barrels, take your place at old tables and benches and perhaps order the *conejo a la jumillana* (fried rabbit served with garlic, onion, bay leaves, rosemary, mint, thyme and oregano).

★ QUIMET I QUIMET   TAPAS €€
Map p302 (☑93 442 31 42; Carrer del Poeta Cabanyes 25; tapas €4-11; ⊗noon-4pm & 7-10.30pm Mon-Fri, noon-4pm Sat & Sun; ⓂParal·lel) Quimet i Quimet is a family-run business that has been passed down from generation to generation. There's barely space to swing a *calamar* in this bottle-lined, standing-room-only place, but it is a treat for the palate, with *montaditos* (tapas on a slice of bread) made to order. Let the folk behind the bar advise you, and order a drop of fine wine to accompany the food.

XEMEI   ITALIAN €€
Map p302 (☑93 553 51 40; Passeig de l'Exposició 85; mains €15-24; ⊗1.30-3.30pm & 9-11.30pm Mon-Fri, 2-4pm & 9pm-midnight Sat & Sun; ⓂPoble Sec) Xemei ('twins' in Venetian, because it is run by twins from Italy's lagoon city) is a wonderful slice of Venice in Barcelona. To the accompaniment of gentle jazz, you might try a starter of mixed *cicheti* (Venetian seafood tapas), followed with *bigoi in salsa veneziana* (thick spaghetti in an anchovy and onion sauce).

LA TOMAQUERA   CATALAN €€
Map p302 (Carrer de Margarit 58; mains €9-15; ⊗1.30-4pm & 8.30-11pm Tue-Sat, closed Aug; ⓂPoble Sec) The waiters shout and rush about this classic place, while carafes of wine are sloshed about the long wooden tables. You can't book, so it's first in, first seated (queues are the norm). Try the house speciality of snails or go for hearty meat dishes. The occasional seafood option, such as *cassola de cigales* (crayfish hotpot), might also tempt. And cash is king.

✗ Sant Antoni

ORXATERIA SIRVENT   ICE CREAM €
Map p302 (☑93 441 76 16; Ronda de Sant Pau 3; horchata from €1.50, ice cream from €1.70; ⊗10am-midnight; ⓂSant Antoni) *Barcelonins'* favourite source of *orxata/horchata* (tiger-nut drink) since 1926, this busy locale serves up the best you'll try without having to catch the train down to this drink's spiritual home, Valencia. You can get it by the glass or take it away. This place also purveys ice cream, *granissat* (iced fruit crush) and *turrón* (nougat).

BODEGA 1900   TAPAS €€
Map p302 (☑93 325 26 59; www.bodega1900.com; Carrer de Tamarit 91; tapas from €4.60; ⊗1-10.30pm Tue-Sat; ⓂSant Antoni) The latest venture from the world-famous Adrià brothers, Bodega 1900 mimics an old-school tapas bar (and calls itself a *'vermutería'*, though it only stocks Martini), but this is no ordinary spit-and-sawdust joint serving *patatas bravas* and tortilla. Witness, for

example, the *mollete de calamars,* probably the best squid sandwich in the world, hot from the pan and served with chipotle mayonnaise, kim chi and lemon zest; or the 'spherified' false olives.

FÀBRICA MORITZ
CATALAN €€

Map p302 (📞93 426 00 50; www.moritz.com; Ronda de Sant Antoni 41; tapas from €3.70; ⊙6am-3am; MSant Antoni) With the help of architect Jean Nouvel and chef Jordi Vilà, this microbrewery from the people behind Moritz beer has been rebuilt and opened with great fanfare as a vast food and drink complex, with wine bar and restaurant. The tapas and more substantial dishes comprise all the cornerstones of Catalan cuisine and plenty more, but be prepared to queue.

BODEGA SEPÚLVEDA
CATALAN €€

Map p302 (📞93 323 59 44; www.bodegasepulved.net; Carrer de Sepúlveda 173; mains €10-20; ⊙1.30-4.30pm & 8pm-12.30am Mon-Sat; MUniversitat) This tavern has been showering tapas on its happy diners since 1952. The range of dishes is a little overwhelming and mixes traditional (Catalan faves like *cap i pota* – stew made with bits of the calf you don't want to think about) with more surprising options like *carpaccio de calabacín con bacalao y parmesán* (thin courgette slices draped in cod and Parmesan). You can hang out until 1am.

The main dining area is out the back and downstairs, with a small, low-ceilinged area upstairs.

★ TICKETS
MODERN SPANISH €€€

Map p302 (www.ticketsbar.es; Avinguda del Paral·lel 164; tapas €6-15; ⊙7-11.30pm Tue-Fri, 1.30-3.30pm & 7-11.30pm Sat, closed Aug; MParal·lel) This is, literally, one of the sizzling tickets in the restaurant world, a tapas bar opened by Ferran Adrià, of the legendary El Bulli, and his brother Albert. And unlike El Bulli, it's an affordable venture – if you can book a table, that is (you can only book online, and two months in advance).

It's a fairly flamboyant and modern affair in terms of decor, playing with circus images and theatre lights, while the food has kept some of the El Bulli greats such as the 'air baguette' – a crust larded with Iberico ham, or the slightly bonkers 'cotton candy tree', with fruit-studded candyfloss clouds served on a small bush. The seafood bar serves a slightly more serious option of oysters, tuna belly, and delicate fish skin in a paper cone.

✕ Sants

ZARAUTZ
BASQUE €€

Map p302 (📞93 325 28 13; www.zarautzbcn.es; Carrer de l'Elisi 13; mains €12-20; ⊙8am-11.30pm Mon-Fri, 9am-11.30pm Sat, closed Aug; MTarragona) A short hop away from the metro station, you can take in some quality Basque tapas at the bar any time of the day, or retire to the restaurant for a full meal, such as *carpaccio de carn amb formatge Idiazábal* (beef carpaccio with a tangy Basque cheese). The owner is a dessert specialist, so save some room. It's a rough-and-tumble-looking joint, but don't let that put you off.

🍷 DRINKING & NIGHTLIFE

A couple of curious bars in El Poble Sec (literally 'Dry Town'!) make a good prelude to the clubs that hold sway up in the wonderfully weird fantasy world of the Poble Espanyol. A couple of clubs on the lower end of Avinguda del Paral·lel are worth seeking out too.

🍷 Montjuïc

LA TERRRAZZA
CLUB

Map p302 (www.laterrrazza.com; Avinguda de Francesc Ferrer i Guàrdia; admission €15-20; ⊙midnight-5am Thu, to 6am Fri & Sat, closed Oct-Apr; MEspanya) One of the city's top summertime dance locations, La Terrrazza attracts squadrons of the beautiful people, locals and foreigners alike, for a full-on night of music and cocktails partly under the stars inside the Poble Espanyol complex.

🍷 El Poble Sec

⭐ LA CASETA DEL MIGDIA   BAR

Map p302 (📞617 956572; www.lacaseta.org; Mirador del Migdia; ⏰8pm-1am Wed & Thu, 8pm-2am Fri, noon-2am Sat, noon-1am Sun, weekends only in winter; Ⓜ Paral·lel, funicular) The effort of getting to what is, for all intents and purposes, a simple *chiringuito* (makeshift cafe-bar) is well worth it. Stare out to sea over a beer or coffee by day. As sunset approaches the atmosphere changes, as lounge music (from samba to funk) wafts out over the hammocks. Walk below the walls of the Castell de Montjuïc along the dirt track or follow Passeig del Migdia – watch out for signs for the Mirador del Migdia.

TINTA ROJA   BAR

Map p302 (📞93 443 32 43; www.tintaroja.cat; Carrer de la Creu dels Molers 17; ⏰8.30pm-1am Wed, to 2am Thu, to 3am Fri & Sat; Ⓜ Poble Sec) A succession of nooks and crannies, dotted with flea market finds and dimly lit in violets, reds and yellows, makes Tinta Roja an intimate spot for a drink and the occasional show in the back – with anything from actors to acrobats. This was once a *vaqueria* (small dairy farm), where they kept cows out the back and sold fresh milk at the front.

🍷 Sant Antoni

BAR CALDERS   WINE BAR

Map p302 (📞93 329 93 49; Carrer del Parlament 25; ⏰5pm-1.30am Mon-Thu, to 2.30am Fri, 11am-2.30am Sat, 11am-midnight Sun; Ⓜ Sant Antoni) It bills itself as a wine bar, but actually the wine selection at Bar Calders is its weak point. As an all-day cafe and tapas bar, however, it's unbeatable, with a few tables outside on a tiny pedestrian side street, and has become the favoured meeting point for the neighbourhood's boho element.

MUSEUM   GAY

Map p302 (Carrer de Sepúlveda 178; ⏰11pm-3am Fri & Sat; Ⓜ Universitat) Explosion in the kitsch factory is the artistic theme here, where chandeliers meet mock Renaissance sculpture and light pop. Drinks are served behind

---

ℹ️ RUTA DEL POBLE SEC

A group of tapas bars in and around the *barrio* (district) organise the 'Poble Sec Route', a suggested bar crawl in which each bar offers a special deal of a beer and a tapa for €2 every Thursday.

---

a stage-lit bar and can be hard to come by from 1.30am. Twinks and muscle builders mix happily in this self-styled 'Video Bar'.

☆ ENTERTAINMENT

SALA APOLO   LIVE MUSIC

Map p302 (📞93 441 40 01; www.sala-apolo.com; Carrer Nou de la Rambla 113; admission club €13-18, concerts vary; ⏰midnight-5am Sun-Thu, 12.30am-6am Fri & Sat; Ⓜ Paral·lel) This is a fine old theatre, where red velvet dominates and you feel as though you're in a movie-set dancehall scene featuring Eliot Ness. 'Nasty Mondays' and 'Crappy Tuesdays' are aimed at a diehard, we-never-stop-dancing crowd. Earlier in the evening, concerts generally take place, here and in 'La 2', a smaller auditorium downstairs. Tastes are as eclectic as possible, from local bands and burlesque shows to big-name international acts.

METRO   GAY

Map p302 (📞93 323 52 27; www.metrodiscobcn. com; Carrer de Sepúlveda 185; admission €19, incl 1 drink; ⏰12.15am-5am Sun-Thu, until 6am Fri & Sat; Ⓜ Universitat) Metro attracts a casual gay crowd with its two dance floors, three bars and very dark room. Keep an eye out for shows and parties, which can range from parades of models to bingo nights (on Thursday nights, with sometimes-interesting prizes). On Wednesday nights there's a live sex show.

BARTS   CONCERT VENUE

Map p280 (Barcelona Arts on Stage; 📞93 324 84 92; www.barts.cat; Avinguda del Paral·lel 62; ⏰5pm-midnight Mon-Thu & Sun, 5pm-2am Fri & Sat; Ⓜ Paral·lel) BARTS hasn't been around very long, but is already hosting the finest rock and pop concerts in the city, thanks to a smart design that combines a comfortable midsized auditorium with excellent acoustics and a supremely professional attitude to sound.

RENOIR FLORIDABLANCA
CINEMA

Map p302 (☑93 426 33 37; www.cinesrenoir.com; Carrer de Floridablanca 135; tickets €6-9; MSant Antoni) With seven screens, this is now the last standing in Barcelona of a small chain of art-house cinemas in Spain showing quality flicks. It is handily located just beyond El Raval, so you can be sure that there is no shortage of postfilm entertainment options nearby.

GRAN BODEGA SALTÓ
LIVE MUSIC

Map p302 (www.bodegasalto.net; Carrer de Blesa 36; ☺7pm-2am Mon-Wed, noon-2am Thu, noon-3am Fri & Sat, noon-midnight Sun; MParal·lel) The ranks of barrels give away the bar's history as a traditional bodega. Now, after a little homemade psychedelic redecoration with odd lamps, figurines and old Chinese beer ads, it's a magnet for an eclectic barfly crowd. Mohicans and tats abound, but the crowd is mixed and friendly, and gets pretty lively on nights when there is live music.

SANT JORDI CLUB
LIVE MUSIC

Map p302 (☑93 426 20 89; Passeig Olimpic 5-7; 🚌55, 150, funicular) With capacity for more than 4500 people, this concert hall, annexed to the Olympic stadium Palau Sant Jordi, is used for big gigs that do not reach the epic proportions of headlining international acts. For concert information, keep your eyes out for listings sections in newspapers, flyers and magazines like the *Guía del Ocio*. Admission prices and opening times vary with the concerts.

SHOPPING

MERCAT DE SANT ANTONI
MARKET

Map p302 (☑93 209 31 58; www.mercatdesantantoni.com; Carrer de Comte d'Urgell 1; ☺7am-2.30pm & 5-8.30pm Mon-Thu, 7am-8.30pm Fri & Sat; MSant Antoni) Just beyond the western edge of El Raval is Mercat de Sant Antoni, a glorious old iron and brick building that is currently undergoing renovation. In the meantime, a huge marquee has been erected alongside to house a food market. The second-hand book market still takes place alongside on Sunday mornings.

GI JOE
FASHION

Map p302 (☑93 329 96 52; www.gijoebcn.com; Ronda de Sant Antoni 49; ☺10am-2pm & 4.30-8.30pm Mon-Sat; MUniversitat) This is the best central army-surplus warehouse. Get your khakis here, along with urban army fashion T-shirts, and throw in a holster, gas mask or sky-blue UN helmet for a kinkier effect.

🏃 SPORTS & ACTIVITIES

PISCINES BERNAT PICORNELL
SWIMMING

Map p302 (☑93 423 40 41; www.picornell.cat; Avinguda de l'Estadi 30-38; adult/child €6.50/4.50; ☺6.45am-midnight Mon-Fri, 7am-9pm Sat, 7.30am-4pm Sun; 🚌50, 61 or 193) Barcelona's official Olympic pool on Montjuïc. On Saturday nights, between 9pm and 11pm, the pool (with access to sauna and steam bath) is open only to nudists. On Sundays between October and May the indoor pool also opens for nudists only from 4.15pm to 6pm.

Day Trips from Barcelona

Girona p196
A splendid cathedral, a maze of narrow cobbled streets and Catalonia's finest medieval Jewish quarter are part of this riverside town's charms.

Figueres p199
The Teatre-Museu Dalí is Spain's most surreal sight, a place of pilgrimage for any fan of Salvador Dalí, and the artist's final resting place.

Montserrat p202
Catalonia's most important shrine is in this spectacularly sited mountain monastery, complete with Europe's oldest choir and superb scenic walks.

Sitges p204
A classy old town and eating scene, superb string of beaches, great nightlife and a hedonistic carnival await visitors at the south coast's premier seaside town.

Tarragona p206
Sunny port city with a beautiful medieval core, boasting some of Spain's most extensive Roman ruins and studded with tempting eating options.

Girona

Explore

Girona's big draw is its old town, a tight huddle of ancient arcaded houses, grand churches and climbing cobbled streets, so head first for the Catedral – either by strolling along the lazy Río Onyar or by taking the high road along the medieval walls. Follow this with a visit to El Call (the medieval Jewish quarter) and the excellent Museu d'Història dels Jueus de Girona before taking your pick of the numerous restaurants in the nearby streets. After lunch, continue your exploration of other old town sights, such as the wonderfully intact Banys Àrabs or the attractive cloisters of the Monestir de Sant Pere de Galligants, before finding a bar around the Plaça de l'Independència to put your feet up for a while.

The Best...

➡ **Sight** Museu d'Història dels Jueus de Girona (p196)

➡ **Place to Eat** El Celler de Can Roca (p199)

➡ **Place to Drink** Bars on Plaça de l'Independència (p198)

Top Tip

For the best city views, take a walk along Girona's medieval walls, known as the Passeig Arqueològic and accessed across from the Banys Àrabs or near Plaça de Catalunya.

Getting There & Away

➡ **Car** Take the AP7 tollway via Granollers.

➡ **Train** Trains and rodalies on the R11 line run from Barcelona (€8.40 to €15.90, 40 minutes to 1½ hours, up to 36 daily).

ⓘ MUSEUM DISCOUNTS

The **GironaMuseus card** (www.gironamuseus.cat), covering six Girona museums, gives useful savings. You pay the full entrance fee at the first museum you visit and then get a 50% discount at the remainder.

Need to Know

➡ **Location** 85km northeast of Barcelona

➡ **Tourist Office** (☑972 22 65 75; www.girona.cat/turisme; Rambla de la Llibertat 1; ☉9am-8pm Mon-Fri, 9am-2pm & 4-8pm Sat, 9am-2pm Sun)

◉ SIGHTS

Most of Girona's sights are concentrated in the lanes of its old town.

★MUSEU D'HISTÒRIA DELS JUEUS DE GIRONA   MUSEUM

(www.girona.cat/call; Carrer de la Força 8; adult/child €4/free; ☉10am-8pm Mon-Sat) Until 1492 Girona was home to Catalonia's second-most important medieval Jewish community (after Barcelona), and one of the finest Jewish quarters in the country. The Call (Catalan for 'ghetto') was centred on the narrow Carrer de la Força for 600 years, until relentless persecution forced the Jews out of Spain. This excellent museum shows genuine pride in Girona's Jewish heritage without shying away from the less salubrious aspects, such as persecution by the Inquisition and forced conversions.

Other well-presented displays deal with Girona's Jewish contribution to medieval astronomy and medicine, the synagogue, everyday life, and rituals in the Jewish community and the diaspora. Standout objects include funerary slabs and the original documents ordering the expulsion of Jews from Spain. Opens shorter hours in low season.

★CATEDRAL   CHURCH

(www.catedraldegirona.org; Plaça de la Catedral; adult/student incl Basílica de Sant Feliu €7/5, Sun free; ☉10am-7.30pm Apr-Oct, 10am-6.30pm Nov-Mar) The baroque facade of the cathedral towers over a flight of 86 steps rising from Plaça de la Catedral. Though the Romanesque **cloister** dates to the 12th century, most of the building is Gothic, with the second-widest nave (23m) in Christendom. The 14th-century gilt-and-silver altarpiece and canopy are memorable, as are the bishop's throne and the museum, which holds the masterly Romanesque *Tapís de la creació* (Tapestry of the Creation) and a Mozarabic illuminated *Beatus* manuscript, dating from 975. The *Creation* tapestry shows God at the epicentre and in the circle around him the creation of Adam, Eve, the animals, the sky, light and darkness.

GIRONA'S JEWS

Girona was one of Catalonia's largest Jewish communities, which lived by and large peacefully alongside their Christian neighbours (in fact, the synagogue was originally located next door to the cathedral), gaining in prosperity and contributing to fields as diverse as astronomy and medicine. In its heyday, the Jewish quarter (the Call) was known as 'the Mother City of Israel'. Little by little, though, and especially with the later crusades in the 12th and 13th centuries, the Jewish community became a ready target for racist attacks. The Call – a maze of tiny alleys, surrounded by a stone wall – went from refuge to ghetto as Jews were gradually confined to their tiny corner of the town. Things came to a head in 1391, when a mob broke into the ghetto, massacring 40 residents. Since the Jews were still under the king's protection, troops were sent in and the survivors were confined to the Galligants Tower 'for their own safety' for 17 weeks, only to find their houses and possessions destroyed upon emerging. Many converted to Christianity in the 15th century, and in 1492 those that remained were expelled from Spain, ending a story that had been over 1500 years in the telling.

MUSEU D'HISTÒRIA DE GIRONA   MUSEUM
(www.girona.cat/museuciutat; Carrer de la Força 27; adult/student/child €4/2/free; ☺10.30am-5.30pm Tue-Sat, to 1.30pm Sun) The engaging and well-presented city history museum does Girona's long and impressive story justice, its displays covering everything from the city's Roman origins, through the siege of the city by Napoleonic troops to the *sardana* (Catalonia's national folk dance) tradition. A separate gallery houses cutting-edge temporary art and photography exhibits.

MUSEU D'ART   GALLERY
(www.museuart.com; Plaça de la Catedral 12; admission €2; ☺10am-7pm Tue-Sat May-Sep, to 6pm Oct-Apr, 10am-2pm Sun) Next door to the cathedral, in the 12th-to-16th-century Palau Episcopal, the art museum collection consists of around 8500 pieces of art from the Girona region, ranging from Romanesque woodcarvings and stained-glass tables to Modernist sculptures by Olot-born Miquel Blay and early-20th-century paintings by Francesc Vayreda.

BANYS ÀRABS   BATHHOUSE
(www.banysarabs.cat; Carrer de Ferràn el Catòlic; adult/child €2/1; ☺10am-7pm Mon-Sat, to 2pm Sun Apr-Sep, 10am-2pm daily Oct-Mar) Although modelled on earlier Muslim and Roman bathhouses, the Banys Àrabs are a finely preserved, 12th-century Christian affair in Romanesque style. This is the only public bathhouse discovered from medieval Christian Spain, where, in reaction to the Muslim obsession with water and cleanliness, washing almost came to be regarded as ungodly. The baths contain an *apodyterium*

(changing room), followed by a *frigidarium* and *tepidarium* (with respectively cold and warm water) and a *caldarium* (a kind of sauna) heated by an underfloor furnace.

BASÍLICA DE SANT FELIU   CHURCH
(Plaça de Sant Feliu; adult/student incl Catedral €7/5, Sun free; ☺10am-5.30pm Mon-Sat, 1-5.30pm Sun) Girona's second great church, with its landmark truncated bell tower, is downhill from the cathedral and entered on a combined ticket. The nave is majestic with Gothic ribbed vaulting, while St Narcissus, the patron of the city, is venerated in an enormous marble-and-jasper, late-baroque side chapel. His remains were formerly held in a glorious 14th-century sepulchre displayed alongside. A decent audioguide tour is included with admission.

MONESTIR DE SANT PERE DE GALLIGANTS   MONASTERY, MUSEUM
(www.mac.cat; Carrer de Santa Llúcia; adult/child €2.30/free; ☺10.30am-1.30pm & 4-7pm Tue-Sat, 10am-2pm Sun) This beautiful 11th- and 12th-century Romanesque Benedictine monastery has a sublime bell tower and a lovely cloister, featuring otherworldly animals and mythical creatures on the capitals of its double columns – there are some great ones in the church too. It's also home to the **Museu Arqueològic**, with old-school exhibits that range from prehistoric to Roman times. Opening hours vary.

MUSEU DEL CINEMA   MUSEUM
(www.museudelcinema.cat; Carrer de Sèquia 1; adult/child €5/free; ☺10am-6pm Tue-Sat; ♿) The Casa de les Aigües houses not only displays tracing the history of cinema from

Girona

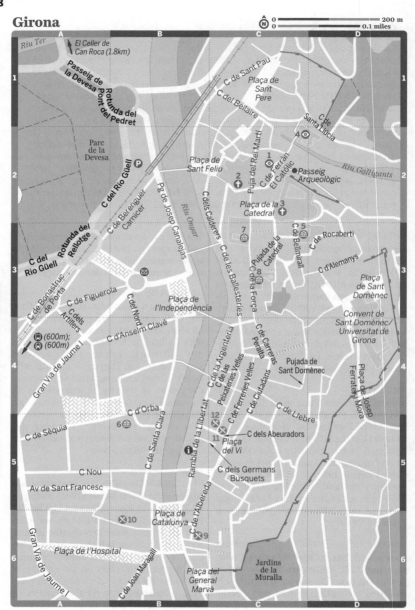

the late-19th-century debut of the Lumiére brothers, but also a parade of hands-on items for indulging in shadow games, optical illusions and the like – it's great for kids. Hours vary, check the website.

EATING & DRINKING

Girona has an excellent range of old town restaurants. For a beer or coffee on a sunny terrace, head to Plaça de l'Independència across the river from the old town.

Girona

+CUB   CAFE €

(www.mescub.cat; Carrer de l'Albereda 15; 3 tapas €10.40; ⊗8am-9pm Mon-Thu, 8am-midnight Fri, 9am-midnight Sat; 🛜🍴) This übercentral cafe is great at any time of day and distinguished by friendly service, innovative tapas – from black pudding with pistachio to salad with black-fig sorbet – fresh fruit-juice combos, shakes and Girona's own La Moska microbrew. There's a great terrace overlooking Plaça de Catalunya.

OCCI   FUSION €€

(www.restaurantocci.com; Carrer dels Mercaders 3; mains €15-23; ⊗1-3.30pm & 8.30-11pm, closed Wed) With elegant contemporary styling and quality glassware and service, this has many elements of a pricier place but remains accessible and welcoming. The menu incorporates Catalan, French and Asian influences, with game dishes featuring in season. Dishes are beautifully presented and delicious. The day they close can vary.

NU   CATALAN €€

(📞972 22 52 30; www.nurestaurant.cat; Carrer d'Abeuradors 4; mains €16-18, degustation menu €50; ⊗1.15-3.45pm & 8.15-10.45pm Tue-Sat, 1.15-3.45pm Mon; 🛜) Sleek and confident, this handsome contemporary old-town spot has innovative, top-notch plates prepared in view by the friendly team. There are always some very interesting flavour combinations, and they work. Great value for this quality.

L'ALQUERIA   CATALAN €€

(📞972 22 18 82; www.restaurantalqueria.com; Carrer de la Ginesta 8; mains €14-20; ⊗1-4pm & 9-11pm Wed-Sat, 1-4pm Tue & Sun) This smart minimalist *arrocería* (rice eatery) serves the finest *arròs negre* (rice cooked in cuttlefish ink) and *arròs a la Catalan* in the city, as well as around 20 other superbly executed rice dishes, including paellas. Eat your heart out, Valencia! It's wise to book ahead for dinner.

★**EL CELLER DE CAN ROCA**   CATALAN €€€

(📞972 22 21 57; www.cellercanroca.com; Carrer Can Sunyer 48; degustation menus €150-180; ⊗1-4pm & 8.30-11pm Tue-Sat Sep-Jul) Named best restaurant in the world in 2013 by The World's 50 Best Restaurants, this place, 2km west of central Girona in a refurbished country house, is run by three brothers. The focus is 'emotional cuisine' through ever-changing takes on Catalan dishes. The style is playful and a full range of molecular gastronomy techniques is employed. The voluminous wine list arrives on a trolley. Book online 11 months in advance; if you haven't, you can join a standby list.

Figueres

Explore

An early start is essential for visiting the incomparable Teatre-Museu Dalí – from midmorning, coachloads of tourists from the Costa Brava can make its narrow corridors quite claustrophobic. You'll want to spend the whole morning here, admiring everything from the exterior to the bizarre decorative touches and Dalí's distinctive works before partaking in some of the finest cuisine in the region, just out of town, or just grabbing a quick bite nearby.

There's more to Figueres than just Dalí, and there are several other attractions worth your time if you have the stamina in the afternoon: the vast Castell de Sant Ferran, perfect for a stroll around, or else the two entertaining museums in the centre.

The Best...

➡ **Sight** Teatre-Museu Dalí (p200)
➡ **Place to Eat** El Motel (p201)
➡ **Place to Drink** Sidrería Txot's (p201)

TOP SIGHT
TEATRE-MUSEU DALÍ

The first name that comes into your head when you sight this red castle-like building, bristling with giant eggs, Oscar-like statues and plaster croissants, is Dalí. An entirely appropriate final resting place for the master of surrealism, it has assured his immortality.

Dalí converted Figueres' former theatre, ruined by fire in 1939, into this place full of surprises, tricks and illusions, which contains a substantial portion of his life's work.

Choice exhibits include **Taxi plujós** (Rainy Taxi): put a coin in the slot and water washes all over the occupant of the car. The **Sala de Peixateries** (Fish Shop Room) holds a collection of Dalí oils. Beneath the former stage of the theatre is the crypt with Dalí's plain tomb, located at 'the spiritual centre of Europe' as Dalí modestly described it.

Gala – Dalí's wife and lifelong muse – is seen throughout, from the **Gala mirando el Mar Mediterráneo** (Gala Looking at the Mediterranean Sea) on the 2nd level, which also appears to be a portrait of Abraham Lincoln from afar, to the classic **Leda atómica** (Atomic Leda).

A separate entrance (same ticket and times) leads into Dalí Joies, a collection of 37 unique Dalí-designed jewels.

DON'T MISS...

➡ The museum's whimsical exterior

➡ Gala mirando el Mar Mediterráneo

PRACTICALITIES

➡ www.salvador-dali.org

➡ Plaça de Gala i Salvador Dalí 5

➡ admission incl Dalí Joies & Museu de l'Empordà adult/child under 9yr €12/free

➡ ⊙9am-8pm Jul-Sep, 9.30am-6pm Tue-Sun Mar-Jun & Oct, 10.30am-6pm Tue-Sun Nov-Feb

Top Tip

It pays to reserve online in advance for the Teatre-Museu Dalí, and to visit outside weekends and public holidays. Get here for opening time to avoid the worst of the crowds.

Getting There & Away

➡ **Car** Take the AP7 tollway via Granollers and Girona.

➡ **Train** Trains and rodalies on the R11 line run from Barcelona (€12 to €16, 1¾ to two hours, at least hourly).

Need to Know

➡ **Location** 118km northeast of Barcelona

➡ **Tourist Office** (☐972 50 31 55; www.visitfigueres.cat; Plaça del Sol; ⊙10am-2pm & 4-6pm Tue-Sat, 10am-3pm Sun & Mon)

⊙ SIGHTS

CASTELL DE SANT FERRAN · · · · · · · · · FORT
(www.lesfortalesescatalanes.info; adult/child €3/free; ⊙10.30am-6pm) This sturdy 18th-century fortress commands the surrounding plains

from a low hill 1km northwest of the centre. Built in 1750 to repel any French invaders and large enough to house 16,000 men, it nevertheless fell to their Gallic neighbours – both in 1794 and 1808. Spain's Republican government held its final meeting of the civil war (on 8 February 1939) in the dungeons. It's a vast complex: the admission fee includes an audioguide; book ahead for other guided tours (€10 to €15) involving jeeps and boats. Opening hours vary seasonally.

MUSEU DE L'EMPORDÀ · · · · · · · · · MUSEUM
(www.museuemporda.org; La Rambla 2; adult/child €4/free; ⊙11am-7pm Tue-Sat, to 2pm Sun) This local museum on the square combines Greek, Roman and medieval archaeological finds with a sizeable collection of art, mainly by Catalan artists, but there are also some works on loan from the Prado in Madrid. Admission is free with a Teatre-Museu Dalí ticket.

MUSEU DEL JOGUET · · · · · · · · · MUSEUM
(www.mjc.cat; Carrer de Sant Pere 1; adult/child €6/free; ⊙10am-6pm Tue-Sat, 11am-2.30pm Sun, closed Jan; ⊡) This museum has more than 3500 toys – from the earliest board

games involving coloured stones and ball-in-a-cup (that timeless classic!) to intricate dolls' houses, 1920s dolls with the creepiest expressions you're ever likely to see, Dinky Toys, and Catalonia- and Valencia-made religious processions of tiny figures. Absolutely mesmerising, and not just for the kids!

EATING & DRINKING

The restaurants closest to the Teatre-Museu Dalí are overpriced, mediocre tourist traps.

SIDRERÍA TXOT'S — BASQUE €

(www.sidreriatxots.com; Avinguda Salvador Dalí 114; dishes €5-11; noon-midnight; wi-fi) Perch on a wooden seat and watch your Basque cider poured from on high from the barrel – the way it's supposed to be – before tucking into cold and hot *pintxos*, tasty burgers, cured meats, cheeses and salads, as well as dishes such as chorizo in cider and L'Escala anchovies on toast. The kitchen's open all afternoon – handy for a post-Dalí meal.

EL MOTEL — CATALAN €€

(Hotel Empordà; 972 50 05 62; www.elmotel.cat; Avinguda Salvador Dalí i Domènech 170; tasting menus €39-60; 7.30-11am, 12.45-3.45pm & 9-11pm; wi-fi) Jaume Subirós, the chef and owner of this hotel-restaurant on a busy road 1km north of the centre, is a seminal figure of the transition from traditional Catalan home cooking to the polished, innovative affair it is today. Highlights are such dishes as sea urchins from Cadaqués and calf's cheek in red wine. There are also appealing rooms at your disposal (singles/doubles €94/109).

SLEEPING

Most people treat Figueres as a day trip from Barcelona or the coast, but it's worth staying overnight if you want to beat the coachloads of tourists to the Dalí museum.

WORTH A DETOUR

DALÍ DELIRIUM

Salvador Dalí was born in Figueres in 1904, but his career took him to Madrid, Barcelona, Paris and the USA. He remained true to his roots and has left his mark in several locations around Catalonia, particularly at his seaside residence in Portlligat and his inland 'castle', Castell de Púbol.

Located by a peaceful cove in **Portlligat**, a tiny fishing settlement a 20-minute walk from Cadaqués, the **Casa Museu Dalí** (972 25 10 15; www.salvador-dali.org; adult/child under 9yr €11/free; 10.30am-6pm Tue-Sun, closed Jan–mid-Feb) – the lifelong residence of Dalí – started life as a mere fisherman's hut, and was steadily altered and enlarged by Dalí, who lived here with his wife from 1930 to 1982. If the Teatre-Museu Dalí is the mask that the showman presented to the world, then this is an intimate glimpse of his actual face. This splendid, bizarre whitewashed structure is a mishmash of cottages and sunny terraces, linked together by narrow labyrinthine corridors and containing an assortment of offbeat furnishings. Compulsory small-group tours are conducted by multilingual guides; booking a day or three ahead – you can do this online or by phone – is essential.

The **Castell de Púbol** (www.salvador-dali.org; Plaça de Gala Dalí; adult/concession €8/6; 10am-6pm Tue-Sun mid-Mar–early Jan), in the village of La Pera, just south of the C66 road between Girona and Palafrugell, is a Gothic and Renaissance mansion, purchased by Dalí in 1969 as a retreat for his wife, Gala, who lived here until her death at 88 in 1982. An inconsolable Dalí then moved in himself, but was removed by friends after starting a fire in 1984. Though much of the castle was decorated according to Gala's taste, Dalí touches do creep in in the form of spindly legged elephant statues in the maze-like garden, a see-through table with a horse visible below and a stuffed giraffe staring at Gala's tomb in the crypt.

For Portlligat, take a **Sarfa** (902 302025; www.sarfa.com) bus to Cadaqués from Figueres (€5.50, one hour, four weekdays); there are also connections from Barcelona and Girona. For the Castell de Púbol, catch a bus to Cruilla de la Pera from Girona (€3, 40 minutes) or Palafrugell, alight at the stop on the C66 and walk 2km to the castle, or take a train from Girona to Flaça (hourly, €2.50, 12 minutes) then take a taxi the last 4km.

HOTEL DURÁN · HOTEL €€

(☑972 50 12 50; www.hotelduran.com; Carrer de Lasauca 5; r €99; P❋☎) Staying at this mid-19th-century hotel is very much in keeping with the Dalí theme as he and his wife used to frequent the place themselves. Successfully blending old-style elegance with contemporary design, the hotel offers modern, good-value rooms and a restaurant like a royal banquet hall, with smooth service and a fantastic €24 lunch menu which features such expertly prepared delights as seared tuna steak and rabbit loin. Breakfast is cheaper if you book online.

Montserrat

Explore

Though the monastery complex itself of this major pilgrimage centre is compact, allow a whole day for the visit if you want to take advantage of the many splendid mountain walks. Take the earliest *cremallera* (rack-and-pinion train) or cable car up the mountain to beat the crowds and begin with the exploration of the monastery complex, paying a visit to the Virgin and then the worthwhile Museu de Montserrat before grabbing an early lunch or, better, a picnic. Season permitting, you might be able to catch a choir performance inside the basilica. Afterwards, ride the funiculars, or else take a walk down to the Santa Cova – the spot where the Virgin was originally found – or up to the Sant Jeroni peak for a splendid view of the valley below.

The Best...

→ **Sight** Monestir de Montserrat (p203)
→ **Place to Eat** Hotel Abat Cisneros (p203)
→ **Walk** Sant Jeroni (p202)

Top Tip

To commune with La Moreneta in solitude and enjoy the stillness and the silence of the mountain, stay overnight to make it to the chapel by the 7am opening time.

Getting There & Away

→ **Train and cable car** The R5 line trains operated by **FGC** (www.fgc.net) run hourly from Plaça d'Espanya station, starting at 8.36am (55 minutes). They connect with the AERI **cable car** (☑93 835 00 05; www.aeridemontserrat.com; one way/return €7/10; ☺9.40am-7pm, closed mid-Jan–Feb) at the Montserrat Aeri stop (every 15 minutes, five minutes) and the **cremallera** (☑902 312020; www.cremallerademontserrat.com; one way/return €5.40/8.60) train at the following stop, Monistrol de Montserrat. There are various train-*cremallera* combo tickets available.

→ **Car** By car take the C16 from Barcelona, then the C58 shortly after Terrassa, followed by the C55 to Monistrol de Montserrat. You can leave the car at the free car park and take the *cremallera* up to the top or drive up and park (cars €5.50).

Need to Know

→ **Location** 50km northwest of Barcelona
→ **Information Office** (☑938 77 77 01; www.montserratvisita.com; ☺9am-5.45pm)

◉ SIGHTS

★**MUSEU DE MONTSERRAT** · MUSEUM
(www.museudemontserrat.com; Plaça de Santa Maria; adult/student €7/6; ☺10am-5.45pm, to 6.45pm Jul-Aug) This museum has an excellent collection, ranging from an Egyptian mummy and Gothic altarpieces to fine canvases by Caravaggio, El Greco, Picasso and several Impressionists, as well as a comprehensive collection of 20th-century classic Catalan art and some fantastic Orthodox icons.

MONTSERRAT MOUNTAIN · MOUNTAIN
You can explore the mountain above the monastery on a web of paths leading to some of the peaks and to 13 empty and rather dilapidated hermitages. The **Funicular de Sant Joan** (one way/return €5.85/9; ☺every 20min 10am-6.50pm, closed mid-Jan–Feb) will carry you up the first 250m from the monastery. If you prefer to walk, the road past the funicular's bottom station leads to its top station in about 45 minutes.

From the top station, it's a 20-minute stroll (signposted) to the **Sant Joan chapel**, with fine westward views. More exciting is the one-hour walk northwest, along a path

TOP SIGHT
MONESTIR DE MONTSERRAT

The monastery – Spain's principal pilgrimage centre after Santiago – was founded in 1025 to commemorate a vision of the Virgin on the mountain, after which the Virgen de Montserrat, allegedly carved by St Luke and hidden here by St Peter, was discovered. Wrecked by Napoleon's troops in 1811, then abandoned after anticlerical legislation in the 1830s, the monastery was rebuilt; today a few dozen monks live here. Pilgrims come from far and wide to venerate the virgin, affectionately known as **La Moreneta** ('the little brown one' or 'the Black Madonna'), a 12th-century dark wooden sculpture of a regal-looking Mary with an elongated nose, holding the infant Jesus and a globe which pilgrims come to touch; she has been Catalonia's patron since 1881 and her blessing is particularly sought by newlyweds.

The 16th-century church's facade, with carvings of Christ and the Apostles, dates from 1901, despite its platteresque style. Stairs to the **Cambril de la Mare de Déu** (⊘7-10.30am & 12.15-6.30pm) FREE, housing La Moreneta, are to the right of the basilica entrance; expect queues. A room off the courtyard is filled with offbeat ex-voto gifts from people crediting the Virgin for all manner of happy events. Barcelona FC dedicate victories to her.

DON'T MISS...

➡ La Moreneta shrine
➡ Montserrat Boys Choir performing at the basilica
➡ A walk up Montserrat's Sant Jeroni peak

PRACTICALITIES

➡ www.abadia montserrat.net
➡ ⊘7am-8pm

---

marked with some blobs of yellow paint, to Montserrat's highest peak, **Sant Jeroni**, from where there's an awesome sheer drop on the north face. The walk takes you across the upper part of the mountain, with a close-up experience of some of the weird rock pillars, all named.

SANTA COVA   CHAPEL

To see the chapel on the spot where the holy image of the Virgin was discovered, you can drop down the **Funicular de Santa Cova** (one way/return €2.20/3.50; ⊘every 20min, closed mid-Jan–Feb), or else it's an easy walk down, followed by a stroll along a precipitous mountain path with fabulous views of the valley below.

ESPAI AUDIOVISUAL   MUSEUM

(adult/child €5/3, with Museu de Montserrat €9; ⊘9am-5.45pm Mon-Fri, to 6.45pm Sat & Sun) This walk-through multimedia space (with images and sounds) illustrates the daily life and activities of the monks and the history and spirituality of the monastery. Extended hours in high season.

★ ENTERTAINMENT

ESCOLANÍA DE MONTSERRAT   CHORAL MUSIC

(www.escolania.cat; ⊘performances 1pm Mon-Fri, noon Sun, 6.45pm Sun-Thu) This famous boys' choir sings in the basilica daily (except school holidays), their clear voices echoing inside the stone walls the way they have done since the 13th century. It is a brief treat; they sing *Virolai,* written by Catalonia's national poet Jacint Verdaguer, and *Salve Regina.* The 40 to 50 *escolanets,* aged between nine and 14, go to boarding school at Montserrat and must endure a two-year selection process to join the choir. See the website for other performances.

🛏 SLEEPING

HOTEL ABAT CISNEROS   HOTEL €€

(📞938 77 77 01; www.montserratvisita.com; s/d €63/108; 🅿🛜) The only hotel in the monastery complex has a super location next to the basilica, and tasteful, spacious rooms, some of which look over Plaça de Santa Maria. There are also inexpensive basic apartments and family packages available. Its restaurant serves imaginative Catalonian dishes (mains €17 to €20).

sitgestur.cat; Plaça de E Maristany 2; ☺10am-2pm & 4-6.30pm or 8pm Mon-Sat, 10am-2pm Sun)

Sitges

Explore

Sitges is perfect for seafront promenading and sun worshipping, so in warmer weather you'll find the most central beaches quite crowded. Luckily, there are quite a few to choose from, so pick your spot for a morning of sunbathing (or skinny dipping off the nudist beach) before choosing a seafood restaurant nearby. But it's not all about the sea here; if you have an interest in contemporary art and in the Modernisme movement, the classy old centre's array of elegant buildings, many housing museums, is well worth some of your time. The gay scene in Sitges – and its vibrant party atmosphere in general – is legendary, so many a day trip ends up the morning after...

The Best...

➡ **Sight** Beaches (p204)
➡ **Place to Eat** eF & Gi (p205)
➡ **Place to Drink** Bar Voramar (p205)

Top Tip

To find out the latest gay nightlife hotspots, head to the **Parrots Hotel** (☎938 94 13 50; www.parrotshotel.com; Calle de Joan Tarrida 16; s/d from €109/120; ☺mid-Feb–Oct; ❇@☎); and if you're coming to Sitges for the bacchanalian weeklong Carnaval in February/March, book well ahead.

Getting There & Away

➡ **Car** The best road from Barcelona is the C32 tollway. More scenic is the C31, which hooks up with the C32 after Castelldefels, but it is often busy and slow.

➡ **Train** From about 6am to 10pm four R2 rodalies trains an hour run to Barcelona's Passeig de Gràcia and Estació Sants (€4.10, 27 to 46 minutes).

Need to Know

➡ **Location** 35km southwest of Barcelona
➡ **Tourist Office** (☎938 94 42 51; www.

◉ SIGHTS

The most beautiful part of Sitges is the headland area, where noble Modernista palaces and mansions strike poses in the streets around the striking **Església de Sant Bartomeu i Santa Tecla**, with the blue sea as a backdrop.

BEACHES BEACHES

The main beach is flanked by the attractive seafront Passeig Maritim, dotted with *chiringuitos* (beachside bars) and divided into nine sections with different names by a series of breakwaters. The **Sant Sebastià**, **Balmins** and **D'aiguadolç** beaches run east of the headland. Though **Bassa Rodona** used to be the unofficial 'gay beach', gay sunbathers are now spread out pretty evenly, while Balmins is the sheltered bay favoured by nudists.

MUSEU ROMÀNTIC MUSEUM

(www.museusdesitges.cat; Carrer de Sant Gaudenci 1; adult/student €3.50/2; ☺10am-2pm & 3.30-7pm Tue-Sat, 11am-3pm Sun) Housed in a late-18th-century Can Llopis mansion, this faded museum recreates with its furnishings and dioramas the lifestyle of a 19th-century Catalan landowning family, the likes of which would often have made their money in South America, and were commonly dubbed *indianos* on their return. Upstairs is an entertaining collection of several hundred antique dolls, some downright creepy. Hours vary seasonally.

★FUNDACIÓ STÄMPFLI ART CONTEMPORANI GALLERY

(www.museusdesitges.cat; Plaça d'Ajuntament; adult/child €3.50/2; ☺3.30-7pm Fri, 10am-2pm & 3.30-7pm Sat, 11am-3pm Sun) This excellent gallery focuses on 20th-century art from the 1960s onwards. The striking paintings and sculptures by artists from all over the world, spread throughout the two renovated historical buildings, include works by Richard 'Buddy' di Rosa, Oliver Mosset and Takis. Extended hours in high season.

★MUSEU CAU FERRAT MUSEUM

(www.museusdesitges.cat; Carrer de Fonollar) Built in the 1890s as a house-cum-studio

CARNAVAL IN SITGES

Carnaval (www.sitges.com/carnaval) in Sitges is a week-long booze-soaked riot made just for the extroverted and exhibitionist, complete with masked balls and capped by extravagant gay parades held on the Sunday and the Tuesday night, featuring flamboyantly dressed drag queens, giant sound systems and a wild all-night party with bars staying open until dawn. Held in February/March; dates change from year to year.

by artist Santiago Rusiñol – a pioneer of the Modernista movement who organised three groundbreaking art festivals in Sitges in the late 19th century – this whitewashed mansion is full of his own art and that of his contemporaries, including his friend Picasso, as well as a couple of El Grecos. The interior, with its exquisitely tiled walls and lofty arches, is enchanting. Under renovation at the time of writing, but due to reopen in 2015.

MUSEU MARICEL DEL MAR MUSEUM

(Carrer de Fonollar; adult/child €6.50/4) This spectacular building houses Catalan art, scuplture and handicrafts from the Middle Ages to the 20th century. Under renovation at the time of writing – though it was open Sundays for guided visits at noon and 1pm, and due to reopen in 2015.

EATING & DRINKING

A couple of local specialities to watch out for are *arròs a la sitgetana* (a brothy rice dish with meat and seafood) and *xató* (a green salad with cod, tuna, anchovies and olives with dressing containing garlic, almonds, hazelnuts, chilli pepper and more).

LA SALSETA CATALAN €€

(938 11 04 19; www.lasalseta.com; Carrer de Sant Pau 35; mains €12-19; 1-4pm daily, 8-11.30pm Wed-Sat) Solicitous service and a sober, attractive interior set the scene for some delicious dishes in this unobtrusive restaurant. They make an effort to source organic and local products, and always have something interesting that's in season. A very satisfying experience.

EL POU TAPAS €€

(www.elpoudesitges.com; Carrer de Sant Pau 5; dishes €4-10; noon-4pm & 8-11.30pm Wed-Mon;) The tiny Wagyu beef burgers at this friendly gourmet tapas place are an absolute delight, and the rest doesn't lag far behind; the traditional *patatas bravas* (potatoes in a spicy tomato sauce) sit alongside the likes of *mojama* (salted dried tuna) with almonds, fried aubergine and *xató*.

LA NANSA SEAFOOD €€

(www.restaurantlanansa.com; Carrer de la Carreta 24; mains €14-22; 1.30-3.30pm & 8.30-11pm Thu-Sat & Mon, 1.30-3.30pm Sun, closed Jan) Cast just back from the town's waterfront and up a little lane in a fine old house is this seafood specialist, appropriately named after a fishing net. It does a great line in paella and other rice dishes, including a local speciality, *arròs a la sitgetana*.

EF & GI FUSION €€€

(www.efgirestaurant.com; Carrer Major 33; mains €18-25; 1-4pm & 7.30-11.30pm Wed-Mon Mar-Jan;) Fabio and Greg (eF & Gi) are not afraid to experiment and the results are startlingly good: the mostly Mediterranean menu, with touches of Asian inspiration, throws out such delights as chargrilled beef infused with lemongrass and kaffir lime, and tuna loin encrusted with peanuts and kalamata olives with mango chutney. Don't skip the dessert, either.

★ BAR VORAMAR BAR

(www.pub-voramar.com; Carrer del Port Alegre 55; 4.30pm-1am Thu-Tue) On Platja de Sant Sebastià, this is a fabulous old-time bar decked out like a ship playing flamenco, jazz and more. They do brilliant caipirinhas, mojitos and more. The chummy booth seating is a Sitges classic.

CASABLANCA BAR

(Carrer Pau Barrabeig 5; 8pm-2am Thu-Sat, Tue-Sun in high season) Classier and less loud than some of the central bars, this welcoming spot is tucked away at the bottom of a flight of stairs and makes a more than decent gin and tonic. You might hear Welsh singing after a few have gone down.

Tarragona

Explore

Since the Museu d'Història de Tarragona – which comprises the main Roman sites – tends to be busiest from midmorning onwards, it's best to start with its Amfiteatre Romà and the Fòrum Provincial first, or the excellent Museu Nacional Arqueològic de Tarragona. Then, head for the Catedral, followed by lunch in one of the many gourmet establishments nearby.

The Roman sights are spread out, so in the afternoon you may want to take a taxi to the Necròpolis Paleocristiana, followed by the Pont del Diable aqueduct. Alternatively, have a peaceful wander along the Passeig Arqueològic Muralles – a walk between the medieval walls – followed by a seafood meal at the fishermen's quarter of Serallo.

The Best...

➡ **Sight** Museu d'Història de Tarragona (p206)

➡ **Place to Eat** Arcs Restaurant (p208)

➡ **Place to Drink** Sha (p208)

Top Tip

Don't visit Tarragona on a Sunday or Monday, as you'll find your sightseeing options drastically curtailed.

Getting There & Away

➡ **Bus** Services from Barcelona (€8.70, 1½ hours, 16 daily) stop at the bus station, a pleasant 20-minute walk from the centre.

➡ **Car** Take the C32 toll road along the coast via Castelldefels or the AP7.

➡ **Train** The local station is a 10-minute walk from the old town while fast AVE trains arrive at Camp de Tarragona station, a 15-minute taxi ride from the centre. Departures from Barcelona include normal trains and rodalies on the R14, R15 and R16 lines (€7 to €38.20, 35 minutes to 1½ hours, every 30 minutes).

Need to Know

➡ **Location** 83km southwest of Barcelona

➡ **Tourist Office** (📷977 25 07 95; www.tarragonaturisme.es; Carrer Major 39; ☺10am-2pm & 3-5pm Mon-Fri, to 7pm Sat, 10am-2pm Sun)

◉ SIGHTS

MUSEU D'HISTÒRIA DE TARRAGONA RUINS
(MHT; www.museutgn.com; adult/child per site €3.30/free, all sites €11.05/free; ☺sites 9am-9pm Tue-Sat, 10am-3pm Sun Easter-Sep, 10am-7pm Tue-Sat, 10am-3pm Sun Oct-Easter) The Museu d'Història de Tarragona consists of various separate Unesco World Heritage Roman sites, as well as some other historic buildings around town. Buy a combined ticket and get exploring!

Fòrum Provincial Pretori i Circ Romans (Plaça del Rei), a sizeable complex with two separate entrances, includes part of the vaults of the Roman circus, where chariot races were once held, as well as the Pretori tower on Plaça del Rei and part of the provincial forum, the political heart of Tarraconensis province. The circus, 300m long, stretched from here to beyond Plaça de la Font to the west.

Near the beach is the well-preserved **Amfiteatre Romà** (Plaça d'Arce Ochotorena), where gladiators hacked away at each other, or wild animals, to the death. In its arena are the remains of 6th- and 12th-century churches built to commemorate the martyrdom of the Christian bishop Fructuosus and two deacons, believed to have been burnt alive here in AD 259. Much of the amphitheatre was picked to bits, the stone used to build the port, so what you see now is a partial reconstruction.

A peaceful walk takes you around the **Passeig Arqueològic Muralles**, part of the perimeter of the old town between two lines of city walls. The inner ones are mainly Roman and date back to the 3rd century BC, while the outer ones were put up by the British in 1709 during the War of the Spanish Succession. Prepare to be awed by the vast gateways built by the Iberians and clamber up onto the battlements from the doorway to the right of the entrance for all-encompassing views of the city. The walk starts from the Portal del Roser on Avenida Catalunya.

Fòrum de la Colònia (Carrer de Lleida), the main provincial forum, occupied most of what is now the old town. Further down the hill, this plaza was occupied by a judicial basilica (where legal disputes were settled) among other buildings. Linked to the site by a footbridge is another excavated area, which includes a stretch of Roman street. The discovery of foundations of a temple to Jupiter, Juno and Minerva suggests the

THE CISTERCIAN ROUTE

Set between Tarragona and Lleida, and a great way to explore inland Catalonia en route between coast and mountains, is a trio of grand Cistercian monasteries along the so-called **Ruta del Cister** (Cistercian Route; www.larutadelcister.info; combined 3-monastery ticket €9).

Following the AP7 freeway southwest from Vilafranca, take the AP2 fork about 18km west, then exit 11 north for the excellent **Reial Monestir de Santes Creus** (Plaça de Jaume el Just, Santes Creus; adult/senior & student €4.50/free; ⊙10am-6.30pm Jun-Sep, 10am-5pm Oct-May). Cistercian monks moved in here in 1168 and from then on the monastery developed as a major centre of learning and a launch pad for the repopulation of the surrounding territory. Behind the Romanesque and Gothic facade lies a glorious 14th-century sandstone cloister, austere chapter house, cavernous dormitory and royal apartments where the *comtes-reis* (count-kings; rulers of the joint state of Catalonia and Aragón) often stayed when they popped by during Holy Week. The church, begun in the 12th century, is a lofty Gothic structure in the French tradition, with a couple of fabulous royal tombs. An audiovisual presentation gives background info.

Back on the AP2, travel another 22km to the medieval town of Montblanc, still surrounded by its defensive walls, and then L'Espluga de Francolí, beyond which you continue 3km to the fortified **Reial Monestir de Santa Maria de Poblet** (www. poblet.cat; Vimbodí-Poblet; adult/student €7/4; ⊙10am-12.45pm & 3-6pm Mon-Sat, 10am-12.30pm & 3-5.30pm Sun), a Unesco World Heritage site. Founded in 1151, it became Catalonia's most powerful monastery and the burial place of many of its rulers. Poblet was sacked in 1835 by marauding peasants as payback for the monks' abuse of their feudal powers, which included imprisonment and torture. A community of Cistercian monks moved back in after the Spanish Civil War and did much to restore the monastery to its former glory. High points include the mostly Gothic main cloister and the alabaster sculptural treasures of the Panteón de los Reyes (Kings' Pantheon). The raised alabaster sarcophagi contain eight Catalan kings, such greats as Jaume I (the conqueror of Mallorca and Valencia) and Pere III.

Swinging away north from Montblanc (take the C14 and then branch west along the LP2335), country roads guide you into the low hills of the Serra del Tallat to **Reial Monestir de Santa Maria de Vallbona de les Monges** (☑973 33 02 66; Carrer Major, Vallbona de les Monges; adult/child €4/1; ⊙10.30am-1.30pm & 4.30-6.45pm Tue-Sat, noon-1.30pm & 4.30-6.45pm Sun Mar-Oct, closes 5.30pm rest of year). It was founded in the 12th century and is where a dozen *monges* (nuns) still live and pray. You will be taken on an informative guided tour (Spanish or Catalan). The monastery has undergone years of restoration, which has finally cleared up most of the remaining scars of civil war damage.

forum was bigger and more important than had previously been assumed.

Pont del Diable, the so-called Devil's Bridge, is actually the Aqüeducte de les Ferreres, an engineering marvel left by the Romans. Its most intact section sits 4km away from the centre, just off the AP7 freeway. It is a fine stretch of a two-tiered aqueduct (217m long and 27m high); in its glory days, it delivered water to over 200,000 people from the Ríu Gayo. Bus 5 to Sant Salvador from Plaça Imperial de Tàrraco, running every 20 minutes, will take you to the vicinity, or park in one of the lay-bys marked on either side of the AP7, just outside the freeway toll gates.

★**MUSEU NACIONAL ARQUEOLÒGIC DE TARRAGONA** MUSEUM
(www.mnat.cat; Plaça del Rei 5; adult/child €2.40/free; ⊙9.30am-6pm Tue-Sat, 10am-2pm Sun) This excellent museum does justice to the cultural and material wealth of Roman Tarraco. Well-laid-out exhibits include part of the Roman city walls, frescoes, sculpture and pottery. The mosaic collection traces the changing trends – from simple black-and-white designs to complex full-colour creations. A highlight is the large, almost complete *Mosaic de peixos de la Pineda*. It's open extended hours in high season.

CATALUNYA'S HUMAN CASTLES

One of the strangest things you'll see in Catalonia are *castells*, or human 'castles' – a sport which originated in Valls, near Tarragona, in the 18th century and which has spread to other parts of Catalonia since. It involves teams of *castellers* standing on each other's shoulders with a death-defying child scrambling up the side of the human tower to perch precariously at the top as the final touch before the whole structure gracefully disassembles itself; towers up to 10 levels high are built. For the most spectacular *castells*, pay a visit to Tarragona's **Festival de Santa Tecla** in mid-September.

NECRÒPOLIS PALEOCRISTIANA　　　RUINS

(www.mnat.cat; Avinguda de Ramón i Cajal 80; admission €2.40; ⊙9.30am-1.30pm & 3-5.30pm Tue-Sat, 10am-2pm Sun) This Roman-Christian city of the dead on the western edge of town consists of over 2000 elaborate tombs. It was used from the 3rd century AD onwards. While you can only look at the tombs through the fence, the museum features funereal objects and sarcophagi. Entry is free if you have already purchased a ticket to the Museu Nacional Arqueològic de Tarragona (p207). It opens extended hours in high season.

★CATEDRAL　　　CATHEDRAL

(www.catedraldetarragona.com; Plaça de la Seu; adult/child €5/3; ⊙10am-7pm Mon-Sat mid-Mar–Oct, 10am-5pm Mon-Fri, 10am-7pm Sat Nov–mid-Mar) Sitting grandly atop town, Tarragona's cathedral has both Romanesque and Gothic features. The cloister has Gothic vaulting and Romanesque carved capitals, one of which shows rats conducting a cat's funeral...until the cat comes back to life! It's a lesson about passions seemingly lying dormant until they reveal themselves. Chambers off the cloister house the **Museu Diocesà**, with an extensive collection.

✗ EATING & DRINKING

The quintessential Tarragona seafood experience can be had in **Serrallo**, the town's fishing port. Plaça de la Font in the old town is great for an outdoor drink.

AQ　　　CATALAN €€

(☎977 21 59 54; www.aq-restaurant.com; Carrer de les Coques 7; degustation menu €40-50; ⊙1.30-3.30pm & 8.30-11pm Tue-Sat) This is a bubbly designer haunt alongside the cathedral with stark colour contrasts (black, lemon and cream linen), slick lines and intriguing plays on traditional cooking. One of the two

degustation menus is the way to go here, or the weekday lunch *menú* for €18.

ARES　　　CATALAN, SPANISH €€

(www.aresrestaurant.es; Plaça del Fòrum; mains €11-19; ⊙1-4pm & 8.30-11.30pm Wed-Sun) Amid a riot of colourful, exuberant Modernista decor, the cordial welcome from this husband-and-wife team guarantees good eating. Some classic Catalan dishes take their place alongside quality ingredients from across Spain: Asturian cheeses, Galician seafood, Burgos black pudding. They are complemented by some re-created Roman dishes. Quality and quantity are both praiseworthy.

BARQUET　　　SEAFOOD €€

(☎977 24 00 23; www.restaurantbarquet.com; Carrer del Gasometre 16; mains €11-18; ⊙1-3.30pm & 9-10.30pm Tue-Sat, 1-3.30pm Mon) This neighbourhood restaurant is a short downhill stroll from the centre. It's deservedly famous for its excellent rice dishes bursting with maritime flavour, and also has great *raciones* of seafood. Cheerful and good value.

ARCS RESTAURANT　　　CATALAN €€€

(☎977 21 80 40; www.restaurantarcs.com; Carrer Misser Sitges 13; mains €18-22; ⊙1-4pm & 8.30-11pm Tue-Sat) Inside a medieval cavern with bright splashes of colour in the form of contemporary art, you are served some wonderful takes on Mediterranean dishes – with lots of delicious seafood carpaccios and tartars. Ingredients are of the highest quality.

SHA　　　CAFE

(Plaça de la Seu; ⊙4pm-midnight Tue-Thu, 4pm-1am Fri & Sat, noon-midnight Sun; 🛜) Part handicrafts shop, part bar-cafe, this place has a prime location just below the cathedral, with great outdoor seating. There's a friendly, hippy vibe and tasty salads, hummus and the like.

🛏 Sleeping

Barcelona has an excellent range of accommodation, with high-end luxury hotels, small-scale boutique lodgings, and a varied spread of midrange and budget selections. The settings offer some fine choices in historic districts, facing the seaside or in the thick of charming neighbourhoods packed with restaurants and nightlife.

Hotels

Hotels cover a broad range. At the bottom end there is often little to distinguish them from better *pensiones* and *hostales,* and from there they run up the scale to five-star luxury. Some of the better features to look out for: rooftop pools and lounges, views (either of the sea or a cityscape – Sagrada Família, Montjuïc, Barri Gòtic) and of course proximity to the important sights. For around €100 to €140 there are extensive options for good doubles across a broad range of hotels and areas. The top-end category starts at €250 for a double, but can easily rise to €500 (and beyond for suites).

Pensiones & Hostales

Depending on the season you can pay as little as €15 to €25 for a dorm bed in a youth hostel. If dorm living is not your thing but you are still looking for a budget deal, check around the many *pensiones* (small private hotels) and *hostales* (budget hotels). These are family-run, small-scale hotels, often housed in sprawling apartments. Some are fleapits, others immaculately maintained gems. You're looking at a minimum of around €35/55 for basic *individual/doble* (single/double) rooms, mostly without a private bathroom. Some places, especially at the lower end, offer triples and quads. If you want a double bed (as opposed to two singles), ask for a *llit/cama* matrimonial (Catalan/Spanish). If your budget is especially tight, check out Barcelona 30.com.

Apartment & Room Rentals

A cosier (and sometimes more cost-effective) alternative to hotels can be short-term apartment rental. A plethora of firms organise short lets across town. Typical prices are around €80 to €100 for two people per night. For four people you might be looking at an average of €160 a night. One of the best options, with hundreds of listings is Air BnB (www.airbnb.com). In addition to full apartments, the site also lists rooms available, which can be a good way to meet locals and/ or other travellers if you don't mind sharing common areas. Prices for a room cost €30 to €60 on average. Other apartment-rental services include the following:

➡ **Oh-Barcelona** (www.oh-barcelona.com)

➡ **Aparteasy** (www.aparteasy.com)

➡ **Feel at Home Barcelona.com** (www.feelathomebarcelona.com)

➡ **Friendly Rentals** (www.friendly rentals.com)

Want to sleep on a local's couch? Try your luck at www.couchsurfing.com. To browse a large selection of accommodation at all price levels, check out Lonely Planet (www.lonelyplanet.com/hotels).

Travellers with Disabilities

Many hotels claim to be equipped for guests with disabilities but reality frequently disappoints. Check out www.accessiblebarcelona.com for help with finding genuinely accessible accommodation. The same people also run www.accessible.travel.

NEED TO KNOW

Price Ranges
These € signs indicate the price of a double room per night during high season. Prices include private bathroom unless otherwise stated.

€	less than €75
€€	€75 to €200
€€€	over €200

Room Tax
Virtually all accommodation is subject to IVA, the Spanish version of value-added tax, at 10%, plus an additional tax of €1.21 per person per night. These charges are usually included in the quoted rate.

Seasonal Rates
Some hotels, particularly at the lower and mid-levels, maintain the same prices year round. Others vary the rates for *temporada alta, temporada media* and *temporada baja* (high, mid- and low seasons). Low season is roughly November to Easter, except during the Christmas/New Year period. Booking on the web is often cheaper than turning up at the door.

Reservations
Booking ahead is recommended, especially during summer. If you arrive without prebooked lodging, the Plaça de Catalunya's tourist office (p255) can help.

Check-In & Check-Out Times
Check-in time is around 2pm or 3pm. Check-out time is generally noon.

Lonely Planet's Top Choices

DO (p212) Magnficent boutique option overlooking the Plaça Reial.

Casa Camper (p214) Stylish option in El Raval with Vinçon furniture and hammocks.

Hotel Casa Fuster (p219) Plush rooms in a Modernista mansion in Gràcia.

Hotel Omm (p218) Fantastical Dalí-esque hotel with a 'peeling' facade.

Best by Budget

€

Casa Gràcia (p219) Stylish hostel with colourful rooms, communal dinners, film screenings and other events.

Amistat Beach Hostel (p215) Small, warm and welcoming hostel, near the beach and restaurants of Poblenou.

Hotel Marina Folch (p215) Family-run budget hotel in Barceloneta.

€€

Five Rooms (p217) Small and charming with beautifully designed rooms.

Poblenou Bed & Breakfast (p216) Great-value spot in one of Barcelona's up-and-coming neighbourhoods.

€€€

Hotel Neri (p213) Beautiful, historic hotel on a tranquil spot in Barri Gòtic.

Hotel Mercer (p213) Peaceful retreat with medieval details and atmospheric rooms.

Best Rooms with a View

El Jardí (p212) Charming views over the picturesque Plaça de Sant Josep Oriol.

Ohla Hotel (p213) Take in the staggering view over the old city from the rooftop terrace.

Barceló Raval (p213) A fabulous roof terrace in El Raval.

Best Hotel Pools

Grand Hotel Central (p215) In a great location on Via Laietana, this place has a rooftop infinity pool.

W Barcelona (p216) Splendid poolside fun just a short stroll from the beach.

Best Style Hotels

Cami Bed & Gallery (p218) Seven unique rooms in an art-filled Modernista building.

Chic & Basic Ramblas (p214) Boasts serious design cred, particularly in the lobby with its vintage decor.

Where to Stay

Neighbourhood	For	Against
La Rambla & Barri Gòtic	Great location, close to major sights; perfect area for exploring on foot; good nightlife and dining options	Very touristy; noisy; some rooms are small, lack windows
El Raval	Central option, with good local nightlife and access to sights; bohemian vibe with few tourists	Can be noisy; seedy and run-down in parts; many fleapits best avoided; feels unsafe to walk late at night
La Ribera	Great restaurant scene and neighbourhood exploring; central; top sights including the Museu Picasso and the Palau de la Música Catalana	Can be noisy; overly crowded; touristy
Barceloneta & the Waterfront	Excellent seafood restaurants; local easygoing vibe; handy access to the promenade and beaches	Very few sleeping options; outside of Barceloneta can be far from the action and better suited to business travellers
La Sagrada Família & L'Eixample	Wide range of options for all budgets; close to Modernista sights; good restaurants and nightlife; prime gay scene (in the 'Gaixample')	Can be very noisy with lots of traffic; not a great area for walking; a little far from the old city
Gràcia & Park Güell	Youthful, local scene with lively restaurants and bars	Far from the old city; few formal options (but lots of rooms for rent)
La Zona Alta	Good nightlife and restaurants in parts	Very far from the action; spread-out area, requires frequent metro travel; geared more towards business travellers
Montjuïc, Poble Sec & Sant Antoni	Near the museums, gardens and views of Montjuïc; great local exploring in El Poble Sec; locations in El Poble Sec are also convenient to El Raval	Somewhat out of the way; can be a bit gritty up by El Sants train station

🛏 La Rambla & Barri Gòtic

La Rambla is lined with boxy hotels, glorious boutique options, *pensiones* and fleapits, and in the labyrinth of the Barri Gòtic are scattered countless others.

ALBERG HOSTEL ITACA   HOSTEL €

Map p276 (📞93 301 97 51; www.itacahostel.com; Carrer de Ripoll 21; dm €21-24, tw/d €60/70, apt €90-150; @🛜; ⓜJaume I) A bright, quiet hostel near the cathedral, Itaca has spacious dorms (sleeping six to 10 people) with parquet floors and spring colours, and two doubles. There's a lively vibe, and the hostel organises activities (pub crawls, flamenco concerts, free daily walking tours), making it a good option for solo travellers.

KABUL   HOSTEL €

Map p276 (📞93 318 51 90; www.kabul.es; Plaça Reial 17; dm €18-29; ❄@🛜; ⓜLiceu) The dorm rooms are small and cramped, the service is brusque, and if you're a light sleeper you can forget about falling asleep before 4am. But for partiers, centrally located Kabul is a top choice. It's easy to meet with other travellers with its nightly activities (pub crawls, club nights) and lively common areas (including a lounge with pool table, and a roof terrace).

VRABAC   GUESTHOUSE €€

Map p276 (📞663 494029; vrabacguesthouse. wordpress.com; Carrer de Portaferrissa 14; d €95-145, s/d without bathroom from €55/65; ❄🛜; ⓜLiceu or Catalunya) In a central location just off La Rambla, Vrabac is set in a beautifully restored heritage building complete with original decorative ceilings, exposed sandstone walls and large oil paintings. Rooms vary in size and equipment – the best have elegant ceramic tile floors and sizeable balconies with private bathrooms. The cheapest are small and basic and lack a bathroom, and aren't recommended. Cash only.

HOTEL COLÓN   HOTEL €€

Map p276 (📞93 301 14 04; www.hotelcolon.es; Avinguda de la Catedral 7; s/d from €130/195; ❄@🛜; ⓜJaume I) The privileged position opposite the cathedral lends this hotel special grace. A range of rooms, from modest singles to light-filled doubles and suites, offers elegant accommodation. Decoration varies considerably (from hardwood floors

to carpet) and the top-floor superior rooms with terrace are marvellous (and go for about €300).

HOTEL CONTINENTAL   HOTEL €€

Map p276 (📞93 301 25 70; www.hotelcontinental.com; La Rambla 138; s/d from €92/101; ❄🛜; ⓜCatalunya) You can imagine being here in 1937, when George Orwell returned from the front during the Spanish Civil War, and Barcelona was tense with factional strife. The Continental's rooms are worn and rather spartan, but have romantic touches like ceiling fans, brass bedsteads and frilly bedclothes. An extra €20 yields a room with a small balcony overlooking La Rambla.

EL JARDÍ   HOTEL €€

Map p276 (📞93 301 59 00; www.eljardi-barcelona.com; Plaça de Sant Josep Oriol 1; d €90-120; ❄🛜; ⓜLiceu) 'The Garden' has no garden but a handful of boxy doubles with balcony overlooking one of the prettiest squares in Barcelona. If you can snag one of them, it is well worth climbing up the stairs. If you can't get a room with a view, you are better off looking elsewhere.

HOTEL RACÓ DEL PI   BOUTIQUE HOTEL €€

Map p276 (📞93 342 61 90; www.hotelh10racodelpi.com; Carrer del Pi 7; d €116-148; ❄@🛜; ⓜLiceu) This hotel was stylishly carved out of a historic Barri Gòtic building, and features 37 rooms with dark wood beams, parquet floors, colourful mosaic-tiled bathrooms and full soundproofing. The rooms' aesthetic is modern: light colours blended with navy blue blankets and the occasional art print. The location is terrific.

BONIC   B&B €€

Map p276 (📞626 053434; www.bonic-barcelona.com; Carrer de Josep Anselm Clavé 9; s €55, d €90-95; ❄@🛜; ⓜDrassanes) Bonic is a small, cosy B&B that has eight rooms in varied styles, with wood or decorative tile floors, tall ceilings and attractive furnishings. Several are bright and cheerfully painted, and some lack exterior windows. Owing to the restrictive layout – all guest rooms share three bathrooms – maximum occupancy is six or seven guests a night, although groups of friends can book the whole place to themselves.

DO   BOUTIQUE HOTEL €€€

Map p276 (📞93 481 36 66; www.hoteldoreial.com; Plaça Reial 1; s/d from €230/280; ❄🛜❄; ⓜLiceu) Overlooking the magnificent plaza for which it is named, this 18-room property has handsomely designed rooms, set with beamed ceilings, wide plank floors and all-important soundproofing. The service is excellent, and the facilities extensive, with roof terrace (with bar in summer), dipping pool, solarium and spa. Its excellent market-to-table restaurants draw in visiting foodies.

HOTEL MERCER
BOUTIQUE HOTEL €€€

Map p276 (📞93 310 74 80; www.mercerbarcelona.com; Carrer dels Lledó 7; d from €385; 🕸🛜; Ⓜ Jaume I) Set on a narrow medieval lane, Hotel Mercer is one of Barcelona's best new hotels. Famed Spanish architect Rafael Moneo stayed true to the building's original Gothic and even Roman elements while creating lavishly designed rooms, some of which overlook an interior garden. There's a lovely rooftop dip pool, stylish cocktail lounge, tapas bar and restaurant, plus wonderfully peaceful common areas.

HOTEL NERI
DESIGN HOTEL €€€

Map p276 (📞93 304 06 55; www.hotelneri.com; Carrer de Sant Sever 5; d from €270; 🕸@🛜; Ⓜ Liceu) This tranquil hotel occupies a beautifully adapted, centuries-old building backing onto Plaça de Sant Felip Neri. The sandstone walls and timber furnishings lend a sense of history, while the rooms feature cutting-edge technology, including plasma-screen TVs and infra-red lights in the stone-clad designer bathrooms. Choose from a menu of sheets and pillows, and sun yourself on the roof deck.

OHLA HOTEL
BOUTIQUE HOTEL €€€

(📞93 341 50 50; www.ohlahotel.com; Via Laietana 49; d from €257; 🕸🛜🏊; Ⓜ Urquinaona) This beautifully designed hotel gets almost everything right, from the top-notch service to the lovely rooftop terrace with pool and twinkling views of Montjuïc. The sleek modern rooms have lavish fabrics, long pendular bedside lights, iPod docks and separate shower cubes that face onto the room (take note if you're travelling with someone who needs a touch more privacy).

There's a Michelin-starred restaurant (Saüc) and enticing cocktail bar presided over by an award-winning mixologist.

HOTEL 1898
LUXURY HOTEL €€€

Map p276 (📞93 552 95 52; www.hotel1898.com; La Rambla 109; d €205-400; 🕸@🛜🏊; Ⓜ Liceu) The former Compañía de Tabacos Filipinas

(Philippines Tobacco Company) has been resurrected as a luxury hotel, complete with an idyllic rooftop bar and pool. Some rooms are smallish, but deluxe rooms and suites have their own terraces. All combine modern comfort and elegance, with hardwood floors and tasteful furniture.

🛌 El Raval

You're right in the thick of things when staying in this mildly wild side of the old city. Accommodation options are broad, from fleapits on dodgy lanes through to the latest in designer comfort. Hostels and cheap hotels abound.

CHIC & BASIC TALLERS
HOSTAL €

Map p280 (📞93 302 51 83; www.chicandbasic.com; Carrer dels Tallers 82; s/d from €71/84; 🕸@; Ⓜ Universitat) The colour scheme here is predominantly white, with exceptions like the screaming orange fridge in the communal kitchen and chill-out area. Rooms are also themed lily white, from the floors to the sheets. Finishing touches include the plasma-screen TVs and the option of plugging your iPod into your room's sound system. The street can get noisy.

HOTEL PENINSULAR
HOTEL €

Map p280 (📞93 302 31 38; www.hotelpeninsular.net; Carrer de Sant Pau 34; s/d €57/80; 🕸@🛜; Ⓜ Liceu) An oasis on the edge of the slightly dicey Barri Xinès, this former convent (which was connected by tunnel to the Església de Sant Agustí) has a plant-draped atrium extending its height and most of its length. The 60 rooms are simple, with tiled floors and whitewash, but mostly spacious and well kept. There are some great bargains to be had on quiet dates.

★ BARCELÓ RAVAL
DESIGN HOTEL €€

Map p280 (📞93 320 14 90; www.barceloraval.com; Rambla del Raval 17-21; r from €128; 🕸@; Ⓜ Liceu) Part of the city's plans to pull the El Raval district up by the bootstraps, this oval-shaped designer hotel tower makes a 21st-century splash. The rooftop terrace offers fabulous views and the B-Lounge bar-restaurant is the toast of the town for meals and cocktails. Rooms have slick aesthetics (white with lime green or ruby-red splashes of colour), Nespresso machines and iPod docks.

CHIC & BASIC RAMBLAS

DESIGN HOTEL €€

Map p280 (☑93 302 71 11; www.chicandbasicramblashotel.com; Passatge Gutenberg 7; s & d €106-116; ❋❂; ⓂDrassanes) The latest in the Chic & Basic chain is the most riotous to date, with quirky and colourful interiors that hit you from the second you walk in and see a vintage Seat 600 in the foyer. The rooms themselves are solid blocks of colour, and each loosely pays homage to an aspect of Barcelona life in the 1960s. All have balconies and small kitchens. Note that the name is misleading – the hotel is a couple of blocks into the Raval.

HOTEL SANT AGUSTÍ

HOTEL €€

Map p280 (☑93 318 16 58; www.hotelsa.com; Plaça de Sant Agustí 3; r from €125; ❋@❂; ⓂLiceu) This former 18th-century monastery opened as a hotel in 1840, making it the city's oldest. The location is perfect – a quick stroll off La Rambla on a curious square. Rooms sparkle, and are mostly spacious and light filled. Consider an attic double with sloping ceiling and bird's-eye views.

HOTEL ESPAÑA

HOTEL €€

Map p280 (☑93 550 00 00; www.hotelespanya.com; Carrer de Sant Pau 9-11; r €164; ❋@❂❂; ⓂLiceu) Best known for its wonderful Modernista interiors in the dining rooms and bar, in which architect Domènech i Montaner, sculptor Eusebi Arnau and painter Ramon Casas had a hand, this hotel offers clean, straightforward rooms in a building that still manages to ooze a little history. In the 1920s it was a favourite with bullfighters.

RAVAL ROOMS

HOSTAL €€

Map p280 (☑93 481 66 70; www.ravalrooms.com; Carrer de Joaquín Costa 44; s/d €90/95; ❋@❂; ⓂUniversitat) There's pea-green and lemon-lime decor in this hip 2nd-floor *hostal* located on a bar-lined lane dominated by resident migrants and wandering bands of uni students. The rooms are pleasant and secure, if snug, and enlivened with colourful artworks.

CASA CAMPER

DESIGN HOTEL €€€

Map p280 (☑93 342 62 80; www.casacamper.com; Carrer d'Elisabets 11; s/d from €238/260; ❋@❂; ⓂCatalunya) The massive foyer looks like a contemporary-art museum, but the rooms are the real surprise. Decorated in red, black and white, each room has a sleeping and bathroom area, where you can put on your Camper slippers, enjoy the Vinçon furniture and contemplate the hanging gardens outside your window. Across the corridor is a separate, private sitting room with balcony, TV and hammock. Get to the rooftop for sweeping cityscapes.

🛏 La Ribera

Several fine hotels are located on the fringes of the busy El Born area and a growing number of the sometimes bombastic buildings on thundering Via Laietana are top-end hotels.

PENSIÓN FRANCIA

HOSTEL €

Map p284 (☑93 319 03 76; www.pensionfrancia-barcelona.com; Carrer de Rera Palau 4; s/d without bathroom €30/55; ❂; ⓂBarceloneta) The homey smell of laundry pervades this quaint little hostel in a great location close to the shore, the Parc de la Ciutadella and the nightlife of El Born. The 11 simple rooms are kept spick and span, with nothing much in the way of frills. Rooms with balconies benefit from plenty of natural light but little noise, as the lane is set away from the busy nearby thoroughfares.

PENSIÓ 2000

PENSIÓN €

Map p284 (☑93 310 74 66; www.pensio2000.com; Carrer de Sant Pere més Alt 6; d €70-80; ❋@❂; ⓂUrquinaona) This 1st-floor, family-run place is opposite the anything-but-simple Palau de la Música Catalana. Seven reasonably spacious doubles have mosaic-tiled floors, and after a recent renovation all have private bathrooms. You can eat your breakfast in the little courtyard.

CHIC & BASIC

DESIGN HOTEL €€

Map p284 (☑93 295 46 52; www.chicandbasic.com; Carrer de la Princesa 50; s €81-87, d €103-150; ❋@❂; ⓂJaume I) This is a very cool hotel indeed, with its 31 spotlessly white rooms and fairy-light curtains that change colour, adding an entirely new atmosphere to the space. The rooms are small, but the ceilings are high and the beds are enormous. Many beautiful old features of the original building have been retained, such as the marble staircase. Chic & Basic also runs a *hostal* in El Raval.

HOTEL BANYS ORIENTALS BOUTIQUE HOTEL €€

Map p284 (☑93 268 84 60; www.hotelbanys-orientals.com; Carrer de l'Argenteria 37; s €96, d €115.50-143; ✳ 🛜; Ⓜ Jaume I) Book well ahead to get into this magnetically popular designer haunt. Cool blues and aquamarines combine with dark-hued floors to lend this clean-lined, boutique hotel a quiet charm. All rooms, on the small side, look onto the street or back lanes. There are more spacious suites in two other nearby buildings.

GRAND HOTEL CENTRAL DESIGN HOTEL €€€

Map p284 (☑93 295 79 00; www.grandhotel-central.com; Via Laietana 30; d €285; ✳ @ 🛜; Ⓜ Jaume I) With super-soundproofed rooms no smaller than 21 sq metres, this design hotel, complete with rooftop infinity pool, is one of the standout hotel offerings along Via Laietana. Rooms are decorated in style, with high ceilings, muted colours (beiges, browns and creams), dark wooden floors and subtle lighting.

🛏 Barceloneta & the Waterfront

The handful of seaside options around Port Vell and La Barceloneta ranges from a rowdy youth hostel to a couple of grand five-stars. Out in the residential neighbourhood of Poblenou, you'll find a mix of low-key B&Bs, appealing hostels and a few stylish top-end options. The waterfront of Port Olímpic is best known for its luxury high-rise hotels.

HOTEL MARINA FOLCH HOTEL €

Map p286 (☑93 310 37 09; Carrer del Mar 16; s/d/tr from €45/65/85; ✳ 🛜; Ⓜ Barceloneta) Simple digs above a busy seafood restaurant, this hotel has just one teeny single and nine doubles of varying sizes and quality. The best are those with small balconies facing out towards the marina. The rooms are basic but well maintained, and the location is unbeatable, just a couple of minutes from the beach.

EQUITY POINT SEA HOSTEL HOSTEL €

Map p286 (☑93 231 20 45; www.equity-point.com; Plaça del Mar 1-4; dm €19-34; ✳ @ 🛜; 🖵 17, 39, 57 or 64, Ⓜ Barceloneta) Perched near the sea in a rather ugly high-rise is this busy backpackers hostel. Rooms are basic, cramped and noisy (bring earplugs) but you will not find a room closer to the beach.

AMISTAT BEACH HOSTEL HOSTEL €

Map p288 (☑93 221 32 81; www.amistatbeach-hostel.com; Carrer Amistat 21; dm €21-33; 🛜; Ⓜ Poblenou) A stylish new addition to Poblenou, Amistat has attractively designed common areas, with a beanbag-filled lounge with DJ set-up, a low-lit TV room and a guest kitchen. The rooms themselves, which sleep from four to 12, are clean, but basic – aside from a splash of colour on the ceilings. Friendly staff organise pub crawls, club nights and other events.

MARINA VIEW B&B €€

Map p286 (☑678 854456; www.marinaviewbcn.com; Passeig de Colom; d without/with view €116/139, tr €136/165; ✳ 🛜; Ⓜ Drassanes) In an excellent location near both the old city and the waterfront, this Irish-run B&B has six airy, comfortably furnished rooms, some with small balconies sporting sunlit views over the marina. The welcome is genuinely warm, and Paddy, the owner, has loads of tips on neighbourhood eateries and how to make the most of your visit.

HOTEL DEL MAR HOTEL €€

Map p286 (☑93 319 30 47; www.gargallo-hotels.com; Pla del Palau 19; d €96-150; ✳ @ 🛜; Ⓜ Barceloneta) The nicely modernised Hotel del Mar is strategically placed between Port Vell and El Born. Rooms are bright, clean and comfortable, though not luxurious. The best chambers have balconies with waterfront views. You're in a fairly peaceful spot but no more than 10 minutes' walk from the beaches and seafood of La Barceloneta, and the nightlife of El Born.

HOTEL 54 HOTEL €€

Map p286 (☑93 225 00 54; www.hotel54barce-loneta.es; Passeig de Joan de Borbó 54; d €153-200; ✳ @ 🛜; Ⓜ Barceloneta) This place is all about location. Modern rooms, with dark tile floors and designer bathrooms, are sought after for the marina and sunset views. Other rooms look out over the lanes of La Barceloneta. You can also sit on the roof terrace and enjoy the harbour views.

BED & BEACH GUESTHOUSE €€

Map p288 (☑630 528156; www.bedandbeach-barcelona.com; Passatge General Bassols 26; d €67-110, s/d without bathroom €39/64; ✳ 🛜; Ⓜ Bogatell) This pleasant eight-room guesthouse is set on a quiet narrow street just a five-minute walk to the beach. Rooms are clean and comfortable, and vary in size and equipment – some lack natural light, others are bright, with simple modern furnishings and in-room kitchens. The rooftop terrace is a fine spot for an afternoon drink, and there's also a shared kitchen for self-caterers.

URBANY BARCELONA HOSTEL €€

(☏93 245 84 14; www.urbanyhostels.com; Avinguda Meridiana 97; dm €20-36, d €75-150; ✳@🛜; ⓂClot, Encants) Near Poblenou, this massive (400-bed) hostel is a good place to meet other travellers with its own bar and airy lounge set amid graffiti-esque artwork, plus a large terrace with views of Jean Nouvel's glowing Torre Agbar. On the downside, rooms are small, and service can be lacklustre. Guests also have access to a pool and gym nearby.

POBLENOU BED & BREAKFAST HOTEL €€

Map p288 (☏93 221 26 01; www.hostalpoble-nou.com; Carrer del Taulat 30; s/d from €50/80; ✳@🛜; ⓂLlacuna) Experience life in this colourful working-class neighbourhood, just back from the beach, a few steps from the restaurant-lined Rambla del Poblenou, and increasingly home to a diverse population of loft-inhabiting gentrifiers. The 1930s house, with its high ceilings and beautiful tile floors, has six appealing rooms, each a little different and all with a fresh feel, light colours, comfortable beds and, occasionally, a little balcony.

EUROSTARS GRAND MARINA HOTEL HOTEL €€€

Map p286 (☏93 603 90 00; www.grandmari-nahotel.com; Moll de Barcelona; r from €200; ✳@🛜🏊; ⓂDrassanes) Housed in the World Trade Center, the Grand Marina has a maritime flavour that continues into the rooms, with lots of polished timber touches and hydro-massage bathtubs. Some rooms on either side of the building offer splendid views of the city, port and open sea. The rooftop gym and outdoor pool have equally enticing views.

W BARCELONA LUXURY HOTEL €€€

Map p286 (☏93 295 28 00; www.w-barcelona.com; Plaça de la Rosa del Vents 1; r from €326; P✳@🛜🏊; 🚌17, 39, 57 or 64, ⓂBarceloneta) This spinnaker-shaped beach-adjacent tower of glass contains 473 rooms and suites that aim for contemporary hotel chic. Self-indulgence is a byword and guests can flit between gym, infinity pool (with bar) and spa.

HOTEL ARTS BARCELONA LUXURY HOTEL €€€

Map p288 (☏93 221 10 00; www.hotelartsbarce-lona.com; Carrer de la Marina 19-21; r from €265; P✳@🛜🏊; ⓂCiutadella Vila Olímpica) Set in a sky-high tower looming above Port Olímpic, this is one of Barcelona's most fashionable hotels. It has more than 480 rooms with unbeatable views, and prices vary greatly according to size, position and time of year. Services range from enticing spa facilities to fine dining in Arola, run by the Michelin-starred Sergi Arola.

MELIÁ SKY BARCELONA LUXURY HOTEL €€€

Map p288 (☏93 367 20 50; www.melia.com; Carrer de Pere IV 272-286; r €152-257; P✳@🛜🏊; ⓂPoblenou) This daring, slim tower, designed by Dominique Perrault, is made from two filigree slabs of glass. It overlooks Jean Nouvel's Parc del Centre del Poblenou and offers designer digs, with city or sea views. The amenities are extensive, including various bars and terraces, an enticing pool and a 24th-floor Michelin-starred restaurant (Dos Cielos).

🛏 La Sagrada Família & L'Eixample

It comes as little surprise that this extensive bourgeois bastion should also be home to the greatest range of hotels in most classes. The grid avenues house some of the city's classic hotels and a long list of decent midrange places.

FASHION HOUSE B&B €

Map p294 (☏637 904044; www.bcnfashion-house.com; Carrer del Bruc 13; s/d €51/91, without bathroom €41/71; ✳🛜; ⓂUrquinaona) The name is a little silly but this typical, broad 1st-floor L'Eixample flat contains eight rooms of varying size done in tasteful style, with 4.5m-high ceilings, parquet floors and, in some cases, a little balcony onto the street. Bathrooms are located along the broad corridor, one for every two rooms.

HOSTAL MUNTANER HOSTAL €

Map p290 (☏93 410 94 74; www.hostalmuntaner.com; Carrer de Muntaner 175; r €60, without bathroom €50; ✳; ⓂHospital Clínic) Within a five-block walk of Passeig de Gràcia and Diagonal, this is a busy residential location surrounded by restaurants and bars (especially along nearby Carrer d'Aribau, a block

GAY BARCELONA

Barcelona has a few excellent gay-friendly options, one in the heart of the old city and fairly simple, another a full design explosion in the heart of the 'Gaixample'. There are a number of gay apartment-rental websites, with a fairly high turnover (since these often enter a slightly grey area, legally).

Hotel Axel (Map p290; ☎93 323 93 93; www.axelhotels.com; Carrer d'Aribau 33; r from €129; ❋@🛜🏊; ⓂUniversitat) Favoured by a mixed fashion and gay set, Axel occupies a sleek corner block and offers modern touches in its 105 designer rooms. A subtle, light colour scheme, plasma TVs and (in the double rooms) king-sized beds are just some of the pluses. The hotel was completely overhauled in 2010. Take a break in the rooftop pool, the Finnish sauna or the spa bath. The rooftop Skybar is open for cocktails from May to September.

Room Mate Pau (Map p294; ☎93 343 63 00; pau.room-matehotels.com; Carrer de Fontanella 7; d €125-170; ❋🛜; ⓂUrquinaona, Catalunya) Just a short stroll from Plaça de Catalunya, Room Mate Pau sits somewhere between upscale hostel and boutique hotel. The rooms are small and minimalist, but cleverly designed (with good mattresses and USB-connected flatscreen TVs). The enticing interior terrace with bar draws a young and hip crowd.

Casa de Billy Barcelona (Map p302; ☎93 426 30 48; www.casabillybarcelona.com; Gran Via de les Corts Catalanes 420; s & d from €40, without bathroom from €35; @; ⓂRocafort) Set in a rambling apartment, a stone's throw from the Gaixample bars, this is an intriguing, gay-friendly stop. The rooms are largely decorated in flamboyant art deco style and guests may use the kitchen. There is a two-night-minimum policy.

---

away). Crisp, simple rooms are comfy and light. Be aware of traffic noise at the front of the house – a room deeper inside will guarantee tranquillity.

HOSTAL OLIVA   HOSTAL €

Map p294 (☎93 488 01 62; www.hostaloliva.com; Passeig de Gràcia 32; d €51-91, r without bathroom €41-71; ❋🛜; ⓂPasseig de Gràcia) A picturesque antique lift wheezes its way up to this 4th-floor *hostal*, a terrific, reliable cheapie in one of the city's most expensive neighbourhoods. Some of the single rooms can barely fit a bed but the doubles are big enough, light and airy (some with tiled floors, others with parquet and dark old wardrobes).

★FIVE ROOMS   BOUTIQUE HOTEL €€

Map p294 (☎93 342 78 80; www.thefiverooms.com; Carrer de Pau Claris 72; s/d from €155/165; ❋@🛜; ⓂUrquinaona) Like they say, there are five rooms (standard rooms and suites) in this 1st-floor flat virtually on the border between L'Eixample and the old centre of town. Each is different and features include broad, firm beds, stretches of exposed brick wall, restored mosaic tiles and minimalist decor. There are also two apartments.

SUITES AVENUE   APARTMENT €€

Map p290 (☎93 487 41 59; www.suitesavenue.com; Passeig de Gràcia 83; apt from €169; P❋@🛜; ⓂDiagonal) Fancy apartment-style living is the name of the game here, and often at an excellent price. Self-contained little apartments with own kitchen and access to a terrace, gym and pool (not to mention the mini-museum of Hindu and Buddhist art) lie behind the daring facade by Japanese architect Toyo Ito.

HOTEL PRAKTIK   BOUTIQUE HOTEL €€

Map p290 (☎93 343 66 90; www.hotelpraktikrambla.com; Rambla de Catalunya 27; r €119-129; ❋🛜; ⓂPasseig de Gràcia) This Modernista gem hides a gorgeous little boutique number. While the high ceilings and the bulk of the original tile floors have been maintained, the 43 rooms have daring ceramic touches, spot lighting and contemporary art. There is a chilled reading area and deck-style lounge terrace. The handy location on a tree-lined boulevard is an added plus.

HOTEL CONSTANZA   BOUTIQUE HOTEL €€

Map p294 (☎93 270 19 10; www.hotelconstanza.com; Carrer del Bruc 33; s/d €80/100; ❋@🛜; ⓂGirona, Urquinaona) This boutique beauty has stolen the hearts of many a visitor to

Barcelona. Design touches abound, and little details like flowers in the bathroom add charm. Suites and studios are further options. The terrace is a nice spot to relax for a while, looking over the rooftops of L'Eixample.

CAMI BED & GALLERY
B&B €€

Map p294 (☑93 270 17 48; www.camibedandgallery.com; Carrer de Casp 22, prl 1º; r from €135, r without bathroom from €110; ✷ 🛜; Ⓜ Catalunya) A new, luxury B&B in a handsome Modernista building that could not be more central, just metres from the Plaça de Catalunya. Seven airy rooms, with high ceilings, are meticulously designed and each is slightly different in character, though only one has a private bathroom. It was conceived by art lovers, and also functions as a gallery, staging exhibtions and cultural events.

CONDES DE BARCELONA
HOTEL €€

Map p290 (☑93 445 00 00; www.condesdebarcelona.com; Passeig de Gràcia 73-75; r €164; 🅿 ✷ @ 🛜 🏊; Ⓜ Passeig de Gràcia) The most attractive half of the Condes de Barcelona occupies the 1890s Modernista Casa Enric Batlló. Across the road stands a more modern extension. Clean, designer lines dominate inside each, with luxurious rooms, hardwood floors and architectural touches reminiscent of the Modernista exterior. The rooftop pool is a great place to relax after a hard day's sightseeing.

HOTEL SIXTYTWO
DESIGN HOTEL €€

Map p294 (☑93 272 41 80; www.sixtytwohotel.com/en; Passeig de Gràcia 62; s/d from €149/164; 🅿 ✷ @ 🛜; Ⓜ Passeig de Gràcia) This 21st-century designer setting, housed in a well-preserved 1930s edifice, boasts Bang & Olufsen TVs and expansive, softly backlit beds. Inside the block is a pretty Japanese garden; you can also opt for a massage in your room. All rooms enjoy designer features (and Etro bath products) but the more tempting (and dearer) ones have balconies or little private terraces.

HCC ST MORITZ
HOTEL €€

Map p294 (☑93 412 15 00; www.hcchotels.com; Carrer de la Diputació 264; r €137; 🅿 ✷ @ 🛜; Ⓜ Passeig de Gràcia) This upmarket hotel, set in a late-19th-century building, has 91 fully equipped rooms and boasts an elegant restaurant, terrace bar and small gym. Some of the bigger rooms, with marble bath-rooms, even have their own exercise bikes. You can dine in the modest terrace garden.

HOTEL ASTORIA
HOTEL €€

Map p290 (☑93 209 83 11; www.hotelastoria-barcelona.com; Carrer de Paris 203; s & d from €103; 🅿 ✷ @ 🛜 🏊; Ⓜ Diagonal) Nicely situated a short walk from Passeig de Gràcia, this three-star hotel is equally well placed for long nights out in the restaurants, bars and clubs of adjacent Carrer d'Aribau. Room decor and types vary wildly. The hotel has its own mini gym and a display of art by Catalan painter Ricard Opisso.

BARCELONA CENTER INN
HOTEL €€

Map p294 (☑93 265 25 60; www.hostalcenter-inn.com; Gran Via de les Corts Catalanes 688; s/d €75/89; ✷ @ 🛜; Ⓜ Tetuan) A charming simplicity pervades the rooms here. Wrought-iron bedsteads are overshadowed by flowing drapes. Room decor varies, with a vaguely Andalucian flavour in the bathrooms. Some rooms have little terraces. Get a back room if you can, as Gran Via is noisy.

HOSTAL GOYA
HOSTAL €€

Map p294 (☑93 302 25 65; www.hostalgoya.com; Carrer de Pau Claris 74; s/d from €74/92; ✷ 🛜; Ⓜ Passeig de Gràcia, Urquinaona) The Goya is a modestly priced gem on the chichi side of L'Eixample. Rooms have a light colour scheme that varies from room to room. In the bathrooms, the original mosaic floors have largely been retained, combined with contemporary design features. The more expensive doubles have a balcony.

SOMNIO HOSTEL
HOSTEL €€

Map p290 (☑93 272 53 08; www.somniohostels.com; Carrer de la Diputació 251; dm €25, d €87, s/d without bathroom €44/78; ✷ @ 🛜; Ⓜ Passeig de Gràcia) A crisp, tranquil hostel with 10 rooms (two of them six-bed dorms and all with a simple white and light-blue paint job), Somnio is nicely located in the thick of things in L'Eixample and a short walk from the old city. Rain showers and thick flex mattresses are nice features in these 2nd-floor digs.

HOTEL OMM
DESIGN HOTEL €€€

Map p294 (☑93 445 40 00; www.hotelomm.es; Carrer de Rosselló 265; s/d from €204/300; 🅿 ✷ @ 🛜 🏊; Ⓜ Diagonal) Design meets plain zany here, where the balconies look like strips of skin peeled back from the shiny hotel surface. The idea would no doubt have appealed to Dalí. In the foyer, a sprawling, minimalist and popular bar opens before you. Light, clear tones dominate in the ultramodern rooms, of which there are several categories.

HOTEL HISPANOS SIETE SUIZA   HOTEL €€€
Map p294 (☑93 208 20 51; www.hispanos7suiza. com; Carrer de Sicilia 255; r for 2 people from €200; P❄️☎️; MSagrada Família) Within spitting distance of the towering madness that is La Sagrada Família is this original lodging option. Wander in past seven vintage Hispano-Suiza cars to one of several apartments, which generally have two double rooms with separate bathrooms (note the super showers!), a lounge, kitchen, washer-drier and terrace.

HOTEL MAJÈSTIC   HOTEL €€€
Map p294 (☑93 488 17 17; www.hotelmajestic.es; Passeig de Gràcia 68; d €251-278; P❄️@☎️; MPasseig de Gràcia) This sprawling, central option has the charm of one of the great European hotels. The rooftop pool is great for views and relaxing, or you can pamper yourself in the spa after a workout in the gym. The standard rooms (no singles) are smallish but comfortable and with marble bathrooms.

MANDARIN ORIENTAL   DESIGN HOTEL €€€
Map p294 (☑93 151 88 88; www.mandarin-oriental.com/barcelona; Passeig de Gràcia 38; d from €425; P❄️@☎️; MPasseig de Gràcia) At this imposing former bank, 98 rooms combine contemporary designer style with subtle Eastern touches. Straight lines, lots of white and muted colours dominate the look. Many of the standard rooms (no smaller than 32 sq metres) have luxurious tubs and all overlook either Passeig de Gràcia or an interior sculpted garden.

🛏️ Gràcia & Park Güell

Staying up in Gràcia takes you out of the mainstream tourist areas and gives you a more authentic feel for the town. All the touristy bits are never far away by metro and the restaurant and bar life in Gràcia is great on its own.

⭐CASA GRÀCIA   HOSTEL €
Map p296 (☑93 187 44 97; www.casagraciabcn. com; Passeig de Gràcia 116; dm from €27, d from €50; ❄️@☎️; MDiagonal) A hostel with a dif-

ference (several differences), the tasteful Casa Gràcia has raised the bar for budget accommodation. There are dorm rooms and a couple of private rooms, and all are decorated in crisp white with bursts of colour. There's a huge terrace where communal dinners are held, along with film screenings and various other events, and art exhibitions adorn its walls. There's also a kitchen and TV room for colder months.

HOTEL CASA FUSTER   DESIGN HOTEL €€€
Map p296 (☑93 255 30 00; www.hotelcasafuster.com; Passeig de Gràcia 132; r from €247; P❄️@☎️; MDiagonal) This sumptuous Modernista mansion, built in 1908–11, is one of Barcelona's most luxurious hotels. Standard rooms are plush, if small. Period features have been restored at considerable cost and complemented with hydro-massage tubs, plasma TVs and king-size beds. The rooftop terrace (with pool) offers spectacular views. The Café Vienés, once a meeting place for Barcelona intellectuals, hosts excellent jazz nights.

🛏️ La Zona Alta

Except for a certain business clientele, this mainly residential area is a little too far from the action for most people. Several exceptional places are well worth considering if being in the centre of things is not a priority.

INOUT HOSTEL   HOSTEL €
(☑93 280 09 85; www.inouthostel.com; Major del Rectoret 2; dm €18; ❄️@☎️; RFGC Baixador de Vallvidrera) 🌿 One of Spain's most extraordinary hostels, Inout is a beautifully located property with a strong social ethos. Over 90% of staff here have disabilities. It's a friendly and welcoming place with extensive facilities, including an enticing pool, sports courts, and a low-key restaurant with panoramic views. It's a 12-minute uphill walk from the Baixador de Vallvidrera FGC station.

HOTEL TURÓ DE VILANA   DESIGN HOTEL €€
Map p298 (☑93 434 03 63; www.turodevilana. com; Carrer de Vilana 7; s/d €105/120; ❄️@☎️; 🚌64, RFGC Les Tres Torres) This bright, friendly hotel is set near the charming residential 'hood of Sarrià. Its 22 rooms feature hardwood floors, a warm colour scheme, marble bathrooms and plenty of natural

SLEEPING GRÀCIA & PARK GÜELL

light. There's not a lot to do in the immediate vicinity, but it's an attractive option for those who like the idea of dipping in and out of central Barcelona.

HOTEL ANGLÍ
HOTEL €€

Map p298 (☎93 206 99 44; www.eurostarshotels.com; Carrer d'Anglí 60; d from €95; ❋@🛜🏊; 🚇Sarrià) Part of the Eurostars chain, Hotel Anglí is a comfortable business option. Glass dominates the three-storey design and the semitransparent tower is lit up in various hues at night. Huge firm beds are set in rooms where floor-to-ceiling windows and expanses of mirrors add to the sense of light. The buffet breakfast is good and from the rooftop pool you can contemplate the Collserola Hills.

ABAC BARCELONA
LUXURY HOTEL €€€

Map p298 (☎93 319 66 00; www.abacbarcelona.com; Av del Tibidabo 1; d from €287; ❋@🛜🏊; 🚇FGC Av Tibidabo) This uber-stylish new addition to Barcelona receives high marks for its beautifully designed rooms, kitted out with Bang & Olufsen TVs, rainfall showerheads, Jacuzzi tubs with aromatherapy and luxury bed linens. A lovely spa and one of the city's best restaurants (with two Michelin stars) add to the appeal.

🛏 Montjuïc, Poble Sec & Sant Antoni

A good area for the cash-strapped, there are several options strung out along and near the El Poble Sec side of Avinguda del Paral·lel, as well as near the train station in Sants.

★HOTEL MARKET
BOUTIQUE HOTEL €

Map p302 (☎93 325 12 05; www.forkandpillow.com; Passatge de Sant Antoni Abad 10; s/d from €72/76; ❋@🛜; 🚇Sant Antoni) Attractively located in a renovated building along a narrow lane just north of the grand old Sant Antoni market (now shut for renovation), this place has an air of simple chic. Room decor is a pleasing combination of white, dark nut browns, light wood and reds.

MELON DISTRICT
HOSTAL €

Map p302 (☎93 329 96 67; www.melondistrict.com; Avinguda del Paral·lel 101; r from €62; ❋@🛜; 🚇Paral·lel) Whiter than white seems to be the policy in this student residence, where the only coloured objects are the green plastic chairs. Erasmus folks and international students are attracted to this hostel-style spot, where you can stay the night or book in for a year. There are meeting lounges, kitchen facilities, a cafe and a laundrette on the premises.

SANT JORDI MAMBO TANGO
HOSTEL €

Map p302 (☎93 442 51 64; www.hostelmambotango.com; Carrer del Poeta Cabanyes 23; dm from €27; @🛜; 🚇Paral·lel) A fun, international hostel to hang out in, the Mambo Tango has basic dorms (sleeping from six to nine people) and a welcoming, somewhat chaotic atmosphere. This playful vibe is reflected in the kooky colour scheme in the bathrooms. Advice on what to do and where to go out is always on hand.

URBAN SUITES
HOTEL, APARTMENT €€

Map p302 (☎93 201 51 64; www.theurbansuites.com; Carrer de Sant Nicolau 3; ste from €130; 🅿❋@🛜; 🚇Sants Estació) Directed largely at the trade-fair crowd, this contemporary spot with 16 suites and four apartments makes for a convenient and comfortable home away from home. You get a bedroom, living room and kitchen, DVD player and free wi-fi, and the configuration is good for families. Prices fluctuate enormously according to demand. Note that there is a two-night minimum stay.

HOSTAL CÈNTRIC
HOSTAL €€

Map p302 (☎93 426 75 73; www.hostalcentric.com; Carrer de Casanova 13; s/d from €75/94; ❋@🛜; 🚇Urgell) The *hostal,* in a good central location just beyond the old city, has rooms starting from basics with shared bathroom and ranging to renovated rooms with private bathroom facilities and aircon. Midrange ones are similar, but a little older and without air-con.

HOTEL MIRAMAR
HOTEL €€€

Map p302 (☎93 281 16 00; www.hotelmiramar-barcelona.com; Plaça de Carlos Ibáñez 3; r €215; ❋🛜; 🚌50 or PM) Welcome to the only hotel on the hill, a designer five-star job. Local architect Oscar Tusquets took the shell of a building built for the 1929 World Fair and later the Barcelona HQ of Spanish national TV (1959–83), and created this olive-green block where all rooms have broad balconies and views over the port, city or park. The modern rooms feature neutral decor, with deep browns, creams and beiges dominating the colour scheme.

Understand Barcelona

Barcelona Today

In 2014 Barcelona commemorated the 300th anniversary of the siege of the city, a watershed event that henceforth placed Catalonia under the dominion of Spain. Whether or not Catalonia will regain its independence, the region will continue to chart its own course ahead – particularly in the realm of architecture, sustainability and cuisine. Meanwhile as in other parts of Spain, the economic crisis continues to have dire consequences, especially for those at the lowest end of the socio-economic spectrum.

Best on Film

All about my Mother (director Pedro Almodóvar, 1999) One of Almodóvar's best-loved films is full of plot twists and dark humour, complete with transsexual prostitutes and doe-eyed nuns.

Vicky Cristina Barcelona (director Woody Allen, 2008) Allen gives Barcelona the *Manhattan* treatment, showing a city of startling beauty and neuroticism.

L'Auberge Espagnol (director Cédric Klapisch, 2002) Warmly told coming-of-age story about a mishmash of foreign-exchange students thrown together in Barcelona.

Barcelona (director Whit Stillman, 1994) A sharp and witty romantic comedy about two Americans living in Barcelona during the end of the Cold War.

Best in Print

Barcelona (Robert Hughes, 1992) Witty and passionate study of 2000 years of history.

Shadow of the Wind (Carlos Ruiz Zafón, 2001) Page-turning mystery set in post-civil-war Barcelona.

Homage to Catalonia (George Orwell, 1938) Orwell's classic account of the early days of the Spanish Civil War.

A Nation in Crisis

Spain's ongoing economic woes showed mild signs of improvement at the end of 2013 and the beginning of 2014, with a projected annual growth rate of 1.2% for the year. This was some small relief for a country that had been mostly in recession since the Global Financial Crisis erupted in 2007. Like many other Spaniards, Catalans have yet to break out the cava. Unemployment remains startlingly high, particularly among young workers (above 40% for those under the age of 25). Meanwhile hardship measures prescribed by bureaucrats – slashing budgets, raising taxes and freezing public sector pay – have done nothing to alleviate the hardship for those struggling to pay their bills.

Last year nearly 16,000 Catalans were evicted from their homes according to figures from the General Council of the Judiciary. Homeowners, unable to meet their mortgage payments, have seen their worlds upended as banks seize their properties. Protests against these evictions have grown in recent years, as *barcelonins* and other Spaniards have taken to the streets in outrage against the austerity measures.

Second-hand stores are one of the few businesses that are doing well. In an era of growing joblessness and tightened purse strings, more and more Catalans are taking to buying and selling used goods. Even Passeig de Gracia, Barcelona's most upscale shopping street, now has a few second-hand stores.

A Bid for Independence

Spain's ongoing financial turmoil has been a catalyst for independence. Ever since the days of Franco – when Catalan was banned in schools and in the media – Catalonia has felt stymied by the sometimes heavy-handed policies of the central government. These days anger revolves around the topic of taxation. Catalonia's economy, one of the best performing in the country, is estimated at $275 billion, accounting for 20% of Spain's GDP. But it suffers a heavy tax burden ('we pay the penalty for Madrid's mistakes' as citizens would say). Not surprisingly, talk of independence has rattled not only Spain but the EU. Catalonia is home to some of the nation's biggest industries, including textiles, car manufacturing and banking, and its succession could cause much turmoil – and more bailouts – in an already troubled Europe.

The fervour has only grown in the last few years. In 2013, on the Catalan National Day (11 September), hundreds of thousands of separatist supporters formed a 400km human chain across Catalonia. It even passed through the centre of Camp Nou, home stadium of FC Barça, long a symbol of pride among Catalans. Recent polls indicate 60% of Catalans support the region becoming a new European state. Madrid, however, has clamped down, with Spanish judges ruling that a vote on independence is illegal, and in clear violation of the Spanish constitution. Many financial analysts and outside observers (such as Moody's Investors Service) believe independence is unlikely for Catalonia. Business interests, while mindful of the heavy tax burden, also don't want to be isolated – as this could lead to an even greater economic crisis.

Redesigning the City

Poblenou, once a centre of industrial activity during the 19th century, went through a time of decay before a slow period of revitalisation that kicked off with the 1992 Olympics. Today Poblenou is once again a hive of activity, and the city's new focal point in the realm of urban renewal. Wild new buildings have arrived in the form of Els Encants Vells market and the monolithic Disseny Hub, which houses the city's newest museum (dedicated to decorative arts, textiles and graphic design). Jean Nouvel's cucumber-like Torre Agbar lies just beyond, adding to the ultramodern architectural landscape. City officials believe the tower, which will be transformed into a hotel in years to come, and other attractions will help make the area a new destination for visitors to Barcelona.

Also part of Poblenou is the zone known as 22@ (vint-i-dos arroba), a 200-hectare district with a staggering number of media, high-tech and design firms. More than 4000 firms have arrived since the turn of the millennium, helping make 22@ Barcelona's leading centre of innovation. Some 47% of the newly opened businesses have been start-ups.

if Barcelona were 100 people

62 would be Catalan
24 would be other Spanish
14 would be non-Spanish

belief systems
(% of population)

90 Roman Catholic

10 Other

population per sq km

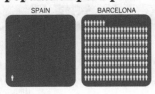

SPAIN   BARCELONA

👤 ≈ 90 people

History

The layered settlement of Barcelona has seen waves of immigrants and conquerors over its 2000-plus years of existence, including Romans, Visigoths, Franks and later Catalans. Barcelona has seen its fortunes rise and fall over the years – from the golden era of princely power in the 14th century to dark days of civil war and the Franco era. A fierce independent streak has always run through Barcelona, which has often put it into conflict with the Kingdom of Castilla – an antagonism that continues to the present, with a desire for more autonomy (full independence say some Catalans) from Spain.

In 1991 the remains of 25 corpses, dating from 4000 BC, were found in Carrer de Sant Pau in El Raval. In those days much of El Raval was a bay and the hillock (Mont Tàber) next to Plaça de Sant Jaume may have been home to a Neolithic settlement.

The Romans

Barcelona's recorded history really begins with the Romans when Barcino (much later Barcelona) was founded in the reign of Caesar Augustus. The Romans were attracted to the location for its possibilities of building a port here.

The heart of the Roman settlement lay within what would later become the medieval city – now known as the Barri Gòtic. The temple was raised on Mont Tàber (three of its columns still stand in a building near Plaça de Sant Jaume). Remains of city walls, temple pillars and graves all attest to what would eventually become a busy and lively town. The Latin poet Ausonius paints a picture of contented prosperity – Barcino lived well off the agricultural produce in its hinterland and from fishing. Oysters, in particular, appeared regularly on the Roman menu in ancient times. Wine, olive oil and garum (a rather tart fish paste and favourite staple of the Romans) were all produced and consumed in abundance.

A stroll through the remnants of former Roman streets in the Museu d'Historia de Barcelona provides a fascinating glimpse of life at that time. There were communal baths, wine-making stores, garum factories, dyeing shops, a laundry (where urine was used as a disinfectant – passersby could make their contribution in pots left outside the building) and upper-class villas (complete with frescoes and mosaic-covered floors). There was even a water drainage system.

TIMELINE	c 4000 BC	218 BC	15 BC
	A Neolithic settlement may have thrived around the present-day Plaça de Sant Jaume at this time, as indicated by jasper implements discovered around Carrer del Paradís.	In a move to block supplies to the Carthaginian general Hannibal, Roman troops under Scipio land at Empúries, found Tarraco (Tarragona) and take control of the Catalan coast.	Caesar Augustus grants the town of Barcino, possibly established under his auspices, the rather long-winded title of Colonia Julia Augusta Faventia Paterna Barcino.

As the Roman Empire wobbled, Hispania (as the Iberian Peninsula was known to the Romans) felt the effects. It is no coincidence that the bulk of Barcelona's Roman walls, vestiges of which remain today, went up in the 4th century AD. Marauding Franks, followed by Romanised Visigoths and other tribes wrought death and destruction on the city; successive waves of invaders flooded across the country like great Atlantic rollers.

Rome's legacy was huge, giving Hispania a road system, aqueducts, temples and the religion that still predominates today, Christianity. Before Rome embraced this monotheistic tradition, however, there were waves of persecutions of early Christians. Santa Eulàlia, who may or may not have existed, is one of the great martyrs of this time. She still plays a role in the city's folklore, with a major festival in her name happening in February each year. Her body is believed to be buried under La Catedral. Christian persecution a few years after her death, when Emperor Constantine declared Christianity the official religion in 312.

Wilfred the Hairy & the Catalan Golden Age

In the 9th century AD, when much of Spain was ruled by the Moors, Louis the Pious – the son of Charlemagne and the future Frankish ruler – conquered Barcelona and claimed it as part of his empire. Barcelona in those days was a frontier town in what was known as the Frankish or Spanish March – a rough-and-ready buffer zone between the Pyrenees and the Moors who had conquered most of the lands to the south.

The March was under nominal Frankish control but the real power lay with local potentates who ranged across the territory. One of these rulers went by the curious name of Guifré el Pelós (Wilfred the Hairy). This was not a reference to uneven shaving habits: according to legend, old Guifré had hair in parts most people do not (exactly which parts was never specified!). He and his brothers gained control of most of the Catalan counties by 878 and Guifré entered the folk mythology of Catalonia.

Guifré consolidated power over Catalunya and ushered in an era of early building projects. He endowed churches and had a new palace for himself in Barcelona (of which nothing remains). His praises were later described by medieval monks and Romantic poets, who credit him with transforming a minor town into the future seat of an empire. If Catalonia can be called a nation, then its 'father' was the hirsute Guifré. He founded a dynasty that lasted nearly five centuries and developed almost independently from the Reconquista wars that were playing out in the rest of Iberia.

Barcelona's first patron saint, Santa Eulàlia (290–304), was martyred for her faith during the persecutory reign of Diocletian. Her death involved 13 tortures (one for each year of her life), including: being rolled in a glass-filled barrel, cutting off her breasts and crucifixion. Some paintings depict her holding a tray containing her cut-off breasts.

AD 415	718	801	878
Visigoths under Athaulf, with captured Roman empress Galla Placidia as his wife, make Barcino their capital. With several interruptions, it remains so until the 6th century.	Only seven years after the Muslim invasion of Spain launched from Morocco at Gibraltar, Barcelona falls to Tariq's mostly Arab and Berber troops on their blitzkrieg march north into France.	After a year-long siege, the son of Charlemagne and future Frankish king Louis the Pious wrests Barcelona from Muslims and establishes the Spanish March under local counts.	Wilfred the Hairy consolidates power throughout Catalonia and founds a long-lasting dynasty with his capital in Barcelona.

Flourishing Culture & Expansion

At the beginning of the second millennium, Catalan culture entered a rich new age. Romanesque churches in the countryside fostered a powerful new style of architecture. Inside lay richly painted frescoes made of the finest pigments and bearing notable Byzantine influences. Some of these works – rescued from churches that later fell into ruin – are beautifully preserved inside the Museu Nacional d'Art de Catalunya (MNAC) on Montjuïc. Commerce was also on the rise, fuelled by a new class of merchants and tradesmen. Shipbuilding, textiles and farming (grain, vineyards) helped power expansion. An even bigger catalyst to Catalonia's growth came in 1137 when Ramon Berenguer IV, the Count of Barcelona, married Petronilla, heir to the throne of neighbouring Aragón, thus creating a joint state that set the scene for Catalonia's golden age.

In the following centuries the regime became a flourishing merchant empire, seizing Valencia and the Balearic Islands from the Moors, and later taking territories as far flung as Sardinia, Sicily and parts of Greece. In the 13th century Barcelona also became the epicentre of a bold experiment in self-government. Jaume I created the Consell dels Cent Jurats (Council of the Hundred Sworn-In) to help run city affairs. Shortly thereafter, Catalonia saw the creation of the Corts Catalanes, a legislative council for Catalonia made up of representatives of the nobility, clergy and high-class merchants to form a counterweight to regal power. Its home was, and remains, the Palau de la Generalitat.

From Gothic Glory to Decline

The 14th century marked the golden age of Barcelona. Its trading wealth paid for the great Gothic buildings that bejewel the city to this day. La Catedral, the Capella Reial de Santa Àgata (inside the Museu d'Història de la Ciutat de Barcelona) and the churches of Santa Maria del Pi and Santa Maria del Mar were all completed during this time. King Pere III (1336–87) later created the breathtaking Reials Drassanes (Royal Shipyards) and also extended the city walls yet again, this time to include the El Raval area to the west.

Preserving the empire began to exhaust Catalonia. Sea wars with Genoa, resistance in Sardinia, the rise of the Ottoman Empire and the loss of the gold trade all drained the city's coffers. Commerce collapsed. The Black Death and famines killed about half of Catalonia's population in the 14th century. Barcelona also lost some of its best merchants when bloodthirsty mobs attacked Jewish businesses and homes in 1391.

After the last of Guifré el Pelós' dynasty, Martí I, died heirless in 1410, Barcelona saw its star diminish, when Catalonia effectively became part of the Castilian state, under the rule of Fernando from the Aragonese

Many Gothic masterpieces were built in the mid-14th century, a time of great suffering in Barcelona. When a wheat crop failed in 1333, the resulting famine killed 10,000 people (a quarter of the city's population). In the 1340s plague devastated the city, killing four of its five counsellors along with many others.

985	1060	1137	1225–29
Al-Mansur (the Victorious) rampages across Catalan territory and devastates Barcelona in a lightning campaign. Much of the population is taken as slaves to Córdoba.	Some 200 years before the Magna Carta, Count Ramon Berenguer I approves the 'Usatges de Barcelona', a bill of rights establishing all free men equal before the law.	Count Ramon Berenguer IV is betrothed to one-year-old Petronilla, daughter of the king of Aragón, creating a new combined state that would be known as the Corona de Aragón.	At age 18 Jaume I takes command; four years later he conquers Muslim-held Mallorca, the first of several dazzling conquests that lead him to be called El Conqueridor (the Conqueror).

throne and Isabel, queen of Castilla. Impoverished and disaffected by ever-growing financial demands from the crown, Catalonia revolted in the 17th century when Catalan peasants gathered on La Rambla outside the walls of the city and began rioting.

They attacked and murdered the viceroy Santa Coloma and sacked and burned his ministers' houses in what was later known as the Guerra dels Segadors (Reapers' War). Under French protection, Catalonia declared itself to be an independent 'republic'. Anarchy ruled over the next few years, until Barcelona was finally besieged into submission by Castile. Little was gained from the effort, though the event was later commemorated as the first great Catalan drive towards independence. The song 'Els Segadors' written down in the 19th century (but with an oral tradition dating back to the 1600s) officially became Catalonia's 'national anthem' in 1993.

Although 11 September reflects the tragic fall of the city, the day is still commemorated as the Diada, the National Day of Catalonia – often a day of political rallies and demonstrations, with independence very much on the agenda.

War of the Spanish Succession

Although Catalonia had only limited autonomy in the late 1600s, things grew worse at the turn of the 18th century when it supported the wrong side in the War of the Spanish Succession. Barcelona, under the auspices of British-backed archduke Charles of Austria, fell after an 18-month siege on 11 September 1714 to the forces of Bourbon king Philip V, who established a unitary Castilian state.

Angered at Catalonia's perceived treachery, the new king abolished the Generalitat and leveled a whole district of medieval Barcelona to build a huge fort (the Ciutadella) to watch over the city. The recently excavated ruins beneath El Born Centre Cultural (which opened in 2013) show what life was like for those living in the 1700s on the future site of the Ciutadella. Their lives changed irrevocably as their homes were destroyed and they were relocated to the soulless new geometric grid of Barceloneta. Not surprisingly, the citadel became the city's most hated symbol among most Catalans. Teaching and writing in Catalan was banned, as Philip V proceeded with a widespread plan of 'castlianisation', in hopes of crushing future dissent. What was left of Catalonia's possessions were farmed out to the great powers.

According to a medieval legend, Barcelona was founded by Hercules himself. Although versions differ, all tell of nine 'barcas' (boats), one of which separates from the others in a storm, and is piloted by Hercules to a beautiful spot on the coast where he founds a city, naming it Barca Nona (Ninth Boat).

A New Boom

After the initial shock, Barcelona found the Bourbon rulers to be comparatively light-handed in their treatment of the city. The big break came in 1778, when the ban on trade with the Spanish American colonies was lifted. In Barcelona itself, growth was modest but sustained. Small-scale manufacturing provided employment and profit, and wages were rising.

1283	1323	1348	1383
The Corts Catalanes, a legislative council for Catalonia, meets for the first time and begins to curtail unlimited powers of sovereigns in favour of nobles and the powerful trading class.	Catalan forces land in Sardinia and launch a campaign of conquest that would only end in 1409. Their fiercest enemy was Eleonora de Arborea, a Sardinian Joan of Arc.	Plague devastates Barcelona. Over 25% of the city's population dies. Further waves of the Black Death, a plague of locusts in 1358 and an earthquake in 1373 deal further blows.	After 50 or so years of frenzied construction the massive Santa Maria del Mar rises above the Ribera. It is one of many Gothic architectural gems completed in the 14th century.

TRAGEDY IN EL CALL

Tucked away in the Barri Gòtic, the narrow medieval lanes of El Call were once home to a thriving Jewish population. Catalan Jews worked as merchants, scholars, cartographers and teachers. By the 11th century, as many as 4000 Jews lived in El Call.

Despite the civic contributions made by Jews, during the 13th century a wave of anti-Semitism swept through Catalonia (and other parts of Europe). In 1243 Jaume I isolated El Call from the rest of the town, and required all Jews to wear identifying badges. When famine struck in the 1330s followed by plague in 1348, it left a wake of devastation, with thousands dead. Trying to make sense of the Black Death, many residents blamed the Jews – for poisoning the wells, sacrificing babies and other grotesque imaginings. Hundreds were tortured to 'confess' their crimes. The harassment continued through the following decades.

The anti-Semitism peaked in 1391 when a frenzied mob tore through El Call, looting and destroying private homes and murdering hundreds of Jews – perhaps as many as a thousand. El Call never recovered, and most of the remaining Jews fled the city.

Barcelona's growth was briefly slowed by the French invasion in 1808, but gradually returned after Napoleon's defeat in 1814. The cotton trade with America helped fuel the boom. In the 1830s, the first steam-driven factories opened in Barcelona, heralding a wave of development that would last for most of the century. Wine, cork and iron industries flourished. From the mid-1830s onwards, steamships were launched off the slipways. In the following decade Spain's first railway line was opened between Barcelona and Mataró.

Justice in feudal days was a little rough by modern standards. As prescribed in a 1060 bill: 'In regard to women, let the rulers render justice by cutting off their noses, lips, ears and breasts, and by burning them at the stake if necessary.'

A Dramatic Redesign

Creeping industrialisation and prosperity for the business class did not work out so well down the line. Working-class families lived in increasingly putrid and cramped conditions. Poor nutrition, bad sanitation and disease were the norm in workers' districts, and riots, predictably, resulted. As a rule they were put down with little ceremony – the 1842 rising was bombarded into submission from the Castell de Montjuïc.

In 1869 a plan to expand the city was begun. Ildefons Cerdà designed L'Eixample (the Enlargement) as a grid, broken up with gardens and parks and grafted onto the old city, beginning at Plaça de Catalunya. The plan was revolutionary. Until then it had been illegal to build in the plains between Barcelona and Gràcia, the area being a military zone. As industrialisation got underway this building ban also forced the concentration of factories in Barcelona itself (especially

1387	1469	1478	1640–52
During the reign of Juan I, Barcelona hosted its first bullfight, according to the city's historical archive. It isn't until the 19th century, however, that bullfighting gains widespread popularity.	Isabel, heir to the Castilian throne, marries Aragonese heir Fernando, uniting two of Spain's most powerful monarchies and effectively subjugating Catalonia to the Castilian state.	Isabel and Fernando, the Reyes Católicos (Catholic Monarchs), stir up religious bigotry and establish the Spanish Inquisition that will see thousands killed until 1834 when it's finally abolished.	Catalan peasants, angered at having to quarter Castilian troops during the Thirty Years War, declare their independence under French protection. Spain eventually crushes the rebellion.

in Barceloneta) and surrounding towns like Gràcia, Sant Martí, Sants and Sant Andreu (all of which were subsequently swallowed up by the burgeoning city).

L'Eixample became the most sought-after chunk of real estate in Barcelona – but the parks were mostly sacrificed to an insatiable demand for housing and undisguised land speculation. The flourishing bourgeoisie paid for lavish, ostentatious buildings, many of them in the unique, Modernista style.

A 19th-Century Renaissance

Barcelona was comparatively peaceful for most of the second half of the 19th century but far from politically inert. The relative calm and growing wealth that came with commercial success helped revive interest in all things Catalan. The Renaixença (Renaissance) reflected the feeling in Barcelona of renewed self-confidence. Politicians and academics increasingly studied and demanded the return of former Catalan institutions and legal systems. The Catalan language was re-adopted by the middle and upper classes and new Catalan literature emerged as well.

In 1892 the Unió Catalanista (Catalanist Union) demanded the re-establishment of the Corts in a document known as the *Bases de Manresa*. In 1906 the suppression of Catalan news sheets was greeted by the formation of Solidaritat Catalana (Catalan Solidarity; a nationalist movement). It attracted a broad band of Catalans, not all of them nationalists.

Perhaps the most dynamic expression of the Catalan Renaissance occurred in the world of art. Barcelona was the home of Modernisme, Catalan art nouveau. While the rest of Spain stagnated, Barcelona was a hotbed of artistic activity, an avant-garde base with close links to Paris. The young Picasso spread his artistic wings here and drank in the artists' hang-out Els Quatre Gats.

An unpleasant wake-up call came with Spain's short, futile war with the US in 1898, in which it lost not only its entire navy, but its last colonies (Cuba, Puerto Rico and the Philippines). The blow to Barcelona's trade was enormous.

Mayhem

Barcelona's proletariat was growing fast. The total population grew from 115,000 in 1800 to over 500,000 by 1900 and over one million by 1930 – boosted, in the early 19th century, by poor immigrants from rural Catalonia and, later, from other regions of Spain. All this made Barcelona ripe for unrest.

CATALAN FLAG

In Catalan folklore, the idea for the Catalan flag – alternating red-and-yellow bars – was born when, during a battle, King Louis the Pious dipped four fingers into the wound of a dying Wilfred the Hairy, and ran them across Wilfred's golden shield. Never mind that Louis died long before Wilfred was born!

1714	1770	1808	1869
Barcelona loses all autonomy after surrendering to the Bourbon king, Felipe V, on 11 September at the end of the War of the Spanish Succession.	A freak hurricane strikes Barcelona, causing considerable damage. Among other things the winds destroy more than 200 of the city's 1500 gaslight street lamps.	In the Battle of Bruc, Catalan militiamen defeat occupying Napoleonic units, yet Barcelona, Figueres and the coast remain under French control until Napoleon's retreat in 1814.	Ildefons Cerdà designs the L'Eixample (the Enlargement) district with wide boulevards and a grid pattern. Modernista architects of the day showcase their creations here.

The city became a swirling vortex of poor workers, Republicans, bourgeois regionalists, gangsters, police terrorists and hired *pistoleros* (gunmen). Among the underclasses, who lived in some of the most abysmal conditions in Europe, there was a deep undercurrent of discontent towards the upper classes, the state and the church (which had long been viewed as an ally to the rich and powerful). When the political philosophy of anarchism began spreading through Europe, it was embraced by many industrial workers in Barcelona, who embarked on a road to social revolution through violent means.

One anarchist bomb at the Liceu opera house on La Rambla in the 1890s killed 22 people. Anarchists were also blamed for the Setmana Tràgica (Tragic Week) in July 1909 when, following a military call-up for Spanish campaigns in Morocco, rampaging mobs wrecked 70 religious buildings and workers were shot on the street in reprisal.

In the post-WWI slump, unionism took hold. This movement was led by the anarchist Confederación Nacional del Trabajo (CNT; National Workers' Confederation), which embraced 80% of the city's workers. During a wave of strikes in 1919 and 1920, employers hired assassins to eliminate union leaders. The 1920s dictator General Miguel Primo de Rivera opposed bourgeois-Catalan nationalism and working-class radicalism, banning the CNT and even closing Barcelona football club, a potent symbol of Catalanism. But he did support the staging of a second world fair in Barcelona, the Montjuïc World Exhibition of 1929.

Rivera's repression only succeeded in uniting, after his fall in 1930, Catalonia's radical elements. Within days of the formation of Spain's Second Republic in 1931, leftist Catalan nationalists of the Esquerra Republicana de Catalunya (ERC), led by Francesc Macià and Lluís Companys, proclaimed Catalonia a republic within an imaginary 'Iberian Federation'. Madrid pressured them into accepting unitary Spanish statehood, but after the leftist Popular Front victory in the February 1936 national elections, Catalonia briefly won genuine autonomy. Companys, its president, carried out land reforms and planned an alternative Barcelona Olympics to the official 1936 games in Nazi Berlin.

But things were racing out of control. The left and the right across Spain were shaping up for a showdown.

The Civil War

On 17 July 1936, an army uprising in Morocco kick-started the Spanish Civil War. The main players in the conflict were the Nationalists, who were allied with conservatives (and the church). Angry at the new leftist direction Spain was heading, they staged a coup, led by General Franco and other rebels, and quickly gained the following of most of the

Ever at the vanguard, Barcelona had the first daily newspaper printed in Spain, its first cinema, public phone and airline (to Majorca). It also built the world's second metropolitan railroad (London was first).

1873	1888	1895	1898
Antoni Gaudí, 21 years old and in Barcelona since 1869, enrols in architecture school, from which he graduates five years later, having already designed the street lamps in Plaça Reial.	Showcasing the grand Modernista touches of recent years (including L'Eixample), Barcelona hosts Spain's first International Exposition, held in the new, manicured Parc de la Ciutadella.	Málaga-born Pablo Picasso, aged 13, arrives in Barcelona with his family. His art-teacher father gets a job in the Escola de Belles Artes, where Pablo enrols as a pupil.	Spain loses its entire navy and last remaining colonies (the Philippines, Cuba and Puerto Rico) in two hopeless campaigns against the USA, dealing a heavy blow to Barcelona businesses.

A CATALAN SUBMARINE

It could have been the Spanish Navy's V2, a late-19th-century secret weapon. Narcis Monturiol i Estarriol (1819–85), part-time publisher and all-round utopian, was fascinated by the sea. In 1859 he launched a wooden, fish-shaped submarine, the *Ictíneo*, in Barcelona. Air shortages made only brief dives possible but Monturiol became an overnight celebrity. He received, however, not a jot of funding.

Undeterred, he sank himself further into debt by designing *Ictíneo II*. This was a first. It was 17m long, its screws were steam driven and Monturiol had devised a system for renewing the oxygen inside the vessel. It was trialled in 1864 but again attracted no finance. Four years later, the vessel was broken up for scrap.

If the Spaniards had had a few of these when they faced the US Navy off Cuba and in the Philippines in 1898, perhaps things might have turned out differently!

army. On the opposite side was the Republican government, which was supported by those loyal to Spain's democratically elected government. Republican supporters were a loose coalition of workers' parties, socialists, anarchists, communists and other left-wing groups.

Barcelona's army garrison attempted to take the city for General Franco but was defeated by anarchists and police loyal to the government. Franco's Nationalist forces quickly took hold of most of southern and western Spain; Galicia and Navarra in the north were also his. Most of the east and industrialised north stood with Madrid. Initial rapid advances on Madrid were stifled and the two sides settled in for almost three years of misery.

For nearly a year, Barcelona was run by anarchists and the Trotskyist militia of the Partido Obrero de Unificación Marxista (POUM; the Marxist Unification Workers' Party), with Companys president only in name. Factory owners and rightists fled the city. Unions took over factories and public services, hotels and mansions became hospitals and schools, everyone wore workers' clothes (in something of a foretaste of what would later happen in Mao's China), bars and cafes were collectivised, trams and taxis were painted red and black (the colours of the anarchists), and one-way streets were ignored as they were seen to be part of the old system.

The anarchists were a disparate lot ranging from gentle idealists to hardliners who drew up death lists, held kangaroo courts, shot priests, monks and nuns (over 1200 of whom were killed in Barcelona province during the civil war), and also burnt and wrecked churches – which is why so many of Barcelona's churches are today oddly plain inside. They in turn were shunted aside by the communists (directed by Stalin from

History Sites

Museu d'Història de Barcelona (p65)

Museu d'Història de Catalunya (p112)

Via Sepulcral Romana (p68)

Museu Marítim (p111)

July 1909	1914	July 1936	March 1938
After the call-up of reserve troops to fight a war in Morocco, *barcelonins* riot. Over 100 are reportedly killed in what's later known as Setmana Tràgica (Tragic Week).	The Mancomunitat de Catalunya, a first timid attempt at self-rule (restricted largely to administrative matters) and headed by Catalan nationalist Enric Prat de la Riba, is created in April.	General Franco launches the Spanish Civil War in Morocco. General Goded leads army units to take Barcelona for Franco but is defeated by left-wing militia, workers and loyalist police.	In just three days of day-and-night air raids on Barcelona carried out by Fascist Italian bombers based in Franco-controlled Mallorca, 979 people are killed and 1500 wounded.

Moscow) after a bloody internecine battle in Barcelona that left 1500 dead in May 1937. Barcelona also suffered aerial bombing raids carried out by Italian bombers sympathetic to Franco. The pockmarked walls around Plaça Sant Felip Neri still bear the scars of one particularly gruesome day of bombardment when dozens of civilians – many of them children – were killed here.

Barcelona became the Republicans' national capital in autumn 1937. The Republican defeat in the Battle of the Ebro in southern Catalonia the following summer left Barcelona undefended. Republican resistance crumbled, in part due to exhaustion, in part due to disunity. In 1938 Catalan nationalists started negotiating separately with the Nationalists. The city fell to Franco's forces in January 1939.

Films set in Franco's Spain

....

Pan's Labyrinth (2006)

....

The Spirit of the Beehive (1973)

....

¡Bienvenido, Mr Marshall! (Welcome, Mr Marshall!; 1952)

....

Las 13 Rosas (The 13 Roses; 2007)

Occupation

Franco's tanks rolled into a strangely silent and empty city. Almost half a million people had fled to the north. The first few months of occupation was a strange hiatus before the onset of the full machinery of oppression. Within two weeks of the city's fall, a dozen cinemas were in operation and the following month Hollywood comedies were being shown between rounds of Nationalist propaganda. The people were even encouraged to dance the *sardana,* Catalonia's national dance, in public (the Nationalists thought such folkloric generosity might endear them to the people of Barcelona).

On the other hand, the city presented an exhausted picture. The metro was running but there were no buses (they had all been used on the front). Virtually all the animals in the city zoo had died of starvation or wounds. There were frequent blackouts, and would be for years.

By 1940, with WWII raging across Europe, Franco had his regime more firmly in place and things turned darker for many. Catalan Francoists led the way in rounding up anarchists and former Republican supporters; up to 35,000 people were shot in purges. At the same time, small bands of resistance fighters continued to harry the Nationalists in the Pyrenees through much of the 1940s. Catalonia's president, Lluís Companys, was arrested in France by the Gestapo in August 1940, handed over to Franco, and shot on 15 October on Montjuïc. He is reputed to have died with the words '*Visca Catalunya!*' ('Long live Catalonia!') on his lips.

The executions continued into the 1950s. Most people accepted the situation and tried to get on with living, while some leapt at opportunities, occupying flats abandoned by 'Reds' who had been forced to flee. Speculators and industrialists allied with Franco were able to earn a lucrative income, but the majority of *barcelonins* were affected by nationwide poverty.

1939	1940	1957	1980
The first of Franco's troops, along with Italian tanks, roll into Barcelona and parade down Avinguda Diagonal. Thousands flee the city towards the French border.	Hitler's henchman and chief of the SS, Heinrich Himmler, visits Barcelona, stays at the Ritz, enjoys a folkloric show at Poble Espanyol and has his wallet stolen.	The Francoist Josep Maria de Porcioles becomes mayor of Barcelona and remains in charge until 1973. He presides over a willy-nilly building spree in the city.	Right-wing Catalan nationalist Jordi Pujol is elected president of the resurrected Catalan regional government at the head of the CiU coalition; he remains in power without interruption until 2003.

Life Under Franco

Franco took a particularly hard line against Barcelona. Catalan monuments in the city were dismantled. He banned public use of Catalan, and had all town, village and street names rendered in Spanish (Castilian). Education, radio, TV and the daily press would henceforth be in Spanish. Independent political activity was banned as was the celebration of traditional Catalan holidays.

In Barcelona, the Francoist Josep Maria de Porcioles became mayor in 1957, a post he held until 1973. That same year, he obtained for the city a 'municipal charter' that expanded the mayor's authority and the city's capacity to raise and spend taxes, manage urban development and, ultimately, widen the city's metropolitan limits to absorb neighbouring territory. He was responsible for such monstrosities as the concrete municipal buildings on Plaça de Sant Miquel in the Barri Gòtic. His rule marked a grey time for Barcelona.

By the 1950s opposition to Franco had turned to peaceful mass protests and strikes. In 1960 an audience at the city's Palau de la Música Catalana concert hall sang a banned Catalan anthem in front of Franco. The ringleaders included a young Catholic banker, Jordi Pujol, who would later rise to pre-eminence in the post-Franco era. For his singing effort he wound up in jail for a short time.

Under Franco a flood of 1.5 million immigrants from poorer parts of Spain, chiefly Andalucía, Extremadura and the northwest, poured into Catalonia (750,000 of them to Barcelona) in the 1950s and '60s looking for work. Many lived in appalling conditions. While some made the effort to learn Catalan and integrate as fully as possible into local society, the majority came to form Spanish-speaking pockets in the poorer working-class districts of the city and in a ring of satellite towns. Even today, the atmosphere in many of these towns is more Andalucian than Catalan. Catalan nationalists will tell you it was all part of a Francoist plot to undermine the Catalan identity.

HISTORY LIFE UNDER FRANCO

Historical Reads

Barcelona (Robert Hughes)

Barcelona – A Thousand Years of the City's Past (Felipe Fernández Armesto)

Homage to Catalonia (George Orwell)

Homage to Barcelona (Colm Tóibín)

The Road to Recovery

When the death of Franco was announced in 1975, *barcelonins* took to the streets in celebration. The next five years saw the gradual return of democracy. In 1977 Josep Tarradellas, who was head of Catalonia's government in exile returned to Barcelona after Franco's death, and was officially recognised by the Spanish government as head of a new Catalan coalition. *Barcelonins* who lived during that time will likely recall the historic words given from the balcony of the Palau de la Generalitat. Before a huge crowd gathered on Plaça de Sant Jaume, he said, *'Ciutadans de Catalunya, ja sóc aquí!'* (Citizens of Catalonia, I am here!).

1992	January 1994	2003	2006
Barcelona takes centre stage as it hosts the summer Olympic Games. In preparation the city undergoes a radical renovation program whose momentum continues today.	The Gran Teatre del Liceu, Barcelona's opera house, burns to the ground as a spark from a welder's blowtorch sets the stage alight. It is rebuilt and reopens in 1999.	Popular former mayor of Barcelona, Pasqual Maragall becomes the first Socialist president of Catalonia in tight elections after Pujol steps aside in favour of CiU's Artur Mas.	The Catalan government negotiates a new autonomy statute with Madrid in a compromise that leaves many unsatisfied and ultimately leads to the fall of Maragall.

Twenty years after his stint in Franco's jails, Pujol (an early ringleader in protests against the Francoists) was elected president of Catalonia in 1980. These were the first free regional elections since before the civil war. A wily antagonist of the central authorities in Madrid, Pujol waged a quarter-century war of attrition, eking out greater fiscal and policy autonomy and vigorously promoting a re-Catalanisation program, with uneven success.

Politics aside, the big event in post-Franco Barcelona was the successful 1992 Olympics, planned under the guidance of the popular Socialist mayor, Pasqual Maragall. The Olympic Games spurred a burst of public works and brought new life to areas such as Montjuïc, where the major events were held. The once-shabby waterfront was transformed with promenades, beaches, marinas, restaurants, leisure attractions and new housing.

After the turn of the millennium, Barcelona continued to invest in urban renewal, with ambitious projects such as the 22@ hi-tech zone in the once-industrial El Poblenou district, the major development around new trade fairgrounds between the city and the airport, and the glimmering Diagonal Mar waterfront development around the Parc del Fòrum at the northeast tip of the city.

Barcelona nearly staged the Olimpíada Popular (People's Olympiad) in 1936, an alternative to the Olympics that was being held in fascist Germany. Around 6000 athletes from 23 countries registered. However, the civil war erupted just before the start. Some athletes who arrived stayed on and joined militias to help defend the republic.

Sustainability & a Catalan Future

Over the last decade, Barcelona has undergone great transformations, with an eye towards sustainability. Since 2000 the city has required all new buildings to install solar panels to provide most of their hot water. Its massive solar panel near the Parc del Fòrum is the largest of any city in Europe. Barcelona's shared bike program, Bicing, launched in 2007, has helped reduce traffic on the road, with some 180,000 subscribers using the service (saving 10 million kg of CO_2 per year). Bicycles aren't the only way Barcelona is reducing its carbon footprint: the city has one of the cleanest bus fleets in Europe, and has become a leader in the realm of electric vehicles, with over 250 charging stations.

The economic crisis that erupted in 2007, however, has largely shifted the topic of conversation away from green initiatives and into the realm of economic recovery. Soaring unemployment and painful austerity measures – not to mention Catalonia's heavy tax burden – has led to anger and resentment towards Madrid, and fuelled the drive towards independence. A referendum on independence was scheduled for November 2014, but was declared illegal by Spanish judges – setting up a showdown between Catalonia and Spain.

2010	2010	March 2014	2026
Pope Benedict XVI consecrates the basilica of Sagrada Família before an audience of 6500, including King Juan Carlos I and Queen Sofia.	Hot on the heels of their victory in the European football championship in 2008, Spain defeats Holland in the World Cup held in South Africa, its first-ever World Cup title.	Six months after a human chain stretches 400km across Catalonia, Spanish judges declare Catalonia's planned referendum on independence unconstitutional.	Builders aim to finish La Sagrada Família on the centenary of the death of its creator Gaudí (1852–1926), which is over 140 years after its construction began.

Catalan Culture

The fortunes of Catalunya have risen and fallen over the years, as Barcelona has gone from wealthy mercantile capital to a city of repression under the Franco regime, followed by the boom and bust of more recent years. Despite today's economic challenges, Catalan culture continues to flourish, with a lively festival calendar and abundant civic pride: manifested in everything from the language spoken on the streets to Barcelona's much-loved football team.

Language

In Barcelona, born and bred locals proudly speak Catalan, a Romance language related to French, Spanish (Castilian) and Italian. It was only relatively recently, however, that Catalan was deemed 'legitimate'. Since Barcelona was crushed in the War of the Spanish Succession in 1714, the use of Catalan has been repeatedly banned or at least frowned upon.

Above Festes de la Mercè (p25)

Franco was the last of Spain's rulers to clamp down on its public use. All that changed in 1980, when the first autonomous regional parliament was assembled and adopted new laws towards *normalització lingüístico* (linguistic normalisation). Today Catalonia's school system is based on bilingual education, with graduates showing equal skill in using either Catalan or Spanish. Around town, Catalan is the *lingua franca:* advertising and road signs tend to be in Catalan, while newspapers, magazines and other publications can be found in both languages (though you'll find about twice as many options in Catalan than in Spanish). You'll also find a mix of Catalan and Spanish programming on radio and TV stations.

Folk Dancing

On weekends year-round devotees of the folk-dance *sardana* gather in front of La Catedral, while a 10-piece band puts everyone in motion. Catalans of all ages come out for the dance, which takes place in a circle, with dancers holding hands. Together they move right, back and then left, hopping, raising their arms and generally building momentum as the tempo picks up. All are welcome to join in, though you'll have to watch a few rounds to get the hang of it.

Festivals

Catalonia's best celebrations tend to revolve around religious holidays. Fests dedicated to Nostra Senyora de la Mercè (Our Lady of Mercy) and Santa Eulàlia – Barcelona's two patron saints – are the city's biggest bashes. You'll see plenty of *sardana* and *castell*-building there. You'll also see *gegants* (huge papier maché giants: lords, princesses, sultans, fisherman and historic and contemporary figures) and *capgrossos* (oversized heads worn by costumed actors). Another feature of these Catalan fests is the *correfoc* (fire run): horned devils brandishing fireworks-spouting pitchforks wreak mayhem in the streets. They are sometimes accompanied by fireworks-spouting dragons, or even wooden carts that are set alight. Full covering (hats, gloves, goggles) are highly recommended for anyone who wants to get near.

Castells

One of the highlights of a traditional Catalan festival is the building of human *castells* (castles), a Catalan tradition that dates back to the 18th century. Teams from across the region compete to build human towers up to 10 storeys tall. These usually involve levels of three to five people standing on each other's shoulders. A crowd of teammates forms a supporting scrum around the thickset lads at the base. To successfully complete the castle, a young (light!) child called the *anxaneta* must reach the top and signal with his or her hand.

FC Barcelona

One of the city's best-loved names is FC Barça, which is deeply associated with Catalans and even Catalan nationalism. The team was long a rallying point for Catalans when other aspects of Catalan culture were suppressed. The club openly supported Catalonia's drive towards autonomy in 1918, and in 1921 the club's statutes were drafted in Catalan. The pro-Catalan leanings of the club and its siding with the republic during the Spanish Civil War earned reprisals from the government. Club president Josep Sunyol was murdered by Franco's soldiers in 1936, and the club building was bombed in 1938. In 1968 club president Narcís de Carreras uttered the now famous words, *El Barça: més que un club* ('more than a club'), which became the team's motto – and emphasised its role as an anti-Franco symbol and catalyst for change in the province and beyond. Today FC Barça is one of the world's most admired teams; in 2014 FC Barcelona's social networks surpassed 100 million followers.

Essential Reading

Barcelona: The Great Enchantress, by Robert Hughes

Barcelonas, by Manuel Vazquez Montalban

Barça: A People's Passion, by Jimmy Burns

At Christmas some rather unusual Catalan characters appear. The *caganer* (crapper) is a chap with dropped pants who balances over his unsightly offering (a symbol of fertility for the coming year). There's also the *caga tío* (poop log), which on Christmas Day is supposed to *cagar* (crap) out gifts.

Architecture

Famed for its architectural treasures, Barcelona has striking Gothic cathedrals, fantastical Modernista creations and avant-garde works from more recent days. The city's great building boom first began in the late Middle Ages, when Barcelona was seat of the Catalan empire. The late 19th century was another time of great ferment, when the city began expanding beyond its medieval confines and bold new thinkers transformed the city. The third notable era of design began in the late 1980s and continues today.

The Gothic Period

Barcelona's first big building boom came at the height of the Middle Ages, when its imposing Gothic churches, mansions and shipyards were raised, together creating what survives to this day as one of the most extensive Gothic quarters in Europe. Most of these architectural treasures lie within the boundaries of the Ciutat Vella but a few examples can be found beyond, notably the Museu-Monestir de Pedralbes in Sarrià.

Historical Roots

This soaring style took off in France in the 12th century and spread across Europe. Its emergence coincided with Jaume I's march into Valencia and the annexation of Mallorca and Ibiza, accompanied by the rise of a trading class and a burgeoning mercantile empire. The enormous cost of building the grand new monuments could thus be covered by the steady increase in the city's wealth.

Perhaps the single greatest building spurt came under Pere III (1319–87). This is odd in a sense because, as Dickens might have observed, it was not only the best of times, but also the worst. By the mid-14th century, when Pere III was in command, Barcelona had been pushed to the ropes by a series of disasters: famine, repeated plagues and pogroms.

Maybe he didn't notice. He built, or began to build, much of La Catedral, the Drassanes, the Llotja stock exchange, the Saló del Tinell, the Casa de la Ciutat (which now houses the town hall) and numerous lesser buildings, not to mention part of the city walls. The churches of Santa Maria del Pi and Santa Maria del Mar were completed by the end of the 14th century.

Architectural Features

The style of architecture reflected the development of building techniques. The introduction of buttresses, flying buttresses and ribbed vaulting in ceilings allowed engineers to raise edifices that were loftier and seemingly lighter than ever before. The pointed arch became standard and great rose windows were the source of light inside these enormous spaces.

Think about the hovels that labourers on such projects lived in and the primitive nature of building materials available, and you get an idea of the awe such churches, once completed, must have inspired. They were not built in a day. It took more than 160 years, a fairly typical time frame, to

---

Gothic Master-pieces

La Catedral

Basílica de Santa Maria del Mar

Església de Santa Maria del Pi

Saló del Tinell (in Museu d'Història de Barcelona)

The Drassanes (Museu Marítim)

CHANGING ATTITUDES TOWARDS GOTHIC STYLES

The lofty Gothic buildings of medieval Europe inspire awe in their modern visitors. But as early as the 16th century, when Renaissance artists and architects turned to the clean lines of classical antiquity for inspiration, all things medieval looked crude, rough and, well, frankly barbarian, just like the ancient Germanic tribes of Goths that had stormed across Europe centuries before. To label something Gothic became the ultimate insult. This attitude spread across Europe. In Barcelona, many private homes built in Gothic style would get a baroque makeover later, but thankfully most of the major monuments were left alone. Not until the 19th century did this extraordinary heritage again awaken admiration, to such an extent that in some north European countries in particular it led to a wave of Gothic revival building.

finish La Catedral, although its facade was not erected until the 19th century. Its rival, the Basílica de Santa Maria del Mar, was one for the record books, taking only 59 years to build.

Catalan Gothic

Catalan Gothic did not follow the same course as the style typical of northern Europe. Decoration here tends to be more sparing and the most obvious defining characteristic is the triumph of breadth over height. While northern European cathedrals reach for the sky, Catalan Gothic has a tendency to push to the sides, stretching its vaulting design to the limit.

Catalonia's vast 14th-century mercantile empire fuelled Barcelona's boom. All manner of goods flowed to and from Sardinia, Flanders, North Africa and other places, with Catalan Jews carrying out much of this trade. The later pogroms, Inquisition and expulsion of Jews had devastating financial consequences and helped reduce Barcelona to penury.

The Saló del Tinell, with a parade of 15m arches (among the largest ever built without reinforcement) holding up the roof, is a perfect example of Catalan Gothic. Another is the present home of the Museu Marítim, the Drassanes, Barcelona's medieval shipyards. In their churches, too, the Catalans opted for a more robust shape and lateral space – step into the Basílica de Santa Maria del Mar or the Església de Santa Maria del Pi and you'll soon get the idea.

Another notable departure from what you might have come to expect of Gothic north of the Pyrenees is the lack of spires and pinnacles. Bell towers tend to terminate in a flat or nearly flat roof. Occasional exceptions prove the rule – the main facade of Barcelona's La Catedral, with its three gnarled and knobbly spires, does vaguely resemble the outline that confronts you in cathedrals in Chartres or Cologne. But then it was a 19th-century addition, admittedly to a medieval design.

Late Gothic

Gothic had a longer use-by date in Barcelona than in many other European centres. By the early 15th century, the Generalitat still didn't have a home worthy of its name, and architect Marc Safont set to work on the present building on Plaça de Sant Jaume. Even renovations carried out a century later were largely in the Gothic tradition, although some Renaissance elements eventually snuck in – the facade on Plaça de Sant Jaume is a rather disappointing result.

Carrer de Montcada, in La Ribera, was the result of a late-medieval act of town planning. Eventually, mansions belonging to the moneyed classes of 15th- and 16th-century Barcelona were erected along it. Many now house museums and art galleries. Although these former mansions appear forbidding on the outside, their interiors often reveal another world, of pleasing courtyards and decorated external staircases. They mostly went through a gentle baroque makeover in later years.

Modernisme

Barcelona's Modernista buildings arose during La Renaixença, a period of great artistic and political fervor that was deeply connected to Catalan identity, and transformed early-20th-century Barcelona into a showcase for avant-garde architecture. Aiming to establish a new Catalan archetype, Antoni Gaudí and other visionary architects drew inspiration from the past, using elements from the Spanish vernacular – shapes, details and brickwork reminiscent of Islamic, Gothic and Renaissance designs.

The Modernistas also revived traditional artisan trades, which you can see in the exquisite stonework and stained-glass windows, and in their artful use of wrought iron, ceramics and mosaic tiles. Nature was celebrated and imitated to perfection in Gaudí's organic forms: leaning tree-like columns, walls that undulate like the sea, and the use of native plants as decorative elements. Inside these buildings, the artistry and imaginative design continues.

For many, Modernisme is synonymous with Gaudí (1852–1926), but he was by no means alone. Lluís Domènech i Montaner (1850–1923) and Josep Puig i Cadafalch (1867–1957) left a wealth of remarkable buildings across the city. The Rome-trained sculptor Eusebi Arnau (1864–1934) was one of the most popular figures called upon to decorate Barcelona's Modernista piles. The appearance of the Hospital de la Santa Creu i de Sant Pau is one of his legacies and he also had a hand in the Palau de la Música Catalana and Casa Amatller. For more information on Modernistas, particularly the celebrated works of Antoni Gaudí, see p146.

Modernista Master-pieces

La Pedrera (p131)

La Sagrada Família (p124)

Palau de la Música Catalana (p98)

Casa Batlló (p130)

Palau Güell (p83)

Casa Amatller (p129)

Hospital de la Santa Creu i de Sant Pau (p133)

ARCHITECTURE MODERNISME

Olympic & Contemporary Architecture

Barcelona's latest architectural revolution began in the 1980s. The appointment then of Oriol Bohigas, who was regarded as an elder statesman for architecture, as head of urban planning by the ruling Socialist party marked a new beginning. The city set about its biggest phase of renewal since the heady days of L'Eixample.

MODERNISME & CATALAN IDENTITY

Modernisme did not appear in isolation in Barcelona. To the British and French the style was art nouveau; to the Italians, Lo Stile Liberty; the Germans called it Jugendstil (Youth Style); and the Austrians, Sezession (Secession). Its vitality and rebelliousness can be summed up in those epithets: modern, new, liberty, youth and secession. A key uniting element was the sensuous curve, implying movement, lightness and vitality. It touched painting, sculpture and the decorative arts, as well as architecture. This leitmotif informed much art nouveau thinking, in part inspired by longstanding tenets of Japanese art.

There is something misleading about the name Modernisme. It suggests 'out with the old, in with the new'. In a sense, nothing could be further from the truth. From Gaudí down, Modernisme architects looked to the past for inspiration. Gothic, Islamic and Renaissance design all had something to offer. At its most playful, Modernisme was able to intelligently flout the rule books of these styles and create exciting new creations.

Aesthetics aside, the political associations are significant, as Modernisme became a means of expression for Catalan identity. It barely touched the rest of Spain; where it did, one frequently finds the involvement of Catalan architects. As many as 2000 buildings in Barcelona and throughout Catalonia display Modernista traces. Everything from rich bourgeois mansion blocks to churches, from hospitals to factories, went up in this 'style', a word too constraining to adequately describe the flamboyant breadth of eclecticism inherent in it.

The Olympic Games Building Boom

The biggest urban makeover in 100 years happened in the run-up to the 1992 Olympics, when more than 150 architects beavered away on almost 300 building and design projects. The city saw dramatic transformations, from the construction of huge arterial highways to the refurbishment of whole neighbourhoods in dire need of repair. In a rather crafty manoeuvre, the city government used national monies to fund urban improvements the capital would never normally have approved. Several kilometres of waterfront wasteland that included Port Vell was beautifully transformed into sparkling new beaches – suddenly Barcelona had prime beachfront real estate. The long road to resurrecting Montjuïc took off with the refurbishment of the Olympic stadium and the creation of landmarks like Santiago Calatrava's Torre Calatrava.

Post-1992, landmark buildings still went up in strategic spots, usually with the ulterior motive of trying to pull the surrounding area up by its bootstraps. One of the most emblematic of these projects is the gleaming white Museu d'Art Contemporani de Barcelona, better known as MACBA, which opened in 1995. The museum was designed by Richard Meier and incorporates the characteristic elements for which the American architect is so well known – the geometric minimalism, the pervasive use of all white with glass and steel – and remains much debated in architectural circles. '...Meier's building was unkind to the art, badly lit and spatially only barely coherent,' wrote the late art critic Robert Hughes.

More widely hailed, the Teatre Nacional de Catalunya, which opened in 1996, is a splendid blend of the neoclassical with the modern. Framed by 26 columns with a single gabled roof and grand entrance steps, the theatre takes the form of a Greek temple, though its all-glass exterior gives it a light and open appearance.

Henry Cobb's World Trade Center, at the tip of a quay jutting out into the waters of Port Vell, has been overshadowed by Ricardo Bofill's hotel, W Barcelona, whose spinnaker-like front looks out to sea from the south end of La Barceloneta's beach strip.

One of the first big projects of the 21st century occurred around Diagonal Mar. A whole district has been built in the northeast coastal corner of the city where before there was a void. High-rise apartments, waterfront office towers and five-star hotels – among them the eye-catching Hotel Me (completed in 2008) by Dominique Perrault – mark this new district. The hovering blue, triangular Edifici Fòrum by Swiss architects Herzog & de Meuron is the most striking landmark here, along with a gigantic photovoltaic panel that provides some of the area's electricity.

Much of the district was completed in 2004, though the area continues to evolve as new buildings are added to the mix. Among the most notable recent additions is a 24-storey whitewashed trapezoidal prism that serves as the headquarters for the national telephone company, Telefónica. Designed by Enric Massip-Bosch and dubbed the Torre ZeroZero, it has a deceivingly two-dimensional appearance upon initial approach. Shortly after its completion in 2011, the Torre was awarded the respected Leading European Architects Forum (LEAF) award for commercial building of the year.

Another prominent addition to the skyline came in 2005. The shimmering, cucumber-shaped Torre Agbar is a product of French architect Jean Nouvel, emblematic of the city's desire to make the developing hi-tech zone of 22@ a reality.

Southwest, on the way to the airport, the new Fira M2 trade fair along Gran Via de les Corts Catalanes is now marked by red twisting twin landmark towers (one the Santos Porta Fira Hotel, the other offices) designed by Japanese star architect and confessed Gaudí fan Toyo Ito.

The Arabs invented the ancient technique of *trencadís*, but Gaudí was the first architect to revive it. The procedure involves taking ceramic tiles or fragments of broken pottery or glass and creating a mosaic-like sheath on roofs, ceilings, chimneys, benches, sculptures or any other surface.

No one longs for the pre-Olympic days when the waterfront was a dangerous and polluted wasteland. However, some old timers still bemoan the loss of its old rickety restaurant shacks, which sat on stilts over the water and served delectable if utterly unfussy seafood.

The heart of La Ribera got a fresh look with its brand-new Mercat de Santa Caterina. The market is quite a sight, with its wavy ceramic roof and tubular skeleton, designed by one of the most promising names in Catalan architecture until his premature death, Enric Miralles. Miralles' Edifici de Gas Natural, a 100m glass tower near the waterfront in La Barceloneta, is extraordinary for its mirror-like surface and weirdly protruding adjunct buildings, which could be giant glass cliffs bursting from the main tower's flank.

The City of Tomorrow

Big projects are slowly unfolding around the city, although the continuing economic crisis has dramatically slowed the pace of construction. The redevelopment of the area near Plaça de les Glòries Catalanes is one of the latest projects underway, with the goal of revitalising the neighbourhood and making it a draw for tourism.

The centerpiece is the new Disseny Hub (which now houses Barcelona's design museum), a building completed in 2013 that incorporates sustainable features in its cantilevered, metal-sheathed building. Vaguely futuristic (though some say it looks like a stapler), it has a rather imposing, anvil-shaped presence over the neighbourhood.

Nearby, stands the Els Encants Vells ('the Old Charms' flea market), which was given a dramatic new look by local architecture firm b720 Fermín Vázquez Arquitectos. Traders now sell their wares beneath a giant, mirrored canopy, situated at geometric angles and held aloft with long, slender poles. It opened to much acclaim in 2013.

In a rather thoughtful bit of recycling, British architect Lord Richard Rogers transformed the former Les Arenes bullring on Plaça d'Espanya into a singular, circular leisure complex, with shops, cinemas and more, which opened in 2011. He did so while still maintaining its red-brick, 19th-century Moorish-looking facade. Perhaps its best feature is the rooftop with 360-degree views from the open-air promenade and cafes and restaurants.

In the *ciutata vela* (old city), El Raval continues to be the focal point for urban renewal. The Filmoteca de Catalunya is a hulking rather brutalist building of concrete and glass, with sharp angles. It was designed by Catalan architect Josep Lluís Mateo and completed in 2011. It sits near the Richard Meier-designed MACBA, which opened in 1995.

Best Contemporary Buildings

Torre Agbar

Teatre Nacional de Catalunya

Mercat de Santa Caterina

Edificio Fòrum

W Barcelona

Santos Porta Fira Hotel (Llobregat)

Les Arenes (Plaça d'Espanya)

ARCHITECTURE OLYMPIC & CONTEMPORARY ARCHITECTURE

Picasso, Miró & Dalí

Three of Spain's greatest 20th-century artists have deep connections to Barcelona. Picasso spent his formative years in the city and maintained lifelong friendships with Catalans. It was Picasso's own idea to create a museum of his works here. Joan Miró is one of Barcelona's most famous native sons. His instantly recognisable style can be seen in public installations throughout the city. Although Salvador Dalí is more commonly associated with Figueres, Barcelona was a great source of inspiration for him, particularly the fantastical architectural works of Antoni Gaudí.

Pablo Picasso

With *Les Demoiselles d'Avignon* (Ladies of Avignon; 1907), Picasso broke with all forms of traditional representation, introducing a deformed perspective that would later spill over into cubism. The subject was supposedly taken from the Carrer d'Avinyó in the Barri Gòtic, in those days populated with a series of brothels.

Born in Málaga in Andalucía, Pablo Ruiz Picasso (1881–1973) was already sketching by the age of nine. As a young boy, he lived briefly in La Coruña (in Galicia), before landing in Barcelona in 1895. His father had obtained a post teaching art at the Escola de Belles Artes de la Llotja (then housed in the stock exchange building) and had his son enrolled there too. It was in Barcelona and Catalonia that Picasso matured, spending his time ceaselessly drawing and painting.

After a stint at the Escuela de Bellas Artes de San Fernando in Madrid in 1897, Picasso spent six months with his friend Manuel Pallarès in bucolic Horta de Sant Joan, in western Catalonia – he would later claim that it was there he learned everything he knew. In Barcelona, Picasso lived and worked in the Barri Gòtic and El Raval (where he was introduced to the seamier side of life in the Barri Xinès).

By the time Picasso moved to France in 1904, he had explored his first highly personal style. In this so-called Blue Period, his canvases have a melancholy feel heightened by the trademark dominance of dark blues. Some of his portraits and cityscapes from this period were created in and inspired by what he saw in Barcelona. A number of pieces from this period hang in the Museu Picasso. By the mid-1920s, he was dabbling with surrealism. His best-known work is *Guernica* (in Madrid's Centro de Arte Reina Sofía), a complex painting portraying the horror of war, inspired by the German aerial bombing of the Basque town Gernika in 1937.

Picasso worked prolifically during and after WWII and he was still cranking out paintings, sculptures, ceramics and etchings until the day he died in 1973.

Joan Miró

By the time the 13-year-old Picasso arrived in Barcelona, his near contemporary, Joan Miró (1893–1983), was still learning to crawl in the Barri Gòtic, where he was born. He spent a third of his life in Barcelona but later divided his time between France, the Tarragona countryside and the island of Mallorca, where he ended his days.

Like Picasso, Miró attended the Escola de Belles Artes de la Llotja. He was initially uncertain about his artistic vocation – in fact he studied commerce. In Paris from 1920, he mixed with Picasso, Hemingway, Joyce and friends, and made his own mark, after several years of struggle,

ART ON THE STREETS

Barcelona hosts an array of street sculpture, from Miró's 1983 *Dona i Ocell*, in the park dedicated to the artist, to *Peix* (Fish), Frank Gehry's shimmering, bronze-coloured headless fish facing Port Olímpic. Halfway along La Rambla, at Plaça de la Boqueria, you can walk all over Miró's *Mosaïc de Miró*.

Picasso left an open-air mark with his design on the facade of the Col·legi Arquitectes opposite La Catedral in the Barri Gòtic. Other works include the *Barcelona Head* by Roy Lichtenstein at the Port Vell end of Via Laietana and Fernando Botero's tumescent *El Gat* on Rambla del Raval. Wander down to the Barceloneta seaside for a gander at Rebecca Horn's 1992 tribute to the old shacks that used to line the waterfront. The precarious stack is called *Homenatge a la Barceloneta* (Tribute to La Barceloneta). A little further south is the 2003 *Homenatge als Nedadors* (Tribute to the Swimmers), a complex metallic rendition of swimmers and divers in the water by Alfredo Lanz.

Heading a little further back in time, in 1983 Antoni Tàpies constructed *Homenatge a Picasso* on Passeig de Picasso; it's essentially a glass cube set in a pond and filled with, well, junk. Antoni Llena's *David i Goliat*, a massive sculpture of tubular and sheet iron, in the Parc de les Cascades near Port Olímpic's two skyscrapers, looks like an untidy kite inspired by Halloween. Beyond this Avinguda d'Icària is lined by architect Enric Miralles' so-called *Pergoles* – bizarre, twisted metal contraptions.

with an exhibition in 1925. The masterpiece from this, his so-called realist period, was *La Masia* (Farmhouse). It was during WWII, while living in seclusion in Normandy, that Miró's definitive leitmotifs emerged. Among the most important images that appear frequently throughout his work are women, birds (the link between earth and the heavens), stars (the unattainable heavenly world, the source of imagination), and a sort of net entrapping all these levels of the cosmos. The Miró works that most people are acquainted with emerged from this time – arrangements of lines and symbolic figures in primary colours, with shapes reduced to their essence. He lived in Mallorca, home of his wife Pilar Juncosa, from 1956 until his death in 1983.

Salvador Dalí

The great Catalan artist Salvador Dalí i Domènech (1904–89) was born and died in Figueres, where he left his single greatest artistic legacy, the Teatre-Museu Dalí. Although few of his famed works reside in Barcelona, the city provided a stimulating atmosphere for Dalí, and places like Park Güell, with its surrealist-like aspects, had a powerful effect on him. Prolific painter, showman, shameless self-promoter or just plain weirdo, Dalí was nothing if not a character – probably a little too much for the conservative small-town folk of Figueres.

The Fundació Joan Miró, housed in an extensive gallery atop Montjuïc, has the single largest collection of Miró's work in the world today.

Every now and then a key moment arrives that can change the course of one's life. Dalí's came in 1929, when the French poet Paul Éluard visited Cadaqués with his Russian wife, Gala. The rest, as they say, is histrionics. Dalí shot off to Paris to be with Gala and plunged into the world of surrealism. In the 1930s Salvador and Gala returned to live at Port Lligat on the north Catalan coast, where they played host to a long list of fashionable and art-world guests until the war years – the parties were by all accounts memorable. They started again in Port Lligat in the 1950s. The stories of sexual romps and Gala's appetite for young local boys are legendary. The 1960s saw Dalí painting pictures on a grand scale, including his 1962 reinterpretation of Marià Fortuny's *Batalla de Tetuán*. On his death in 1989, he was buried (according to his own wish) in the Teatre-Museu he had created on the site of the old theatre in central Figueres, which also houses an awe-inspiring Dalí collection.

Music & Dance

Barcelona's vibrant music and dance scene has been shaped by artists both tradi-tional and cutting edge. From Nova Cançó, composed during the dark years of the dictatorship, to the hybridised Catalan rumba to hands-in-the air rock ballads of the 1970s and '80s, Barcelona's music evolves constantly. Today's groups continue to push musical boundaries, blending rhythms from all corners of the globe. In the realm of dance, flamenco has a small loyal following, while the old-fashioned folk dance *sardana* continues to attract growing numbers.

Contemporary Music

Around the same time Nova Cançó singers were taking aim at the Franco regime, folk singers from Latin America were decry-ing their own corrupt military dictatorships. Songs by Victor Jara of Chile, Mercedes Sosa of Argentina and Chico Buarque of Brazil helped unite people in the fight against oppression.

Nova Cançó

Curiously, it was probably the Franco repression that most helped foster a vigorous local music scene in Catalan. In the dark 1950s the Nova Cançó (New Song) movement was born to resist linguistic oppression with music in Catalan (getting air time on the radio was long close to impossible), throwing up stars that in some cases won huge popularity throughout Spain, such as the Valencia-born Raimon. More specifically loved in Cata-lonia as a Bob Dylan–style 1960s protest singer-songwriter was Lluís Llach, much of whose music was more or less anti-regime. Joan Manuel Serrat is another legendary figure. His appeal stretches from Barcelona to Buenos Aires. Born in the Poble Sec district, this poet-singer is equally at ease in Catalan and Spanish. He has repeatedly shown that record sales are not everything to him. In 1968 he refused to represent Spain at the Eurovision song contest if he were not allowed to sing in Catalan. Accused of being anti-Spanish, he was long banned from performing in Spain.

Born in Mallorca, the talented singer Maria del Mar Bonet arrived in Barcelona in 1967, and embarked on a long and celebrated singing career. She sang in Catalan, and many of her searing and powerful songs were banned by the dictatorship. On concert tours abroad, she attracted world-wide attention, and she has performed with distinguished groups and solo-ists across the globe.

Rock Català

A specifically local strand of rock has emerged since the 1980s. Rock Català (Catalan rock) is not essentially different from rock anywhere else, except that it is sung in Catalan by local bands that appeal to local tastes. Among the most popular groups of years past include Sau, Els Pets, Lax'n Busto and the Valenciano band, Obrint Pas.

The Pinker Tones are a Barcelona duo that attained international suc-cess with an eclectic electronic mix of music, ranging from dizzy dance numbers to film soundtracks. Another Barcelona band with international ambitions and flavours is Macaco, a group that sings in different languages – Catalan, Spanish (Castilian), English and Portuguese among others – and blends Latin rhythms and electronica in their rock anthems. When people talk about 'Raval sound' (after the name of the still somewhat seedy old-city district), this is the kind of thing they mean.

RETURN OF LA RUMBA

Back in the 1950s, a new sound mixing flamenco with salsa and other Latin sounds emerged in *gitano* (Roma people) circles in the bars of Gràcia and the Barri Gòtic. One of the founders of rumba Catalana was Antonio González, known as El Pescaílla (married to the flamenco star Lola Flores). Although he was well-known in town, the Mataró-born *gitano* Peret later took this eminently Barcelona style to a wider (eventually international) audience. By the end of the 1970s, however, rumba Catalana was running out of steam. Peret had turned to religion and El Pescaílla lived in Flores' shadow in Madrid. But Buenos Aires–born Javier Patricio 'Gato' Pérez discovered rumba in 1977 and gave it his own personal spin, bringing out several popular records, such as *Atalaya*, until the early 1980s. After Pérez, it seemed that rumba was dead. Not so fast! New rumba bands, often highly eclectic, have emerged in recent years. Ai Ai Ai, Barrio Negro, El Tío Carlos and La Pegatina are names to look out for.

Far greater success across Spain has gone to Estopa, a male rock duo from Cornellà, a satellite suburb of Barcelona. The guitar-wielding brothers sing a clean Spanish rock, occasionally with a vaguely flamenco flavour. Along the same vein, the Barcelona hit trio Pastora peddles a successful brand of Spanish pop, mixing electric sounds with a strong acoustic element. Hailing from Barcelona, Mishima is an indie pop band which has recorded a mix of albums in English and Catalan. They remained largely obscure prior to the release of their 2007 album *Set tota la vida,* which earned accolades across the music industry.

Born in El Raval, Cabo San Roque is an even more experimental group, incorporating huge soundscapes, powerful rhythms and mechanical accents often using nontraditional John Cage–style instruments in their avant-garde performances. In one show, the five-person group shared the stage with a polyphonic washing machine powered by a bicycle chain.

Another key name on El Raval's scene is 08001 (which is El Raval's postcode). This ever-evolving collective brings together musicians from all across the globe, fusing unusual sounds from hip-hop, flamenco, reggae and rock to styles from Morocco, West Africa, the Caribbean and beyond. *No Pain no Gain* (2013) is the latest album of 08001.

Classical, Opera & Baroque

Spain's contribution to the world of classical music has been modest, but Catalonia has produced a few exceptional composers. Best known is Camprodon-born Isaac Albéniz (1860–1909), a gifted pianist who later turned his hand to composition. Among his best-remembered works is the *Iberia* cycle. Montserrat Caballé is Barcelona's most successful voice. Born in Gràcia in 1933, the soprano made her debut in 1956 in Basel (Switzerland). Her hometown launch came four years later in the Gran Teatre del Liceu. In 1965 she performed to wild acclaim at New York's Carnegie Hall and went on to become one of the world's finest 20th-century sopranos. Her daughter, Montserrat Martí, is also a singer and they occasionally appear together. Another fine Catalan soprano was Victoria de los Ángeles (1923–2005), while Catalonia's other world-class opera star is the renowned tenor Josep (José) Carreras.

Jordi Savall has assumed the task of rediscovering a European heritage in music that predates the era of the classical greats. He and his late wife, soprano Montserrat Figueras, have, along with musicians from other countries, been largely responsible for resuscitating the beauties of medieval, Renaissance and baroque music. In 1987 Savall founded La Capella Reial de Catalunya and two years later he formed

PAU CASALS

Born in Catalonia, Pau Casals (1876–1973) was one of the greatest cellists of the 20th century. Living in exile in southern France, he declared he would not play in public as long as the Western democracies continued to tolerate Franco's regime. In 1958 he was a candidate for the Nobel Peace Prize.

LONGING FOR CUBA

The oldest musical tradition to have survived to some degree in Catalonia is that of the *havaneres* (from Havana) – nostalgic songs and melancholy sea shanties brought back from Cuba by Catalans who lived, sailed and traded there in the 19th century. Even after Spain lost Cuba in 1898, the *havanera* tradition (a mix of European and Cuban rhythms) continued. A magical opportunity to enjoy these songs is the Cantada d'Havaneres (www.havanerescalella.cat, in Catalan), an evening concert held on the Costa Brava in early July. Otherwise, you may stumble across performances elsewhere along the coast or even in Barcelona, but there is no set program.

---

the baroque orchestra Le Concert des Nations. You can sometimes catch their recitals in locations such as the Gran Teatre del Liceu or the Basílica de Santa Maria del Mar.

Dance

Flamenco

For those who think that the passion of flamenco is the preserve of the south, think again. The *gitanos* (Roma people) get around, and some of the big names of the genre come from Catalonia. They were already in Catalonia long before the massive migrations from the south of the 1960s, but with these waves came an exponential growth in flamenco bars as Andalucians sought to recreate a little bit of home.

First and foremost, one of the greatest *bailaoras* (flamenco dancers) of all time, Carmen Amaya (1913–63) was born in what is now Port Olímpic. She danced to her father's guitar in the streets and bars around La Rambla in pre–civil war years. Much to the bemusement of purists from the south, not a few flamenco stars today have at least trained in flamenco schools in Barcelona – dancers Antonio Canales and Joaquín Cortés are among them. Other Catalan stars of flamenco include *cantaores* (singers) Juan Cortés Duquende and Miguel Poveda, a boy from Badalona. He took an original step in 2005 by releasing a flamenco album, *Desglaç*, in Catalan. Another interesting flamenco voice in Catalonia is Ginesa Ortega Cortés, actually born in France. She masters traditional genres ably but loves to experiment. In her 2002 album, *Por los espejos del agua* (Through the Water's Mirrors), she does a reggae version of flamenco and she has sung flamenco versions of songs by Joan Manuel Serrat and Billie Holiday.

An exciting combo formed in Barcelona in 1996: the seven-man, one-woman group Ojos de Brujo (Wizard's Eyes), which melded flamenco and rumba with rap, ragga and electronic music. Unfortunately, the band split up in 2013, with lead singer Marina setting off to pursue a solo career as 'Marinah'.

Sardana

The Catalan dance *par excellence* is the *sardana,* whose roots lie in the far northern Empordà region of Catalonia. Compared with flamenco, it is sober indeed but not unlike a lot of other Mediterranean folk dances.

The dancers hold hands in a circle and wait for the 10 or so musicians to begin. The performance starts with the piping of the *flabiol,* a little wooden flute. When the other musicians join in, the dancers start – a series of steps to the right, one back and then the same to the left. As the music 'heats up' the steps become more complex, the leaps are higher and the dancers lift their arms. Then they return to the initial steps and continue. If newcomers wish to join in, space is made for them as the dance continues and the whole thing proceeds in a more or less seamless fashion.

Top Albums

Techari, Ojos de Brujo

Anells d'Aigua, Maria del Mar Bonet

Verges 50, Lluís Llach

Wild Animals, Pinker Tones

Set tota la vida, Mishima

Voràgine, 08001

Rey de la rumba, Peret

X anniversarium, Estopa

Survival Guide

Transport

ARRIVING IN BARCELONA

Most travellers enter Barcelona through El Prat airport. Some budget airlines use Girona-Costa Brava airport or Reus airport.

Flights from North America take about eight hours from the east coast (10 to 13 hours typically, with a stopover); from the west coast count on 13 or more hours including a stopover. Flights from London take around two hours; from Western Europe it's about two to three hours.

Travelling by train is a pricier but perhaps more romantic way of reaching Catalonia from other European cities. The new TGV takes around around seven hours from Paris to Barcelona. Long-distance trains arrive in Estació Sants, about 2.5km west of La Rambla.

Long-haul buses arrive in Estació del Nord.

Flights, tours and rail tickets can be booked online at lonelyplanet.com.

El Prat Airport

Barcelona's **El Prat airport** (☑902 404704; www.aena.es) lies 17km southwest of Plaça de Catalunya at El Prat de Llobregat. The airport has two main terminal buildings: the new T1 terminal and the older T2, itself divided into three terminal areas (A, B and C).

In T1, the main arrivals area is on the 1st floor (with separate areas for EU Schengen Area arrivals, non-EU international arrivals and the Barcelona–Madrid corridor). Boarding gates for departures are on the 1st and 3rd floors.

The main **tourist office** (☉8.30am-8.30pm) is on the ground floor of Terminal 2B. Others on the ground floor of Terminal 2A and in Terminal 1 operate the same hours. Lockers (which come in three sizes) can be found on the 1st floor of Terminal 1. Lost-luggage offices can be found by the arrivals belts in Terminal 1 and on the arrivals floor in Terminals 2A and 2B.

Bus

The **A1 Aerobús** (Map p302; ☑902 100104; www.aerobusbcn.com; one way/return €5.90/10.20) runs from Terminal 1 to Plaça de Catalunya (30 to 40 minutes depending on traffic) via Plaça d'Espanya, Gran Via de les Corts Catalanes (corner of Carrer del Comte d'Urgell) and Plaça de la Universitat every five to 10 minutes from 6.10am to 1.05am. Departures from Plaça de Catalunya are from 5.30am to 12.30am and stop at the corner of Carrer de Sepúlveda and Carrer del Comte d'Urgell, and at Plaça d'Espanya.

The A2 Aerobús from Terminal 2 (stops outside ter-

CLIMATE CHANGE & TRAVEL

Every form of transport that relies on carbon-based fuel generates CO_2, the main cause of human-induced climate change. Modern travel is dependent on aeroplanes, which might use less fuel per kilometre per person than most cars but travel much greater distances. The altitude at which aircraft emit gases (including CO_2) and particles also contributes to their climate change impact. Many websites offer 'carbon calculators' that allow people to estimate the carbon emissions generated by their journey and, for those who wish to do so, to offset the impact of the greenhouse gases emitted with contributions to portfolios of climate-friendly initiatives throughout the world. Lonely Planet offsets the carbon footprint of all staff and author travel.

minal areas A, B and C) runs from 6am to 1am with a frequency of between 10 and 20 minutes and follows the same route as the A1 Aerobús.

Buy tickets on the bus or from agents at the bus stop. Considerably slower local buses (such as the No 46 to/from Plaça d'Espanya and a night bus, the N17, to/from Plaça de Catalunya) also serve Terminals 1 and 2.

Mon-Bus (www.monbus. cat) has regular direct buses (which originate in central Barcelona) between Terminal 1 only and Sitges (€4). In Sitges you can catch it at Avinguda de Vilanova 14. The trip takes about 40 minutes and runs hourly.

Alsa (☎902 422242; www. alsa.es) runs the Aerobús Rápid service several times daily from El Prat airport to various cities including Girona, Figueres, Lleida, Reus and Tarragona. Fares range from €8/15 one way/return to Tarragona and up to €28/50 one way/return to Lleida.

Plana (☎977 553680; www. busplana.com) has services between the airport and Reus (one way/return €15/27), stopping at Tarragona, Port Aventura and other southwest coastal destinations nearby along the way.

Train

Train operator Renfe runs the R2 Nord line every halfhour from the airport (from 5.42am to 11.38pm) via several stops to Barcelona's main train station, **Estació Sants** (Plaça dels Països Catalans; ⓂEstació Sants), and Passeig de Gràcia in central Barcelona, after which it heads northwest out of the city. The first service from Passeig de Gràcia leaves at 5.08am and the last at 11.07pm, and about five minutes later from Estació Sants. The trip between the airport and Passeig de Gràcia takes 25 minutes. A one-way ticket costs €4.10.

The airport train station is about a five-minute walk from Terminal 2. Regular shuttle buses run from the station and Terminal 2 to Terminal 1 – allow an extra 15 to 20 minutes.

Taxi

A taxi between either terminal and the city centre – about a half-hour ride depending on traffic – costs around €25. Fares and charges are posted inside the passenger side of the taxi – make sure the meter is used.

Girona-Costa Brava Airport

Girona-Costa Brava airport (☎902 404704; www. aena.es) is 12km south of Girona and 92km northeast of Barcelona. You'll find a tourist office, ATMs and lost-luggage desks on the ground floor.

Regular **Renfe** (☎902 320320; www.renfe.es) train services run between Girona and Barcelona (€8.40 to €11.25, around 1½ hours). Speedier Avant trains get there in 38 minutes (one way €16).

Sagalés (☎902 130014; www.sagales.com) runs hourly bus services from Girona-Costa Brava airport to Girona's main bus/train station (€2.75, 30 minutes) in connection with flights. The same company runs direct **Barcelona Bus** (Map p294; ☎902 130014; www.barcelonabus.com) services to/from **Estació del Nord** (Map p294; ☎902 260606; www.barcelonanord. cat; Carrer d'Ali Bei 80; ⓂArc de Triomf) bus station in Barcelona (one way/return €16/25, 75 minutes).

A taxi ride into Girona from the airport costs €20 to €26. To Barcelona you would pay around €140.

Reus Airport

Reus airport (☎902 404704; www.aena.es) is 13km west of Tarragona and 108km southwest of Barcelona. The tourist office and lost-luggage desks are in the main terminal building.

Hispano-Igualadina (Map p302; ☎902 292900; www.igualadina.net; Estació Sants) buses run between Reus airport and **Estació d'Autobusos de Sants** (Map p302; Carrer de Viriat; ⓂEstació Sants) to meet flights (one way €16, 1½ hours). Local bus 50 (www. reustransit.cat) serves central Reus (€3, 20 minutes) and other buses run to local coastal destinations.

Estació Sants

The main train station in Barcelona is **Estació Sants** (Plaça dels Països Catalans; ⓂEstació Sants), located 2.5km west of La Rambla. Direct overnight trains from Paris, Geneva, Milan and Zurich arrive here. From here it's a short metro ride to the Ciutat Vella or L'Eixample.

Estació Sants has a tourist office, a telephone and fax office, currency exchange booths open between 8am and 10pm, ATMs and leftluggage lockers.

Estació del Nord

Long-distance buses leave from **Estació del Nord** (Map p294; ☎902 260606; www.barcelonanord.cat; Carrer d'Ali Bei 80; ⓂArc de Triomf). A plethora of companies operates to different parts of Spain, although many come under the umbrella of **Alsa** (☎902 422242; www.alsa.es). For other companies, ask at the bus station.

There are frequent services to Madrid, Valencia and Zaragoza (20 or more a day) and several daily departures to distant destinations such as Burgos, Santiago de Compostela and Seville.

Eurolines (www. eurolines.es), in conjunction with local carriers all over Europe, is the main international carrier. Its website provides links to national operators; it runs services across Europe and to Morocco from Estació del Nord, and Estació d'Autobusos de Sants, next to Estació Sants in Barcelona. Another carrier is **Linebús** (www.linebus.com).

GETTING AROUND BARCELONA

Barcelona has abundant options for getting around town. The excellent metro can get you most places, with buses and trams filling in the gaps. Taxis are the best option late at night.

Metro

The easy-to-use **TMB Metro** (☑010; www.tmb.net) system has 11 numbered and colour-coded lines. It runs from 5am to midnight Sunday to Thursday and holidays, from 5am to 2am on Friday and days immediately preceding holidays, and 24 hours on Saturday.

Ongoing work to expand the metro continues on several lines. Lines 9 and 10 will eventually connect with the airport (2016 at the earliest).

Suburban trains run by the **Ferrocarrils de la Generalitat de Catalunya** (FGC; ☑93 205 15 15; www.fgc.net) include a couple of useful city lines. All lines heading north from Plaça de Catalunya stop at Carrer de Provença and Gràcia. One of these lines (L7) goes to Tibidabo and another (L6 to Reina Elisenda) has a stop near the Monestir de Pedralbes. Most trains from Plaça de Catalunya continue beyond Barcelona to Sant Cugat, Sabadell and Terrassa. Other FGC lines head west from Plaça d'Espanya, including one for Manresa that is handy for the trip to Montserrat.

Depending on the line, these trains run from about 5am (with only one or two services before 6am) to 11pm or midnight Sunday to Thursday, and from 5am to about 1am on Friday and Saturday.

Bus

Transports Metropolitans de Barcelona (TMB; ☑010; www.tmb.net) buses run along most city routes every few minutes between 5am and 6.30am to between around 10pm and 11pm. Many routes pass through Plaça de Catalunya and/or Plaça de la Universitat. After 11pm a reduced network of yellow *nitbusos* (night buses) runs until 3am or 5am. All *nitbus* routes pass through Plaça de Catalunya and most run every 30 to 45 minutes.

Taxi

Taxis charge €2.10 flag fall plus meter charges of €1.03 per kilometre (€1.30 from 8pm to 8am and all day on weekends). A further €3.10 is added for all trips to/from the airport, and €1 for luggage bigger than 55cm x 35cm x 35cm. The trip from Estació Sants to Plaça de Catalunya, about 3km, costs about €11. You can flag a taxi down in the streets or call one:

Fonotaxi (☑93 300 11 00)

Radio Taxi Barcelona (☑902 222111, 93 293 31 11)

Radio Taxi BCN (☑93 225 00 00; www.radiotaxibcn.org)

The call-out charge is €3.40 (€4.20 at night and on weekends). In many taxis it is possible to pay with a credit card and, if you have a local telephone number, you can join the T033 Ràdio taxi service for booking taxis online (www.radiotaxi033.com, in Spanish). You can also book online at www.catalunyataxi.com.

TICKETS & TARGETES

The metro, FGC trains, *rodalies/cercanías* (Renfe-run local trains) and buses come under one zoned-fare regime. Single-ride tickets on all standard transport within Zone 1 cost €2.15.

Targetes are multitrip transport tickets. They are sold at all city-centre metro stations. The prices given here are for travel in Zone 1. Children under four years of age travel free. Options include the following:

➡ Targeta T-10 (€10.30) – 10 rides (each valid for 1¼ hours) on the metro, buses, FGC trains and *rodalies*. You can change between metro, FGC, *rodalies* and buses.

➡ Targeta T-DIA (€7.60) – unlimited travel on all transport for one day.

➡ Two-/three-/four-/five-day tickets (€14/20/25.50/30.50) – unlimited travel on all transport except the Aerobús; buy them at metro stations and tourist offices.

➡ T-Mes (€52.75) – 30 days' unlimited use of all public transport.

➡ Targeta T-50/30 (€42.50) – 50 trips within 30 days, valid on all transport.

➡ T-Trimestre (€142) – 90 days' unlimited use of all public transport.

Taxi Amic (📞93 420 80 88; http://rtljtic.wix.com/taxiamic) is a special taxi service for people with disabilities or difficult situations (such as transport of big objects). Book at least 24 hours in advance if possible.

Women passengers who feel safer with taxis driven by women can order one on the **Línea Rosa** (📞93 330 07 00; www.servitaxi.com).

Tram

TMB (📞902 193215; www.trambcn.com) runs three tram lines (T1, T2 and T3) into the suburbs of greater Barcelona from Plaça de Francesc Macià and is of limited interest to visitors. The T4 line runs from behind the zoo (near the Ciutadella Vila Olímpica metro stop) to Sant Adrià via Glòries and the Fòrum. The T5 line runs from Glòries to Badalona (Gorg stop). The T6 runs between Badalona (Gorg) and Sant Adrià. All standard transport passes are valid. A more scenic option is *tram blau* (blue tram), which runs up to the foot of Tibidabo.

Cable Car

Several aerial cable cars operate in Barcelona and provide great views over the city. The **Transbordador Aeri** (Map p286; www.telefericodebarcelona.com; Passeig Escullera; one way/return €11/16.50; ⏰11am-7pm; 🚌17, 39 or 64, Ⓜ Barceloneta) travels between the waterfront southwest of Barceloneta and Montjuïc. The two-stage **Telefèric de Montjuïc** (return €10.80; ⏰10am-9pm) runs between Estació Parc Montjuïc and the Castell de Montjuïc.

Bicycle

Over 180km of bike lanes have been laid out across the city, so it's possible to commute on two environmentally friendly wheels. A waterfront path runs northeast from Port Olímpic towards Riu Besòs. Scenic itineraries are mapped for cyclists in the Collserola parkland, and the *ronda verda* is an incomplete 75km cycling path that extends around the city's outskirts. You can cycle a well-signed 22km loop path (part of the *ronda verda*) by following the seaside bike path northeast of Barceloneta.

You can transport your bicycle on the metro on weekdays (except between 7am and 9.30am or 5pm and 8.30pm). On weekends and holidays, and during July and August, there are no restrictions. You can use FGC trains to carry your bike at any time and Renfe's *rodalies* trains from 10am to 3pm on weekdays and all day on weekends and holidays.

Hire

Countless companies around town offer bicycles (including tandems and tricycle carts). They include the following:

BarcelonaBiking.com (Map p276; 📞656 356300; www.barcelonabiking.com; Baixada de Sant Miquel 6; bike hire per hr/24hr €5/15, tour €21; ⏰10am-8pm, tour 11am daily; Ⓜ Jaume I or Liceu)

Biciclot (Map p286; 📞93 221 97 78; bikinginbarcelona.net; Passeig Marítim de la Barceloneta 33; bike hire per hr/day €5/17; ⏰11am-6pm Mon-Fri, 10am-8pm Sat & Sun; Ⓜ Ciutadella Vila Olímpica)

Fat Tire Bike Tours (Map p276; 📞93 342 92 75; http://fattirebiketours.com; Carrer Sant Honorat 7; bike hire per hr/half-day €3/8, tour €24; ⏰10am-8pm; Ⓜ Jaume I or Liceu)

My Beautiful Parking (Map p284; 📞93 186 73 65; www.mybeautifulparking.com; Carrer Viagatans 2; bike hire per 2hr/24hr €6/15; ⏰10am-9pm Mon-Sat; Ⓜ Jaume I or Liceu)

Rent Electric (📞902 474474; www.rentelectric.com; Plaça del Mar 1; bike hire per 2/4hr €8/12; ⏰10am-7pm; Ⓜ Barceloneta)

Un Cotxe Menys (📞93 268 21 05; www.bicicletabarcelona.com; Carrer de l'Esparteria 3; bike hire per hr/day/week €5/15/55; ⏰10am-7pm; Ⓜ Jaume I)

Car & Motorcycle

With the convenience of public transport and the high price of parking in the city, it's unwise to drive in Barcelona. However, if you're planning a road trip outside the city, a car is handy .

Hire

Avis, Europcar, National/Atesa and Hertz have desks at El Prat airport, Estació Sants and Estació del Nord. Rental outlets in Barcelona include the following:

Avis (📞902 110275; www.avis.com; Carrer de Còrsega 293-295; Ⓜ Diagonal)

Cooltra (📞93 221 40 70; www.cooltra.com; Passeig de Joan de Borbó 80-84; Ⓜ Barceloneta) You can rent scooters here for around €35 (plus insurance). Cooltra also organises scooter tours.

Europcar (📞93 302 05 43; www.europcar.com; Gran Via de les Corts Catalanes 680; Ⓜ Girona)

Hertz (📞902 998707; www.hertz.com; Carrer del Viriat 45; Ⓜ Sants)

MondoRent (📞93 295 32 68; www.mondorent.com; Passeig de Joan de Borbó 80-84; Ⓜ Barceloneta) Rents scooters (including stylish Vespas) as well as electric bikes.

National/Atesa (📞93 323 07 01; www.atesa.es; Carrer de Muntaner 45; Ⓜ Universitat)

Directory A–Z

Discount Cards

The **ISIC** (International Student Identity Card; www.isic.org) and the **European Youth Card** (www.euro26.org) are available from most national student organisations and allow discounted access to some sights. Students generally pay a little more than half of adult admission prices, as do children aged under 12 and senior citizens (aged 65 and over) with appropriate ID.

Possession of a **Bus Turístic** (☑93 285 38 32; www.barcelonabusturistic.cat/en; day ticket adult/child €27/16; ☉9am-8pm) ticket entitles you to discounts at some museums.

Articket (www.articketbcn.org; per person €30) gives admission to the following six sights for €30 and is valid for six months. You can pick up the ticket at the tourist offices at Plaça de Catalunya, Plaça de Sant Jaume and Estació Sants train station.

➡ Museu Picasso
➡ Museu Nacional d'Art de Catalunya (MNAC)
➡ Museu d'Art Contemporani de Barcelona (MACBA)
➡ Fundació Antoni Tàpies
➡ Centre de Cultura Contemporània de Barcelona (CCCB)
➡ Fundació Joan Miró

Arqueoticket is for those with a special interest in archaeology and ancient history. The ticket (€13) is available from participating museums and tourist offices and grants free admission to the following sights:

➡ Museu Marítim
➡ Museu d'Història de la Ciutat
➡ Museu d'Arqueologia de Catalunya (MAC)
➡ Museu Egipci

Barcelona Card (www.barcelonacard.com) is handy if you want to see lots in a limited time. It costs €34/44/52/58 for two/three/four/five days. You get free transport (and 20% off the Aerobús), and discounted admission prices (up to 30% off) or free entry to many museums and other sights, as well as minor discounts on purchases at a small number of shops, restaurants and bars. The card costs about 50% less for children aged four to 12. You can purchase it at tourist offices and online (buying online saves you 10%).

The **Ruta del Modernisme** (www.rutadelmodernisme.com; €12) pack is well worth looking into for visiting Modernista sights at discounted rates.

Electricity

Spain uses 220V, 50Hz, like the rest of continental Europe.

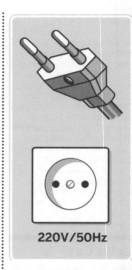

220V/50Hz

Emergency

The following are the main emergency numbers:

Ambulance (☑061)
Catalan police (Mossos d'Esquadra;☑088)
EU standard emergency number (☑112)
Fire brigade (Bombers; ☑080, 085)
Guardia Civil (Civil Guard; ☑062)
Guardia Urbana (Local Police;☑092; La Rambla 43; Ⓜ Liceu)
Policía Nacional (National Police;☑091)

Tourist Police (☑93 256 24 30; La Rambla 43; ⊘24hr; ⓂLiceu)

Internet Access

In an increasingly wired city (where many folks have smartphones or web-enabled devices), internet cafes are a disappearing breed. Aside from an internet cafe, look also for *Locutorios* (public phone centres), which often double as internet centres.

Bornet (☑93 268 15 07; Carrer Barra de Ferro 3; per 15min/hr €1/2.80; ⊘11am-midnight Mon-Thu, to 2.30am Fri-Sun; ⓂJaume I) A cool little internet centre and art gallery.

Medical Services

All foreigners have the same right as Spaniards to emergency medical treatment in public hospitals. EU citizens are entitled to the full range of health-care services in public hospitals, but must present a European Health Insurance Card (enquire at your national health service) and may have to pay upfront.

Non-EU citizens have to pay for anything other than emergency treatment. Most travel-insurance policies include medical cover.

For minor health problems you can try any *farmàcia* (pharmacy), where pharmaceuticals tend to be sold more freely without prescription than in places such as the USA, Australia or the UK.

If your country has a consulate in Barcelona, its staff should be able to refer you to doctors who speak your language. Hospitals include the following:

Hospital Clínic i Provincial (☑93 227 54 00; Carrer de Villarroel 170; ⓂHospital Clínic)

Hospital Dos de Maig (☑93 507 27 00; Carrer del Dos de Maig 301; ⓂSant Pau–Dos de Maig)

WI-FI ACCESS

Most hotels, hostels, guesthouses and apartment rentals offer their guests wi-fi access (not always for free). A growing array of city bars and restaurants are latching on to the service – look for the black-and-white wi-fi signs.

The city also has dozens of free public wi-fi hotspots. Look for the small blue signs with the blue 'W' symbol. You can find a complete list of sites here: www.bcn.cat/barcelonawifi/en.

Places in this guide that offer wi-fi have the symbol 🛜.

Some 24-hour pharmacies:

Farmàcia Castells Soler (Passeig de Gràcia 90; ⊘24hr; ⓂDiagonal)

Farmàcia Clapés (La Rambla 98; ⊘24hr; ⓂLiceu)

Farmàcia Torres (www.farmaciaabierta24h.com; Carrer d'Aribau 62; ⊘24hr; ⒭FGC Provença)

Money
ATMS

Barcelona abounds with banks, many of which have ATMs. ATMs are also in plentiful supply around Plaça de Catalunya, Plaça de Sant Jaume (in the Barri Gòtic) and La Rambla.

Changing Money

You can change cash or travellers cheques in most major currencies without problems at virtually any bank or *bureau de change* (usually indicated by the word *canvi/cambio*).

The foreign-exchange offices that you see along La Rambla and elsewhere are open for longer hours than banks, but they generally offer poorer rates. Also, keep a sharp eye open for commissions at *bureaux de change*.

Credit Cards

Major cards such as Visa, MasterCard, Maestro and Cirrus are accepted throughout Spain. They can be used in many hotels, restaurants and shops. If your card is lost, stolen or swallowed by an ATM, you can telephone toll free to immediately stop its use:

Amex (☑902 375637)
Diners Club (☑900 801331)
MasterCard (☑900 971231)
Visa (☑900 991124)

Travellers Cheques & Moneycards

Travellers cheques are far less convenient than simply using bank cards at ATMs. If you do opt for this old-school option, Amex and Visa are widely accepted brands. For lost cheques, call a **24-hour freephone number** (for Amex ☑900 810029, for Visa ☑900 948978).

The **Travelex Cash Passport** (www.travelex.com) and **Thomas Cook Travel Moneycard** (www.thomascookmoney.com) are prepaid cards. You can load funds onto them before you travel and use them like any card in ATMs, restaurants or shops worldwide.

Opening Hours

Standard opening hours are as follows:

Restaurants lunch 1pm to 4pm, dinner 8.30pm to midnight

Shops 9am or 10am to 1.30pm or 2pm and 4pm or 4.30pm to 8pm or 8.30pm Monday to Saturday

Department stores 10am to 10pm Monday to Saturday

Bars 6pm to 2am (closing at 3am on weekends)

Clubs midnight to 6am Thursday to Saturday

Banks 8.30am to 2pm Monday to Friday; some also 4pm to 7pm Thursday or 9am to 1pm Saturday

Museums & art galleries Opening hours vary considerably, but generally fall between 10am and 8pm (some shut for lunch from around 2pm to 4pm). Many museums and galleries are closed all day on Monday and from 2pm on Sunday

Post

Correos is Spain's national postal service. Barcelona's **main post office** (Map p276; Plaça d'Antoni López; ⊙8.30am-9.30pm Mon-Fri, to 2pm Sat; Ⓜ Jaume I) is a lovely fresco-filled building just opposite the northeast end of Port Vell at Plaça d'Antoni López.

Another handy **post office branch** (Map p290; Carrer d'Aragó 282; ⊙8.30am-8.30pm Mon-Fri, 9.30am-1pm Sat; Ⓜ Passeig de Gràcia) lies just off Passeig de Gràcia at Carrer d'Aragó 282. Many other branches tend to open between 8.30am and 2.30pm Monday to Friday and from 9.30am to 1pm on Saturday.

Segells/sellos (stamps) are sold at most *estancos* (tobacconists' shops) and at post offices throughout the city.

Public Holidays

New Year's Day (Any Nou/Año Nuevo) 1 January

Epiphany/Three Kings' Day (Epifanía or El Dia dels Reis/Día de los Reyes Magos) 6 January

Good Friday (Divendres Sant/Viernes Santo) March/April

Easter Monday (Dilluns de Pasqua Florida) March/April

Labour Day (Dia del Treball/Fiesta del Trabajo) 1 May

Day after Pentecost Sunday (Dilluns de Pasqua Granda) May/June

Feast of St John the Baptist (Dia de Sant Joan/Día de San Juan Bautista) 24 June

Feast of the Assumption (L'Assumpció/La Asunción) 15 August

Catalonia's National Day (Diada Nacional de Catalunya) 11 September

Festes de la Mercè 24 September

Spanish National Day (Festa de la Hispanitat/Día de la Hispanidad) 12 October

All Saints Day (Dia de Tots Sants/Día de Todos los Santos) 1 November

Constitution Day (Día de la Constitución) 6 December

Feast of the Immaculate Conception (La Immaculada Concepció/La Inmaculada Concepción) 8 December

Christmas (Nadal/Navidad) 25 December

Boxing Day/St Stephen's Day (El Dia de Sant Esteve) 26 December

Safe Travel

It cannot be stressed enough that newcomers to Barcelona must be on their guard. Petty theft is a problem in the city centre, on public transport and around main sights. Report thefts to the **tourist police** (☎93 256 24 30; La Rambla 43; ⊙24hr; Ⓜ Liceu) office on La Rambla. You are unlikely to recover your goods but you will need to make this formal *denuncia* (police report) for insurance purposes. To avoid endless queues at the *comisaría* (police station), you can make the report by phone (☎902 102112) in various languages. The following day you go to the station of your choice to pick up and sign the report (for a list of *comisarías*, go to the website www.policia.es under 'Denuncias').

Taxes & Refunds

Value-added tax (VAT) is also known as IVA (*impuesto sobre el valor añadido;* pronounced 'EE-ba'). IVA is 10% on accommodation and restaurant prices and is usually (but not always) included in quoted prices. On most retail goods the IVA is 21%. IVA-free shopping is available in duty-free shops at all airports for people travelling between EU countries.

Non-EU residents are entitled to a refund of the 21% IVA on purchases costing more than €90 from any shop, if the goods are taken out of the EU within three months. Ask the shop for a Cashback (or similar) refund form showing the price and IVA paid for each item and identifying the vendor and purchaser. Then present the form at the customs booth for IVA refunds when you depart from Spain (or elsewhere in the EU). You will need your passport and a boarding card that shows you are leaving the EU, and your luggage (so do this before checking in bags). The officer will stamp the invoice and you hand it in at a bank at the departure point to receive a reimbursement.

Telephones

Public telephones The blue payphones are easy to use for international and domestic calls. They accept coins, *tarjetas telefónicas* (phonecards) issued by the national phone company Telefónica and, in some cases, credit cards. *Tarjetas telefónicas* are sold at post offices and tobacconists.

Call centres A few *locutorios*, which also double as internet centres, are scattered around El Raval (look around Carrer de Sant Pau and Carrer de l'Hospital). Check rates before making calls.

Making calls To call Barcelona from outside Spain, dial the international access code, followed by the code for Spain (34) and the full number (including Barcelona's area code, 93, which is an integral part of the number). To make an international call, dial the international access code (00), country code, area code and number.

Operator Services

➡ International operator for reverse-charge calls: ☎1408

➡ International directory enquiries: ☎11825

➡ Domestic operator for a domestic reverse-charge call *(llamada por cobro revertido)*: ☎1409

➡ National directory enquiries: ☎11818

Mobile Phones

Mobile-phone numbers start with 6 or 7. Numbers starting with 900 are national toll-free numbers, while those starting with numbers between 901 and 905 come with varying conditions. A common one is 902, which is a national standard-rate number. In a similar category are numbers starting with 803, 806 and 807.

Spain uses GSM 900/1800, compatible with the rest of Europe and Australia but not with the North American GSM 1900 or the system used in Japan. If your phone is tri- or quadriband, you will probably be fine. You can buy SIM cards and prepaid call time in Spain for your own national mobile phone (provided what you own is a GSM, dual- or tri-band cellular phone and not code-blocked). You will need your passport to open any kind of mobile-phone account, prepaid or otherwise.

Time

Spain is one hour ahead of GMT/UTC during winter, and two hours ahead during daylight saving (the last Sunday in March to the last Sunday in October). Most other Western European countries are on the same time as Spain year-round. The UK, Ireland and Portugal are one hour behind. Spaniards use the 24-hour clock for official business (timetables etc) but generally switch to the 12-hour version in daily conversation.

Tourist Information

Several tourist offices operate in Barcelona. A couple of general information telephone numbers worth bearing in mind are ☎010 and ☎012. The first is for Barcelona and the other is for all Catalonia (run by the Generalitat). You sometimes strike English speakers, although for the most part operators are Catalan/Spanish bilingual. In addition to tourist offices, information booths operate at Estació del Nord bus station and at Portal de la Pau, at the foot of the Mirador de Colom at the port end of La Rambla. Others set up at various points in the city centre in summer.

Plaça de Catalunya (Map p290; ☎93 285 38 34; www.barcelonaturisme.com; underground at Plaça de Catalunya 17-S; ⊗9.30am-9.30pm; ⓂCatalunya)

Plaça Sant Jaume (Map p276; ☎93 285 38 32; Carrer de la Ciutat 2; ⊗8.30am-8.30pm Mon-Fri, 9am-7pm Sat, 9am-2pm Sun & holidays; ⓂJaume I)

Estació Sants (Map p302; ⊗8am-8pm; ⓇEstació Sants)

El Prat Airport (Terminal 1 arrivals, Terminal 2B arrivals hall; ⊗8.30am-8.30pm)

La Rambla Information Booth (Map p276; www.barcelonaturisme.com; La Rambla dels Estudis 115; ⊗8.30am-8.30pm; ⓂLiceu)

Palau Robert Regional Tourist Office (Map p290; ☎93 238 80 91, from outside Catalonia 902 400012; www.gencat.net/probert; Passeig de Gràcia 107; ⊗10am-8pm Mon-Sat, to 2.30pm Sun; ⓂDiagonal) A host of material on Catalonia, audiovisual resources, a bookshop and a branch of Turisme Juvenil de Catalunya (for youth travel).

Travellers with Disabilities

Some hotels and public institutions have wheelchair access. All buses in Barcelona are wheelchair accessible and a growing number of metro stations are theoretically wheelchair accessible (generally by lift, although there have been complaints that they are only any good for parents with prams). Lines 2, 9, 10 and 11 are completely adapted, as are the majority of stops on Line 1. In all, about 80% of stops have been adapted (you can check which ones by looking at a network map here: www.tmb.cat/en/transport-accessible). Ticket vending machines in metro stations are adapted for the disabled and have Braille options for the blind.

Several taxi companies have adapted vehicles including **Taxi Amic** (☑93 420 80 88; http://rtljtic.wix.com/taxiamic) and **Gestverd** (☑93 303 09 09).

Most street crossings in central Barcelona are wheelchair-friendly.

For more information on what the city is doing to improve accessibility check out the council's *Accessible Barcelona Guide* in several languages (www.barcelona-access.com).

Other services include the following:

Barcelona Turisme (www.barcelonaturisme.com) Barcelona's official tourism organisation maintains a website devoted to making the city accessible to visitors with a disability (www.barcelona-access.com).

ONCE (Map p302;☑93 325 92 00; Carrer de Sepúlveda 1; ⓂPlaça d'Espanya) The national organisation for the vision-impaired can help with information, including lists of places such as restaurants where Braille menus are provided.

Visas

Spain is one of 25 member countries of the Schengen Convention, under which 22 EU countries (all but Bulgaria, Cyprus, Ireland, Romania and the UK) plus Iceland, Norway and Switzerland have abolished checks at common borders.

EU nationals require only their ID cards to visit Spain. Nationals of many other countries, including Australia, Canada, Israel, Japan, New Zealand and the USA, do not require visas for tourist visits to Spain of up to 90 days. Non-EU nationals who are legal residents of one Schengen country do not require a visa to visit another Schengen country.

All non-EU nationals entering Spain for any reason other than tourism (such as study or work) should contact a Spanish consulate, as they may need a specific visa and will have to obtain work and/or residence permits. Citizens of countries not mentioned above should check with their Spanish consulate whether they need a visa.

Women Travellers

Think twice about going by yourself to isolated stretches of beach or down empty city streets at night. It's inadvisable for women to hitchhike – either alone or in pairs.

Topless bathing is OK on beaches in Catalonia and also at swimming pools. While skimpy clothing tends not to attract much attention in Barcelona and the coastal resorts, tastes in inland Catalonia tend to be somewhat conservative.

Ca la Dona (Map p276;☑93 412 71 61; www.caladona.org; Carrer de Ripoll 25; ⓂUrquinaona) The nerve centre of the region's feminist movement, Ca la Dona (Women's Home) includes many diverse women's groups.

Centre Francesca Bonnemaison (Map p284;☑93 268 42 18; www.labonne.org; Carrer de Sant Pere més Baix 7; ⓂUrquinaona) A women's cultural centre where groups put on expositions, stage theatre productions and carry out other cultural activities.

Institut Català de les Dones (Map p280;☑93 495 16 00; www.gencat.net/icdona; Plaça de Pere Corominas 1; ⓂLiceu) It can point you in the right direction for information on marriage, divorce, rape/assault counselling and related issues. The 24-hour hotline for victims of assault is ☑900 900120.

Language

Catalan (català) and Spanish (español, more precisely known as castellano, or Castilian) both have official-language status in Catalonia. Aranese (aranés), which is a dialect of Gascon, is also an official language in the Val d'Aran. In Barcelona, you'll hear as much Spanish as Catalan, so we've provided some Spanish as well as Catalan basics here to get you started.

Most Spanish sounds are pronounced the same as their English counterparts. If you follow our coloured pronunciation guides, you'll be understood. Note that the kh is a throaty sound (like the 'ch' in the Scottish loch), ly is pronounced as the 'lli' in 'million', ny as the 'ni' in 'onion', th is pronounced with a lisp, and r is strongly rolled. In our pronunciation guides, the stressed syllables are in italics.

Where necessary, masculine and feminine forms are given for the words and phrases in this chapter, separated by a slash and with the masculine form first, eg perdido/a (m/f). Where both polite and informal options are given, they are indicated by the abbreviations 'pol' and 'inf' respectively.

BASICS

Hello.	Hola.	o·la
Goodbye.	Adiós.	a·dyos
How are you?	¿Qué tal?	ke tal
Fine, thanks.	Bien, gracias.	byen gra·thyas
Excuse me.	Perdón.	per·don
Sorry.	Lo siento.	lo see·en·to
Yes./No.	Sí./No.	see/no

WANT MORE?

For in-depth language information and handy phrases, check out Lonely Planet's Spanish Phrasebook. You'll find it at **shop.lonelyplanet.com**, or you can buy Lonely Planet's iPhone phrasebooks at the Apple App Store.

Please.	Por favor.	por fa·vor
Thank you.	Gracias.	gra·thyas
You're welcome.	De nada.	de na·da

My name is ...
Me llamo ...   me lya·mo ...

What's your name?
¿Cómo se llama Usted?   ko·mo se lya·ma oo·ste (pol)
¿Cómo te llamas?   ko·mo te lya·mas (inf)

Do you speak (English)?
¿Habla (inglés)?   a·bla (een·gles) (pol)
¿Hablas (inglés)?   a·blas (een·gles) (inf)

I (don't) understand.
Yo (no) entiendo.   yo (no) en·tyen·do

ACCOMMODATION

I'd like to book a room.
Quisiera reservar una   kee·sye·ra re·ser·var oo·na
habitación.   a·bee·ta·thyon

How much is it per night/person?
¿Cuánto cuesta por   kwan·to kwes·ta por
noche/persona?   no·che/per·so·na

Does it include breakfast?
¿Incluye el desayuno?   een·kloo·ye el de·sa·yoo·no

hotel	hotel	o·tel
guesthouse	pensión	pen·syon
youth hostel	albergue juvenil	al·ber·ge khoo·ve·neel

I'd like a ... room.	Quisiera una habitación ...	kee·sye·ra oo·na a·bee·ta·thyon ...
single	individual	een·dee·vee·dwal
double	doble	do·ble

air-con	aire acondicionado	ai·re a·kon·dee·thyo·na·do
bathroom	baño	ba·nyo
window	ventana	ven·ta·na

KEY PATTERNS

To get by in Spanish, mix and match these simple patterns with words of your choice:

When's (the next flight)?
¿Cuándo sale   kwan·do sa·le
(el próximo vuelo)?   (el prok·see·mo vwe·lo)

Where's (the station)?
¿Dónde está   don·de es·ta
(la estación)?   (la es·ta·thyon)

Where can I (buy a ticket)?
¿Dónde puedo   don·de pwe·do
(comprar   (kom·prar
un billete)?   oon bee·lye·te)

Do you have (a map)?
¿Tiene (un mapa)?   tye·ne (oon ma·pa)

Is there (a toilet)?
¿Hay (servicios)?   ai (ser·vee·thyos)

I'd like (a coffee).
Quisiera (un café).   kee·sye·ra (oon ka·fe)

I'd like (to hire a car).
Quisiera (alquilar   kee·sye·ra (al·kee·lar
un coche).   oon ko·che)

Can I (enter)?
¿Se puede (entrar)?   se pwe·de (en·trar)

Could you please (help me)?
¿Puede (ayudarme),   pwe·de (a·yoo·dar·me)
por favor?   por fa·vor

Do I have to (get a visa)?
¿Necesito   ne·the·see·to
(obtener   (ob·te·ner
un visado)?   oon vee·sa·do)

DIRECTIONS

Where's ...?
¿Dónde está ...?   don·de es·ta ...

What's the address?
¿Cuál es la dirección?   kwal es la dee·rek·thyon

Could you please write it down?
¿Puede escribirlo,   pwe·de es·kree·beer·lo
por favor?   por fa·vor

Can you show me (on the map)?
¿Me lo puede indicar   me lo pwe·de een·dee·kar
(en el mapa)?   (en el ma·pa)

at the corner	en la esquina	en la es·kee·na
at the traffic lights	en el semáforo	en el se·ma·fo·ro
behind	detrás de	de·tras de
far (away)	lejos	le·khos
in front of	enfrente de	en·fren·te de
left	izquierda	eeth·kyer·da
near	cerca	ther·ka
next to	al lado de	al la·do de
opposite	frente a	fren·te a
right	derecha	de·re·cha
straight ahead	todo recto	to·do rek·to

EATING & DRINKING

I'd like to book a table for ...	Quisiera reservar una mesa para ...	kee·sye·ra re·ser·var oo·na me·sa pa·ra ...
(eight) o'clock	las (ocho)	las (o·cho)
(two) people	(dos) personas	(dos) per·so·nas

What would you recommend?
¿Qué recomienda?   ke re·ko·myen·da

What's in that dish?
¿Que lleva ese plato?   ke lye·va e·se pla·to

I don't eat ...
No como ...   no ko·mo ...

Cheers!
¡Salud!   sa·loo

That was delicious!
¡Estaba buenísimo!   es·ta·ba bwe·nee·see·mo

Please bring the bill.
Por favor nos trae   por fa·vor nos tra·e
la cuenta.   la kwen·ta

Key Words

appetisers	aperitivos	a·pe·ree·tee·vos
bar	bar	bar
bottle	botella	bo·te·lya
bowl	bol	bol
breakfast	desayuno	de·sa·yoo·no
cafe	café	ka·fe
children's menu	menú infantil	me·noo een·fan·teel
(too/very) cold	(muy) frío	(mooy) free·o
dinner	cena	the·na
food	comida	ko·mee·da
fork	tenedor	te·ne·dor
glass	vaso	va·so
highchair	trona	tro·na
hot (warm)	caliente	ka·lyen·te
knife	cuchillo	koo·chee·lyo
lunch	comida	ko·mee·da
main course	segundo plato	se·goon·do pla·to
market	mercado	mer·ka·do
menu (in English)	menú (en inglés)	oon me·noo (en een·gles)

CATALAN

The recognition of Catalan as an official language in Spain is the end result of a regional government campaign that began when the province gained autonomy at the end of the 1970s. Until the Battle of Muret in 1213, Catalan territory extended across southern France, taking in Roussillon and reaching into the Provence. Catalan was spoken, or at least understood, throughout these territories and in what is now Catalonia and Andorra. In the couple of hundred years that followed, the Catalans spread their language south into Valencia, west into Aragón and east to the Balearic Islands. The language also reached Sicily and Naples, and the Sardinian town of Alghero is still a partly Catalan-speaking outpost today. Catalan is spoken by up to 10 million people in Spain.

In Barcelona you'll hear as much Spanish as Catalan. Your chances of coming across English speakers are also good. Elsewhere in the province, don't be surprised if you get replies in Catalan to your questions in Spanish. However, you'll find that most Catalans will happily speak to you in Spanish, especially once they realise you're a foreigner. This said, the following Catalan phrases might win you a few smiles and perhaps help you make some new friends.

Hello.	*Hola.*	**Monday**	dilluns
Goodbye.	*Adéu.*	**Tuesday**	dimarts
Yes.	*Sí.*	**Wednesday**	dimecres
No.	*No.*	**Thursday**	dijous
Please.	*Sisplau./Si us plau.*	**Friday**	divendres
Thank you (very much).	*(Moltes) gràcies.*	**Saturday**	dissabte
You're welcome.	*De res.*	**Sunday**	diumenge
Excuse me.	*Perdoni.*		
May I?/Do you mind?	*Puc?/Em permet?*	1	un/una (m/f)
I'm sorry.	*Ho sento./Perdoni.*	2	dos/dues (m/f)
		3	tres
What's your name?	*Com et dius?* (inf)	4	quatre
	Com es diu? (pol)	5	cinc
My name is ...	*Em dic ...*	6	sis
Where are you from?	*D'on ets?*	7	set
Do you speak English?	*Parla anglès?*	8	vuit
I understand.	*Ho entenc.*	9	nou
I don't understand.	*No ho entenc.*	10	deu
Could you speak in	*Pot parlar castellà*	11	onze
Castilian, please?	*sisplau?*	12	dotze
How do you say ... in	*Com es diu ... en*	13	tretze
Catalan?	*català?*	14	catorze
		15	quinze
I'm looking for ...	*Estic buscant ...*	16	setze
How do I get to ...?	*Com puc arribar a ...?*	17	disset
Turn left.	*Giri a mà esquerra.*	18	divuit
Turn right.	*Giri a mà dreta.*	19	dinou
near	*a prop de*	20	vint
far	*a lluny de*	100	cent

Signs

Abierto	Open
Cerrado	Closed
Entrada	Entrance
Hombres	Men
Mujeres	Women
Prohibido	Prohibited
Salida	Exit
Servicios/Aseos	Toilets

plate	plato	pla·to
restaurant	restaurante	res·tow·ran·te
spoon	cuchara	koo·cha·ra
supermarket	supermercado	soo·per·mer·ka·do
vegetarian food	comida vegetariana	ko·mee·da ve·khe·ta·rya·na
with/without	con/sin	kon/seen

Meat & Fish

beef	carne de vaca	kar·ne de va·ka
chicken	pollo	po·lyo
duck	pato	pa·to
lamb	cordero	kor·de·ro
lobster	langosta	lan·gos·ta
pork	cerdo	ther·do
prawns	camarones	ka·ma·ro·nes
tuna	atún	a·toon
turkey	pavo	pa·vo
veal	ternera	ter·ne·ra

Fruit & Vegetables

apple	manzana	man·tha·na
apricot	albaricoque	al·ba·ree·ko·ke
artichoke	alcachofa	al·ka·cho·fa
asparagus	espárragos	es·pa·ra·gos
banana	plátano	pla·ta·no
beans	judías	khoo·dee·as
beetroot	remolacha	re·mo·la·cha
cabbage	col	kol
carrot	zanahoria	tha·na·o·rya
celery	apio	a·pyo
cherry	cereza	the·re·tha
corn	maíz	ma·eeth
cucumber	pepino	pe·pee·no
fruit	fruta	froo·ta
grape	uvas	oo·vas

lemon	limón	lee·mon
lentils	lentejas	len·te·khas
lettuce	lechuga	le·choo·ga
mushroom	champiñón	cham·pee·nyon
nuts	nueces	nwe·thes
onion	cebolla	the·bo·lya
orange	naranja	na·ran·kha
peach	melocotón	me·lo·ko·ton
peas	guisantes	gee·san·tes
(red/green) pepper	pimiento (rojo/verde)	pee·myen·to (ro·kho/ver·de)
pineapple	piña	pee·nya
plum	ciruela	theer·we·la
potato	patata	pa·ta·ta
pumpkin	calabaza	ka·la·ba·tha
spinach	espinacas	es·pee·na·kas
strawberry	fresa	fre·sa
tomato	tomate	to·ma·te
vegetable	verdura	ver·doo·ra
watermelon	sandía	san·dee·a

Other

bread	pan	pan
butter	mantequilla	man·te·kee·lya
cheese	queso	ke·so
egg	huevo	we·vo
honey	miel	myel
jam	mermelada	mer·me·la·da
oil	aceite	a·they·te
pasta	pasta	pas·ta
pepper	pimienta	pee·myen·ta
rice	arroz	a·roth
salt	sal	sal
sugar	azúcar	a·thoo·kar
vinegar	vinagre	vee·na·gre

Drinks

beer	cerveza	ther·ve·tha
coffee	café	ka·fe
(orange) juice	zumo (de naranja)	thoo·mo (de na·ran·kha)
milk	leche	le·che
tea	té	te
(mineral) water	agua (mineral)	a·gwa (mee·ne·ral)
(red) wine	vino (tinto)	vee·no (teen·to)
(white) wine	vino (blanco)	vee·no (blan·ko)

EMERGENCIES

Help!	¡Socorro!	so·ko·ro
Go away!	¡Vete!	ve·te

Call ...!	¡Llame a ...!	lya·me a ...
a doctor	un médico	oon me·dee·ko
the police	la policía	la po·lee·thee·a

I'm lost.
Estoy perdido/a.   es·toy per·dee·do/a (m/f)

I had an accident.
He tenido un   e te·nee·do oon
accidente.   ak·thee·den·te

I'm ill.
Estoy enfermo/a.   es·toy en·fer·mo/a (m/f)

It hurts here.
Me duele aquí.   me dwe·le a·kee

I'm allergic to (antibiotics).
Soy alérgico/a a   soy a·ler·khee·ko/a a
(los antibióticos).   (los an·tee·byo·tee·kos) (m/f)

SHOPPING & SERVICES

I'd like to buy ...
Quisiera comprar ...   kee·sye·ra kom·prar ...

I'm just looking.
Sólo estoy mirando.   so·lo es·toy mee·ran·do

Can I look at it?
¿Puedo verlo?   pwe·do ver·lo

I don't like it.
No me gusta.   no me goos·ta

How much is it?
¿Cuánto cuesta?   kwan·to kwes·ta

That's too expensive.
Es muy caro.   es mooy ka·ro

Can you lower the price?
¿Podría bajar un   po·dree·a ba·khar oon
poco el precio?   po·ko el pre·thyo

There's a mistake in the bill.
Hay un error en   ai oon e·ror en
la cuenta.   la kwen·ta

ATM	cajero automático	ka·khe·ro ow·to·ma·tee·ko
internet cafe	cibercafé	thee·ber·ka·fe
post office	correos	ko·re·os
tourist office	oficina de turismo	o·fee·thee·na de too·rees·mo

TIME & DATES

What time is it?
¿Qué hora es?   ke o·ra es

It's (10) o'clock.
Son (las diez).   son (las dyeth)

Half past (one).
Es (la una)   es (la oo·na)
y media.   ee me·dya

morning	mañana	ma·nya·na
afternoon	tarde	tar·de
evening	noche	no·che
yesterday	ayer	a·yer
today	hoy	oy
tomorrow	mañana	ma·nya·na

Monday	lunes	loo·nes
Tuesday	martes	mar·tes
Wednesday	miércoles	myer·ko·les
Thursday	jueves	khwe·bes
Friday	viernes	vyer·nes
Saturday	sábado	sa·ba·do
Sunday	domingo	do·meen·go

January	enero	e·ne·ro
February	febrero	fe·bre·ro
March	marzo	mar·tho
April	abril	a·breel
May	mayo	ma·yo
June	junio	khoo·nyo
July	julio	khoo·lyo
August	agosto	a·gos·to
September	septiembre	sep·tyem·bre
October	octubre	ok·too·bre
November	noviembre	no·vyem·bre
December	diciembre	dee·thyem·bre

TRANSPORT

boat	barco	bar·ko
bus	autobús	ow·to·boos
plane	avión	a·vyon
train	tren	tren

first	primer	pree·mer
last	último	ool·tee·mo
next	próximo	prok·see·mo

Question Words

What?	¿Qué?	ke
When?	¿Cuándo?	kwan·do
Where?	¿Dónde?	don·de
Who?	¿Quién?	kyen
Why?	¿Por qué?	por ke

I want to go to ...
Quisiera ir a ... kee·sye·ra eer a ...

What time does it arrive/leave?
¿A qué hora llega/sale? a ke o·ra lye·ga/sa·le

Does it stop at ...?
¿Para en ...? pa·ra en ...

Can you tell me when we get to ...?
¿Puede avisarme pwe·de a·vee·sar·me
cuando lleguemos a ...? kwan·do lye·ge·mos a ...

What stop is this?
¿Cuál es esta parada? kwal es es·ta pa·ra·da

I want to get off here.
Quiero bajarme aquí. kye·ro ba·khar·me a·kee

a ... ticket	*un billete de ...*	oon bee·lye·te de ...
1st-class	*primera clase*	pree·me·ra kla·se
2nd-class	*segunda clase*	se·goon·da kla·se
one-way	*ida*	ee·da
return	*ida y vuelta*	ee·da ee vwel·ta

aisle seat	*asiento de pasillo*	a·syen·to de pa·see·lyo
cancelled	*cancelado*	kan·the·la·do
delayed	*retrasado*	re·tra·sa·do
platform	*plataforma*	pla·ta·for·ma
ticket office	*taquilla*	ta·kee·lya
timetable	*horario*	o·ra·ryo
train station	*estación de trenes*	es·ta·thyon de tre·nes
window seat	*asiento junto a la ventana*	a·syen·to khoon·to a la ven·ta·na

I'd like to hire a ...	*Quisiera alquilar ...*	kee·sye·ra al·kee·lar ...
bicycle	*una bicicleta*	oo·na bee·thee·kle·ta
car	*un coche*	oon ko·che
motorcycle	*una moto*	oo·na mo·to

Numbers

1	*uno*	oo·no
2	*dos*	dos
3	*tres*	tres
4	*cuatro*	kwa·tro
5	*cinco*	theen·ko
6	*seis*	seys
7	*siete*	sye·te
8	*ocho*	o·cho
9	*nueve*	nwe·ve
10	*diez*	dyeth
20	*veinte*	veyn·te
30	*treinta*	treyn·ta
40	*cuarenta*	kwa·ren·ta
50	*cincuenta*	theen·kwen·ta
60	*sesenta*	se·sen·ta
70	*setenta*	se·ten·ta
80	*ochenta*	o·chen·ta
90	*noventa*	no·ven·ta
100	*cien*	thyen
1000	*mil*	meel

diesel	*gasóleo*	ga·so·lyo
helmet	*casco*	kas·ko
mechanic	*mecánico*	me·ka·nee·ko
petrol/gas	*gasolina*	ga·so·lee·na
service station	*gasolinera*	ga·so·lee·ne·ra

(How long) Can I park here?
¿(Por cuánto tiempo) (por kwan·to tyem·po)
Puedo aparcar aquí? pwe·do a·par·kar a·kee

The car has broken down.
El coche se ha averiado. el ko·che se a a·ve·rya·do

I have a flat tyre.
Tengo un pinchazo. ten·go oon peen·cha·tho

I've run out of petrol.
Me he quedado sin me e ke·da·do seen
gasolina. ga·so·lee·na

GLOSSARY

Items listed below are in Catalan/Spanish (Castilian) where they start with the same letter. Where the two terms start with different letters, or where only the Catalan or the Spanish term is provided, they are listed separately and marked (C) for Catalan or (S) for Spanish. If an entry is not marked at all, it is because it takes the same form in both languages.

ajuntament/ayuntamiento – town hall

artesonado (S) – Mudéjar wooden ceiling with interlaced beams leaving a pattern of spaces for decoration

avinguda (C) – avenue

barcelonin (C) – inhabitant/native of Barcelona

Barcino – Roman name for Barcelona

barri/barrio – neighbourhood, quarter of Barcelona

caganer (C) – the crapper, a character appearing in Catalan nativity scenes

El Call (C) – the Jewish quarter in medieval Barcelona

capella/capilla – chapel

carrer/calle – street

casa – house

castellers (C) – human-castle builders

cercanías (S) – local trains serving Barcelona's airport, suburbs and some outlying towns

comte/conde – count

correfoc (C) – appearance of firework-spouting devils at festivals; literally 'fire runs'

església (C) – church

farmàcia/farmacia – pharmacy

festa/fiesta – festival, public holiday or party

FGC (C) – Ferrocarrils de la Generalitat de Catalunya; local trains operating alongside the Metro in Barcelona

fundació/fundación – foundation

garum – a spicy sauce made from fish entrails, found throughout the Roman Empire

gegants – huge figures paraded at *festes*

Generalitat (C) – Catalan regional government

guiri – foreigner (somewhat pejorative)

hostal – commercial establishment providing one- to three-star accommodation

iglesia (S) – church

IVA – *impost sobre el valor afegit/impuesto sobre el valor añadido*, or value-added tax

masia – Catalan country farmhouse

mercat/mercado – market

Modernisme (C) – the turn-of-the-19th-century artistic style, influenced by art nouveau, whose leading practitioner was Antoni Gaudí

Modernista – an exponent of Modernisme

Mudéjar (S) – a Muslim living under Christian rule in medieval Spain; also refers to their decorative style of architecture

palau (C) – palace

passatge (C) – laneway

pensió/pensión – commercial establishment providing one- to three-star accommodation

plaça/plaza – plaza

platja/playa – beach

Renaixença – rebirth of interest in Catalan literature, culture and language in the second half of the 19th century

rodalies (C) – see *cercanías*

saló (C) – hall

sardana – traditional Catalan folk dance

s/n (S) – *sin número* (without number)

tablao – restaurant where flamenco is performed

teatre – theatre

terrassa/terazza – terrace; often means a cafe or bar's outdoor tables

trencadís – a Modernista style of mosaic, created using broken tiles

turista – second class; economy class

Behind the Scenes

SEND US YOUR FEEDBACK

We love to hear from travellers – your comments keep us on our toes and help make our books better. Our well-travelled team reads every word on what you loved or loathed about this book. Although we cannot reply individually to your submissions, we always guarantee that your feedback goes straight to the appropriate authors, in time for the next edition. Each person who sends us information is thanked in the next edition – the most useful submissions are rewarded with a selection of digital PDF chapters.

Visit **lonelyplanet.com/contact** to submit your updates and suggestions or to ask for help. Our award-winning website also features inspirational travel stories, news and discussions.

Note: We may edit, reproduce and incorporate your comments in Lonely Planet products such as guidebooks, websites and digital products, so let us know if you don't want your comments reproduced or your name acknowledged. For a copy of our privacy policy visit lonelyplanet.com/privacy.

OUR READERS

Many thanks to the travellers who used the last edition and wrote to us with helpful hints, useful advice and interesting anecdotes: Caroline Amukusana, Filippo Aroffo, Sylvia Campbell, Liesbeth Cobbaut, Tom Drinkwater, Shailendra Singh, Chris Watts, Guy Winker

AUTHOR THANKS

Regis St Louis

I'm grateful to the many friends and acquaintances who provided guidance and tips along the way. Biggest thanks go to coauthor Sal Davies for her hard work, Manel Casanovas for gourmet insight at Barcelona Turisme, Sol Polo and friends, Margherita Bergamo, Carine Ferry, Gonzalo Salaya, Anna Aurich, Núria Rocamora, Manel Baena, Malén Gual and Bernardo Laniado-Romero. Thanks also to Alan Waterman for making the trip down from London. Finally, big hugs to my family for all their support.

Sally Davies

Those without whom in Barcelona include Nora Vos Lizari, Julie Prat Dedé, Ada Rodríguez, Zéphyr Hervelin, Mia Planas, Esther Torres and Mireia Coll. In Melbourne and London they include Dora Whitaker and Kristin Odijk, but special thanks for endless patience and guidance on the technical side of things go to Jo Cooke and Regis St Louis. Extra special thanks go to Tess, for her unstinting enthusiasm as a research assistant.

Andy Symington

I owe gratitude to many people in tourist offices, on streets, in cabs. Particular thanks to the Lonely Planet team, Regis St Louis, my coauthors and to my family for their constant support. I also owe thanks for various favours to José Eliseo Vázquez González, Javier De Celis Sánchez, Richard Prowse and Mike Burren.

ACKNOWLEDGMENTS

Transports Metropolitans de Barcelona map © Ferrocarril Metropolità de Barcelona, SA 2011.

Illustrations pp126-7, pp182-3 by Javier Zarracina.

Cover photograph: La Pedrera, Gregory Wrona/Alamy.

THIS BOOK

This 9th edition of Lonely Planet's *Barcelona* guidebook was researched and written by Regis St Louis, Sally Davies and Andy Symington. The 8th edition was written by Regis St Louis, Anna Kaminski and Vesna Maric, and the previous edition was written by Damien Simonis. This guidebook was commissioned in Lonely Planet's London office, and produced by the following:

Commissioning Editor Dora Whitaker

Destination Editor Jo Cooke

Coordinating Editors Carolyn Boicos, Kristin Odijk

Senior Cartographer David Kemp

Book Designer Katherine Marsh

Assisting Editors Justin Flynn, Anne Mulvaney

Senior Editor Karyn Noble

Cover Researcher Naomi Parker

Illustrator Javier Zarracina

Thanks to Penny Cordner, Ryan Evans, Larissa Frost, Genesys India, Jouve India, Virginia Moreno, Wayne Murphy, Claire Naylor, Martine Power

Index

See also separate subindexes for:

✗ **EATING P270**

● **DRINKING & NIGHTLIFE P271**

☆ **ENTERTAINMENT P271**

🔒 **SHOPPING P272**

🏃 **SPORTS & ACTIVITIES P273**

🛏 **SLEEPING P273**

INDEX SPORTS & ACTIVITIES

Barcelona Maps

Sights

- Beach
- Bird Sanctuary
- Buddhist
- Castle/Palace
- Christian
- Confucian
- Hindu
- Islamic
- Jain
- Jewish
- Monument
- Museum/Gallery/Historic Building
- Ruin
- Sento Hot Baths/Onsen
- Shinto
- Sikh
- Taoist
- Winery/Vineyard
- Zoo/Wildlife Sanctuary
- Other Sight

Activities, Courses & Tours

- Bodysurfing
- Diving
- Canoeing/Kayaking
- Course/Tour
- Skiing
- Snorkelling
- Surfing
- Swimming/Pool
- Walking
- Windsurfing
- Other Activity

Sleeping

- Sleeping
- Camping

Eating

- Eating

Drinking & Nightlife

- Drinking & Nightlife
- Cafe

Entertainment

- Entertainment

Shopping

- Shopping

Information

- Bank
- Embassy/Consulate
- Hospital/Medical
- Internet
- Police
- Post Office
- Telephone
- Toilet
- Tourist Information
- Other Information

Geographic

- Beach
- Hut/Shelter
- Lighthouse
- Lookout
- Mountain/Volcano
- Oasis
- Park
- Pass
- Picnic Area
- Waterfall

Population

- Capital (National)
- Capital (State/Province)
- City/Large Town
- Town/Village

Transport

- Airport
- Border crossing
- Bus
- Cable car/Funicular
- Cycling
- Ferry
- Metro station
- Monorail
- Parking
- Petrol station
- S-Bahn/Subway station
- Taxi
- T-bane/Tunnelbana station
- Train station/Railway
- Tram
- Tube station
- U-Bahn/Underground station
- Other Transport

Note: Not all symbols displayed above appear on the maps in this book

Routes

- Tollway
- Freeway
- Primary
- Secondary
- Tertiary
- Lane
- Unsealed road
- Road under construction
- Plaza/Mall
- Steps
- Tunnel
- Pedestrian overpass
- Walking Tour
- Walking Tour detour
- Path/Walking Trail

Boundaries

- International
- State/Province
- Disputed
- Regional/Suburb
- Marine Park
- Cliff
- Wall

Hydrography

- River, Creek
- Intermittent River
- Canal
- Water
- Dry/Salt/Intermittent Lake
- Reef

Areas

- Airport/Runway
- Beach/Desert
- Cemetery (Christian)
- Cemetery (Other)
- Glacier
- Mudflat
- Park/Forest
- Sight (Building)
- Sportsground
- Swamp/Mangrove

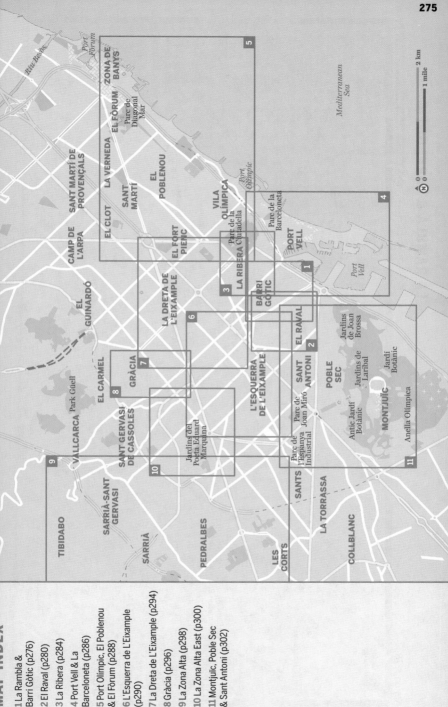

LA RAMBLA & BARRI GÒTIC

Key on p278

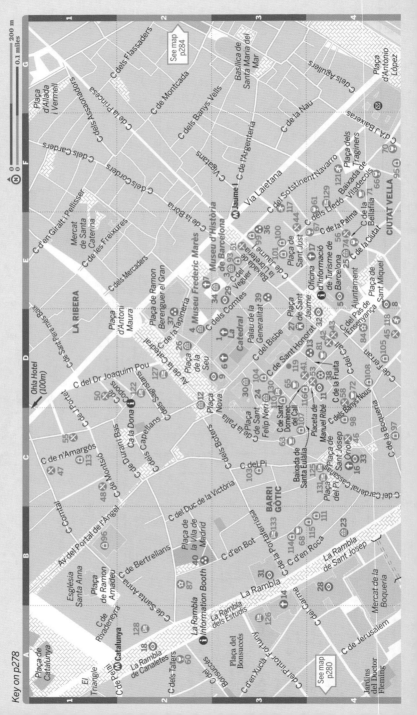

0.1 miles
200 m

See map p284

See map p280

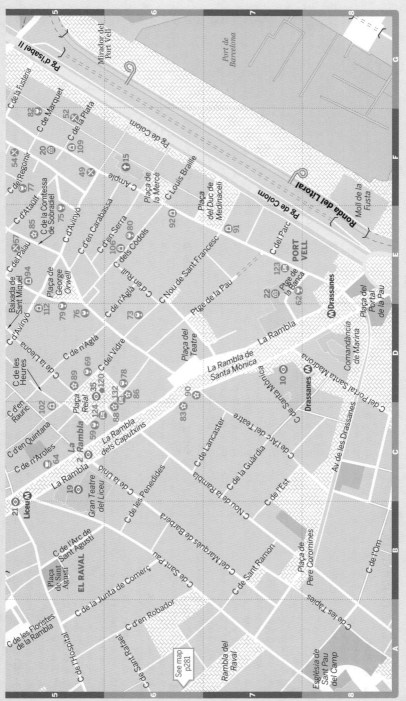

Pg d'Isabel II

Mirador del
Port Vell

Port de
Barcelona

C de la Fusteria

82

C de Marquet

52

C de la Plata

109

20

Pg de Colom

54

C del Regomir

77

49

C Ample

Plaça de
la Mercè

15

C de Louis Braille

Plaça del
Duc de
Medinaceli

85

C de la Comtessa
de Sobradiel

75

C d'Ataülf

57

94

C del Palau

C d'Avinyó

C d'en Carabassa

106

C d'en Serra

80

C dels Còdols

92

91

C del Parc

PORT
VELL

Moll de la
Fusta

Ronda del Litoral

Pg de Colom

Baixada de
Sant Miquel

Plaça de
George
Orwell

112

79

76

C d'en Rull

C de n'Aglà

73

C Nou de Sant Francesc

Ptge de la Pau

123

Pge de
la Banca

22

62

Drassanes

Plaça del
Portal
de la Pau

C d'Avinyó

C del Vidre

69

89

C de les
Heures

C de la Lleona

Plaça del
Teatre

La Rambla

La Rambla de
Santa Mònica

Comandància
de Marina

C del Portal Santa Madrona

C d'en
Rauric

102

124

35

120

132

86

88

78

Plaça
Reial

59

La Rambla
dels Caputxins

La Rambla
dels Caputxins

90

83

C de Santa Mònica

10

Drassanes

Av de les Drassanes

C d'en Quintana

64

C de n'Aroles

La Rambla

2

C de Lancaster

C de l'Arc del Teatre

C de la Guàrdia

21

Liceu

19

Gran Teatre
del Liceu

C de la Unió

C de les Penedides

C Nou de la Rambla

C de l'Est

Plaça de
Pere Coromines

C de l'Om

C de l'Arc de
Sant Agustí

Plaça
de Sant
Agustí

EL RAVAL

C del Marquès de Barberà

C de Sant Pau

C de Sant Ramon

C de les Tàpies

C de les Floristes
de la Rambla

C de l'Hospital

C de la Junta de Comerç

C de Sant Rafael

C d'en Robador

Rambla del
Raval

Església de
Sant Pau
del Camp

See map
p281

LA RAMBLA & BARRI GÒTIC *Map on p276*

EL RAVAL

Key on p282

200 m
0.1 miles

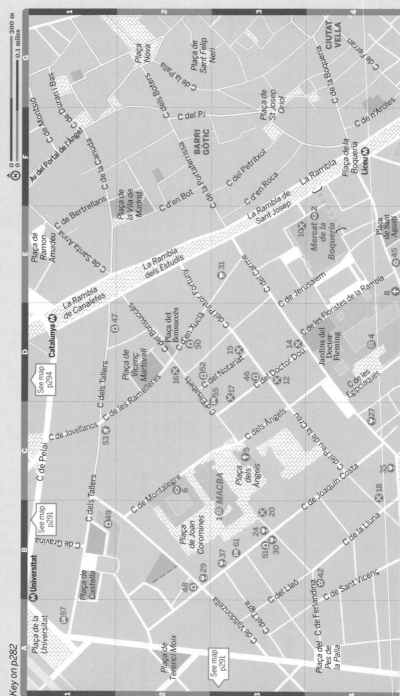

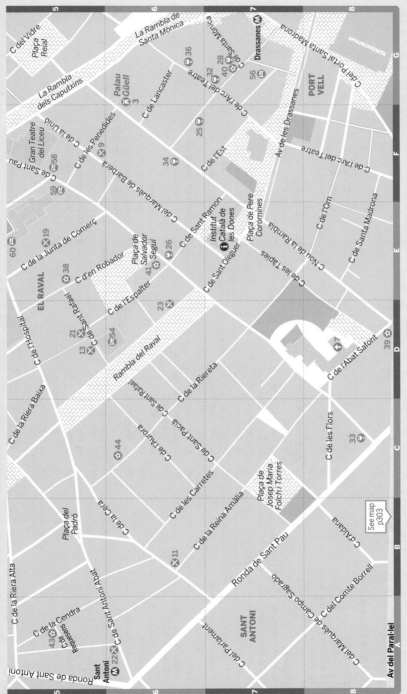

EL RAVAL

C del Vidre

Plaça Reial

La Rambla de Santa Mònica

C de Santa Mònica

Drassanes

C del Portal Santa Madrona

PORT VELL

36

32

40 28

C de l'Arc del Teatre

56

La Rambla dels Caputxins

Palau Güell
3

C de Lancaster

25

Av de les Drassanes

C de l'Arc del Teatre

C de la Unió

Gran Teatre del Liceu

C de les Penedides

58

9

C de la Unió

34

C de l'Est

C de l'Om

C de Santa Madrona

59

C de Sant Pau

C del Marquès de Barberà

Institut Català de les Dones

Plaça de Pere Coromines

19

C de la Junta de Comerç

38

C d'en Robador

Plaça de Salvador Seguí

26

C de Sant Ramon

C Nou de la Rambla

C de les Tàpies

60

EL RAVAL

C de l'Hospital

21

C de Sant Rafael

41

C de l'Espalter

23

C de Sant Oleguer

54

13

Rambla del Raval

C de la Riereta

7

C de l'Abat Safont

39

C de la Riera Baixa

C de Sant Rafael

C de Sant Pacià

C de la Reina Amàlia

C de les Flors

33

C de l'Aurora

44

C de les Carretes

Plaça de Josep Maria Folch i Torres

See map p303

C d'Aldana

Plaça del Padró

C de la Cera

C de la Reina Amàlia

Ronda de Sant Pau

C del Marquès de Campo Sagrado

C del Comte Borrell

C de la Riera Alta

11

C del Parlament

SANT ANTONI

43

C de la Cendra

C de Requesens

22

C de Sant Antoni Abat

Sant Antoni

Ronda de Sant Antoni

Av del Paral·lel

EL RAVAL *Map on p280*

LA RIBERA *Map on p284*

Key on p283

LA RIBERA

See map p295

See map p276

See map p276

Arc de Triomf M

C de Girona
C d'Ali Bei
Ronda de Sant Pere
4

C de Méndez Núñez
C de Lluís el Pladós
34
13
Plaça de Sant Pere

C del Bruc
Pg de Lluís Companys

Plaça del Comerç

Ptge de Sert
C de Sant Pere més Alt

C d'en Cortines
C del Portal Nou

C d'Ortigosa
C de Sant Pere més Alt
C d'en Mònec
30
C del Comerç

Palau de la Música Catalana
3

C d'en Llàstics
C dels Meigs
Plaça de Sant Agustí Vell

C de Sant Pere Mitjà
C de Sant Pere més Baix
Plaça del Pou de la Figuera

Casal Lambda
C de Mare de Déu del Pilar
C d'en Giralt i Pellisser
38
C de Jaume Giralt
Former Convent de Sant Agustí
51
5

C de Verdaguer i Callís
74
37
32
Plaça d'Allada i Vermell
18

Centre Francesca Bonnemaison
C del Fonollar
40

C General Alvarez de Castro
Mercat de Santa Caterina
C dels Carders
C dels Assaonadors

LA RIBERA
69
31
16
25
14
7

C del Dr Joaquim Pou
Av de Francesc Cambó
C de les Freixures
C de Colomines
C dels Corders
41

Plaça d'Antoni Maura
C dels Mercaders
Museu Picasso
2
Palau dels Cervelló
63

Av de la Catedral
72
20
C de Montcada
8
17

Plaça de la Seu
C de Santa Llúcia
C de la Tapineria
19
C de la Bòria
53
59
64
21
35
44

Plaça de Ramon Berenguer el Gran
Carrer dels Cotoners
50
54

C de Santa Llúcia
C dels Comtes
Plaça de l'Àngel
52
70
73
C Vigatans
C del Bro Solí
C dels Mirallers
65
1

C del Bisbe
C de l'Argenteria
58
Basílica de Santa Maria del Mar
46

Via Laietana
C de Manresa
C de Basea
27
Carrer de les Caputxes

C de la Llibreteria
C de Jaume I
C del Sotstinent Navarro
C de la Nau

BARRI GÒTIC
Plaça de Sant Jaume
Plaça de Sant Just
C dels Lledó
CIUTAT VELLA
66

C del Call

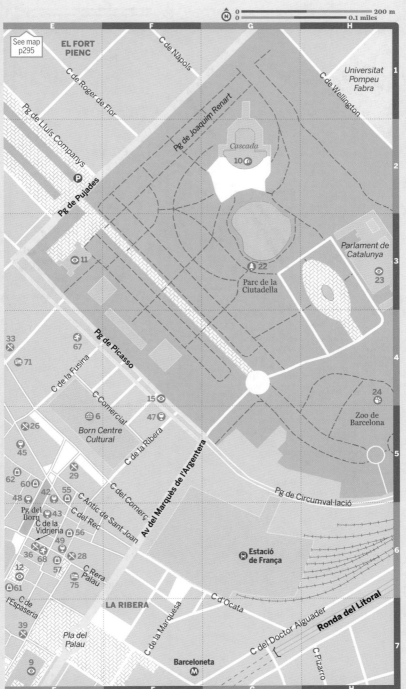

LA RIBERA

See map p295

EL FORT PIENC

C de Nàpols

C de Roger de Flor

Pg de Lluís Companys

Pg de Joaquim Renart

Universitat Pompeu Fabra

C de Wellington

P
Pg de Pujades

11

Cascada
10

22
Parc de la Ciutadella

Parlament de Catalunya

23

33
71

67
Pg de Picasso

C de la Fusina

C Comercial

15

6
Born Centre Cultural

47

C de la Ribera

24

Zoo de Barcelona

26

45

29

C del Comerç

62 60
48 42 55
Pg del Born
C de la Vidrieria
36 68
12
61

43
C del Rec
56
49
28
57
75
C Rera Palau

C Antic de Sant Joan

Av del Marquès de l'Argentera

Pg de Circumval·lació

Estació de França

39

C de l'Espaseria

LA RIBERA

Pla del Palau

C de la Marquesa

C d'Ocata

C del Doctor Aiguader

Ronda del Litoral

C Pizarro

9

Barceloneta
M

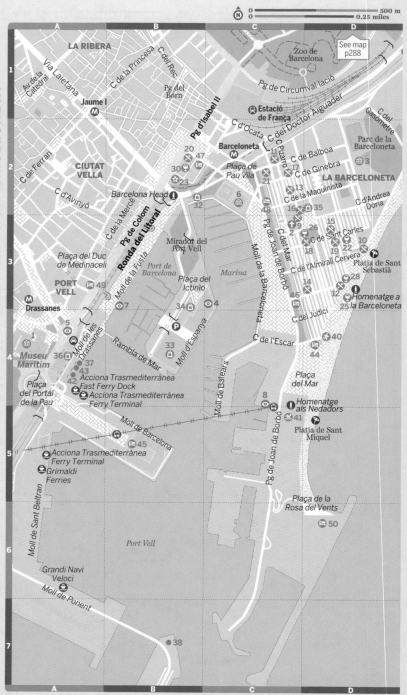

PORT VELL & LA BARCELONETA

0 — 500 m
0 — 0.25 miles

See map
p288

LA RIBERA

Via Laietana

Av de la Catedral

C de la Princesa

C del Rec

Pg del Born

Pg de Circumval·lació

Zoo de Barcelona

Jaume I

C de la Princesa

Pg d'Isabel II

Estació de França

C d'Ocata

C del Doctor Aiguader

C del Gasòmetre

Parc de la Barceloneta

C de Ferran

CIUTAT VELLA

C d'Avinyó

Barceloneta

Plaça de Pau Vila

C Pizarro

C de Balboa

C de Ginebra

LA BARCELONETA

C d'Andrea Doria

20
47
30
23

Barcelona Head

32

6

48

11
17
21
13
16
35
29
2
26
18
19
15
C de Sant Carles
10

C de la Maquinista

C de la Mercè

Pg de Colom

Ronda del Litoral

Mirador del Port Vell

Port de Barcelona

Plaça del Ictínio

Marina

Moll de la Barceloneta

Pg de Joan de Borbó

C del Mar

C de l'Almirall Cervera

Platja de Sant Sebastià

28
12
25

Homenatge a la Barceloneta

Plaça del Duc de Medinaceli

PORT VELL

49

Drassanes

Moll de la Fusta

5

7

34
4

14
46

C del Judici

Museu Marítim

36

Moll de les Drassanes

1

33

Rambla de Mar

Moll d'Espanya

C de l'Escar

40
44

Plaça del Mar

Moll de Balears

Plaça del Portal de la Pau

37
43
42

Acciona Trasmediterránea Fast Ferry Dock

Acciona Trasmediterránea Ferry Terminal

8

Homenatge als Nedadors

41

Platja de Sant Miquel

Moll de Barcelona

45

Acciona Trasmediterránea Ferry Terminal

Grimaldi Ferries

Pg de Joan de Borbó

Plaça de la Rosa del Vents

50

Moll de Sant Beltran

Port Vell

Grandi Navi Veloci

Moll de Ponent

38

Av del Litoral
Peix Sculpture
C de Ramon Trias Fargas

Platja de la Barceloneta

Mediterranean Sea

PORT VELL & LA BARCELONETA

PORT OLÍMPIC, EL POBLENOU & EL FÓRUM

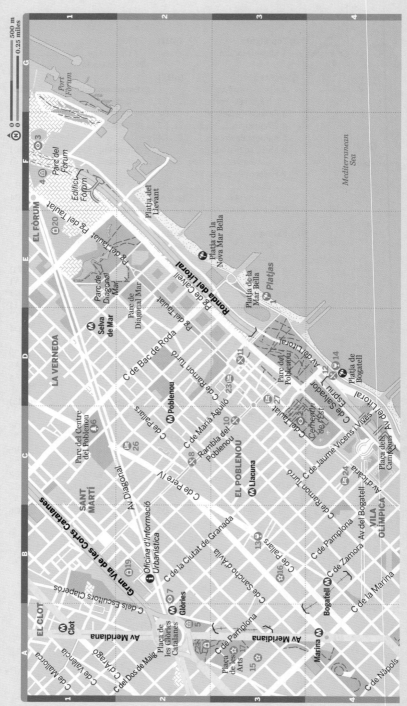

500 m
0.25 miles

Port Fòrum

Parc del Fòrum

Edifici Fòrum

EL FÓRUM

Pg del Taulat

Parc de Diagonal Mar

Platja del Llevant

Platja de la Nova Mar Bella

Platja de la Mar Bella

Platjas

Mediterranean Sea

Pg de Calvell

Ronda del Litoral

LA VERNEDA

Selva de Mar

Parc de Diagonal Mar

Pg del Taulat

C de Bac de Roda

C de Ramon Turró

Poblenou

Parc del Poblenou

Av del Litoral

Platja de Bogatell

Parc del Centre del Poblenou

C de Pallars

C de Maria Aguiló

Rambla del Poblenou

Cementiri del Est

C del Taulat

C de Salvador Espriu

SANT MARTÍ

Av Diagonal

Oficina d'Informació Urbanistica

C de Pere IV

EL POBLENOU

Llacuna

C de Ramon Turró

C de Jaume Vicens Vives

Plaça dels Camp Nous

VILA OLÍMPICA

Av d'Icària

EL CLOT

Clot

Av Meridiana

Gran Via de les Corts Catalanes

C dels Escultors Claperós

Plaça de les Glòries Catalanes

Glòries

C de la Ciutat de Granada

C de Sancho d'Àvila

C de Pallars

C de Pamplona

C de Zamora

Av del Bogatell

Bogatell

C de la Marina

C de Mallorca

C de València

C d'Aragó

C del Dos de Maig

Av Meridiana

Plaça de les Arts

C de Pamplona

Av Meridiana

Marina

C de Nàpols

PORT OLÍMPIC, EL POBLENOU & EL FÒRUM

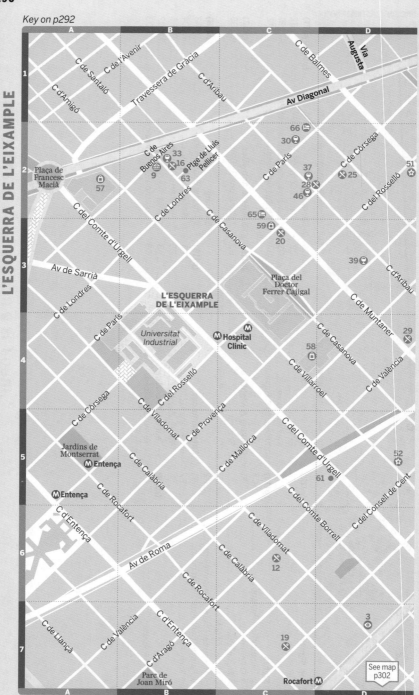

L'ESQUERRA DE L'EIXAMPLE

C de Santaló
C de l'Avenir
C d'Amigó
Travessera de Gràcia
C d'Aribau
C de Balmes
Via Augusta
Av Diagonal

C de Buenos Aires
Ptge de Lluís Pellicer
C de París
C de Còrsega
C del Rosselló

Plaça de Francesc Macià
57
33
16
9
63
37
28
46
25
51
30
66
65
59
20

C del Comte d'Urgell
C de Londres
C de Casanova

Av de Sarrià
C de Londres

L'ESQUERRA DE L'EIXAMPLE

Plaça del Doctor Ferrer Cajigal
39
C d'Aribau

Universitat Industrial
C de París
C del Rosselló
C de Còrsega
C de Viladomat
C de Provença
C de Mallorca

Ⓜ Hospital Clínic
Ⓜ
C de Muntaner
C de Casanova
29
58
C de Villarroel
C de València

Jardins de Montserrat
Ⓜ Entença
C de Calàbria
52
C del Comte d'Urgell
61
C del Comte Borrell
C del Consell de Cent

Ⓜ Entença
C de Rocafort
C d'Entença
Av de Roma
C de Viladomat
C de Calàbria
12

C de Rocafort
C de Llançà
C de València
C d'Entença
C d'Aragó
3
19

Parc de Joan Miró
Rocafort Ⓜ

See map p302

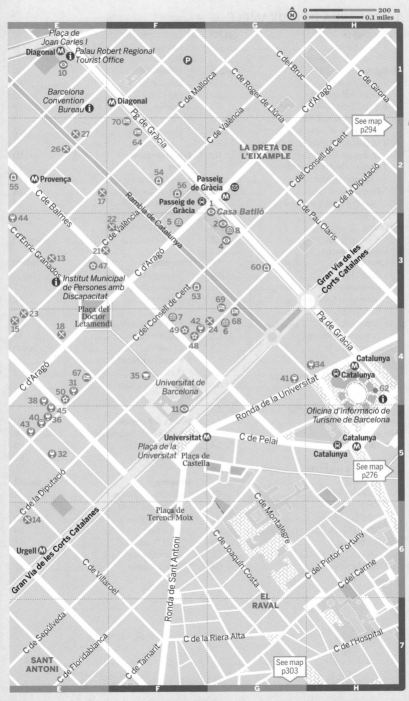

0   200 m
0   0.1 miles

Plaça de
Joan Carles I
Diagonal Ⓜ Ⓘ Palau Robert Regional
Tourist Office
10 Ⓟ

C del Bruc
C de Girona
C de Mallorca
C de Roger de Llúria

Barcelona
Convention
Bureau Ⓘ Ⓜ Diagonal
C de Mallorca
70 📷
64
Pg de Gràcia
C de València

C d'Aragó

LA DRETA DE
L'EIXAMPLE

C del Consell de Cent
C de la Diputació

See map
p294

55 Ⓐ Ⓜ Provença
C de Balmes
54
Ⓐ
56
Passeig
de Gràcia
Ⓜ
5 Ⓐ
Passeig de
Gràcia Ⓐ 1
Ⓐ Casa Batlló
2 Ⓐ
8 🏛
4 Ⓐ
C de Pau Claris

17
Rambla de Catalunya
22
C de València
21
47
Institut Municipal
de Persones amb
Discapacitat
13
C d'Enric Granados
44

C d'Aragó
60 Ⓐ
Gran Via de les
Corts Catalanes

53 Ⓐ
Plaça del
Doctor
Letamendi
C del Consell de Cent
7 🏛
42
49 Ⓐ
24 🍴
48
69 📷
68 🏛
6

23
15
18

67 Ⓐ
31
50
35 🍴
Universitat de
Barcelona
11 Ⓐ
41 🍴
34 🍴
Catalunya
Ⓡ Catalunya
Ⓜ
62
Ⓘ
C d'Aragó
38
45
40
36
43
Ⓡ

Ronda de la Universitat
Oficina d'Informació de
Turisme de Barcelona

32
Universitat Ⓜ
Plaça de la
Universitat
Plaça de
Castella
C de Pelai
Catalunya
Ⓜ
Catalunya

See map
p276

14
Plaça de
Terenci Moix
C de la Diputació

Urgell Ⓜ
Gran Via de les Corts Catalanes
C de Villarroel
C de Joaquín Costa
C de Montalegre
C del Pintor Fortuny
C del Carme
Ronda de Sant Antoni

EL
RAVAL

C de Sepúlveda
C de Floridablanca
C de Tamarit
C de la Riera Alta
C de l'Hospital

SANT
ANTONI

See map
p303

L'ESQUERRA DE L'EIXAMPLE *Map on p290*

LA DRETA DE L'EIXAMPLE *Map on p294*

LA DRETA DE L'EIXAMPLE

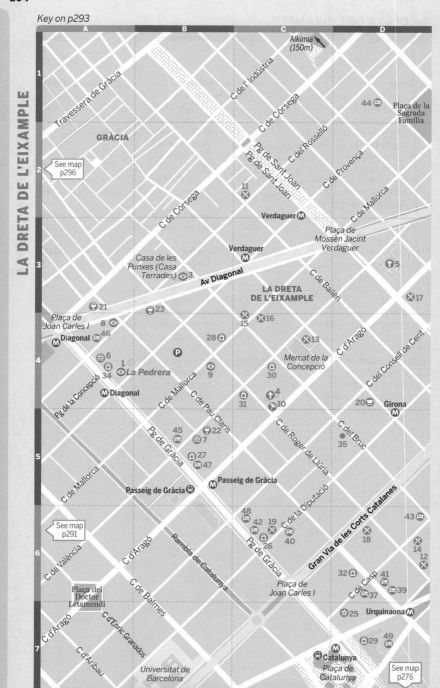

LA DRETA DE L'EIXAMPLE

Alkímia
(150m)

Plaça de la
Sagrada
Família

44

Travessera de Gràcia

GRÀCIA

See map
p296

C de l'Indústria

C de Còrsega

C de Còrsega

C del Rosselló

Pg de Sant Joan
Pg de Sant Joan

C de Provença

C de Mallorca

11

Verdaguer Ⓜ

Verdaguer Ⓜ

Plaça de
Mossèn Jacint
Verdaguer

Casa de les
Punxes (Casa
Terrades) 3

C de Còrsega

Av Diagonal

C de Bailén

5

LA DRETA
DE L'EIXAMPLE

21

23

15

16

17

Plaça de
Joan Carles I

8

Ⓜ Diagonal 46

28

13

C d'Aragó

C del Consell de Cent

6

1

34 La Pedrera

Ⓟ

9

30

Mercat de la
Concepció

20 Girona Ⓜ

Pg de la Concepció

Ⓜ Diagonal

C de Mallorca

C de Pau Claris

31

4

10

C de Roger de Llúria

45

22

7

C del Bruc

35

C de Mallorca

27

47

Passeig de Gràcia

Ⓜ Passeig de Gràcia

Passeig de Gràcia Ⓡ

C de la Diputació

Gran Via de les Corts Catalanes

See map
p291

C de València

C d'Aragó

Rambla de Catalunya

Pg de Gràcia

48

42 19

26

40

43

18

14

12

C de Balmes

32

41

37 39

C de Casp

Plaça del
Doctor
Letamendi

Plaça de
Joan Carles I

25

Urquinaona Ⓜ

C d'Aragó

C d'Enric Granados

C d'Aribau

Universitat de
Barcelona

29

49

Ⓡ Catalunya

Plaça de
Catalunya

See map
p276

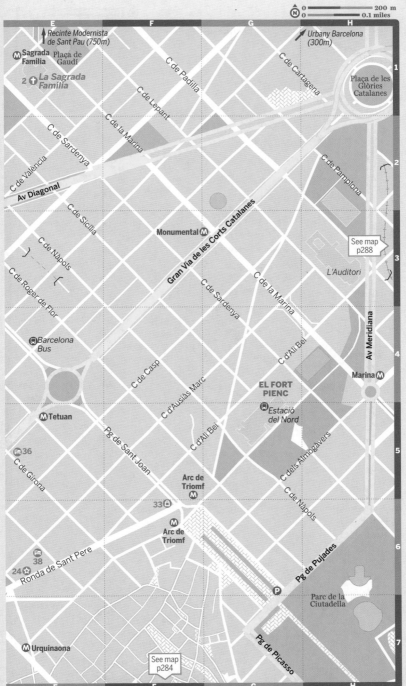

N 0 ———————— 200 m
0 ———————— 0.1 miles

Recinte Modernista
de Sant Pau (750m)

Urbany Barcelona
(300m)

Ⓜ Sagrada
Família

Plaça de
Gaudí

2 ⊕ La Sagrada
Família

C de Padilla

C de Cartagena

Plaça de les
Glòries
Catalanes

1

C de Lepant

C de València

C de la Marina

C de Sardenya

C de Pamplona

2

Av Diagonal

C de Sicília

C de Nàpols

Monumental Ⓜ

Gran Via de les Corts Catalanes

See map
p288

3

C de Roger de Flor

C de Sardenya

C de la Marina

L'Auditori

C d'Ali Bei

4

Ⓑ Barcelona
Bus

C de Casp

EL FORT
PIENC

Marina Ⓜ

Av Meridiana

Ⓜ Tetuan

C d'Ausiàs Marc

Ⓑ Estació
del Nord

Pg de Sant Joan

C d'Ali Bei

C dels Almogàvers

5

Ⓑ 36

C de Girona

Arc de
Triomf
Ⓜ

C de Nàpols

33 🔒

38 🛏

24 ✴

Ⓜ
Arc de
Triomf

Ronda de Sant Pere

6

Pg de Pujades

P

Parc de la
Ciutadella

Ⓜ Urquinaona

See map
p284

Pg de Picasso

7

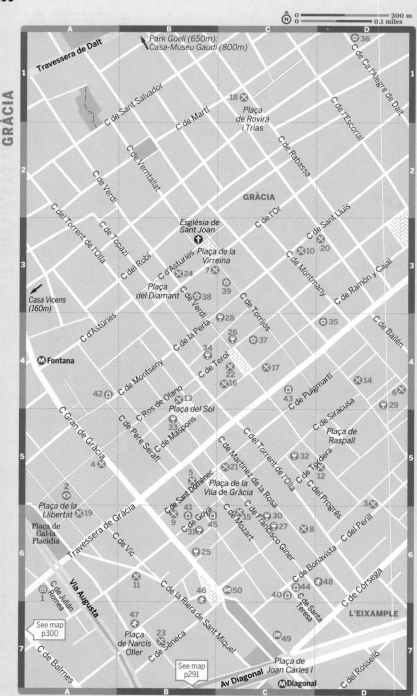

See map p300

See map p291

GRÀCIA

LA ZONA ALTA

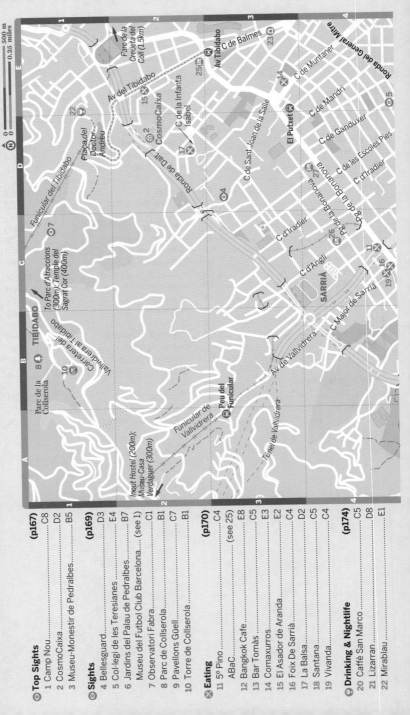

0   500 m
0   0.25 miles

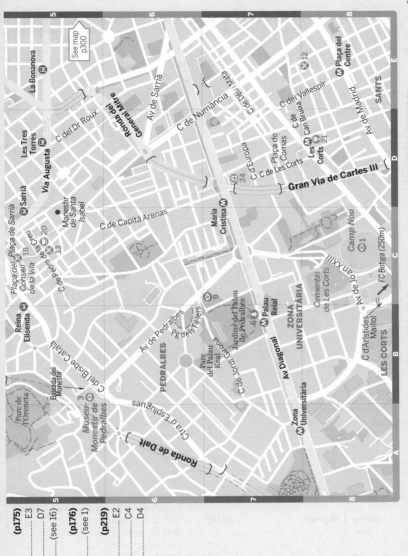

LA ZONA ALTA

LA ZONA ALTA EAST

MONTJUÏC, POBLE SEC & SANT ANTONI *Map on p302*

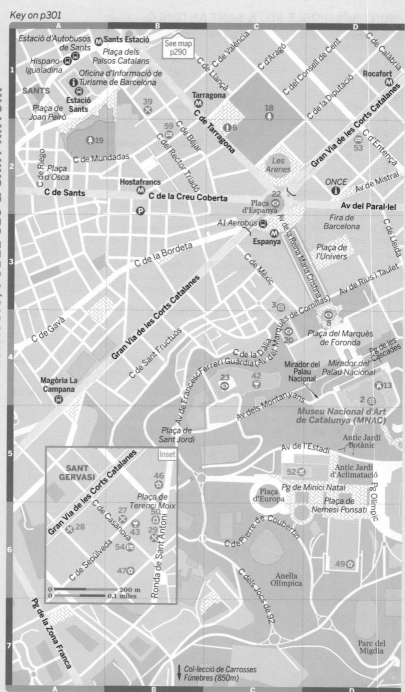

Key on p301

MONTJUÏC, POBLE SEC & SANT ANTONI

Estació d'Autobusos de Sants
Sants Estació
Plaça dels Països Catalans
Hispano-Igualadina
See map p290
Oficina d'Informació de Turisme de Barcelona
SANTS
Estació Sants
Plaça de Joan Peiró
C de València
C d'Aragó
C de Llança
C del Consell de Cent
Rocafort
C de Calàbria
C de la Diputació
Tarragona
18
39
C de Béjar
59
C de Tarragona
6
C del Rector Triadó
Gran Via de les Corts Catalanes
53
C d'Entença
19
C de Riego
C de Mundadas
Plaça d'Osca
Les Arenes
ONCE
Av de Mistral
Hostafrancs
C de Sants
C de la Creu Coberta
22
Av del Paral·lel
Plaça d'Espanya
Fira de Barcelona
A1 Aerobús
Espanya
C de Lleida
Plaça de l'Univers
C de la Bordeta
C de Mèxic
Av de la Reina Maria Cristina
Av de Rius i Taulet
Gran Via de les Corts Catalanes
3
8
C de Gavà
C de Sant Fructuós
20
Plaça del Marquès de Foronda
Pg de les Cascades
C de la Dàlia (Av del Marquès de Comillas)
C de Francesc Ferreri Guàrdia (Av
23
42
Mirador del Palau Nacional
Mirador del Palau Nacional
2
13
Magòria La Campana
Av dels Montanyans
Museu Nacional d'Art de Catalunya (MNAC)
Plaça de Sant Jordi
Antic Jardí Botànic
Av de l'Estadi
Inset
SANT GERVASI
Gran Via de les Corts Catalanes
46
Antic Jardí d'Aclimatació
52
Pg de Minici Natal
Plaça d'Europa
Pg Olímpic
Plaça de Terenci Moix
27
50
28
C de Casanova
43
29
C de Sant Antoni
Ronda de Sant Antoni
Plaça de Nemesi Ponsati
C de Pierre de Coubertin
54
C de Sepúlveda
47
49
0   200 m
0   0.1 miles
Anella Olímpica
C dels Jocs de 92
Pg de la Zona Franca
Parc del Migdia
Col·lecció de Carrosses Fúnebres (850m)

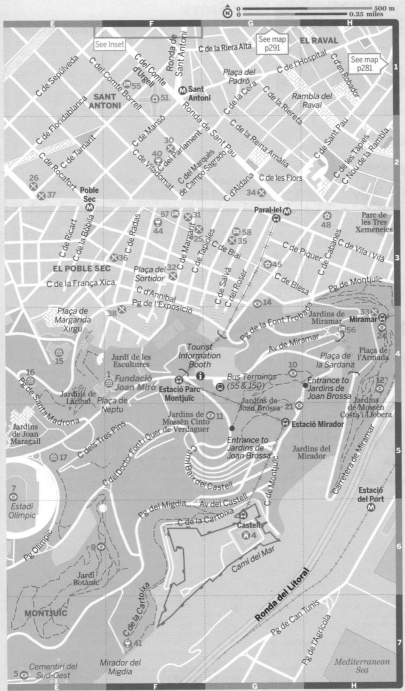

0   500 m
0   0.25 miles

EL RAVAL

See map p291

See map p281

C de Sepúlveda

C del Comte Borrell

C de Floridablanca

C del Comte d'Urgell

Ronda de Sant Antoni

C de la Riera Alta

C de l'Hospital

C d'en Robador

SANT ANTONI

55

51

Sant Antoni M

Plaça del Padró

C de la Cera

C de la Riereta

Rambla del Raval

C de Manso

C de Tamarit

C de R C de Tamarit

C de Rocafort

Ronda de Sant Antoni

C del Parlament

30

40

C de Viladomat

Ronda de Sant Pau

C del Marquès de Campo Sagrado

C de la Reina Amàlia

C de Sant Pau

C de les Tàpies

C Nou de la Rambla

26

37

Poble Sec M

C d'Aldana

C de les Flors

34

Paral·lel M

Parc de les Tres Xemeneies

C de Ricart

C de la Bòbila

C de Radas

57

44

31

48

C de Vila i Vilà

C de Margarit

25

C de Tapioles

58

35

EL POBLE SEC

C de la França Xica

36

Plaça del Sortidor

32

C d'Annibal

C de Salvà

C del Roser

C de Blai

C de Piquer

C de Cabanes

45

C de Blesa

Pg de Montjuïc

Plaça de Margarida Xirgu

38

Pg de l'Exposició

14

Pg de la Font Trobada

Jardins de Miramar

33

Miramar

24

Tourist Information Booth

56

Av de Miramar

Plaça de la Sardana

Plaça de l'Armada

Jardí de les Escultures

15

Fundació Joan Miró

1

Estació Parc Montjuïc

Bus Terminus (55 & 150)

10

Entrance to Jardins de Joan Brossa

12

16

Pg de Santa Madrona

Jardins de Laribal

Plaça de Neptú

Jardins de Mossèn Cinto de Verdaguer

11

Jardins de Joan Brossa

21

Estació Mirador

Jardins de Mossèn Costa i Llobera

Jardins de Joan Maragall

17

C dels Tres Pins

C del Doctor Font i Quer

Entrance to Jardins de Joan Brossa

Jardins del Mirador

Carretera de Miramar

7

Estadi Olímpic

Camí Baix del Castell

Pg del Migdia

Av del Castell

C de Montjuïc

Estació del Port M

Pg Olímpic

9

C de la Cartoixa

Castell

4

Camí del Mar

MONTJUÏC

Jardí Botànic

C de la Cartoixa

Ronda del Litoral

Pg de Can Tunis

Pg de l'Agrícola

5

Cementiri del Sud-Oest

41

Mirador del Migdia

Mediterranean Sea

Our Story

A beat-up old car, a few dollars in the pocket and a sense of adventure. In 1972 that's all Tony and Maureen Wheeler needed for the trip of a lifetime – across Europe and Asia overland to Australia. It took several months, and at the end – broke but inspired – they sat at their kitchen table writing and stapling together their first travel guide, *Across Asia on the Cheap*. Within a week they'd sold 1500 copies. Lonely Planet was born.

Today, Lonely Planet has offices in Franklin, London, Melbourne, Oakland, Beijing and Delhi, with more than 600 staff and writers. We share Tony's belief that 'a great guidebook should do three things: inform, educate and amuse'.

Our Writers

Regis St Louis

Coordinating Author; La Rambla & Barri Gòtic; Barceloneta & the Waterfront; Camp Nou, Pedralbes & La Zona Alta Regis first fell in love with Barcelona and Catalonia on a grand journey across Iberia in the late 1990s. Since then he has returned frequently, learning Spanish and a smattering of Catalan, and delving into the rich cultural history of this endlessly fascinating city. Favourite memories from his most recent trip include earning a few scars at a wild *correfoc* (fire run) in Gràcia, watching brave *castellers* build human towers at the Santa Eulàlia fest, and feasting on *navallas* (razor clams), *pop á feira* (Galician-style octopus) and *carxofes* (artichokes) all across town. Regis is also the author of *Discover Barcelona*, and he has contributed to *Spain, Portugal* and dozens of other Lonely Planet titles. He lives in Brooklyn, New York. Regis also wrote the majority of the Plan Your Trip chapters, the Understand Barcelona and Survival Guide sections, and cowrote the Sleeping chapter.

Sally Davies

El Raval; La Ribera; La Sagrada Família & L'Eixample; Gràcia & Park Güell; Montjuïc, Poble Sec & Sant Antoni Sally landed in Seville in 1992 with a handful of pesetas and five words of Spanish, and, despite a complete inability to communicate, promptly snared a lucrative number handing out leaflets at Expo '92. In 2001 she settled in Barcelona, where she is still incredulous that her daily grind involves researching fine restaurants, wandering around museums and finding ways to convey the beauty of this spectacular city. Sally also wrote the Entertainment and Shopping chapters and cowrote the Sleeping chapter.

Andy Symington

Day Trips Andy hails from Australia but has been living in Spain for over a decade, where, to shatter a couple of stereotypes of the country, he can frequently be found huddled in subzero temperatures watching the tragically poor local football team. He has authored and coauthored many Lonely Planet guidebooks and other publications on Spain and elsewhere; in his spare time he walks in the mountains, embarks on epic tapas trails, and co-bosses a rock bar.

Published by Lonely Planet Publications Pty Ltd
ABN 36 005 607 983
9th edition – Nov 2014
ISBN 978 1 74220 892 3
© Lonely Planet 2014   Photographs © as indicated 2014
10 9 8 7 6 5 4 3 2 1
Printed in China